THE CURIA IS THE POPE

.

Published by
Mount Salus Press
Kholisa. Easton, Delgany
Co. Wicklow, A63TD74

Email: mountsaluspress@gmail.com
www.mountsaluspress.com

Copyright © 2020, by John O'Loughlin Kennedy

Amazon edition 2020

ISBN 978-1-8382945-2-6

"The Curia is the Pope"

and why it cannot listen

John O'Loughlin Kennedy

Mount Salus Press
Delgany, Ireland

Power tends to corrupt and absolute power corrupts absolutely.
Great men are almost always bad men,
even when they exercise influence and not authority.
There is no greater heresy than that the office sanctifies the holder of it.

—Lord Acton, *Letter to Archbishop Creighton*.

To attain the hight and depth of thy eternal ways
All human thoughts come short, Supreme of things;
Thou in thyself art perfect, and in thee
Is no deficience found; not so is man …

—John Milton, *Paradise Lost*

Dedication
for Raymond, Mike, David, and Breffni
Irish Spiritan Missionaries
and
Sr. Joseph Lemass
Irish Dominican Teacher
Requiescant in Pace

Contents

Acknowledgements

This book has taking shape over a lifetime. For years, my sense of loyalty to the Church made me think I should keep my observations to myself. Then gradually the same sense of loyalty, but this time to Jesus Christ, convinced me I should write it. Foremost among the encouragers was the late Sr Margaret MacCurtain, O.P. known in another era by her religious name, Benvenuta. There was also a highly stimulating "Theology Day" in Maynooth where, quite by chance, I found myself lunching with Prof. Enda McDonagh and the late Dr Denis Carroll. They were thought provoking and encouraging. Dr Carroll's idea that Christianity always includes a subversive element resonates with me still. More recently, Prof. Richard Gaillardetz, without seeing the manuscript, kindly guided me to several authoritative studies that I would otherwise have missed.

I am indebted to so many people who helped me over the years that I cannot begin to list them now. I am grateful to all. Reading Marie Keenan's book on the systemic dimension of the paedophile crisis and having the opportunity to talk with her and Anne Cleary in the Sociology Department of UCD was empowering. Among the more recent helpers who read and commented on the manuscript or individual chapters from it were Micheál Ross, Monica Kerrane, Pádraig McCarthy, Joe Mulvaney, Sarah Ingle, Gina Menzies, Angela Hanley, Donal Moore, Joan McGee, and Paul Fairbrook. John Heffernan's detailed examination was painstaking on his part and challenging on mine. My thanks to all. I think I can say that all their suggestions were carefully considered. The decisions as to what went in, stayed in, got dropped or amended were mine as is the responsibility for the final content.

Since my beloved Kay died, my son Paul, his wife Alva and two granddaughters, Sophie and Alice, have made me part of their family, providing me with bed and board, a place for books and a quiet workspace. Without their patience, generosity, and support, this book would never have seen the light of day.

There is printing and publishing in my DNA from both sides of the family. When I started Mount Salus Press in Dalkey, my ambition was that printing would develop into publishing. More than seventy years later, the eponymous limited company has come and gone, and I am grateful for the many capable and talented people who kept it alive in the intervening years. With some assistance from Colm Holmes, the name has now become the imprint for this book, belatedly realising my teenage ambition. *Deo Gratias.*

Preface

The Second Vatican Council, the highest authority in the Roman Catholic Church, was virtually unanimous, in agreeing at least ten major changes of policy or doctrine.

The implementation of the new policies was left to the papacy although the curial leaders had resisted the changes throughout the debates. The curia is the dominating element in the papacy. It is a bureaucracy that manages overworked popes, who mostly allow themselves to be managed. It controls access to the popes, outlives them and exercises their legally unlimited power. It selects and controls the bishops and is thus the effective government of the Church.

In the words of Pope John Paul II, "The curia *is* the pope".

Many of the intended changes posed a threat to the hegemony of the curia; something that no bureaucracy will tolerate willingly. The curia, however, could not be seen to openly reject the Council decisions. So, it blocked what it could by stealth and weakened more, by claiming to be correcting misinterpretations.

The curia fears reform and ignores or denigrates Catholics who campaign for it. Arguments based on Council decisions, on humanity or human rights, on efficiency, effectiveness, experience, or a waning priesthood can all be dismissed by reference to doctrine. And doctrine and practice are given a pretence of infallibility as if they cannot change, although, the record disproves this comprehensively. (See page 114)

It is not the people in top management that are to blame but the structure and system that they have inherited. The necessary reform is opposed by the group dynamic and the fiction and conviction that current structures and ecclesiology are part of some eternal and unchanging divine plan.

This book makes the case for reform and provides historical and theological justification together with evidence that many teachings presented as infallible are open to revision. It looks for a change of focus from the profession of a set of beliefs to the practice of a Christly way of life—to a united discipleship of active unselfish love and care for our brothers and sisters and for the environment on which the quality, and indeed the very continuity, of human life depend.

It identifies the inappropriate management structure and practices and suggests practical steps to enable Church governance to be more loving and forgiving, to pursue the kind of unity Christ prayed for, and to give the top priority they deserve to his foundational mandates:

"Make disciples of all the nations" and "Do This in commemoration of me".

Introduction

"You couldn't work for a so-called Catholic newspaper without being an atheist"
—Patrick Kavanagh

The idea that the present governance structure of the Roman Catholic Church accurately follows some eternal unchanging divine plan is comforting for those directly involved but is historically unsustainable. Moreover, it seems unlikely that God would insist on something quite so unfit for purpose.

The primary task of the church is to make disciples of all the nations. The greatest sustained evangelisation the world has ever known, however, came from an island which had never been touched by the administrative system of the Roman Empire on which the official structure of the Church is modelled, nor by the overwhelming influence of Roman Law. This was Ireland, the Island of Saints and Scholars. It proves, at least, that the divine plan can be implemented in more than one way.

Roman Law may have been the greatest system of law ever devised, but it was not what Jesus was about … and it provided for his crucifixion. In advance of setting up his church, he had expressed his disapproval of the domination/subordination paradigm of leadership as practised by the pagan rulers of his day and had warned his followers against adopting it. "…their great men make their authority felt. This is not to happen among you" (Mt 20:26). His followers do not listen. They are more concerned with which of them might be the greatest. Over the centuries, Christian leaders have allowed a system to develop with multiple titles, rankings, dignities, and special dress, each matched by a higher level of deference, privilege, and authority. This reached a zenith in 1870 at Vatican I when the pope was made infallible and given jurisdiction over the entire church; a legal manoeuvre that gifted the curia with immense power. Lord Acton anticipated the corrupting effect.

"You couldn't work for a so-called Catholic newspaper without being an atheist". Patrick Kavanagh is credited with this comment. Since he was a poet, we should have looked for the serious meaning behind the quip. He was a regular contributor to *The Standard* newspaper—"Catholic Ireland's National Weekly"— which our family, being consciously Catholic and nationalist, read regularly. As an insider, Kavanagh must have been aware of what the paper could not publish. Stories about corruption of clergy or church institutions undoubtedly circulated within the office, but that was as far as they could go—out of loyalty to the Church and deference to the sensitivities of the readership. The paper did its share of denouncing people and organisations it disagreed with but never published stories that might reflect badly on the church. Initially, even the secular media in Ireland suppressed reports of clergy sex abuse.

Ireland, in those days, was schooled in religious decorum. "Let it not so much as be named among you as becometh saints" (Eph. 5:3) could have been a national maxim. For example, court reports in Irish newspapers never used the word

1

'prostitute'. How could they? The street-girls had been charged and sentenced for the offence of 'loitering with intent to commit a felony'. It simply would not do, to admit openly and in print that such a thing as prostitution existed in holy Ireland. That would be to spread 'bad example'. The same attitude prevailed regarding the abuse of children. Some people in authority knew it was happening, but it was better not spoken about.

As we now know, allegations of abuse were made at the time, but officials of both church and state were too inhibited to investigate them properly. Irish bishops, when faced with the problem, followed the standard Roman prescription; they moved the perpetrator to an unsuspecting parish or diocese, enjoined silence on the victims and their advocates and kept the matter subject to 'pontifical secrecy'. They had little choice. It was secrecy or excommunication. Rome wanted no criminal charges or civil investigations. They might have caused scandal! For decades, not a whiff of these abuses or allegations appeared in the media.

The denial or suppression of truth, however well-intentioned, generally does more harm than good. If the Gárda Síochána (the Irish police force) and the press, not to mention the Departments of Education and of Justice, had been less inhibited about investigating the allegations of abuse, whether of children or adults, whether in church or state institutions, the problem itself and the issue of dereliction of duty by those in authority, would have been tackled decades earlier, and the ruin of many young lives avoided.

This is not another book about child sexual abuse by clergy. It is directed, however, at a management structure that has failed to deal with abuse—a system that bound bishops (under threat of excommunication) to keep cases secret from 1922 until 2019, and that looked on victims as 'enemies' of the Church. A system that is still unwilling to accept that the pattern of training, employment and deployment of priests contributes significantly to the problem.[1] It inquires why the curia, which manages and briefs the pope, has been unable to grapple with the complex situational, organizational, and institutional forces at work, and act more effectively in dealing with the causes.

The revelation of a policy of toleration over a long period of time—in relation to the Sixth Commandment, no less—poses a hitherto unthinkable question. What

---

[1] Cf. The work of Marie Keenan, psychotherapist and social scientist at University College Dublin *Child Sexual Abuse and the Catholic Church: Gender, Power, and Organizational Culture, OUP, 2011.* Some of Dr Keenan's conclusions appear in a chapter in *Broken Faith: Why Hope Matters,* Bern, Peter Lang, 2013. This is online at
https://www.academia.edu/31095343/Child_Sexual_Abuse_and_the_Cathlic_Church_A_Multi-layered_Perspective?email_work_card=title
Cf also Revista Comunicación. Volumen 19, año 31, No. 2, Agosto-Diciembre, 2010 (pp. 20-26). There is an imperfect English translation at
https://www.academia.edu/23081874/Systemic_Practice_in_a_Complex_Sys-tem_Child_Seual_Abuse_and_the_Catholic_Church?email_work_card=interaction_paper

other forms of abuse are being tolerated by church authorities? Are there other areas where the organisational needs and priorities are being allowed to obstruct the very objectives for which it was founded? The short answer of this book is 'Yes'.

In several areas the governing policies and priorities conflict with the purpose. In secular organisations, this sort of danger is the everyday concern of audit committees. To answer the question in relation to the Roman Catholic Church is difficult because, despite Christ's disapproval of oaths and secretiveness, the Roman authorities have for centuries made an art form of secrecy and prioritised it among its officials as a virtue[2] although a culture of secrecy is known to facilitate corruption.

This study attempts to light a few candles in the darkness. It is an assessment from the pew of how some current weaknesses of the Church might be overcome. If some people in the management of the Church think that this study—or any other based solely on the evidence available to the faithful—is mistaken or incomplete, they have a remedy; take heed of Christ's condemnation and prioritise truth and transparency ahead of 'pious fibs' and institutional secrecy.

People who confuse Rome with the Church itself might construe this book as an attack on the Church by one of its enemies. They would be doubly mistaken.

Firstly, it is a critique of the management structure and its disordered priorities. The curia is a religious bureaucracy that continues to exhibit the group dynamics of any secular bureaucracy. It prioritises its own continuance and aggrandisement over its appointed mission. While ostensibly acting as the pope's administration, it has established itself as a tier of governance between the pope and the bishops, exercising the powers of the former and arrogating the authority of the latter, while leaving both with their officially defined responsibilities. The bureaucracy, as we shall see, is the effective government of the Roman Catholic Church and is humanly responsible for its condition today. It makes profligate use of a large number of talented and very dedicated people. It is a major part of the problem itself. Incapable of reforming itself, it will never reform the Church. Shuffling personnel and rewriting departmental responsibilities will not be enough. The problem goes deeper than that. This book makes a case for dismantling part of it and decentralising its necessary work in a spirit of reliance on the Holy Spirit and on the many capable and prayerful people who have dedicated their lives to the service of the Church.

Pope Francis apparently wants to make significant changes but is encountering powerful resistance. For forty years the papacy has been manifestly opposing the implementation of Vatican II while protesting the contrary. In refusing to engage with calls for reform, from clergy and faithful alike, it has been blindly walking the

---

[2] Divulging a 'Secret of the Holy Office' otherwise 'Pontifical Secrecy' incurs automatic excommunication that can only be lifted by the pope personally—Kieran Tapsell, The Second Cover-up, in *The Swag*, Autumn 2014, accessed on www.v2catholic.com, August 2019. Note 1. Since 1974, the excommunication is no longer automatic. Note 2. On December 17th, 2019, Pope Francis removed clerical sex abuse cases from the scope of Pontifical Secrecy.

Church that Christ prayed should be one, in the direction of another failed reformation and further fragmentation.

Secondly, I am no enemy of the Church, but a committed member, concerned at how easily religion can obscure rather than illuminate the Way, and dutifully offering my ten cents worth as requested by Vatican II. *(Lumen Gentium* §37) and by Pope John Paul II who invited suggestions, in his encyclical, *Ut Unum Sint,* on how the papacy could facilitate a unified church.

The current Pope, Francis, is a remarkable man. A product of the system himself, he can see some of its weaknesses. He has a *titulo* (diploma) in chemistry and worked as a chemist before joining the Jesuits. He understands Barry Commoner's first law of ecology: *"Everything is connected to everything else".* [3] His reform agenda recognises that the church is an integral part of creation, affected by it and affecting it. He knows that the reform of systems is always complex. He needs the support of pressure from the faithful seeking reform.

A word about words. Several words that are very relevant to this study have more than one meaning and the research for this book has pointed up not a few important ones that have changed their meaning, or had their meaning changed, over time.

When Roman Catholics refer to "The Church", they can mean any one of eight things: The Mystical Body of Christ, the Universal Church of Christ, the Roman Catholic Church, the teaching authority of Rome, the current top management team, the People of God, the local community with whom we worship or the building in which we gather. The confusion is sometimes exploited to deceive. I shall try to avoid ambiguity. The word 'love', which is crucial to this study, covers such an impossible range of meanings—from attitude to action, from making to sacrificing from concern for self to altruism—that one must rely on the context for the meaning. The word 'pope' means a person and must be clearly distinguished from the papacy—an institution made up of the pope and the bureaucracy known as the curia. *Presbyter* has progressed from meaning 'appointed elder' to 'ordained priest', as the *episcopos* [4] had earlier gone from being the overseer or organiser of the local church to consecrated bishop, archbishop, cardinal, or pope.

The term 'Christian' has acquired so much baggage over the centuries that it no longer means similarity to Christ. For this use, I prefer the term 'Christly'.

Some churchmen use Latin phrases as if they should terminate the discussion, as if the fact that they are in a 'holy' language adds some special authority. In writing about the faith, however, one cannot avoid Latin words, so I have added a small glossary to avoid confusion.

---

[3] Barry Commoner, *The Closing Circle.* 1971. This is the book that initiated the modern environmental movement. The other three laws are: *Everything has to go somewhere, Nature knows best,* and *There is no such thing as a free lunch.*

[4] Presbyter comes from Greek *presbus,* =old man, comparative *presbuteros* =elder. Bishop from Greek *episcopos* =overseer. In early occurrences, they are not always clearly distinguished.

Chapter 1

Uncertainty creates the gods & the tribe

"In this world, nothing is certain except death and taxes"
—Benjamin Franklin

To be a person is to be physical, spiritual, rational, social, and able to make choices. Together these characteristics imply society, order, and organisation, to which the individual relates in freedom. Humans have the unique ability to discern truth. which speaks with its own authority. Individuals cannot do the discerning alone. They rely on the guidance of others to survive, learn, and flourish.

In human affairs, uncertainty has always been the only real certainty. The consequent insecurity spawned the gods and the tribe. Primitive societies must have been challenged to understand the seemingly capricious and random events that shaped their lives. Some unseen spirits or gods, had to be in charge of weather, trees, rivers, health, fertility, wars, fire, the harvest, the sea, the north wind, rain. Too much for one to handle. Obviously, there had to be many.

Conceived in the human imagination, the gods reflected the human form albeit with fewer limitations and some added capabilities. Being powerful, they were modelled on humans who wielded power. So, they were expected to be touchy, selfish, tyrannical, and apt to be vengeful, vindictive, and vicious if upset. So better not do anything to offend them, even inadvertently. They must be flattered and appeased or they may exercise their caprice at our expense. To keep on their good side, we should reassure them regularly that their wishes are our top priority. We must worship them and offer them honour, praise, and gifts.

Sacrifice is found in so many primitive societies that it may have arisen spontaneously in different places and times. It appears to have been invented by humans to fill a human need in a very uncertain world; to demonstrate respect for the gods or to appease their possible wrath. Better to anticipate them with expiation for any possible offences rather than risk their ire and retribution.

The authorities in Ancient Rome shared this view and were taking no unnecessary chances. They were very conscious of the gods and did not expect them to be very forgiving or even discriminating when it came to expressing anger. Thus, Roman Law, being very rational, required all citizens (male only, of course— women and children did not count any more than household pets) to attend public worship regularly, lest one man's disrespect would provoke wrath on the entire community. After the fire of Rome, the Christians were blamed for provoking disaster by worshipping the wrong deities.

Roman priests were trained to offer the appropriate sacrifices to the various gods. It was considered important that the established rituals be observed in precise detail.

This required years of training at special colleges. Like any priestly caste or class, their perceived ability to warn of impending godly anger gave them substantial political power. In ancient Rome, the priestly profession was held in high esteem and was so powerful that the head priest competed with the Emperor for the title of *'Pontifex Maximus'* and held it for most of the time.

Uncertainty also creates anxiety and the tribe.

At a more earthly level, uncertainty generates anxiety and insecurity, even when there is no immediate threat. In primitive societies, a man could not hope to protect his family and possessions and be a hunter-gatherer on his own. There is safety and strength in numbers. Initially the extended family provides a degree of security then the tribe develops, in part to match the strength of neighbouring tribes. A strong tribe offers an assurance of future safety, security, and comfort.

Readiness to defend tribal interests thus assumes paramount importance. Men are conditioned from boyhood to risk anything, even life itself, in their defence. Absolute loyalty by each male to the tribal story, generally part myth and part history, and to the group self-image, slogans, traditions, ambitions, and self-interest is expected. Any focus on inconvenient facts, any suggestion of an alternative perspective or a different emphasis is seen as having the potential to destabilise and is deemed a betrayal. It may lead to severe disapproval, sanctions, or expulsion from the group.

TRIBAL CHARACTERISTICS OF BUREAUCRACIES.

Every bureaucracy is tribal. While the incidence of turnover among personnel can lessen individual dependence, the bureaucracy can evoke stronger fidelity because it provides each of its members with immediate and ongoing rewards: security, status, a standard of living, and possibly a pension, with the added hope of betterment into the future. The peer pressure on members who are perceived to be ambivalent about institutional self-serving can be powerful. Much of this applies to the bureaucracy that runs the Catholic Church, the Roman curia.

The late Dr Jerry Pournelle (1933-2017) was a prolific lecturer, columnist, and author. He formulated several "Laws". "Pournelle's Iron Law of Bureaucracy" is his best known, possibly because it resonates with peoples' experience.

> "...in any bureaucratic organization there will be two kinds of people: those who work to further the actual goals of the organization, and those who work for the organization itself ... The Iron Law states that in all cases, the second type of person will always gain control of the organization and will always write the rules under which the organization functions".

The overarching priority of a bureaucracy is to protect and perpetuate itself, by garnering additional power, influence and control over its environment and resisting any change that might threaten it. In its search for security and power, a bureaucracy will seek to weaken or eliminate any potentially competing power centre that it cannot control.

By enhancing the power and influence of its leader, a bureaucracy grows stronger and secures its future and the security of each individual member. The lust for additional power is proportional to its size. Its attainment is limited by public law, competition, its own statutes, and by public opinion. The group dynamic can distract from or overwhelm the original purposes for which the bureaucracy was established. It can create its own myths and tribal culture.

The altruism that motivates a person as an individual gets a low priority in his decision making as a bureaucrat. He must apply the rules of the organisation and seek its best interests. He must protect his colleagues and their livelihood. Thus, a group pursues its common ends. In the group dynamic altruism can be tolerated only if it promises a more-than-compensating return in security, PR, votes, or income. Compassion and truth take second, or third, place.

Homogeneous sub-groups and committees

A sub-group within a bureaucracy will tend to prioritise the bureaucracy's needs unless the subgroup is homogeneous enough and their common interest is affected in which case the sub-group's needs will dominate. Unselfishness is not a natural characteristic of committees and the more alike the membership, the more certain that their common interest will prevail. Homogeneous committees can make very partisan decisions.

Sometimes it seems that a group can arrive at a decision that each of the members as an individual would reject or for which no individual member would wish to be personally responsible. Dr John Crown, a respected oncologist in Dublin, has commented on this:

> " … individuals, lovely people. I once wrote there was an inverse moral synergy in the Civil Service. You put a whole lot of good and decent people together and collectively they acted in a most abominable fashion when they formed an organisation".[5]

THE CURIA SHARES CHARACTERISTICS OF SECULAR BUREAUCRACIES

Bureaucracies tend to be rule bound. When rules appear petty, the bureaucrat conforms, if only out of habit or because there may be a rationale of which he is unaware. Characteristically, however, rules that run counter to his own instincts or convictions, are also obeyed. Sociologists of military organisation and government have been intrigued to understand why. Max Weber has explained that the honour of the civil servant is "vested in his ability to execute conscientiously the order of superior authorities, exactly as if it agreed with his own conviction". Weber sees this as involving "moral discipline and self-denial in the highest sense, [without which] the whole apparatus would fall to pieces"[6].

---

[5]—Dr John Crown being interviewed by Eamonn Dunphy on RTÉ, 15/11/2007. 16 minutes into podcast)

[6] Gerth and Mills, eds., *From Max Weber,* London, Routledge and Kegan Paul, 1970 p. 95

In the curia, the link between superiors and inferiors has the added strength of religious commitment, deference based on rank, and oaths of loyalty. This enables individuals, to shrug off personal responsibility while playing their parts in decisions and procedures that contravene any normal standards of jurisprudence or indeed of morality. Putting the organisation first can assuage the individual conscience. Regrettably, a bureaucracy has no conscience to take its place.

> The great theologian Yves Congar … speaks of being "crushed, destroyed, excommunicated by a pitiless system which can neither emend itself nor even recognise its errors, but which is run by men who are disarming in their goodness and piety".[7]

Congar is not alone. He is one of a noble line of theologians, that have challenged the myths and the sanitised history of the institution and have suffered for their devotion to truth. In the Roman curia, it appears that obedience to superiors, or to bureaucratic precedent, is the paramount virtue.[8] It can be used by officials to absolve themselves of responsibility for actions that would otherwise be considered morally reprehensible.

This is perilously close to the thinking that enabled normal people to play their individual roles in the bureaucratic process that sustained the Holocaust.[9] Obedience and commitment to the institution was habitual. Each official knew he was only one cog in the machine. If he refused to play his part, he would be replaced immediately. He might ruin his career, but it would not stop the process. His sacrifice to principle would benefit nobody. What he had to do might be distasteful, but the service of the institution provided justification.

There is no comparison between the objectives of the CDF and those of the German bureaucracy of the time, but the principles involved and the sociological forces at work in the watchdog of orthodoxy and morality of the Roman Catholic Church are terrifyingly similar. All this explains how we can find people in history, plenty of them, whose lives were dedicated to the service of God, torturing other people, and dutifully condemning them to be burnt alive as a public spectacle. "The hour cometh, that whosoever killeth you will think that he doth a service to God" (Jn. 16:2). Thus, good people in a bureaucratic structure can become more concerned for the church organisation than its mission.

Misdirected devotion

The curial system rewards ambition. It rewards the service of the system rather than the service of God. It tries to equate the two services and ends up confusing them. It is prone to corruption, not just because power tends to corrupt,

---

[7]—Geoffrey Robinson, *Confronting Power and Sex in the Catholic Church,* quoting from Alain Woodrow, *Congar's Hard-Won Victory,* The Tablet, 28th April 2001, p 605.

[8] "…namely obedience. This virtue is the font and origin of all virtues"—Leo X, Bull, *Exsurge Domine,* 1520 www.papalencyclicals.net, accessed 2 June 2017.

[9] Cf. Gerald E. Markle, *meditations of a holocaust traveller.* Chapter 3 describes in detail the essential role of bureaucracy in the systematic murder of five or six million people.

but also because it traditionally disdains the separation of powers which is the best defence against abuse of power in human affairs. It justifies its structures and actions by suitable supporting doctrines and –since Vatican 1–by pretending that a plethora of rules and teachings are infallible and irreformable.[10]

Bishop Geoffrey Robinson, from whose book the above extract from Congar is taken goes on to draw the conclusion:

> The fundamental problem does not lie in the individual persons who make up the curia, but in the system that they are bound to uphold.[11]

Speaking to members of the curia before Christmas 2014, Pope Francis listed 15 'Curial Diseases': pitfalls that every member should be on guard against. He was warning his listeners about the pursuit of false values: security, power, prestige, wealth, image, convenience, and control. Without a "vital, personal, authentic and solid relationship with Christ" a member would simply "become a bureaucrat". Francis did not limit these dangers to individuals but linked them specifically to "every curia … and ecclesial movement". He was talking from his own experience of people working in religious organisations and was asking members of the curia to oppose the group dynamic, individually and spiritually.

The Roman curia is a large bureaucracy of long standing. Although charged with serving the Pope and the Church, it has generally displayed the normal characteristics of a secular bureaucracy. Accordingly, in making decisions it tends to prioritise its own power, authority, security, and ambitions … sometimes at the expense of truth, justice, and charity.

Surprisingly, the curia as at present constituted has no justification in scripture. Its origins go back beyond the start of Christianity into the pagan religious bureaucracy of ancient Rome which was Christianised abruptly when Christianity became the religion of the Empire. Thus, it cannot claim to be part of any eternal divine plan. Yet, in everyday operation, it is the more powerful part of the papacy. When Cardinal Evaristo Arns suggested that the Pope was giving the curia too much free rein, John Paul II responded:

> "You are mistaken. The curia is the pope".

The curia *is* the pope![12] And who better to tell us than Pope John Paul II after 17 years' experience of the office. While the curia and the pope together form the

---

[10] The reader may well ask why the author continues to be a member of a church of which he is so critical. The answer is that I am critical, not of the Church, but of the self-renewing curial structure that has developed into a governing layer between the successor of Peter and the successors of the apostles. It has made a virtue of building its power and influence. Poor management would be a poor reason for abandoning the Church that Jesus Christ gave us.

[11] —Geoffrey Robinson, *Confronting Power and Sex in the Catholic Church,* p128 quoting from Alain Woodrow, *Congar's Hard-Won Victory,* The Tablet, 28th April 2001, p 605.

[12] —*National Catholic Reporter. 11 October 1996.* https://www.thefreelibrary.com/Cardinal+Arns+says-+pope+gives+his+curia+free+rein%3a+the+pope+replies%2c...-a018777581 Retrieved 01 Sep. 2019.

papacy, the curia manages the pope and dominates in the medium and long term. The curia is the effective government of the Church.

Since the 1950s, economists have been aware of the tendency of the regulator to become captive of the entity that he is charged with regulating. This is more likely to happen when the appointed expert has years of experience of working in the relevant sector. Not only do most popes fit this category, but since all popes are managed by the bureaucracy that they are supposed to be governing, some degree of regulatory capture seems inevitable.

Historically, popes reign for an average of less than nine years. while the curia continues. Building an ever more centralised system, it writes the laws. It selects bishops and controls them through vows of obedience, oaths of loyalty and a system of pettifogging approvals. It controls its own recruitment and promotes only those who support the policies of the bureaucracy wholeheartedly. So, the ethos does not change. It maintains a tradition whereby those who rise to be prefects of certain congregations get to be cardinals. These curial cardinals, as a group, have the greatest single influence in the selection of a pope. The bureaucracy has thus structured itself to make change virtually impossible.

The conclave that elected Cardinal Bergoglio was looking for reform. They elected the first Jesuit pope, the first from the southern hemisphere, the first from outside Europe in more than a millennium. They chose someone who could rise above curial groupthink.

If Pope Francis can make his changes take root, he may well succeed against the odds. In the meantime, he is showing the world the difficulties of moving forward when influential members of the team want to hold back. Everybody knows the curia will outlast him and can wait to undo his work. The bishops, in consequence, are faced with an unenviable choice between the short-term and the long, between the principled and the pragmatic, between obedience to a transient pope and cultivation of relations with a recalcitrant bureaucracy.

In Chapter 6 we will look at a number of important decisions made in the name of the papacy that seemed to owe more to group self-interest than to the inspiration of the Holy Spirit. This will lead us to question whether the curia, or indeed any self-regulating bureaucracy can properly serve an organisation that is concerned with the things of the spirit.

The Church preaches the Cross, where Christ sacrificed himself for others. The world sees this as folly. Bureaucracies are naturally self-centred. They have difficulty understanding the folly of the Cross. Every large organisation needs the services of a bureaucracy, but no Church should be governed by one.

A fortiori, the Catholic Church should not be governed by a homogeneous one.

Chapter 2

The Incarnation and church purpose

I came into the world for this; to bear witness to the truth and all who are on the side of truth listen to my voice.

—Jesus to Pilate, (Jn. 18:37)

AMAZING MESSAGE

The purpose of Christianity can be defined in relatively uncontroversial terms. It is to bring the message and Spirit of the Lord Jesus Christ, the Son of God, to all the world over time. For this, the message must be simple enough to touch the uneducated and profound enough to capture the minds of the most philosophical.

And what a message. It changed the world. His message was utterly amazing at the time. There is only one God and he loves us like a father or mother. He wants us to love one another. Jesus conveyed the message primarily by the example of his life, death, and resurrection. St Francis of Assisi reflected on the method: "Evangelise always, sometimes use words". Christ revealed things that the best philosophers could never have proven for us and left remarkably simple instructions for those who would answer his invitation to follow him.

Reassurance and Challenges

Good News. Five essential things of which people who believe in the resurrection of Jesus Christ, the Son of God, can rest assured:

1. There is only one God, the Creator of all that is.
2. God loves us, and all that he has made.
3. God is magnanimous and ever ready to forgive us our failings.
4. God will reward the good with eternal life; he will judge our lives using one criterion only; what we have done in freedom out of love.
5. As a loving Father, he wishes his children to return his love and to love one another.

There are three mandates. His followers are expected and empowered to:

1. "Do this, in commemoration of me" along with "take this, all of you, and eat" and "take this, all of you and drink".
2. "Go, make disciples of all the nations, baptize them in the name of the Father, the Son and the Holy Spirit and teach them to observe all the commands I gave you".
3. Love God by loving your neighbour and the ecology on which life depends. Christ's moral theology ("All the Law and the prophets") derives from this.

They are inseparable; If you love me, "Feed my lambs and my sheep". We are blessed with love of him when we take loving care of his other children and his creation.

The Way we should carry out the mandates:

1. Humbly. When you are in authority you must not lord it over people as the pagan rulers do. "No, the greatest among you must behave as if he were the youngest, the leader as if he were the one who serves":

2. In Unity. "That they all may be one, as thou, Father, in me, and I in thee"

3. Lovingly. "Love one another as I have loved you".

4. Prayerfully. "When you pray, say this:

> Our Father, Who art in heaven,
> Hallowed be Thy name,
> Thy kingdom come,
> Thy will be done on earth as it is in heaven,
> Give us this day our daily bread
> And forgive us our trespasses
> as we forgive those who trespass against us,
> And lead us not into temptation but deliver us from evil."[13]

And finally, the Promise:

> "And know that I am with you always; yes, to the end of time".

We will refer to this simply as the Promise. It is important to understand that in keeping the Promise, Christ assures us as a group that we will never lack for his guidance. But he never overrides the freedom of decision on which our capacity to love depends.

UNCONDITIONAL LOVE: FORGIVENESS AND A PROMISE AND A WAY

Love is the common thread in the Good News, the Mandates, the Way, and the Promise. Jesus defines his followers exclusively in terms of love. *By this shall all men know that you are my disciples; because you have love, one for another*. The equation works both ways. His disciples are those who love. All who love are his disciples. He wishes us to love him in our brothers and sisters and teaches that if we do, we will be united to him and to the Father. It is of the nature of an invitation that it can be accepted or declined. He respects our freedom.

He defined love at its very greatest; that a man should lay down his life for his friends. He then went on to exemplify it for us by his ultimate self-sacrifice. We humans tend to prioritise our own selfish ends and ambitions. In contrast, Christ's life teaches us to love the Father and obey his will, as we understand it, in all things.

---

[13] We start with a summary of Christ's message because it tends to get obscured by religious detail. Furthermore, it may seem superfluous to spell out the Lord's Prayer when most readers can rattle it off by heart. If, in doing so, we could understand what it means and mean what it says, books like this would not need to be written. It encapsulates all.

Christ's life and the manner of his death set a new example for all mankind and for all time—that in loving the Father and doing his will, feeding the lambs and the sheep, there should be, literally, no limits. This has evoked unselfishness and self-denial to a heroic degree from many saints and mystics.

It is interesting to note in passing that St Patrick's total and unconditional self-giving, in coming back permanently to the land of his earlier enslavement, bore fruit abundantly. He set the example for the extraordinary tradition of life-long dedicated overseas evangelisation by monks from Ireland that lasted for almost six hundred years. But more of that later.

Ancient philosophers could see the necessity of a Creator with supreme wisdom and intelligence, probably limitless. Humans share in this rationality but in a finite way. We learn from one another; each is both learner and teacher. The search for truth is not a job for one. It is humanity's search. Deception is a betrayal of our shared humanity.

Faith can be rational

Jesus, being both God and man, taught us things that we could not otherwise have known or been sure of. Believing that he was both God and man, it becomes perfectly rational to accept that some of the things he revealed would be beyond our ken; outside the logic of the time-space-energy-matter ecosystem of which we form part. Accepting that there are some mysteries of religion is thus perfectly rational. Even the most intransigent rationalist can accept that the human mind and imagination grapple rather inadequately with the infinite.

Nor do we abandon rationality when we accept something humbly on the authority of those who are wiser or better informed than we are. In its original meaning, 'apostolic succession' meant the reassurance and trust that the revealed truth had been passed on in a sequence of teacher-disciple-teacher relationships originating with the apostles. Trust, however, only extends as far as the integrity, honesty and openness of the teacher can support it. It would be irrational to trust one who stoops to deception. This puts a heavy responsibility on those who have taken on responsibility for teaching, sanctifying, and governing,

The Way

In an unforgettable exchange, he exasperates Peter by enquiring three times: Do you love me Peter? Each time Peter said "Yes" Jesus exhorts him to feed the lambs and sheep. This text has been used to justify the claim of Peter's successors to a primacy of jurisdiction. In face of that, how can a pope tolerate any set of human regulations that prevents a growing proportion of Christ's followers from sharing the Lord's Supper together on the Lord's Day? And from receiving the bread of heaven when they desire it? Or the sacrament of reconciliation. Is that feeding?

Jesus was not just speaking to Peter at this point. While the questions were put to the founding leader of the Church, in the answer Jesus is telling all who would love him how he wants them to behave: take care of others, especially those in need; feed

THE CURIA IS THE POPE

them spiritually and physically, literally and metaphorically. We serve the needs of others, not just in the caring professions as nurses, doctors, ministers, and teachers, but also in everyday economic activity as bus drivers, builders, legislators, traders, farmers, artists. Caring is as varied as peoples' needs. It generally involves some sacrifice of self-interest. However, when we give top priority to our own needs, feelings, and ambitions, we are caring for ourselves, not loving. "Self-indulgence is the opposite of the Spirit"(Ga. 5:17)

Christ set out clearly the one criterion on which our lives will be judged. Surprisingly for his listeners, this will not be by reference to our sins, or to the ten commandments, or the Mosaic or Canon Law, or even orthodox adherence to doctrine. Nor will we be judged on whether we managed to stay in full communion with Rome, Canterbury, or Mecca. We will be judged on our readiness to love. *"As long as you did it to one of these, my least ones …"*.

Of course, if we look for the unifying element in the ten commandments, we find that it is love: love for God, and for our brothers and sisters. When the lawyer asked him to define the greatest commandment, Christ responded that, taken together, love is the fundamental commandment. *"On these depend all the law and the prophets"*. While this is foundational it needs to be repeated time and again because it tends to be obscured by doctrinal and disciplinary detail. The Catechism of the Catholic Church runs to 700 pages; the Code of Canon Law to over 500. The *condensed* version of Fr Prummer's Manual of Moral Theology also runs to more than 500 pages. Is it any wonder that the fundamental message often gets obscured and that priorities get confused?

Forgiveness Linked to Love

Thus, Christly moral theology is based on love. St Thomas Aquinas had little difficulty in reconciling Aristotle's ethics with Christian morality, but Christ did not come on earth to confirm the philosopher's ethics. He asks much more. He taught us by example to love the Father, and his will, without limit and to love and care for one another. This requires some degree of unselfishness. The modern ecological movement, and notably Fr Seán McDonagh and Pope Francis, have shown us that this inevitably includes a call to everyone "to care for the earth"[14] by being less selfish in many small ways. One person's impact on the environment, affects the well-being of everyone else. As the leaf, so the forest.

So, our consciences consistently reprove us when we stoop to selfish behaviour.

Forgiveness and love are intimately linked. Forgiveness is like mercy. "It is twice blest; It blesseth him that gives and him that takes". One forgives because one loves, the recipient loves because he has been forgiven. As Jesus explained, the sinner came to love greatly, because 'much had been forgiven her'.[15] Christ was always ready to forgive, whether forgiveness was requested or not. His first words to the paralysed

---

[14] Cf. Seán McDonagh, *To care for the Earth,* 1986, Geoffrey Chapman
[15] Not the other way around as Luke 7:47-48 has often been mistranslated.

14

man were: *"Son, thy sins are forgiven thee"*. (Luke 5:18) I like to think that this man may not have been afraid of death so much as terrified of the retribution to come for some things he had done in life. Christ did not ask for a recital of sins. He just forgave them, gratuitously. Similarly, with the good thief. With no judging, no enquiry about what sin or how often, no thought for purgatory[16] and no regard for the 'temporal punishment due to sin', Christ reassured him with the promise: *"This day you will be with me in paradise"*. He did not seem to share the obsession with detailed laws and regulations that characterised the religious leaders of his time. He was always magnanimous and amazingly gentle in dealing with sinners. His gratuitous, generous forgiveness generally came first.

He did an utterly amazing, unthinkable, and unexpected thing—never anticipated by the philosophers, or in all the literature of the Roman or Greek gods or in the Old Testament—when he handed his disciples the authority to forgive sins.

All this does not mean that he considered sin unimportant. He expressed unequivocal disapproval of four specific failings that make a rather chastening list for Christians today:

> 1. Hypocrisy, particularly religious hypocrisy,
> 2. Scandal, particularly the scandalising of children,
> 3. Oaths (Mt. 5:33-34)
> 4. Secretive ways, because they facilitate evildoing, (Jn 3:19-21)

The Promise and the message

The Promise relates, among other things, to the truths that Jesus revealed to us. It preceded the structure of popes, bishops, and priests. It was addressed to his followers, to all the People of God. We are entitled to rely on it. Its most recent formulation in relation to the faith we profess comes from *Lumen Gentium* (§12) using a phrase from St Augustine in the fourth century:

> "The body of the faithful as a whole, anointed as they are by the Holy One, cannot err in matters of belief. Thanks to a supernatural sense of the faith which characterises the People as a whole, it manifests this unerring quality when 'from the Bishops down to the last of the laity', it shows universal agreement in matters of faith and morals". (LG §12) [17]

A related phrase from Augustine had a formative impact on Newman: *"Securus iudicat orbis terrarum"* (the verdict of the world is conclusive). Newman interprets this as "The universal Church, in her judgments, is sure of the Truth". This echoes very closely the teaching of Augustine quoted above.

---

[16] His oversight here need not surprise us. Purgatory did not become Catholic teaching until 500 years later, with Pope Gregory the Great.—See Peter Watson, *Ideas,* Phoenix, Orion Books Ltd ISBN 0 7538 2089-7 p317.

[17] Walter M. Abbott, S.J., Ed., *The Documents of Vatican II,* London – Dublin, Geoffrey Chapman, 1966, *p*29.

It is therefore in the beliefs of the People of God that the charism of infallibility resides. And it is on this that the teaching authority of Church leaders depends. Christians trust in the Holy Spirit to maintain this in a general way while re cognising that, apart from the basics reflected in the Creeds and the Lord's Prayer, it is notoriously difficult to articulate in detail what the beliefs of the People of God are.

St Paul implies that the purpose and challenge of the Church is vested in the entire Church. The individual members have their own charisms, duties, strengths, and opportunities. The growth of the Church is not the responsibility of any one person or group but is shared by all inspired by the Spirit. St Paul sees the charisms that unify and build up the church as being widely distributed among the faithful as gifts.

> "And to some his gift was that they should be apostles; to some, prophets; to some, evangelists; to some pastors and teachers; so that the saints together make a unity in the work of service, building up the body of Christ. In this way we are all to come to unity in our faith and in our knowledge of the Son of God . . . " (Eph. 4:11-13)

Thus, Christianity is a Spirit-coordinated movement. However, for it to be effective in a world of human beings, time and place, a visible organisation that includes a teaching authority is undoubtedly needed.

But Jesus was not a micro-manager. While the general instructions are clear, he was not into writing procedures or manuals. He founded a Church, based on his apostles and disciples. He did not write a legal constitution for his church, but gave us the guiding principles, sometimes illustrating them with parables. He taught by example. His entire life as recorded in the gospels and passed down to us by apostolic tradition was a demonstration of how our creator God wishes us to live. He invites us, his followers, to learn of him in the community of the church and help one another to follow his example in the details of our lives. While he made it very clear how the superiors were to relate to the inferiors, he left no detailed treatise on how his followers were to go about fulfilling the mandates in the myriad different circumstances of billions of lives in changing times and cultures. The followers were to work this out for themselves and this has turned out to be a continuous process as the Church has grown in scale and complexity and adapted itself more or less successfully to a changing world.

Like St Thomas the Apostle, we might well ask how we can possibly know the will of the Father in all of life's different situations. The answer would be the one Christ gave to Thomas: *"I am the way, the truth and the life"*. It is a matter of loving and caring for one another; in responding to the everyday situations and opportunities of our lives. Christ answered John the Baptist's enquiry by describing what he was doing. *"The blind see, the lame walk ... and the poor have the gospel preached to them"*. (Matt 11.5)

Structure, law, liturgy, prayer, other sacraments, ministers, church buildings, hospitals, schools, management, rules, regulations, ecclesial offices, titles, ranks, regalia, traditions and so on, are necessary elements ordered towards the objective. They are all good and useful in different ways but can easily become ends in themselves, obscuring the purpose and objective. As the world changes, the Church is continually in need of reform. The management must always strive to identify and clarify the Christly priorities, for all to follow .

Recapitulation

To sum up, the purpose of the Church, the People of God, is to spread the Good News—that the one and only God, our creator, loves us and forgives us—to all the people so that they too can learn to love and forgive and thus become disciples, carrying out Christ's mandates and perpetuating the memory of his teaching, his example, and his ultimate self-sacrifice. Christ has promised to be with his followers in pursuing this purpose, but he never takes away our freedom of decision. The purpose demands organisation made up of a tangible structure and many other elements. These are all good but can easily become ends in themselves, obscuring the real purpose and objective. The Church therefore always needs teachers, and a management that is continually attuned to the purpose and aware of the signs of the times.

Chapter 3

The Roman contribution

It is often overlooked that from the latter part of the 3rd century onward the leading bishops possessed a previous training in the Roman Civil law.

—Charles Sherman

THE CENTRALITY OF ROME

The first reference to the church as 'Catholic' is in the writing of St Ignatius, Bishop of Antioch[18] at the start of the second century[19]. The word catholic signifies universal. Thus, in the title 'Roman Catholic Church' the two adjectives sit rather uneasily together. How can something universal have a geographical limitation? Still, the title is true to history if not to logic or geography. By the second century, the Roman See had something of a claim to primacy in the universal church, if only because both Peter and Paul had preached the faith and suffered martyrdom there. Its foremost position as an arbiter of orthodoxy was invoked by St Irenaeus (d. 202 AD), whose authority as a teacher in the apostolic succession (in the original meaning of the phrase) is unrivalled. He had learned the Way from St Polycarp who in turn had learned it from St John the Evangelist. He was therefore an authentic source of apostolic teaching. He was a lively opponent of heresy two centuries before the Roman Empire adopted Christianity as the state religion.

Historically, the position of Rome as the centre of governance and of communication in the Empire gave everything Roman a pre-eminence. Although the capital of the Empire had moved to Constantinople before the it abandoned its many gods in favour of the one God, the administrative department concerned with religious affairs and the training of priests had remained in Rome. When the Patriarchates of Jerusalem, Antioch and Alexandria were overrun by the Muslims, only the relative newcomer, Constantinople, was left to vie with Rome. This it did. The See of Constantinople was much less venerable, but since Constantinople was to be the 'New Rome', it tried to be equal to or better than the old in all respects. Furthermore, its

---

[18] Ignatius was a towering figure in the ancient church, martyred in Rome. History has given him the title of bishop, although the episcopacy as we know it had not developed in his day. —John Behr, *The formation of Christian Theology*, Volume 1, pp 81-82 Footnote (2). Behr quotes: Cf. A. Brent, *The Relations between Ignatius of Antioch and the Didascalia", Second Century, 8.3 (1991), 129-56:* "However, this emphasis on the role of the bishop, monoepiscopacy, should be neither overstated nor construed in terms of the later "monarchical" bishop".

[19] Owen Chadwick, *A History of Christianity*, London Weidenfeld & Nicholson, 1995, *p286*

Patriarch had the advantage of being close to the levers of power. Being part of the court intrigue and having the ear of the Emperor, or indeed the Empress, was crucial in those turbulent times when an allegation of heresy could exile a bishop and create a covetable vacancy.

The Emperor no longer borrowed the title of *Pontifex Maximus,* but as head of everything, he was the unquestioned head of the Church. Even before Christianity became the state religion, it was the Emperors who summoned ecumenical councils. The Councils that are recognised by virtually all Christian denominations as properly ecumenical were all summoned by Emperors.

Christianity was officially tolerated in the Roman Empire following an edict of Galerius in 311 AD, confirmed by Constantine in the Edict of Milan two years later. This tolerated variety in religious practice. For Christianity, however, Constantine went far beyond toleration. He actively encouraged and favoured it, introducing the Christian Sunday as a day of rest throughout the Empire[20] and providing elegant buildings for the Bishop of Rome and his staff.

At the time, nobody knew how long the official toleration would last. The possibility of renewed persecution was always there. It became an immediate threat when Julian the Apostate became the sole Emperor in 361. He had plans to institute a new state church that would have been more directly under his control. (Incidentally, one of the characteristics he wanted his new church to preserve was the notably Christian tradition of looking after the needy). This threat ended providentially when Julian was killed in battle in 363 A.D. The possibility of renewed persecution finally ended when Theodosius promulgated the Edict of Thessalonica in 380, making Christianity the religion of the Empire.

WHAT CHRISTIANITY ACQUIRED

There has been no shortage of debate as to whether the Roman empire absorbed Christianity or *vice versa.* What we inherited was certainly permitted by God but that does not mean that every detail was a direct expression of the divine will for his church, then or since. Good in so many ways, but by no means perfect in all respects. What Christianity acquired included:

1. The definitive end to persecution of Christians by imperial authorities.

2. A professional lifelong priesthood restricted to men and, by default, the official invention of the laity.

3. A long-established and powerful religious bureaucracy headquartered in Rome.

4. The dominance of the Latin language in Church affairs.

---

[20]See: Ed. Schillebeeckx, *The Church with a Human Face,* New York, The Crossroad Publishing Co., 1985, p 142.

5. The pervading influence of Roman Law on Church law and ultimately on the civil legal systems of Europe.

6. Law, with its emphasis on externalities, assumed a centrality not accorded to it by Jesus or St Paul.

7. A new understanding of Baptism.

8. The slaughter policy for heresy.

9. Clergy participation in the machinery of the Roman Empire, including security, postal services, travel privileges, and salaries.

10. The diocesan structure of governance and finance.

11. Ecumenical Councils

So many changes in so short a time must have been cataclysmic for the leaders of the church. As we consider the changes individually, we shall see that many had long-term effects. Traces of some are with us still.

1) Persecution turns to encouragement, belief no longer life-threatening

The threat of persecution had reduced gradually during the fourth century. While the Edict of Milan legalised all religions, Constantine restored Christian church property which had been confiscated during the persecutions. He introduced the Christian Sunday throughout the empire and enabled the Church to receive legacies. He provided accommodation for the Bishop of Rome (probably Pope Miltiades (311-314) which later became known as the Lateran Palace and was still the pope's residence a thousand years later. In summoning the important Council of Nicaea, Constantine would not have known the religious significance of what he was doing. His primary objective was probably to promote the peace of the realm rather than the good of the church.

The Edict of Thessalonica made Christianity the state religion in 380 AD, ending the threat of persecution but the Emperor Theodosius seems to have tolerated paganism. (His son and successor in the Eastern part of the Empire, Constantius, went so far as to persecute pagans). Christian men and women, who had traditionally met in one another's houses and celebrated the Lord's Supper privately, could now build churches with confidence, and attend worship openly in large numbers, as male Roman citizens had been required to do for centuries.

2) An ordered priesthood

The Edict of Thessalonica is admirably succinct. It changed the world in 123 words! Only *"Catholic Christianity"* would be allowed and the touchstone of *"this faith is that we should believe, in accordance with apostolic discipline and Gospel teaching, that there is one Godhead, Father, Son and Holy Spirit, in an equal Majesty and a holy Trinity"*. Christian leaders must have had a hand in drafting the edict. The definition ruled out Arianism, making it heretical in civil law. The Edict set out the principle and left the implementation to be worked out by others—with a threat of physical force if needed in the service of orthodoxy.[21]

The lifelong, professional pagan priesthood was part of the imperial civil service. The fear of incurring the wrath of the various gods had bred an obsession with the scrupulous performance of defined sacrificial liturgies. The Roman priesthood was made up of men who had undergone extensive training at one of the priestly colleges, augmented at times by men who had achieved positions of high honour in Roman society.

For hundreds of years, religious management had been part of the administrative structure of the Roman Empire which was as patriarchal as Roman society of the time. This is probably where the link between ordination and administrative responsibility originated. It may have contributed to the phasing out of women from the ministry in the Church.

While there were some priestesses in ancient Rome, female officials were an anomaly in the patriarchal society. The Vestal Virgins were an exception. They had regular roles as acolytes in some public rituals, but they had to bring in a male priest for the annual ritual of quenching and re-lighting the sacred fire. Their *raison d'être* was in worshiping female deities such as Bona Dea, Ceres and Vesta. Their duties were principally to keep the sacred fire burning and to safeguard important civil archives. When the worship of female gods came to an end, the Vestal Virgins were redundant. They were disbanded in or before 394 AD and allowed to marry.

The Edict of Thessalonica did not provide for a transition period, but the pagan priests had probably seen it coming with the growing influence of the Christians in Roman society, the army, and politics. They would have been conscious of the signs of the times. They probably grumbled when their world was turned upside down but there is no evidence that they went on strike. Roman paganism was not a religion of the heart. They were civil servants. They complied. They had to accept baptism like other law-abiding Romans, and they learned from the Christian leaders how to celebrate the Lord's Supper in place of their diverse traditional pagan sacrifices.

With the influx of new Christians and the inclusion of women, the congregations suddenly grew much larger. Needing to be seen and heard, the priests continued the Roman custom of using raised altars. It is very probable that in return for being instructed in the Christian way of worship, the priestly civil servants allowed some of the *presbyteri* and *episcopi* to join their ranks. The commitment of the pious Christian Emperor, Theodosius, would have facilitated this. The religious bureaucracy certainly accepted the Bishop of Rome as its new leader.

---

[21] Sidney Z. Ehler & John B. Morall, (Trs & Eds) *Church and State through the Centuries,* Westminster, Maryland, The Newman Press (1954) p.7.

When the Roman priests, who had been trained meticulously in the various forms of sacrifice appropriate to the different gods, became Christians they would naturally have focused on uniformity in the liturgy and on the sacrificial element. This may have contributed to the change of emphasis as the sacrificial element in the Lord's Supper overtook and gradually surpassed the commemorative dimension.

Now that Christians could worship openly and publicly in large numbers, the domestic celebration of the Lord's Supper fell into disuse, although it resembles more closely the example of Jesus. It would be an understandable error if the faithful of the time considered the domestic celebration as nothing more than a carry-over from the furtive days of intermittent persecution when public celebration would have been imprudent and provocative. Domestic celebration may have been actively discouraged by the professional priests.

Whatever the reason for its demise, the domestic celebration was a great loss. With it went the small-scale fellowship that later played an evangelising role in Ireland under penal laws, in the base communities of Latin America[22] and in the cellular structure used so successfully today by some Protestant churches. The full personal involvement of his followers in celebrating the life, death and resurrection of Jesus, and in offering themselves as 'living sacrifices' as taught by both Peter and Paul, was lost.[23] One wonders if a lively tradition of offering themselves in union with Christ's sacrifice, without reference to the earthly time frame, would not have overcome the Protestant Reformers' diffidence about *repeating* Christ's sacrifice.

Lost also was the strengthening of faith that comes simply from praying and witnessing together in small intimate groups. The sharing of celebration and spiritual experience was overtaken by the Roman *obligation* to *attend* in a largely passive way. At some point, in an extraordinary departure from the example of Jesus, the faithful were discouraged from taking communion as a normal part of the ceremony.[24] The breaking of bread together was reduced to an option as Mass was regularly celebrated with the celebrant alone receiving. This downplayed the unifying symbolism of the Eucharist and further limited the participation of the laity. St Paul's characterisation of the Christian community as a priestly people was disregarded for 1500 years (despite a reminder from Martin Luther, and others, along the way) until Vatican II revived it in teaching, if not in practice. Guarding against any possible encroachment,

---

[22] "I think that we should continue on our way of evangelisation, especially creating the small church communities, which we call the small basic church communities. They are necessary to create the spirit in which people know one another, in which people truly participate."—Cardinal Aloisio Lorscheider, Archbishop of Fortaleza quoted by Joseph Dunn in *No Vipers in the Vatican,* Dublin, Columba Press, 1996 *p204*

[23] See 1 Peter 2:4-5,9; Rom. 12:1

[24] As a young woman, St. Thérèse of Lisieux expressed distress that she was "allowed" to receive Holy Communion only on the…"great feasts. Alas how far apart they seemed". —From her autobiography: *A little white flower,* London. Burns Oates & Washbourne, 1926, p71.

Canon Law to this day lays down that deacons and lay persons are *not permitted* to say the prayers with the priest, especially the eucharistic prayer.[25]

All this is not to say that Masses for large gatherings of the faithful have no place in the life of the Church. Of course, they have, but not to the exclusion of the small. Nor is it to say that the professional clergy have no place. They do, but not to the point of denying the faithful the grace of the Sacrament that forms the source and summit of our spiritual life, as happens in places where there is a shortage of clergy.

3) A well-established bureaucracy

The Emperor's word was law. The powerful and established Roman Religious Bureaucracy—then more than 600 years old—may well have welcomed the official change. Its influence had been waning for almost seventy years under a succession of Emperors who favoured Christianity (broken only by Julian). Welcome or not, they had no choice but to accept the edict, adopt Catholic Christianity promptly in compliance with imperial wishes, and get busy introducing the new state religion and liturgical rules to all the regions of the far-flung Empire. They also had the challenge of absorbing the existing Christian communities, including that of Rome, into the administrative structures. The College of Pontiffs was the core of the pagan bureaucracy responsible for managing religious affairs. throughout the Empire. The head of the College had the official title of *Pontifex Maximus*. Although some Emperors appropriated this title to themselves from time to time, it was normally held by the head priest. When translated, the title means *Greatest Bridge-builder*. It must have lost its literal meaning through usage before Christians could tolerate its use for their earthly leader. Its literal meaning is undeniably heretical. Despite this, early in the fifth century, the title of *Pontifex Maximus* had passed exclusively, and permanently, to the Bishop of Rome.

An immediate effect of the Edict of Thessalonica, however, must have been to land the Bishop of Rome with the leadership of the religious bureaucracy. There was a major challenge in the education, retraining and redeployment of personnel including the heads of religious affairs in the various provinces and dioceses. He would have needed to transfer some knowledgeable and experienced personnel from his own curia to key positions in the bureaucracy. He may well have merged the two, at least to an extent. The pope's secretariat thus became a part of the Imperial Civil Service. Thus, the primacy of jurisdiction of the Bishop of Rome became an official part of the administrative structure for several hundred years, with the pope subservient only to the Emperor. Authority for maintaining exacting standards in the liturgy would have led the bureaucracy to continue its roles as training institute and final arbitrator on issues of practice, and ritual. A version of the aphorism *"Lex Orandi, Lex Credendi"*

---

[25] Canon 907, 1983 Code.

dates from the early fifth century.[26]   One can see how the bureaucracy under the Pontifex Maximus inevitably developed the further primacies; of orthodoxy and jurisdiction. Roman power and control had its foundations in the pagan state church and was underpinned by the Emperor—in the West until the collapse of the Western Empire (476 AD) and in the East for five centuries waning gradually until it came to an end with the East/West schism in 1054. As the Church re-established itself in the West independently of the Empire, Christians in the West continued to look to the Roman See as the touchstone of orthodoxy and the centre of unity.

Rome was not satisfied with the pre-eminence accorded it by the bishops of the world. The primacy of honour and recognition as the court of final appeal was not enough. The bureaucracy had governed before and would have felt it was entitled to govern again. The Roman mind-set required that this should be established in law as well as in tradition. The Roman ambition to dominate has been a recurring feature of Church history ever since. It reached its zenith in the adoption of the twin dogmas of Papal Infallibility and Universal Jurisdiction at Vatican I.

Unfortunately, any collaboration by equals ends when one claims dominance. Others must then resist or submit. The relationship under which bishops monitored their neighbours for orthodoxy under the guidance of the Spirit, suffered when one bishop laid claim to overall power and control. Pope Victor I (189-198) has the dubious honour of being the earliest recorded Bishop of Rome claiming the right to interfere in other churches. At one point, he purported to exclude all the churches of Asia Minor from communion, not only with Rome, but with the church generally. As far as is known, Pope Stephen I (254-257) was the first to find a doctrinal basis for Roman primacy—in the Lord's charge to Peter (Matt. 16:18), coupled with his own claim to hold the succession from Peter,[27] although there is no evidence of Peter being styled Bishop of Rome in his lifetime and he certainly never had the title of pope or *Pontifex Maximus*. The history of the papacy laying claims to special authority, titles, and powers for itself could doubtless fill a separate volume.

4) Latin as the language of the Church.

We got the advantages of the Latin language along with its inadequacies. In time it replaced Greek which had a more precise philosophical vocabulary. Latin later became a key part of the mystique of the profession, invested with attributes entirely inappropriate to a language, like holiness and authority. This sort of carelessness could only serve to obscure the true meaning of holiness and authority in the mind of the faithful.

A universal language in a universal church enabled a unity of liturgy and law and created a sense of community even among peoples who had never met. As it became

---

[26] The Catechism of the Catholic Church, (1124) quoting Prosper of Acquitane. In English: "The law of prayer is the law of faith"

[27] J.N.D. Kelly, *Oxford Dictionary of Popes,* paperback updated 2005, p 12

a dying or dead language, Latin may have suffered less from the tendency for words to change their meaning over time. This did not necessarily prevent the underlying reality from changing but it has helped to protect the meaning of many essential documents, particularly the scriptures and the writings of the early Fathers, although very few of these originated in Latin. Centuries later, when the everyday use of Latin was limited to the educated and the aristocracy of Europe, the predominant use of the language in religious affairs helped to divide the community by putting the clergy in a class apart from their flocks, more like the aristocracy. Moreover, it ensured that most of the faithful were kept in ignorance of the scriptures. This effect was copper fastened by a ban on the publication of vernacular translations of the scriptures, which was not finally lifted until the end of the nineteenth century.

It was a faulty translation of the Greek text of Romans 5:12 that led St Augustine to develop his interpretation of Original Sin which has greatly influenced the Church in the West [28]in regard to the conditions for salvation and in its attitude to sexuality.

A final problem with Latin is that it lacks the extensive and subtle vocabulary developed by the more philosophical Greeks. For the developing church, Latin suffered from a lack of precision in two critically important words.

First: *Castus.* The Romans used the same word, *castus,* to refer to chastity, to ritual abstinence, to holiness and to unselfishness. We know that language and concepts influence one another, and that people often mistake the word for the thing. This suggests that the distinction between chastity and unselfishness may not always have been clear in Latin conversation or documentation. Christ's moral teaching is founded on love of other and this love presupposes a level of practical unselfishness, which is thus (or should be) a foundational concept in Christly moral theology. Latin was the language of moral theology for 1800 years.

The lack of precision in distinguishing between holiness, unselfishness and chastity may have contributed to the enduringly negative attitude to sex and pleasure. It undoubtedly helped to obscure the centrality of unselfish love in the theology of discipleship and to facilitate the substitution by the Roman authorities of a system of detailed rules and regulations that owed far more to Judaic tradition, to Roman Law and to the Roman obsession with meticulous liturgical ritual than to the example of Jesus Christ or the preaching of St Paul. It might also help to explain the preoccupation with things and acts as values in themselves at the expense of motivation, consequences, love, and conscience which would be the pillars of a Christly Moral Theology. This is dealt with in more detail in Chapter 14.

Second: *Ordinatio.* The same word, *Ordinatio,* was used in Latin, to cover two different concepts, distinguished in Greek as *cheirotonia* and *cheirothesia*. The first means selection and appointment, the second, the ceremony of consecration. At the

---

[28] Dale Moody, *The Word of Truth: A Summary of Christian Doctrine Based on Biblical Revelation,* Grand Rapids, MN, Wm B. Eerdmans Publishing Company, 1981, *p*289

beginning of the fifteenth century Macarius of Ancyra can still write that the choice of a community makes someone a bishop; here the laying on of hands is secondary.[29] (Augustine, remember, became the bishop at the insistence of the community). Great theological importance has been attached to maintaining consistency in the precise form of the *cheirothesia*, in the words used and especially in the *impositio manuum* (imposition of hands). The more important business of selection and appointment, however, has been taken out of the hands of the community altogether. In the second millennium, the appointment of bishops became something for princes and popes to negotiate between them and synods and councils found it necessary to condemn simony repeatedly. In the twentieth century, after centuries of struggle, the papacy finally prevailed. As the power of the bishops waned and loyalty to one's bishop gave way to loyalty to Rome, secular governments had less need to control religious appointments and these finally became the exclusive prerogative of the Roman bureaucracy. The legislation now provides that the pope's assent to the selection is an essential prerequisite for the episcopal consecration that makes the priest into a bishop. The community has no say. As a formality, the pastors are sometimes con-sulted in advance, but their input appears to have little effect on the choice. It is not unusual for an appointee to be unknown to the faithful in his new diocese, and even to the pastors. His contacts with the bureaucracy in Rome or with the local Nuncio are what gets him the job. In the pontificates of John Paul II and Benedict XVI, docility and a readiness to profess the Roman party line on certain non-infallible hot-button issues were essential attributes. This has had its effect on the standing of the bishops, the quality of management and the life of the Church.

Furthermore, it has significant implications for the ecumenicity and authority of any future church council, even within the Roman Catholic Church itself. How can a bishop who does not know his people witness to their beliefs? *A fortiori,* how can he know what they think, if discussion of hot button issues is suppressed? Any future instance of moral unanimity among bishops will not reflect the *sensus fidelium* but rather the criteria that guided the central selection committee during the immediately preceding decades. The very concept of an ecumenical council has been undermined by central selection of homogeneous bishops.

5) The pervading influence of Roman Law.

The Roman Empire was ruled by law and Roman Law had a powerful influence on the development of the Church and its laws. The Bishop of Rome became the head of the religious bureaucracy with the same title, *Pontifex Maximus,* as his pagan predecessors. The bureaucracy continued to be part of the Roman administrative sys-tem, with the popes directly accountable to the Emperors. They became powerful as

---

[29] —Edward Schillebeeckx, *The Church with a Human Face,* New York, The Crossroad Publishing Co., 1985, p 139.

the Christianised church bureaucracy continued to manage religious affairs under Roman law and custom.

The transition from Paganism to Christianity throughout the Empire must have required many changes in the meticulous regulations for religious celebrations and in administrative responsibilities. Thus, the early Christian liturgical and disciplinary rules would have taken the form of amendments to Roman administrative law. At very least, they would have been fitted to the structure and format of Roman Law. William Ball LLD writes:

> There is no doubt "that Roman jurisprudence provided early Christian teachers" from the times of the Apostles themselves in the 1st century "with language and modes of thought by means of which they (these Christian teachers) might give expression to the truths they desired to propagate".[30]

Charles Sherman, former Professor of Roman Law at Yale, writes

> [I]t is often overlooked that from the latter part of the 3rd century onward the leading bishops possessed a previous training in the Roman Civil law. St Cyprian, St Ambrose, St Augustine, St Paulinus of Nola, and St John Chrysostom had practised law either as teachers or advocates at the Bar. Furthermore, St Ambrose and St Paulinus had held high administrative and judicial offices of State.[31]

Three hundred years later the Code of Justinian openly reflected the lack of a distinction between civil and church law.

Roman Law was based on the tacit assumption that women were rather less than human. They did not share the rights, dignity, and freedoms of Roman citizens. The law saw them more akin to chattels than to human beings. In adopting the Christian religion, the empire did not revise the Law to reflect Christ's attitude to women, and Roman Law has influenced Church and European Law right up to the present day. In the thirteenth Century St Thomas Aquinas could still classify women as incapable of eminence and in a state of subjection.

6) Law becomes paramount

The Church is a community of worship. The service of God must come from the heart or it loses the reality of worship. If it springs from constraint, or the threat of sanctions, here or hereafter, it is servitude at worst or at best informed long-term self-interest. The basis of Christian worship must be knowledge and love; law comes second or third. When law takes priority, then we must ask: is it law that is being worshipped?

Constantine encouraged Christianity, although not officially a Christian himself until his final days. He had arranged to be baptised on his deathbed. He would have

---

[30] William Edward Ball, LLD, *St Paul and Roman Law,* p. vii, quoted by Charles P. Sherman in *Brief History of Imperial Roman Canon Law,* 7 Cal. L. Rev. 93 (1919).

[31] Charles P. Sherman, Brief History of Imperial Roman Canon Law, 7 Cal. L. Rev. 93 (1919).

been aware of the teaching that Baptism wipes away all previous sin, so he was keeping his freedom to do things his own way in life while yet ensuring his 'visa' for heaven would be valid. He would not have agreed with Pearse who wrote in his own *apologia pro vita sua,* a poem entitled 'The Fool:[32]

> "For this I have heard in my heart, that a man
> … shall not bargain or huckster with God".

Constantine's bargaining strategy reflects a legalistic, debtors and creditors ledger, approach to salvation from which the Latin Church has never been entirely free.

Law is essential. In an institution devoted to the spirit, however, it should be subordinate. St Augustine, although a lawyer himself, could say:

> "Love, and do what thou wilt …
> let the root of love be within,
> of this root can nothing spring but what is good".

Law, unfortunately, tends towards the black or white, the yes or no, the on or off, the binary option. But the things of the spirit tend to come in imperceptible gradations. Human love, hope, faith, compassion, kindness, trust, prudence, strength, and fortitude are all continua. In the Latin Church, law has assumed a sovereignty not accorded to it by Jesus or St Paul. This facilitates control, but at a cost; the letter overwhelms the spirit, the theoretical outshines the actual, the legal fiction can supersede the fact, profession can easily be equated with belief.

The Roman officials adopted Christianity as individuals, but the bureaucracy resisted conversion. As we have seen, bureaucracies don't do compassion. They are so essentially self-centred that they have trouble understanding the dynamics of love. Power and control are what they understand. Consequently, they prioritise rules. The Roman bureaucracy of today gives many of St Augustine's opinions a quasi-scriptural status, but it does not make a guideline of his advice to "love and do what thou wilt".

7) A new understanding of Baptism.

The Edict of 380 AD did not provide for a phased introduction. It was by implication immediate and it must have provided an enormous headache for the civil servants and a challenge to the existing Christians. It was not all implemented in a day, however, and we can only imagine how it played out.

Up to then, neophyte Christians, known as *catechumens,* were expected to demonstrate their belief while under instruction over a period of six months or more before being admitted to full membership of the community, marked by the reception of baptism. The Edict brought an end to persecution and the need for a candidate to prove his belief, for his own sake and to avoid betrayal of the Christian community. Roman Law required worship and the Emperor had now stipulated that all worship was to be Christian. Consequently, law-abiding Romans must have been queueing up

---

[32] Poem by Pádraig Pearse, *The Fool.*

to become Christians. Who could refuse them? The Christian communities had many good reasons to co-operate with the Emperor. This must have hastened the end of the catechumenate as the standard entry system. Baptism now had to become the start of the process, as it had been in Apostolic times. A simple request followed by an acceptance of the Nicene/Constantinopolitan Creed would be enough. Hopefully, the sacrament would achieve what it symbolised. The parallel with the oath of loyalty for new recruits joining the Roman Army, the *sacramentum,* was so immediate that the word sacrament became a vital part of the Christian lexicon and has been with us ever since.

8) Slaughter policy for heretics.

The Roman gods were typical pagan gods; believed to be capricious, vindictive, vengeful, and easily offended. Natural or man-made disasters were thought to be expressions of their anger. Since one man's offence could bring retribution on the whole community, Roman Law required each *pater familias* to attend public worship regularly and to provide for private rites in the home. Refusing to worship the customary gods was a legal offence punishable by death. The Edict of Thessalonica replaced the gods with God. It did not repeal the legal requirement to worship with its gruesome sanction.

Jesus brought the good news that our Creator loves us, is ready to forgive our sins, and wants us to reciprocate in love. Love, of its very nature, must be voluntary. Logically then, the Christianised Empire should have abandoned the obligatory element of worship. Making Christianity obligatory involved a basic misunderstanding of the gospel. The death penalty for heresy remained a feature of Roman Law although, mercifully, the full rigour of the law was not generally applied against those who remained pagan at the time. Justinian's codification of Roman Law in the sixth century, however, included the death penalty for heresy and his Code became the foundational model for civil law in many parts of Europe. Consequently, Christians in Europe, whose forbears had been thrown to the lions or burnt as human torches for being Christian, saw their own clergy complicit in burning people at the stake a thousand years later for not being sufficiently orthodox Christians; or for refusing to profess beliefs they did not share. There was a tradition that clergy should not shed human blood, so their role was to test a person who had been denounced as a heretic. Testing by torture was routine. If the victim could not prove his orthodoxy or identify his (anonymous) accuser and show that there was an ulterior motive for the denunciation, the clerics could find him guilty of heresy, and hand him over to the civil authorities to carry out the ceremonial public killing. It was known for bishops to enhance the influence of their office by presiding over this depraved form of entertainment. It had the useful effect of deterring others from expressing unorthodox views; or even from disagreeing with the bishop.

The Biblical parallel—of the Jewish high priests trying Jesus by their law and delivering him to the Roman Governor for execution—does not seem to have occurred to anyone, or if it did, it was no deterrent. Heretics were executed in England until 1612. In Spain, the last was hanged in 1826 at Valencia.

9) Missionary opportunity.

The pagan religious bureaucracy had access to the communication systems of the empire and this privilege would have continued when Christianity became the state religion. Within the Roman Empire, ships were required to carry authorised government officials as passengers free of charge. This system would have greatly facilitated the movement of Christian preachers undertaking missionary journeys. Many itinerant Christian preachers would have been dependent on the approval of the Roman authorities to qualify for the privilege.

10) Dioceses and Bishops.

The administrative structure of the Empire was designed to secure the borders, maintain tranquillity, regulate courts, and remit taxes to Rome. It was a hierarchical system where officers were given substantial power and the necessary wide discretion to govern their defined areas. It is clear from the terminology used by the church today, *provinces, dioceses, vicars, presbyters etc.,* that the structure of church administration mimicked the civil administration of which at one time it was an integral part. At other times although separate, it was scarcely distinguishable. Confusion arises because, with the passage of time, the meaning and usage of several important words have changed. In addition, some were used loosely and interchangeably, even at the time.

A *diocese,* in Roman civil affairs, was a huge area, encompassing several *provinces.* In church affairs, it came to relate to a much smaller territory ruled over by a bishop. The word 'bishop' springs from *'episcopos'.* The underlying reality developed from that of overseer or manager of a local church to diocesan monarch and back, in more recent times, to little more than diocesan manager.

The terms *episcopos* and *presbyteros* in some ancient documents have the distinct meanings of 'overseer' and 'elder' respectively. In others, one of these terms is used to indicate both offices. The term *presbyteri* later came to be used for priests and *episcopii* for diocesan (or titular) bishops. It is thus difficult to be sure what the terms really meant in different places and times in antiquity. To add to the confusion, some translators of ancient documents have given these words their modern meaning. *Presbyteros* is often rendered anachronistically as 'priest', and this can be misleading.[33]

In his epistle, St Paul tells Titus to complete the organisation of the Churches in Crete. It is evident that Paul had preached to communities of Christians in the towns

---

[33] An important example of this occurs in St Paul when he tells Titus to appoint *presbyteri* in the cities of Crete (Titus 1:5). Twenty-two English translations render the word as 'elders', where the Douay/Rheims translation, used exclusively for centuries by Roman Catholics, gives 'ordain priests'. This has helped to obscure the historically late development of the office of priest among Christians. The Jerusalem Bible, which is probably the most scholarly uses "appoint elders".

of the island but had not got around to making such appointments. He had taught them to celebrate the Lord's Supper without designating who would preside or lead. When he was among them as a visitor instructing them, it would have been natural for him to preside. Titus was instructed to select suitable men or women from among the faithful and appoint them as presbyters. In this text, Paul seems to equate elders and overseers.[34] Maybe he just meant leaders.

One thing is clear however: St Paul does not mean priests. As a Jew and a Roman citizen, he knew the word for priest, but he did not use it. When he converted the people, and instructed them in the practice of the faith, he taught them how to celebrate the Lord's Supper as the ritual that unified the churches and sanctified the faithful. As Paul sees it, there is no need for a priest; the Christians are already a priestly people. Christians need no intermediary; They have 'put on Christ' and Christ is both God and man. They need no specialist to offer sacrifice on their behalf. Individual priests were a late arrival in Christianity, probably influenced by Roman and Jewish religious practice. We will return to this issue in a more appropriate context.

Catholicism as the state religion had about a hundred years in which to establish itself before the Western Empire was overrun. The distinction between civil and religious rule would not always have been very sharply defined but there must have been some officials with direct responsibility for overseeing religious affairs in the provinces; *episcopii* in fact and possibly in title becoming what we know as bishops. They would have reported to the religious bureaucracy in Rome. Christianity as a state activity collapsed with the withdrawal of the Imperial officials. But that was not the end of the matter. By that time there must have been many bishops, independently loyal to Jesus Christ and their flocks rather than to the Empire, who, like the Irish bishops under Penal Laws, kept the faith with their flocks when the salaries stopped coming. Not all the native populations were wiped out or uprooted by the barbarian invaders. Pockets of Catholicism must have survived. Those left without an *episcopos* would have appointed one. As we have said, Christianity as a religious practice enforced by civil law involved a profound misunderstanding of the gospel. Nevertheless, there is evidence that many bishops understood better and remained with their flocks, even taking on some duties of civil leadership when their colleagues withdrew. They would certainly have kept contact with the Christianised religious bureaucracy in Rome. Thus, the Roman diocesan framework survived while the church communities in areas under barbarian control were rebuilding.

There were many such communities, administratively united by the diocesan structure. What united them spiritually, however, was their faith in the risen Lord, faithfulness to the apostolic teachings, and the celebration of the Eucharist.

---

[34] This is noted four centuries later by St Jerome in his letter to Evangelus.
—http://www.newadvent.org/fathers/3001146.htm, accessed March 2017

11) Ecumenical Councils

As we have seen in Chapter 3, it was the Emperor, Constantine, who conceived the idea of a General or Ecumenical Council. Although Christianity was not yet the state religion of the Empire and Constantine himself had not yet been baptised, he summoned, participated, and presided. His objective was peace and peace depended on unity. He had to settle the differences in belief that were being exploited. He knew that a simple majority vote would leave the Church as divided as before, so he set a high bar for all major decisions. They would require the virtual unanimity that would express the mind of the Church authoritatively and would thus encourage a very small minority to rethink their convictions. He was happy that this was achieved.[35] His providential precedent has been honoured at every Council since then with only one exception. At Vatican I, Pope Pius IX, conscious of the substantial opposition to the definition of the two dogmas, changed the procedures, ruling that a simple majority would suffice. Constantine would have foreseen the divisive result. The definitions have turned the papacy into the biggest obstacle to unity among Christians.

It is worth noting that the seven Ecumenical Councils that are recognised by all Christians were summoned by Roman Emperors. The idea that only a pope can convoke a Council was a controlling provision, included in the 1917 Code of Canon Law (Cn 222) and repeated in 1983 (Cn 338 §1). It confers an arbitrary legal power on the papacy and blocks any global initiative of the bishops. The law has no basis in theology or biblical studies. It means that were a pope were to be insane or otherwise incapacitated, the bishops of the world would be unable to call a legal General Council or even a meeting of the College of Bishops itself to deal with the situation.

In *Lumen Gentium,* chapter 3, the bishops affirm their shared responsibility for the universal church. In concert with the bishop of Rome, they form one of two supreme authorities—a self-contradictory expression. They were not ready to openly question the dogmas of 1870, repeatedly protesting continuity with Vatican I while approving radical changes, including governance by the College of Bishops. Even the carefully nuanced John W. O'Malley, suggests that they 'protested too much'. [36]

The 1983 revision of Canon Law, precluded the bishops from taking any initiative:

> It belongs to the Roman Pontiff to select and promote, according to the needs of the Church, ways in which the College of Bishops can exercise its office in respect of the universal church in a collegial manner. (Cn 337 §3).

No papacy has suggested a way for the College of Bishops to fulfil its role. Under the same Canon, however, any pope acting independently of the curia could legally superimpose a Governing Body representing the Bishops under his leadership and charge it with creating its own constitution, procedures and standing orders.

---

[35]See Constantine, Letters: http://www.constantinethegreatcoins.com/Constantine/Book2.html
[36] John W. O'Malley, *Vatican I, the Council and the Making of the Ultramontane Church,* Cambridge MA, The Belknap Press of Harvard University Press, 2018, p 242

Chapter 4

Church structure develops

There is a tendency in matter
"to complexify upon itself and at the same time to increase in consciousness.

—Pierre Teilhard de Chardin

OVERSEERS AND ELDERS DEVELOP THE DIGNITY OF BISHOPS AND PRIESTS.

The apostles started their mission as itinerant preachers. They appointed elders, *(presbyteri)* and overseers *(episcopi)* for the local communities of believers that they founded. The two functions were not always clearly distinguished. At times, one may have included the other[37]. The meaning of the terms is often uncertain. It changed as the church developed. We might safely call them the leadership committee. Their functions appear to have been to show the Way and to organise the people with various charisms and talents to which St Paul witnesses.

The itinerant preachers would generally have presided as they taught the new Christians to celebrate the Lord's Supper. Thereafter, while the Lord's Supper still took the form of a celebratory meal in a private house, the host or hostess would sometimes have presided. As Christian communities grew and coalesced, particularly in cities, gifted organisers became influential and were known as bishops (derived from *episcopi*, overseers,). They tended to be chosen by the community although, for a time, they were part of the imperial administrative system, under the Christianised religious bureaucracy in Rome. With the Roman tradition of giving officials wide discretion, they became powerful in their own diocese in the fourth and fifth centuries. (St Ignatius of Antioch was something of an exceptional case, ahead of his time in this respect[38])

As the leader of a significant and united section of the population the bishop gained civil influence and power in addition to his ecclesiastic authority, even if he was not a civil servant. He became something of a dignitary. His pre-eminence ensured that if he were present at the Lord's Supper, he would normally preside. For a time, the *episcopus* became the *only* person who could preside, so he became a *sine qua*

---

[37] Titus 1:5 and 1 Timothy 3:2. The meaning of the terms *presbyteros* and *episcopos* have presented difficulties for translators. Different translations use 'elder' or 'overseer' interchangeably. In Titus, the Jerusalem Bible uses the word 'president'. The Douai/Rheims Bible, long the standard in Catholicism, used 'priest' and 'bishop'. This is an anachronism and helped to obscure the fact that an ordained priest was not required until the third or fourth century. Originally, it was the community that celebrated the Lord's Supper when they dined together.

[38] —John Behr, *The formation of Christian Theology,* Volume 1, pp 81-82 Footnote (2). Behr is quoting: Cf. A. Brent, *The Relations between Ignatius of Antioch and the Didascalia,* Second Century, 8.3 (1991), pp 129-56

non for the event. St Ignatius of Antioch describes the grandeur of the presiding bishop flanked by his *presbyteri*. As Christian groups multiplied, this pattern proved unsustainable and the *episcopi* started to delegate the right to celebrate to *presbyteri*. Robert Taft S.J writes:

> "from the fourth century we see a growing consciousness that presbyters celebrating the eucharist together with the bishop are doing something that the laity cannot do, something only they have the mandate to perform".[39]

Generally, however, the *presbyteri* and *episcopi* would have been the ones to preside in the early, small, communities. These offices were taken seriously. St Paul was aware that appointment as an elder sometimes went to a person's head. (1 Tm 3:6)

What must be distinguished here is 'mandate' and 'power'. Even in the earliest times, there was need of regulation for such a sacred gathering. An orderly celebration required that people be allocated different tasks. Among these, that of leading the proceedings was obviously important and carried some prestige. In some cases, it must have been rotated among the more sophisticated or literate members who would have been able to preside. In others it would have devolved regularly on the same person.[40] At times the person chosen as overseer/manager might himself or herself have been the only one capable of presiding.

Sacerdotal offices and a hierarchy of titles and dignities emerge.

The transition from being an elder or overseer who presides well, to being the one who normally presides is scarcely noticeable. Once established, for others to intrude on this pattern of service could be considered an affront, an impertinence, unmannerly or even offensive. Function can generate status and status prerogatives, so it is easy to see how the normal president could become a fixture. From there to sole celebrant is not a big step. Having the job of presiding at the sacred mysteries could easily be confused with having the power to effect them.

All this occurred in different places at various times over a long period. As we shall see later, it came to fruition more abruptly in areas under Roman control when the citizens, including the pagan priests, were required by edict to become Christian without a transition period and the overseers or bishops became state appointees.

Thus, what Paul described as works of service became offices. Offices gave rise to a class of officeholders which in due course became a profession. This would have been influenced by the conversion of Jewish priests and, after the Edict of Thessalonica, by the absorption of the Roman priestly profession. This naturally developed a pecking order, with titles, privileges, powers, and a professional code. The profession monopolised the priesthood which up to then had resided in the Christian

---

[39] Robert Taft S.J., Ex Oriente Lux ? Some reflections on Eucharistic Celebrations, in *Worship* 54, (1980) p 318

[40] Charismatic leaders would often have been chosen. Although the culture of the time undervalued women in general, among the Christians there were many women in leadership.

community because that is what being 'a priestly people' meant. Bradshaw says that the fourth century…

> [M]arks the beginning of a further shift in the whole understanding of the liturgical role of the bishop and presbyters, away from the notion of presiding over a rite celebrated corporately by the whole church to the idea of their doing something for and on behalf of the people. It was not until sometime later, however, that the term 'priest', which had been applied to the bishop since at least the beginning of the third century, began also to be used of presbyters individually, and not just in their association with the bishop.[41]

Schillebeeckx deals with this point extensively. Let it suffice here to quote excerpts from one page:

> Of course, for the early church the community itself is the active subject of the *offerimus panem et calicem* … The active subject of the eucharist was the community … So, at that time concelebration did not mean a common celebration of the eucharist by concelebrating priests but was the term for the concelebration by the whole of the believing people who were present.[42]

Once the idea of the individual priest became established, the presbyters leap-frogged over the order of deacons which had been established by the apostles but who had never been given official permission to preside. The preoccupation with their own dignity and the importance of pecking order was still echoing the concern of the twelve as to who would be the 'greatest'. The Council of Arles (314) was aware that 'in many places' deacons were celebrating mass and forbade this in Canon 15. Apparently, the deacons and senior deaconesses *(presbytides)* of those times must have been seen as getting above their station. Canon 18 instructs the deacons to respect the presbyters and do nothing without their knowledge and approval, About the same time (mid fourth century) the Synod of Laodicea banned the appointment of any further *presbytides*. It also ruled: "It is not right for deacons to sit in the presence of presbyters unless he be bidden by the presbyter to sit down. Likewise, the deacons shall have worship of the sub-deacons and all the [inferior] clergy" (Cn 20)[43]. Apparently, the issue of relative dignity was still important among the successors of the apostles. The Council of Nicaea had illustrated the same preoccupation.

Gradually, the profession became sacralised and took control of the charismatic activities, the distributed 'gifts' that Paul had identified as being important for maintaining unity in the faith or turned them into subordinated offices. (The monopoly included evangelisation and teaching, which made it quite easy to erase the priesthood of the community from Catholic awareness for 1500 years.) What had started as elders and overseers thus developed a sacerdotal dignity and became priests and bishops.

---

[41] Paul Bradshaw, *Liturgical Presidency in the Early Church,* Bramcote, Notts. Grove Books, Grove Liturgical Studies No 36 p27

[42] Edward Schillebeeckx, *The Church with a Human Face,* New York, Crossroad, 1985, p 146

[43] Charles J. Hefele, Bishop of Rottenburg, *A History of the Councils,* pp 165-6. Already Christ's instruction on the exercise of authority was being threatened by social convention.

The priests were associated with local churches while bishops came to manage and govern a cluster of churches in a specified area. The bishops were deemed to be the successors of the apostles although they were definitely not itinerant, each being theoretically 'wedded' to his own see. When a bishop moved to a more desirable see, as sometimes happened, this was disapproved of[44] and was sometimes called 'adultery'. As the bishop's area of responsibility grew larger, it was referred to as a diocese, a title copied from the Roman civil system. Bishops came to need secretarial and administrative staff. These were known collectively as a curia.

As successors of the apostles, bishops might have been deemed equal but for administrative purposes they were grouped under four patriarchates, Jerusalem, Antioch, Alexandria, and Rome. At an early stage, the Roman See was accorded a Primacy of Honour by all the others. The Roman penchant for legal definition, however, coupled with the empire-wide authority in matters religious to which the pagan bureaucracy had been accustomed and which the Christianised bureaucracy exercised for a hundred years, led to expectations and tensions. Later, Constantinople, as the New Rome, became recognised as a fifth patriarchate. When Jerusalem, Antioch and Alexandria were overrun by Islam, the New Rome was left to vie with the Old Rome for the leadership. And it did.

The importance of order

Christ gave us the institutional Church as part of his Promise to be with his followers until the end of time. We would quite literally be lost without it. It is very reasonable to infer some form of hierarchical intention, and indeed the primacy of Peter, from Christ's description of Peter as the rock on which the Church was to be founded and from his instruction to Peter to *'confirm the brethren'*. That the primacy should continue after Peter's death is equally reasonable. Its link to the Bishop of Rome may well be providential. The way it has been exercised throughout history, however, is very human. The great church historian, Lord Acton, had the papacy in mind when he wrote: *"Power tends to corrupt and absolute power corrupts absolutely"*.[45]

What did the word 'hierarchy' mean then? Does it mean the same thing now? In the very early days, the hierarchical structure was composed of the *presbyteri* and *episcopi* who were part of the local church community and were left in charge when an Apostle decided it was time to resume his missionary journey and to spread the good news further afield. He prayerfully entrusted the community he was leaving to the guidance of the Holy Spirit. When a major disagreement arose, the protagonists sought out Peter and the brethren in Jerusalem. Invoking the Spirit, they exchanged experiences and a lively debate ensued. The mind of the People of God emerged in discussion

---

[44] The movement of *presbyteri* was disapproved of. The Council of Arles (314 AD) was prepared to tolerate one move but called for those who moved more than once to be deposed.

[45] Lord Acton, *Letter to Archbishop Creighton*. Given as the correct version in an obituary in the *Telegraph* for the 4th Lord Acton who died 10th October 2010.

and guided the decision on what was to be taught or what was to be done. It is interesting to note that the Jerusalem council made its decision by consensus and propounded the principle that people who believe should not be burdened unnecessarily. Regrettably, this sound decision has often been ignored since then.

Later, as *episcopi* developed into bishops, each new bishop was elected or selected by the community, i.e. members of the local church or churches.[46] Schillebeeckx, as we shall see, reckons that appointment made him a bishop sacramentally. He was then consecrated by nearby bishops, generally three or more. Once appointed, bishops were responsible to God for the governance of their dioceses and for ensuring that apostolic teaching was preserved intact. Since they were deemed to be 'married' to their dioceses, promotion to a wealthier or more influential one was condemned by several ecumenical councils, which tells us that it continued to happen.

PRESERVING THE BELIEFS OF THE FAITHFUL

Christ's promise to be with us has been interpreted from post-apostolic times as meaning that he would ensure that the beliefs of his followers arising from the truths he had revealed would be preserved free from significant error. Vatican II quoted St Augustine's formula:

> Thanks to a supernatural sense of the faith which characterises the People as a whole, it manifests this unerring quality when, "from the bishops down to the last member of the laity" it shows universal agreement in matters of faith and morals. *(Lumen Gentium* §12)

Thus, infallibility in faith is promised to, and grounded in, the beliefs of the faithful as a whole. The pillar and ground of truth is the People of God. Knowing exactly what his followers believe, however, has always proved difficult. There will always be questions also about the scope of the promise and the implied granularity, and the timescale. St Augustine's formula would seem to limit the extent to the essentials, and the degree of detail to the basics while leaving open the question of timescale.

Synods and Councils

The task of articulating the faith would have rested primarily on the elders, and 'prophets' (as teachers) initially. Bishops, as they developed from being organisers, became the authoritative teachers. They appear to have monitored one another and local synods and councils were held to resolve differences. This led to development of better understanding and more detailed teaching some of which had to be modified as human understanding and knowledge, both sacred and profane, developed. The idea of a humble 'pilgrim church' being led by the Spirit to 'all truth' remained valid. Temporary errors of individual bishops or communities did not negate the overall Promise.

---

[46] When Christianity was the State Church bishops would have been civil servants. Augustine was selected by public clamour, and apparently confirmed subsequently by the religious authorities in Rome.

The spread of Arianism among the bishops themselves, however, led to bishops being deposed, exiled, replaced and, in some cases, restored. The doctrinal question became entangled with issues of politics, personalities, positions, power and possibly wealth. Local councils were too divided and partisan to settle the Arian issue and it grew into much more than a local issue. Unity in faith was lost and with it, the unity of charity. The latter may have happened first.

The Emperor, Constantine, summoned all the bishops to the great Council of Nicaea in 325, to settle the doctrinal and disciplinary issues and to restore peace. He introduced the principle of moral unanimity for conciliar decisions. Unity was important to him, if only because it would restore peace in the realm. There were some arguments about offices and episcopal boundaries, but the outstanding work of the Council was the virtually unanimous agreement on the essentials of the Creed.[47] Fortunately, the idea of infallibility had not yet been thought of, leaving it possible for some of the formulations of Nicaea to be refined at the Council of Chalcedon. Since then it has been widely accepted that moral (or virtual) unanimity at a council of all the bishops (or equivalents), with perhaps some other dignitaries and sages added, is the highest authority in the Church, but not necessarily infallible.

This was confirmed at the Council of Florence (1414-18) which ended the Western Schism but was doubly overturned by the definition of the Dogma of Infallibility at Vatican I (1869-70) by resorting to majority vote.

HIERARCHICAL STRUCTURE DEVELOPS OVER TIME

Virtually every encyclical, whatever the subject, stresses at some point the vital importance of the hierarchical structure of the Church that Christ founded. This is repeated so often that one might infer that the faithful and their pastors pose some threat to the hierarchy. But the threat does not come from below. The real damage has been inflicted from above.

Roman Catholicism preserves all the hierarchical ranks and titles, but the basic principle of hierarchical structure—that an office or a position should carry authority commensurate with its responsibilities—has been largely forgotten. The principle of subsidiarity, much preached to others, is routinely turned on its head in the Church's own affairs. The bishops who are in theory responsible for provision of the sacraments in their dioceses find their hands tied behind their backs. They are not allowed to get on with doing their defined job.

Current Church structure may meet the dictionary meaning of 'hierarchy'. But is it anything like what Christ meant or what the Apostles put in place? There are at least 27 steps in the hierarchical ladder from Sub-Deacon to Pope, while leaving out

---

[47] The shift in emphasis from a religion that was characterised by the way of life of its adherents to one defined by its set of beliefs is sometimes seen as the downside of the Council of Nicaea. It may have been happening already.

the pecking orders within the Vatican diplomatic corps, the curial dicasteries and the many congregations of consecrated religious.

The focus on dignity starts on day one of a vocation to the priesthood. The last man to arrive at the seminary is the lowest in dignity. He leads the formal procession into the church at the start of the liturgy. Over the years he gradually works his way towards the rear to where those who are highest in dignity are found.[48]

After ordination he starts again at the bottom of a new life-long system of priestly precedence that depends on innumerable ranks, length of service within that rank, titles and honours.[49] Popes have seen fit to rail against careerism among the clergy[50] but, in all fairness, the individual cannot be blamed. It is the system. Pastors must conform to the system in which they find themselves if they are to carry out their duties effectively and avoid causing disruption.

We can presume that each of the offices and ranks was instituted to fill a pastoral or organisational need identified at the time. At the same time, we cannot deny that, taken all together, they have created career paths that can attract ambitious and self-centred personnel to the system.

At times in the past, the career path enabled some prelates to live like medieval princes on the revenues of wealthy, and sometimes distant, dioceses. This gave rise to simony. Repeated condemnations at synods and councils bear witness to its persistence. Seminarians who show ambition to become bishops or cardinals are not unknown today. They are called 'alpinists' because of their propensity to climb and are sometimes aptly described as suffering from scarlet fever!

Making Hierarchy Less Fit for Purpose

At significant steps in the ladder of promotion, from the position of parish priest and higher, the candidate is nowadays required to promise under oath to be loyal to the Papacy and to support current orthodoxy and discipline without exception. As we have seen above, the practice of requiring an oath is not Christly. Furthermore, it betrays a lack of trust in the selection process and it inhibits freedom, discretion, creativity and honesty in the diocesan hierarchy and the lower clergy.

The oath was ostensibly introduced to safeguard eternal truth and strengthen the hierarchical institution. However, the two objectives tend to conflict, and the practice has worked to the detriment of both. It has helped to elevate the opinions and practices approved by current management to the status of unchallengeable truth. (Pope

---

[48] Dignity plays a disproportionate role in the system. In Chapter 12 we will consider Msgr. (later Cardinal) Desmond Connell's contribution to the debate on women's ordination delivered to the Canon Law Society of Great Britain and Ireland (21/5/1986). In it he mentions dignity no less than six times.

[49] As at last count, Wikipedia was listing 119 different titles governing precedence. https://en.wikipedia. org/wiki/Order_of_precedence_in_the_Catholic_Church

[50] Among them, John Paul II, and Francis.

Francis has been demonstrating the practical limitations of his power in this regard). It has undermined the preaching of virtually every Catholic priest and bishop. The faithful, knowing of the oaths, are apt to wonder if the preacher is saying something because he really believes it or because his job depends on it. They sense his less-than-honest reserve on certain topics or that he avoids preaching on them at all. The priest who says things in private that he cannot say in his homily is a commonplace. If, as has been said, the faith is caught not taught, it tends to be caught from people we know and respect and whom we can trust to tell the truth about what they believe themselves.

Moreover, if people are entitled to truth, keeping it from them deliberately is a form of deceit, with the consequent danger of drifting into hypocrisy. How can we hope to bring people to 'The Truth' except by ruthlessly prioritising truth?

Obedience and responsibility

The effectiveness of the institution has been weakened also by making obedience to one's superiors the virtue above all others.[51] It can even override doctrine. Omitting to consult him can be interpreted as implying disrespect for a superior or his preferences. The effect is to inhibit creativity and innovation and to push decision making farther and farther up the line and towards the centre. This turns the hierarchical structure into a monarchical or oligarchical one and concentrates power in the hands of the pope's immediate circle of officials.

Downgrading bishops' conferences

Exaggeration of the scope of papal infallibility combined with unlimited central jurisdiction and modern communications have undermined the bishops as leaders, as managers, and as teachers. Routinely, minor discretionary decisions 'delegated' to the episcopal conferences must be submitted back to the Apostolic See for its approval before implementation. For example, after the Council had decided to re-establish the permanent diaconate, rules were introduced requiring each bishop's conference to get specific permission from Rome. In this way the conferences were kept under tight control. As in the case of the individual bishop, a conference that shows too much independence or creativity can find that various legal permissions, approvals, and dispensations from Rome get held up indefinitely.

Bishops' Conferences now need courage if they are to follow a reforming pope when his initiatives are seen to be opposed by the curia. They know that the curia will outlast the pope and they are conscious of the need to maintain a good working relationship into the future. Furthermore, ambitious bishops need to keep open the paths to promotion.

---

[51] "…namely obedience. This virtue is the font and origin of all virtues"—Leo X, Bull, *Exsurge Domine,* 1520 www.papalencyclicals.net, accessed 2 June 2017.

The Decree on the Bishops' Pastoral Office was approved at Vatican II by moral unanimity. The vote was: *Placet-* 2,319; *Non Placet-* 2. It approved of national episcopal conferences in general and it recommended that they be set up wherever they were lacking. It also called for contacts between conferences on a regional basis to 'promote and safeguard their higher welfare'. It described episcopal conferences as jointly exercising the pastoral office of the bishops and prescribed that the planned revision of Canon Law should provide a legal framework to give effect to the Decree. Since the Council, national and regional conferences have become a normal part of Church structure.

This could have provided a way, however, whereby bishops could act in concert and push back against the control of the curia. The bureaucracy has reacted with statements and by imposing statutes that undermine the authority and effectiveness of the Conferences. We will revert to this in Chapter 13. When Fr John Courtney Murray was being persecuted by the Holy Office and Cardinal Ottaviani for his theories on religious freedom, he was supported by some prominent US bishops. The cardinal was annoyed by their independence of mind and lack of 'loyalty'. He was advised to adopt a policy of appointing more docile bishops who could be depended upon to support the Roman position in future disagreements![52] Evidently, the advice was taken.

Selection of bishops

As more and more educated populations with increasing life-style choices have become accustomed to democratic decision making, the selection of bishops has moved the other way. It has been vested by Canon Law in the papacy with virtually no participation by the pastors or faithful of the dioceses concerned. This is the reverse of 'reading the signs of the times' as recommended by Vatican II. Selection is now done by a committee dominated by curial insiders relying on secret information provided by the Vatican diplomatic corps. It is an open secret that the criteria for episcopal appointments during the papacies of John Paul II and Benedict XVI have hinged on the readiness to profess current orthodoxy in relation to celibacy, contraception, and the refusal of ordination for women—the three issues on which the *sensus fidelium* is most obviously at variance with the Roman authorities.[53] On the personal characteristics of candidates during these papacies, the evident policy was to filter out those who had displayed undue independence of thought or leadership.[54] While this filter has not always been effective, it has worked to make the conferences of bishops more docile in their actions and more timid in public utterances. It has

---

[52]The advice was given by Msgr. Joseph Fenton who was Ottaviani's *peritus* subsequently at the Council. —Robert Nugent, *Silence Speaks, Teilhard de Chardin, Yves Congar, John Courtney Murray, and Thomas Merton*, Mahwah, NJ, Paulist Press, 2011, *p*52.

[53] This raises an interesting question about our dwindling congregations: Have the People moved away from the leadership or has the leadership distanced itself from the People?

[54] A more courageous promotions policy might to result in a more agile and resilient organisation.

also weakened the authority of the Synods because the attending bishops tend to reflect central selection criteria rather than the beliefs, or judgements of their flocks.

The Primacy too has changed over the centuries. There is clear confirmation of Peter's special position among the Apostles in Paul (Gal 2:11) reporting on Peter's visit to Antioch: "*I told him straight to his face*". One does not boast of speaking openly and directly to one's peer. Paul recognised Peter as the leader. There is a delicious irony, however, in the fact that the same passage that copper-fastens Peter's position as leader also depicts him as being, well, not exactly infallible. He seems to have had the grace and humility to accept that his earlier action was misjudged, and Paul's implementation of the Gospel message was right.

In the twentieth century, the President of the Leadership Conference of Women Religious, Sr Theresa Kane, spoke to Pope John Paul II publicly. Like St Paul, she *told him straight to his face*:

> "We have heard the powerful message of our church addressing the dignity and reverence of all persons … As women, we have pondered these words".

She went on to draw the conclusion that the Church should follow the high standards it proposes to others, and implement its own teaching:

> "by providing the possibility of women as persons being included in all ministries".

The successor of St Peter, could not listen. He could only respond in silent anger.

Pope John Paul II was not listening then and was still unable to listen after twenty years of failure to convince the faithful. In 1994, he created a new doctrine by edict:

> "I declare that the Church has no authority whatsoever to confer priestly or-dination on women and that this judgement is to be definitively held by all the Church's faithful".

The People of God have rejected this teaching. The Roman prejudice against women was too blatant.

The authority to ordain priests derives from the two mandates. Neither of these is gender dependent. The Church has exactly the same authority to ordain women priests as it has to ordain men. (See Chapter 12.)

There are stark contrasts between St Peter and many of the popes of history. The itinerant preacher and martyr had 'neither gold nor silver' and never styled himself as bishop of Rome, let alone as pope, holy father, or *pontifex maximus*. Through the ages his successors amassed physical wealth and acquired many titles of honour. Innocent III was not satisfied with the title 'Vicar of Peter' and elevated himself to 'Vicar of Christ' instead. The office of pope developed power and wealth and attracted some very unscrupulous occupants. For centuries, popes lived like royalty and exercised spiritual and temporal power. As Peter's successors, they claimed things he had never claimed; like inerrancy, *plenitudo potestatis*, varying levels of ecclesiastical and temporal authority and ultimately, infallibility.

The most senior churchmen have been free to follow the inspiration of the Holy Spirit or to choose their own preferred paths. Like the rest of us, popes and cardinals are sinners in need of forgiveness. But forgiveness does not undo the consequential damage. And the more powerful the position, the greater the potential for damage. At times, it would appear that the Holy Spirit has guided the Church on its pilgrim way despite the actions of some of its leaders.[55]

ABERRANT MANAGEMENT STYLE

Right up to the Last Supper the Apostles were deeply concerned with pecking order, arguing among themselves as to who should be the greatest although they knew that Jesus disapproved of this. He had spoken to them about the style of management he wanted.. But they were not good at listening. In this respect Fr Wilfred Harrington O.P. has called attention to a "strange and disturbing feature".

> "Simply stated, it is this: the clearer the words of Jesus in regard to Christian conduct, the more certainly have Christians done exactly the opposite!"[56]

To illustrate his point, Fr Harrington quotes five instances in which Jesus told his disciples that authority in his church was to be exercised humbly and as a servant. He goes on to contrast that with the readiness of Church authorities to adopt: "the trappings and the titles and the style of the Roman Empire, and later, of Feudalism!"

He could also have contrasted it with the attitude of Pope Pius IX who changed the voting rules at Vatican I to exalt his own position 'irrevocably' and require all Catholics who wished to be saved to believe that he, the Pope, was infallible and furthermore that there was no limit to his power in ruling the church.[57] Far from repudiating this extraordinary conduct, the modern papacy has recently conferred on him the title of 'Saint' and approved his cult, insofar as such a thing may have existed anywhere outside of the Roman bureaucracy.

In a wider context, Fr. Harrington could have added the way in which the curia, in the past and in our own day, has emulated the totalitarian tyrants in their inhuman treatment of those who have dared to criticise management behaviour, to share inconvenient truths with the faithful or to offer insights that might call for modification of current teaching or structures. The CDF does this in face of Jesus's clear commandment to his disciples:

> Be compassionate as your Father is compassionate. Do not judge and you will not be judged yourselves; do not condemn and you will not be condemned yourselves; grant pardon and you will be pardoned (Luke 6:36).

---

[55] Cf, Barbara W. Tuchman, *The March of Folly,* London, Abacus, a division of Little, Brown & Co., particularly Chapter Three: The Renaissance Popes Provoke the Protestant Secession, 1470-1530.

[56] Wilfred J. Harrington OP, *Scribalism in the Church,* in Angela Hanley and David Smith (Eds.) Quench not the Spirit, Dublin, The Columba Press, 2005. We revert to Fr Harrington on page 265

[57] Universal Jurisdiction with *plenitudo potestatis.*

The coercive methods employed are supposedly justified by the need to protect the truths of the Faith. What they are protecting is the authority of the papacy and they use the supposed ends to justify the means. One cannot defend the Faith by flouting Gospel standards. Furthermore, if the truths being protected are important, they will survive the cauldron of discussion. That is our understanding of the Promise. The elevation of any body of human knowledge, even that of the Roman Magisterium, to the point where it cannot be questioned must surely be wrong, a kind of idolatry. Only God is absolute.

Some other examples spring to mind of clear instructions that the management of the Church has chosen to ignore consistently:

"You must call no one on earth your father since you have only one Father, and he is in heaven" (Matt 23:9).

1. This must be interpreted in the context of its time. It has a different meaning in today's culture. In Aramaic, *Abba* (Father) was a title of honour as was *Rabbi* (Master). It is fair, however, to interpret Jesus as inveighing against titles of honour. The papacy knows that a bishop should have a flock. To confer the dignity and honour without the responsibilities, however, it appoints titular bishops, linked to phantom dioceses with no Catholics or even no people.

The obsession with pecking order in the Catholic Church has given rise to an entire structure of titles and honorifics. Kissing feet is no longer expected but kissing of rings and the demand for veiled coiffure for ladies survived into the third millennium.

2. "And when he saw the crowds, he felt sorry for them because they were harassed and dejected, like sheep without a shepherd. Then he said to his disciples, 'the harvest is rich, but the labourers are few, so ask the Lord of the harvest to send labourers into his harvest'" (Mt 9:36-37) (Lk 10:2).
So, what do we do in practice? We make it unnecessarily difficult for men to become shepherds and we rule out women entirely from all levels of the priestly ministry! Christ clearly foresaw the need for more labourers in his metaphorical 'vineyard', but the current overseers maintain high walls and gates lest others venture to help.

3. "[I]t was said to our ancestors: You must not break your oath but must fulfil your oath to the Lord. But I say this to you: do not swear at all … All you need say is "Yes" if you mean yes, "No" if you mean no: anything more than this comes from the evil one" *(Matt 5)*.

With little thought for being obedient themselves, church authorities impose life-long vows of obedience on candidates at ordination and oaths of fidelity to the pope and the current teaching at each stage of promotion. There is, notably, no oath of fidelity to Jesus. Even if some exegetes have managed to reconcile them with the gospel, these oaths remain counterproductive.

If taken seriously by the candidates, these vows downgrade the importance of personal responsibility and conscience in the minds of the clergy. They tend to create a culture that 'prizes loyalty above honesty' and can give a face of virtuous obedience to careful careerism. They impugn the integrity of pastors who are prevented from preaching the truth as they know it and inhibited from clarifying the distinction between infallible and fallible teaching, between the essentials and the trivialities. Consequently, the essentials tend to be obscured. The vows are dangerous. They facilitate corruption. People are horrified when they learn how Marcial Maciel Degollado, the notorious founder of the Legion of Christ, used the congregation he founded to create a cover and provide a source of funding for the most grotesque immorality.

An experienced Vatican correspondent of long standing, Valentina Alazraki, speaking to the papal summit on sex abuse has said:

> One need not forget that in the Legion there was a fourth vow according to which if a Legionary saw something he was uncertain of regarding a superior, he could neither criticize much less comment about it. Without this censure, without this total concealment, had there been transparency, Marcial Maciel would not have been able, for decades, to abuse seminarians and to have three or four lives, wives, and children.[58] … What is the Church's mission? To preach the Gospel. But to do so she needs [to be] a moral guide; coherence between what one preaches and what one lives is the basis of being a credible institution, worthy of trust and respect.

The statutes of religious congregations such as the Legion of Christ are among the things that, under current canon law, require the detailed approval of the Holy See. It is not too surprising that the danger of corruption inherent in the fourth vow would have escaped the examining bureaucrat. Rome has required its own 'fourth vow' in the form of the oath of fidelity since 1910 (with a break between 1967 and 1989).[59] Although much more nuanced,[60] in this strictly hierarchical organisation, it further inhibits challenges to the judgement, actions or behaviour of a superior. If more clerics had the courage of St Paul who was ready to challenge St Peter 'to his face', or of Sr Theresa Kane with Pope John Paul II, the corruption that tolerated a culture of sexual abuse would have come to light much sooner.

The institutional Church has developed gradually over the centuries. It is thus a self-serving distortion when members of the church hierarchy claim the current structure as the necessary and only possible implementation of the Divine will.

---

[58] Veteran Vatican reporter, Valentina Alazraki of Mexico's Noticieros Televisa, speaking at the abuse summit in the Vatican 21-24th February 2019.
[59] Loyalty oaths were known in the time of Pope Paschal II (1099-1118). He probably felt he needed them. He had to cope with no fewer than four anti-popes during his reign!
[60] The current version of the oath was published in Osservatore Romano, Weekly Edition English, 15 July 1998, p3. The text is available online: https://www.ewtn.com/library/curia/cdfoath.htm

Chapter 5

An alternative structure

This island always has an abbot for its ruler, who is a priest,
to whose authority the whole province, including its bishops are subject

—Venerable Bede, writing about Iona

A Development on the Periphery

While God permitted a development modelled on the Roman Empire, this was not the only possible structure for his church. He allowed an alternative structure to flourish on a small island on the edge of the known world that the Romans had failed to conquer, Ireland. This demonstration site lasted for almost 600 years. Time enough to become part of European history.

The influence of the monasteries

St. Patrick was the Apostle of Ireland. He established the See of Armagh, probably informally. As his successors, Archbishops of Armagh could later claim a Primacy of Ireland, but their influence did not always match their claims. While there were bishops, Ireland did not have a normal diocesan system in operation until the twelfth century. Without the precedent of the Roman apparatus of governance, the monarchical diocesan system remained undeveloped in what was a non-urban society. The link between administrative authority and the sacramental functions of the bishop, so natural in the Roman system, had not been established. In contrast, the monasteries flourished under their elected abbots and the larger ones tended to control several scattered churches not necessarily in one continuous area. In addition to abbots and bishops, there was a functionary, known as a *coarb* who seems to have been concerned mainly with church temporalities. "Most church heads noticed in the annals throughout the period studied [650-1000 AD] are described in 'abbatial[61]' or 'coarbial' terms but many are identified as bishops". There were thus, bishops, abbots and coarbs. While a man might have more than one function, the bishop as overall ruler of the church in his diocese had not yet emerged in Ireland. Local Christian communities tended to look to the monasteries for teaching, example, and pastoral care.

Monasteries tended to spring up around men, and sometimes women, some of them living as hermits (a state of life known as Green Martyrdom), whose reputation

---

[61] Colmán Etchingham, *Church Organisation in Ireland,* Maynooth, Laigin Publications, 1999, p 104

for sanctity and wisdom attracted followers. [62] Holiness can be magnetic, fascinating, even to the unbeliever. Cardinal Ó Fiaich comments:

"… problem which has always plagued men who have abandoned the world. The world they had fled from pursued them – even into the cloister"[63].

These communities seem to have maintained traditions of holiness and learning long after the founding personality had died or moved on. Monasteries were also founded and endowed by kings, chieftains, and wealthy individuals. There seems to have been no shortage of vocations to the monastic life. There was a convention that subsequent abbots should be elected from the clan of the founder or failing that, of the person who supplied the land, and this could continue for generations. Importantly, the convention left some room for choice of the most suitable person from the loosely defined group and those doing the choosing would have been in a position to know something of the character and capabilities of the candidates being considered.

Monasteries tended to attract further endowment and legacies which enabled them to grow and the more famous ones became wealthy and powerful and established lesser or 'daughter' monasteries, sometimes at quite a distance. They also controlled individual churches in scattered locations without any geographical boundaries. There were several outbreaks of plague in the seventh and eighth centuries and monasteries took over isolated churches that had lost their congregations and pastors.[64] This was a source of contention between the weak diocesan system and the larger monasteries. Without the precedent of the Roman apparatus of civil government, the growth of the monasteries limited the development of the diocesan system. The link between the sacramental functions of the bishop and his authority in administrative or temporal matters, which we take for granted now, was not a feature of the Irish Church in the seventh, eighth and ninth centuries. This may have left the bishops with extra time for prayer and preaching. It left the dioceses with modest income, so any tithes they might remit to Rome would have been small.

Thus, the monasteries, particularly the larger ones, tended to be more influential than the dioceses. It was not unusual for a bishop to live in a monastery, subject to the abbot and the rule.

Bede, writing about Ireland from an Anglo-Saxon perspective, describes Iona and St Columcille:

"This island always has an abbot for its ruler, who is a priest, to whose authority the whole province, including its bishops are subject—an unusual order of things in which they follow the example of their first teacher who was not a bishop, but a priest and monk".[65]

[62] See Dáibhí Ó Cróinín, *Early Medieval Ireland,* Longmans, 1995, p 203
[63] Tomás Ó Fiaich, *Columbanus, in his own words,* Dublin, Veritas 1974, p 30
[64] Dáibhí Ó Cróinín, *op. cit.* p 160.
[65] Dáibhí Ó Cróinín, *op. cit.* P. 147.

Saints Columcille and Columbanus

The 'first teacher' in Iona, St Columcille was hugely influential in the evangelisation of Scotland and the north of England. To him is attributed the theory that a monastery should not number more than 150 monks. When that number was exceeded, 12 volunteers and one leader would set out to find communities to whom they could bring the knowledge and love of Christ. The monastery would kit them out with a boat, liturgical books, seeds, tools and so on. They would set out for Scotland or Europe, often with no definite idea of where they might end up. They trusted in the guidance of the Spirit. Following the example of St Patrick, they went for life. This was called White Martyrdom:

> "When he separates for the sake of God from everything he loves, although he suffer fasting or labour thereat".[66]

It sustained an amazing flow of missionaries to Europe that lasted for almost 600 years, going farther and farther afield. There are 800 sites of churches or monasteries known to be associated with the Irish monks, stretching from Scotland well into Eastern Europe.

The greatest of these monks, with a confusingly similar name, is St Columbanus. With his twelve companions, he traversed modern France three times setting up several monasteries before heading over the Alps to found the famous monastery at Bobbio in a large barracks abandoned long before by the Roman army. His journey can be traced in the many churches dedicated to him and in the towns and villages, hills and mountains that bear his name to this day.[67] His first monastery at Annegray in France had led to the setting up of the ultimately more famous one at nearby Luxeuil. When he earned the enmity of the local Queen Brunhilde, he and the remaining Irish monks were expelled from there under armed guard. Brunhilde's plan to put them forcibly on a boat sailing to Ireland was thwarted providentially, and they were able to make their way back via Paris, Metz and Koblenz to Basle and Lake Constance.

One of his companions, Gall, who was his best linguist, took sick and could not face the journey over the Alps. He wanted to settle in a quiet place and spend his final years in prayer and contemplation. Columbanus continued angrily on the journey without him, but banned him from saying Mass. Gall's sanctity, however, attracted a following and led to the formation of yet another monastery near the site of his hermitage. This ultimately grew into a town and then a city, known to this day as St Gallen in Switzerland. Fittingly, when Columbanus was dying, he ordered that his abbatial staff be sent to Gall as a token of his esteem and forgiveness.[68]

---

[66] Text and translation in Stokes and Strachan, *Thesaurus Palaeohibernicus,* Cambridge 1901-3, quoted by Dáibhí Ó Cróinín, *Early Medieval Ireland,* Longmans, 1995.

[67] Cf. Tomás Ó Fiaich, *Columbanus, in his own words,* Veritas, Dublin 1974.

[68] Among dozens of books about Columbanus, I have drawn on that by Cardinal Tomás Ó Fiaich: Dublin, Veritas, 1974

St Killian is credited with the evangelisation of the Franks, a people who later became very powerful and, under Pepin the Short came to the rescue of papacy and the city of Rome and donated the Papal States to Pope Stephen II. St Killian is still honoured in Wurzburg where he was martyred. His relics are paraded through the streets on his feast day and put on display in the cathedral which is named after him. He is celebrated annually in the *Kiliani-Volksfest*.

There were many others less famous. It would be easy, and mistaken, to paint a picture of Europe in total chaos under the barbarians. It would be equally simplistic to credit the Irish alone with restoring Christianity and civilisation. But the "Island of Saints and Scholars" is not mythological. The eight hundred surviving sites of Irish monastic evangelism provide ample evidence of the scale of missionary commitment that the Irish Church sustained for over half a millennium.

Is everything sacred?

The Irish monks were not greatly concerned about the distinction between sacred and profane learning. They saw the Creator in every aspect of creation. It did not matter if one was studying Astronomy, Scripture, Music or Greek or planting turnips, building cells, milking cows, or copying and illustrating manuscripts. For the Celtic monk, everything was sacred. Whatever he was studying, teaching or working on, it was to God's world he was contributing. His life was one of worship in everything he did.[69] He worked in co-operation with others, under obedience to an elected Abbot.

Celtic Christianity was literally down to earth. It had no sense of a two-kingdom spirituality or of a rigid dichotomy between the secular and the sacred.[70]

Presiding at the Lord's Supper

It is widely accepted that, after his time as a slave in Ireland, St Patrick studied with St Germanus of Auxerre and was consecrated as an *episcopos* by him before returning to Ireland in or about 432 AD. (The date is debated among the scholars.) This would have authorised Patrick in turn to consecrate other *episcopi*. Like St Paul, however, he would have wanted to get his Christian communities established before selecting and appointing officials.[71]

St Patrick had grown up on the periphery of the Roman Empire. He writes in his *Confessio* that his father was a deacon and his grandfather a presbyter. In the early fourth century, the term presbyter probably meant an elder rather than a priest, and while either father or grandfather might well have presided when the community met for 'the breaking of bread', neither would have had the 'powers' of the ordained priesthood. The earliest surviving mention of *transforming the body and blood* in a rite of

---

[69] In today's terms, he would understand that the butcher, the baker, the candle-stick maker, the bus driver, the housewife or the bishop, all give glory to God by following their calling in a spirit of loving care for those they serve.

[70] —John Scally, 'The Celtic church and lessons for the future', from *Quench not the Spirit*, ed Angela Hanley and David Smith, Dublin, The Columba Press, 2005 P167

[71] Titus 1:5

ordination is in the Gelasian Sacramentary[72] which dates from the end of the seventh or early eighth century. In his youth, before he was captured, Patrick was probably accustomed to the celebration of the Lord's Supper on a domestic scale with one or two members leading the community. The combination of sociability and intimate unaffected witness would have facilitated the development of a lively faith.

With the Irish population responding so well to his preaching and having no churches initially, he doubtless followed the apostolic practice of teaching his new converts to mark the Lord's Day by coming together for prayer and celebration of the Lord's Supper as a community. This might help to explain the enduring legend that St Brigid presided at Mass in her monastery in Co Kildare. The standard explanation, that she was consecrated as a bishop by mistake, is charming but a bit far-fetched.[73] When St Patrick was learning the faith, one did not need ordination to preside; priestly ordination was a relatively new idea and the need for an ordained president would have taken some time to get established on the periphery of the Empire. The people celebrated as a priestly community as mandated by Christ. Brigid, as abbess, would have been the natural person to preside. Judging by the scale of her monastic 'city' in Kildare, she had that charism of leadership that so often accompanies holiness.

The dating of Easter

Computus was the use of astronomy to calculate the date for Easter on which the bulk of the liturgical calendar depended, including Pentecost and Lent. Unfortunately, there was a dispute within Christianity as to how the date should be calculated. In practice this caused administrative problems wherever different systems adjoined one another. Scotland and northern England that had been evangelised by Colmcille followed the Irish formula while the rest of the island followed the Roman way introduced by Augustine of Canterbury. The Synod of Whitby (664 AD) was called to resolve the problem. The Irish claimed to be following scripture and accused the Romans of attempting to find a way to avoid coinciding with the Jewish Passover. Their opponents won the day. After the debate, Oswiu, the King of Northumbria, who had chaired the proceedings, gave his judgement. The main concern he displayed was for himself in the afterlife. He explained that he wanted no argument with St Peter at the pearly gates, so he ruled in favour of the Roman formula.

---

[72] John Bligh S.J., *Ordination to the Priesthood,* London & New York, Sheed and Ward, 1956, p 19 footnote

[73] The story is that her ageing friend, St Mel, while intending to install her as Abbess, read the wrong prayer and consecrated her a bishop by mistake. This sounds like a subsequent fabrication to avoid admitting that Church practice in earlier centuries was different. It would have explained away the scandal of a woman, un-ordained, celebrating the Lord's Supper without a priest. How could she have done such a thing and still be considered a saint? The nice theological debate as to the invalidity of an unintentional consecration can be left for another time and place.

Having lost the debate, the Irish monks seem to have accepted the Roman method of *computus,* the monks on the *Sceilig Mhichíl* being the exception.[74] The Irish acceptance of the ruling meant that their European converts were spared the problems of having competing dates for Easter as the great missionary epoch continued.

Decline and end

The monasteries suffered grievously from the plundering of the Norse raiders in the ninth and tenth centuries. They were already in decline when the Anglo/Norman invasion brought further depredations. Two events in the next century sealed their fate.

As the influence of the monasteries weakened, the diocesan bishops asserted their role in line with Roman reform policy of the time. The Synod of Rath Breasail in 1111 made a start on revising the diocesan boundaries. When St Malachy, as Archbishop of Armagh, went to Rome in 1139 seeking the pallium for several bishops, he was told that the authority of a National Synod would be essential. He was appointed as Papal Legate with the objective of organising the Irish dioceses into suffragan groups headed by Archbishops. This was finally achieved at the synod of Kells in 1172. Pope Eugene III (1145-1153) had already approved four metropolitan sees. Geoffrey Keating, the greatly respected historian, suggests that Rome's determination to 'reform' the Irish church was not prompted by any moral or spiritual shortcomings, but had more to do with establishing a revenue stream. The Roman ambition to centralise power and control, given a great impetus by Pope Gregory VII, had been intensifying for half a century, leaving the papacy chronically short of cash. Diocesan tithes would provide a regular source of income.

The other event was the arrival of the Normans in 1169. This invasion was facilitated by the Bull *Laudabiliter* of the pro-Norman Pope Hadrian IV (an Englishman who, as legate of Anastasius IV had established the remittances of Peter's Pence from Norway and Sweden). The Bull encouraged Henry II to incorporate Ireland into the English realm[75] and 'reform' the Irish Church. The authenticity of *Laudabiliter* is challenged by historians. Even if it was forged, however, it facilitated the conquest, by weakening the resistance of the clergy at least. In those days, the teaching was that the pope had divine authority to dispose of kingdoms as well as depose monarchs. Anyone having the temerity to question a papal edict would be deemed a heretic, destined for hell. Doubtless the newly appointed monarch would be happy to ensure the questioner arrived there without delay! Thus started 700 years of colonial rule for Ireland. The monasteries that outlived Henry II did not survive the depredations of Henry VIII.

---

[74] For a time, it was possible to get married on *Sceilig Mhichíl,* the monastic rock off the south-west coast, after Shrove Tuesday because Lent had not yet started on the rock.

[75] Kelly, J.N.D., *Oxford Dictionary of Popes,* Oxford University Press, Paperback, Rev. 2005, P. 175.

The loss of the monastic structure and the Norman invasion finally brought to an end the greatest and most sustained missionary movement the world has ever seen. Rome does not seem to have appreciated the Irish contribution to the re-conversion of Europe which by then had been largely accomplished. Nor did Rome realise that it was helping to bring an end to a glorious chapter in the story of Christianity. 'The Island of Saints and Scholars' was passing into history.

Was the monastically dominated structure of the Irish Church a success? Emphatically "Yes". Pope Francis never tires of reminding us that the essential characteristic and primary task of the church is missionary. Moreover, if we use the criterion 'By their fruits ye shall know them' and consider its effectiveness in 'making disciples of all the nations', the Irish monastic system of the sixth to the eleventh century equals or outshines anything else in the history of the Church.

This digression into Irish history is most definitely not intended to suggest that the Church should try a first millennium solution to a third millennium problem. The Irish experience, however, even if somewhat exaggerated and romanticised at times, proves conclusively that the current structure of the Church cannot be considered to be the only valid implementation of God's eternal plan. This has very significant consequences for the development of ecumenism.

Chapter 6

Bureaucracy builds its power base

These leading men accordingly spoke to the King. 'Let this man be put to death'… 'He is in your hands as you know,' King Zedekiah answered, 'for the King is powerless against you.' So, they took Jeremiah and threw him into the well

— (Jr 38).

POWER IN THE PAPACY

The papacy is composed of the pope and the Roman curia, which is a bureaucracy of about 3,000, mainly laity. In canon law, however, all decision-making positions are reserved to ordained priests. It is modelled on a medieval court and took its present shape in 1588 under Pope Sixtus V. The key dicasteries and congregations (departments) are headed up by Cardinals. While we think of the papacy as a monarchy, it really forms a continuing oligarchy. The top officials exercise the pope's power and prerogatives. The Cardinal Secretary of State approximates to a prime minister who does not have to answer to a parliament. He leads the core group that manages the pope, and controls access to him. Only the most capable of popes have been able to manage the curia. Only the holiest of popes can challenge curial thinking. Its top personnel change very slowly, carefully perpetuating its ethos by promoting like-minded clerics. In effect, the curia governs the Church.

Popes come and go like political leaders. The bureaucracy continues, like the civil service. It is more powerful, relatively speaking, than the civil service of a modern state because there is no constitution to set boundaries and because it does not have to answer to a government or legislature. Furthermore, the normal separation of powers is not applied. It combines Legislative, Executive and Judicial powers and has a seven-hundred-year history of claiming, in the name of the pope, that it cannot err. It functions also as the professional institute, setting standards for all priests and bishops and controlling their training and conditions of employment. It is jealous of its power and autonomy and vigilant in preventing the development of competing power centres. While popes have vindicated the right of workers to organise, the curia has victimised priests who have formed independent associations, particularly those promoting reform. It has denigrated the authority of local and regional assemblies of bishops. Its greatest fears are the loss of power that would arise from an effective College of Bishops or from progress in Christian unity. It has legislated to disempower the first and promoted barriers against the second. It responds rapidly to any perceived challenge to its authority or power and incredibly slowly to any allegation of inappropriate structures, policies, or behaviour. It could be described as a typical bureaucracy, except that it has fewer internal and external constraints, and its decision-makers lack variety of training and experience.

In current canon law, the theoretical power of the pope is unlimited (Cn 331). His physical power was very real, however, in the days when he had a police force, an army, and an Inquisition, and when the faithful were taught that the kingdom of God was promoted by burning heretics. In those days, the faithful were led to believe that there was no salvation outside the Church, and that excommunication left God with absolutely no option but to consign the victim to hell for all eternity. Wise people did not tangle with popes or bishops. The *sensus fidelium* was effectively silenced for centuries.

Papal power probably peaked in the reign of Pope Innocent III at the beginning of the thirteenth century. It is now much more tenuous. It now depends on a lived faith in Jesus Christ on the part of individuals and the derived respect for the leadership of his Church. With growing levels of education, communication and democratisation, this respect is no longer automatic, but is conditioned by events and perceptions and by comparison of actions with gospel values. It must now be earned anew with every generation.

A Christianised bureaucracy

The religious bureaucracy of the empire, continued to manage religious affairs through a period of radical transition from Pagan ritual to Christian worship.[76] The change would have been very challenging—from a religion of obligatory external observance to an interior one inspired by love. It would not have been total. Even the most genuine converts tend to carry forward something of their earlier attitudes and convictions.

After the loss of the Western Empire the bureaucracy continued to administer religious affairs in the East under the authority of the Emperor. In the West it started to rebuild Christianity, this time on the mandate of Jesus Christ alone, and as we have seen with some help from the Irish. As time went by, the scale of the latter activity overtook and exceeded the former. The last pope who needed to get approval from the Emperor in Constantinople before being consecrated was Gregory III in 751 AD.

Losing and gaining power

From about the end of the third century, the influence of the pagan religious bureaucracy had been reduced by the transfer of the court and the rest of the imperial administration away from Rome; first to Milan in 286 AD, to Ravenna a century later and ultimately to Constantinople. It would be further threatened by the collapse of the Western Empire. As the Roman bureaucracy became more distanced from the

---

[76] John A. Dick, Ph.D., S.T.D. Vice President of the Association for the Rights of Catholics in the Church has an interesting comment in an email circulated 5/1/2019. "Thanks to Constantine and the Council of Nicaea, institutional Christianity shifted its identity focus from correct Christian conduct to doctrinal fidelity and institutional obedience. It was indeed a major shift".

imperial court and the levers of power in Constantinople, its influence in the East began to erode. It reacted as would any secular bureaucracy by trying to strengthen its position. The Roman See was already accepted as the court of final appeal to settle religious disputes. Conscious of the civil power it had enjoyed previously, it began to demand, more stridently as time went on, that the pre-eminence accorded to it by the other patriarchates should be extended legally to a primacy of jurisdiction. This would have re-established its earlier position of governing all religious affairs and would even extend it beyond the limits of the empire.

Rome had never been the mother church of the Christians. That distinction historically rested with Jerusalem. In pagan days, however, and for a hundred years after Christianity became the religion of the empire, Rome had dominated as the centre of religious governance and management, subject only to the Emperor himself. As the Emperor's concern for the defence of Rome faded, so did his influence. Rome asserted its right independently to govern the Church and resisted the efforts of the See of Constantinople to make itself into a counterweight.

East-West tension

The bishops are undoubtedly the successors of the Apostles in one respect; in their capacity to argue over who should be the greatest. The records suggest that there was quite a lot of time spent at the great councils arguing about boundaries, dignities, powers, legal distinctions, pecking order and benefices. From the perspective of the twenty-first century, some of the arguments over legalities, doctrines and heresies look like turf wars. They were trials of strength, concerned with establishing authority as often as truth. The roots of the East-West Schism of 1054 can be clearly discerned seven hundred years earlier in the tensions preceding the Council of Sardica which met in 343 AD. At that time, the brotherhood of bishops was beginning to divide into two camps; the Western one that supported Roman claims to dominance and the Eastern one that opposed it.[77] It is surprising that a level of unity and harmony between the churches survived so long in the face of one See's determination to dominate over all the others.

There was more to the tension, however, than the issue of supreme control. Hellenic philosophy permeated the church in the East, maintaining a focus on the spiritual and a more immediate consciousness of the workings of the Holy Spirit. This philosophy could tolerate a structure of relatively autonomous churches, united by the celebration of the Eucharist and the message of Christ in the gospels. They did not share the inherited veneration of Roman Law which prompted the Western church to rely on legislation, power, and enforcement.

---

[77] Pope Stephen I, (254-257 AD) was the first pope, so far as is known, to find a doctrinal basis for Roman primacy, basing it on Matt. 16:18 (You are Peter and on this rock I will build my church . . .) —J.N.D. Kelly, *Oxford Dictionary of Popes,* Oxford, Updated 2005, p 21.

The Papal States

The shift of the Imperial Court to (the more defendable) Constantinople created a further problem for the Duchy of Rome, that of military security. The City was sacked three time in the space of one hundred and fifty years. By the eighth century, and having lost virtually all the Western Empire, the Emperors in Constantinople had no interest in the defence of Rome. When the Lombards captured the Exarchate of Ravenna, 'the last Western stronghold of the Byzantine Empire', and some other areas adjacent to Rome, they then threatened the Duchy itself. The Emperor Constantine V made no attempt at defence and Pope Gregory III (731–741) found it necessary to appeal for support to Charles Martel, the ruler of Franconia. Although the Franks were powerful and, as we have seen, had been converted to Christianity at that stage no support was forthcoming.

Gregory's successor, Pope Stephen II (752-757) had more success. He enlisted the aid of Pepin the Short who had by then become the King of the Franks. Pepin forced Aistulf, King of the Lombards, to surrender the captured territories. He then donated them to the pope, giving the papacy full political sovereignty for the first time. The Duchy of Rome now became the capital of the Papal States. The religious administration expanded to include civil governance. (The boundaries between the two were often fuzzy). With the pope as monarch, the Papal States would last for over 1,000 years. For a time, it was church doctrine that the existence of the Papal States was essential to the life of the Church.[78]

At times, the governance of the Papal States became very corrupt. This is not surprising. The pope and his ministers were already the leaders of Christendom, when to this was added the combined functions of temporal legislators, judiciary and executive. The papacy was now an absolute monarchy in spiritual and temporal matters. It took on the trappings of a medieval court. It was permanent and answerable to nobody. Well, that is not quite true. It was answerable to the pope. But the pope, like King Zedekiah, was powerless without his ministers.

It is hard to conceive of a structure better calculated to exploit human weakness and breed ambition, corruption, and abuse. The theory of the Separation of Powers would not be popularised by Montesquieu until a thousand years later. His ideas would have seemed irrelevant to the papal bureaucracy whose members have always tended to see the *status quo* as a direct expression of the divine will. Pope Gelasius 1, at the end of the fifth century had expounded the theory of two powers, the spiritual and the temporal. He claimed that the spiritual was inherently the greater since it provided for the salvation of the other.[79] From the time of Gregory VII (11th century), the papacy displayed an insatiable lust for temporal power and attempted, with some

---

[78] The denial of this was condemned by Pius IX in the Syllabus of Errors
[79] Kelly, *Oxford Dictionary of Popes,* p 48

success, to establish the doctrine that the pope could depose kings at will and absolve feudal subjects from their oaths of loyalty, the moral force of which bound feudal society together. The concern of the papacy had shifted from supernatural to supranational dominance. With no constitutional restraints, the secular ambitions of the bureaucracy exploited the claim of its leader to unchallengeable divine authority.

The teaching that all temporal authorities should be subject to the spiritual authority served the ambitions of the papacy but was based on a remarkably strained interpretation of scripture.

Self-serving interpretation of scripture

At the Last Supper, the disciples were continuing to argue about who should be the greatest. They were failing to grasp what Jesus was trying to tell them about his imminent death, and about their future need to exercise normal prudence in spreading the gospel and not presume on automatic miraculous interventions. When Christ said by way of example that one might need to sell a cloak to buy a sword[80], they seemed to hear only the word 'sword'. They responded: "See, Lord, here are two swords", and Jesus replied: "That's enough". Maybe he meant "That's quite enough"!

They were about to go out in the dark to pray at the Mount of Olives, without the benefit of street lighting or a police escort. The narrative required the introduction of a sword at this stage to explain why Peter was carrying one when their prayers were interrupted by the arrest of Jesus. At that point, Peter used it to cut off the right ear of the servant of the high priest. Jesus healed it and rebuked Peter: "Put your sword back, for all who draw the sword will die by the sword". There is a prophetic irony here. By giving the scriptural reference to two swords a far-fetched interpretation that bolstered its own international temporal claims, and by ignoring entirely Christ's disapproval of Peter's recourse to arms, the papacy, undoubtedly, caused many people to 'die by the sword'.

It was a fanciful and self-serving way to use scripture, but Rome had long been claiming exclusive authority in interpreting revelation. It is hard to see how any authority, even a God-given one, could survive such abuse. The interpretation occasioned immense damage. It can be argued that the obsession of the papacy with its own untrammelled authority and power, in both spiritual and temporal affairs, has been the common factor in all the disasters that have riven Catholic Christianity.

CONTROLLING THE INTERPRETATION OF SCRIPTURE

The books of the bible were written for the people of their time and this complicates the process of interpretation. The Old Testament contains some amazing, encrypted foreknowledge of Jesus Christ. The New Testament is our written record of his life and teaching. The books were written within the cultures of their time. Had

---

[80] Luke 22:23-38, John 18:10, Matt 26:52

they, by some miracle, anticipated our modern knowledge of geography, astronomy, human physiology, quantum physics, evolution, the structure of the atom or space/time theory they would have been unintelligible in their own day and consequently would not have survived, let alone become the world's all-time bestseller.

The Canon of Scripture is no longer a matter of controversy among Christians, but its translation and interpretation will probably always be. The People of God need the guidance of the Spirit if they are to begin to understand its implications. Philip[81] asked the eunuch who was reading Isaiah in his chariot: "Do you understand what you are reading?" "How can I" was the reply, "unless I have someone to guide me". The faithful always need teachers.

Centuries of rabbinical studies had failed to see what the prophesies about the Messiah really meant, until Jesus overtook two dispirited disciples on the road to Emmaus. He explained the scriptures to them sweeping away confusion and replacing it with a convincing clarity. Then they 'recognised him in the breaking of bread' and their faith in Jesus was restored.

Our teachers are the successors of the apostles who hand on the traditional beliefs which, together with the scriptures, form Christ's revelation. To make it our own individually, however, still requires interpretation and implementation.

The faithful share the responsibility of safeguarding the truth of revelation, of interpreting the parts in the context of the whole and relating them to everyday life in succeeding eras. The Papacy, however, has long claimed to do this authoritatively.

Awesome responsibility

It is an awesome responsibility that can brook no distortion of truth or intrusion of unworthy motivation. And yet, in history and even today, there is evidence of distortion and unworthy motivation.

As noted earlier, a bureaucracy tends to give top priority to its own perpetuation, power, and the control of its environment. Bureaucracies are not good at being unselfish. As a rule, the altruists get overwhelmed. Even the most unselfish and dedicated member cannot escape the pressure to safeguard the interests and privileges of the group. The common denominator among the members of every bureaucratic committee is their commitment to, and personal dependence on, the bureaucracy itself. Decisions in committee tend to hinge on the shared ethos and common concerns of the members. The effect of the decision on the bureaucracy itself is always an important factor even if not adverted to. The more homogeneous the membership: the narrower the vision. Broader considerations and collateral damage can be dismissed as being outside the defined area of responsibility of the group.

Decision-making in the Roman religious administration, in both its Pagan and Christian phases, has always been the preserve of the clergy. Since the Council of Trent, the key personnel have a great deal in common, sharing an effective formation

---

[81] Acts 7:6

programme, life-long commitment and dependency, celibacy, centralisation and over-arching respect for rank and dignity, which makes groupthink almost irresistible. The appointment of outside directors, including women, which has been shown to add balance in secular organisations, would be considered almost heretical in Rome. Because of its structure, therefore, and despite all the excellent people involved, the group dynamic in the curia will always tend to prioritise the group ambitions and the needs of the profession over the promptings of the Spirit.

Interpretation must be related to current realities.

Interpretation of revelation in relation to everyday life must change with our grow-ing understanding of the world we live in. This would be easier to understand if the focus was still on how we live rather than what we profess. The papacy, however, is obsessed with maintaining its own inerrancy and the long-standing claim that its con-clusions continue to be right even when the reasoning is seen to be wrong. The bureaucracy only tolerates a change if it promises an early dividend in power and control (or possibly a trophy of Anglican converts with their pastors). Fear of losing authority, makes Rome reluctant to change interpretations, even when they no longer fit with mankind's grasp of reality …and a superior grasp of reality is one character-istic of effective leadership. Regrettably, the papacy has lost credibility at times through collective fear that honest re-interpretation might erode its claim to divine authority. It has resisted, at times for over a hundred years, before accepting that new knowledge and new understanding may call for revised interpretation.

When the late Cardinal Martini, on his deathbed, dared to say that the church authorities are "two hundred years out of date", he was probably not referring to his twentieth-century colleagues but to the group dynamic of a large bureaucracy that finds security in resisting change.

Sr Margaret Farley R. S. M. speaking in June 2012 to the Catholic Theological Society of America, said:

> "We clearly have grown in many spheres of knowledge -- about humans, about the way the universe runs," said Farley. "It seems reasonable … that if we come to know even a little bit more than we knew before, it might be that the conclusions that we had previously drawn need to be developed. Or maybe even let go of … Because it would be a contradiction to Roman Catholic frameworks for doing moral theology to say that we can't. That would be to imply that we know everything we can know and there's nothing more to be done." [82]

Both Cardinal Martini and Sr Margaret are supported by history. We will settle for three examples:

1. Galileo was judged to be a heretic because his observation of the heavens showed that Rome was not the centre of the universe. This contradicted the

---

[82] www.ncronline.org/news/spirituality/vatican-criticized-nun-addresses-fellow-theologians

derived biblical doctrine of the time which boosted Roman importance. He escaped the consequences by pretending to recant in a half-hearted way. Having friends in high places probably helped to make this acceptable.

2. Contraception and masturbation were condemned as akin to murder[83] before the contribution of female ovulation was proved in 1827. Up to then it was quite reasonable to think that the male 'seed' contained a tiny little person[84] and the woman only contributed an environment that facilitated its development before birth.

3. The theory of evolution was dismissed for generations, despite mounting evidence, because it demanded an allegorical rather than a literal interpretation of the Genesis account of Adam and Eve as our first parents. In turn, evolution raised awkward questions about the literal interpretation of the "Fall" on which was based the doctrine of Original Sin and St Augustine's conclusion that God had no option but to consign millions of innocent unbaptised infants to eternal punishment.

Listening to the Spirit

Here, I am not suggesting that the Church authorities have ever lacked the promptings of the Holy Spirit. No! The weakness, however, lies in the response—in man's unwillingness to listen and be guided—in the obsession of a group with its own perceived interests. The Roman claim to authority would be meaningless without the Promise, but the papacy operates as if divine inspiration has been channelled exclusively through itself and, crucially, as if its officials have always implemented the inspiration exactly—both suppositions being far from true.

The Spirit inspires, but never takes away the freedom to choose on which our capacity to love depends. Christ keeps his promise and is still with his pilgrim church, despite the sins, the pride, and the faulty map-reading of some of its greatest leaders and members.

Historically, the curia and the popes have often had difficulty in listening, particularly to the inspiration that comes indirectly, through the faithful or their pastors. They have divorced their infallibility from the *sensus fidelium* on which it was originally based. They have often abused the authority entrusted to them. Over the centuries and more particularly since 1870, they have enhanced their own power by making a monopoly of the Promise. They have presented this almost as if it were an automatic service for propositions that is provided solely through their offices, and that it is specific and immediate, and precludes uncertainty or mistakes. Being committed to this fiction, the bureaucracy cannot admit that a specific teaching might have been

---

[83] St John Chrysostom quoted by Uta Ranke-Heinemann, *Eunuchs for the Kingdom of Heaven,* New York, Penguin Books, 1991, paperback, p 74

[84] Cf. St Justin, Apologia 1, Chapter 19

wrong[85], until it has faded safely from the minds of the faithful. The papacy, like a bad professor, confuses teaching authority with always being right. As humanity has become more widely educated, a process to which the church itself contributed enormously, the faithful find the notion of on-demand, single channel, divine direction less and less convincing. Recent exposures of deceit, secrecy, sexual immorality among the clergy, scandals, financial irregularities, lies and cover-ups have done nothing to counter this. While these issues are coming to light in our time, there is no evidence to suggest that they are new phenomena in church management. In the past it was possible to keep them secret. They need to be ended or at least reduced by introducing the separation of powers.

THE WILL TO POWER IN THE HISTORY OF THE BUREAUCRACY.

While Christ's commands apply to all the faithful, somehow the matching powers and authorisations implicit in them are generally deemed to be the divinely restricted prerogatives of the ordained professionals (with occasional exceptions to cover exigencies). Examples are celebrating the Lord's Supper, preaching in the liturgy, forgiving sins, validating marriages, invoking blessings, together with legislating, decision making, and administration of church affairs.

One does not need to be a cynic to observe how often in the broad sweep of history papal policy and doctrinal pronouncements have combined to advance the power and control exercised by the Roman bureaucracy directly or through the priesthood which it controls. Only God can judge the motives of those making the decisions. Relying on Newman's 'cumulative probabilities' however, we can safely infer that the bureaucracy generally serves its own needs and ambitions in ways that show little need of inspiration from the Holy Spirit.

Out of a myriad of decisions in the history of twenty centuries, we will limit ourselves to twenty examples on significant issues.

Decision 1: Temporal power

For many centuries, the papacy (popes *and* curia) taught that the reference to the 'two swords' in Luke 22:38 endowed the papacy with the supreme right to rule in temporal matters. (See page 57) We can now see this as a self-serving interpretation and an undeniable abuse of religious authority to further secular ambitions.

Decision 2: The power to confect the Eucharist.

When the early Christians met for the Lord's Supper in apostolic and post-apostolic times it was a memorial meal to celebrate the life, teaching and self-sacrificing

---

[85] This inability was demonstrated when Pope Benedict XVI erased Limbo from Catholic teaching. He felt he had to deny that it had ever been part of the teaching of the Church. He was referring artfully to defined magisterial teaching. In truth, although it was part of tradition for fifteen hundred years, it never was defined officially. Benedict pretended that it was simply a theory among some theologians. His distinction could have the effect of undermining some other doctrines which have never needed papal or conciliar definition.

death and resurrection of Jesus. As much as the food, it is the attendance that makes a meal a celebration. It was the community of his followers that were celebrating. This needed an organiser to arrange, food, cooking, a doorkeeper, crockery, servers, and a venue. When it came to the focal point of the gathering, somebody had to lead those present; in a word, to preside. While the celebration was still a domestic event, this would have been the host or hostess or an elder or overseer *(presbyter* or *episcopus),* a visiting preacher, or whoever was familiar with the customary practices.[86]

The practice of having an ordained individual confect the Eucharist on behalf of the community had not been introduced in Rome itself at the middle of the third century when Pope Fabian divided the city into seven ecclesiastical districts. He placed "a deacon, supported by a sub-deacon and six junior assistants in charge of each".[87] Deacons were ministering and administering staff who assisted a bishop as needs arose. Although ordained, they were never priests. It is evident that the churches in Rome were still celebrating the Lord's Supper as communities up to that time at least, only sixty years before the edict of Milan.

It is quite possible that the practice of having a priest leading the ceremony developed independently among those Jewish converts who continued to keep the Law of Moses. They had demonstrated an unwillingness to let go of other traditional practices. As we have noted above, even the most complete converts tend to carry forward some of their earlier attitudes. As Jews they were accustomed to having priests intercede for them and offer sacrifice on their behalf. The Acts reports that "the number of disciples in Jerusalem was greatly increased, and a large number of priests made their submission to the faith".[88] Of course, the Jewish people were also part of the Roman sphere of influence where the role of a priest in offering sacrifice to the various Roman gods was part of the culture.

Modifying Christ's instruction to "Do this", the authorities forbade the 'laity' from celebrating,[89] although still requiring them to attend. This new arrangement would have called for a significant number of ordained *presbyteri* and could only have become normalised in different places during the fourth and fifth century. We have noted above that the earliest record of an ordination or consecration rite that references the power of consecrating the Eucharist comes from the eighth century.[90] We can assume that for some time before that, it had become normal for the community to have an ordained president to pronounce the words of consecration.

When sacramental ordination was introduced it came to be understood as confer-ring on the priest of the *power* to *confect* the Eucharist. This became a cornerstone of

---

[86] In describing the Christian celebration in *Apologia 1, Chapter 65,* St Justin Martyr refers to the part played by 'the president', not the 'celebrant'.

[87] J.N.D. Kelly, *Oxford Dictionary of Popes,* OUP, updated 2005, *p*16, quoting the Liberian Catalogue

[88] Acts 6:7

[89] This is still with us. v. Code of Canon Law, 1983, Canon 907.

[90] The Gelasian Sacramentary

the prestige and mystique of the Christian priesthood but is theologically insupportable. Below we quote Thomas Aquinas in another context: "The sacrament is not wrought by … the celebrant or the recipient, but by the power of God". All the Church authorities can do is to give authority in accordance with their regulations governing the implementation of the command to 'Do This'.

Ordination sprang from the need for *order*. It marked the appointment of a man to an official position of leadership and authorised him to act for the community. The sacrament of the Eucharist is a symbolic commemoration of Christ's life and ultimate sacrifice. It is Christ's offering. In presiding the priest is acting *in persona Christi* and symbolises Christ. If we give *persona* its original Latin meaning of theatrical 'role' it becomes less pretentious, but it still distracts from the essential idea that every member of the congregation is part of the Mystical Body—both as offering and offeror. It has blurred Paul's objective; that every Christian should be able to say: 'It is not I who live but Christ who lives in me' and that this should guide him in everything he does. The awareness that Christ lives in us and we in Christ[91] is weakened when the exercise of the charisms distributed among the Pauline community are become the official prerogative of one person. St Paul would have each one of the priestly people offer himself or herself at the Lord's Supper along with Jesus and be a prophet, evangeliser, healer, preacher, counsellor, administrator, or influencer according as Christ allots his gifts[92]. The involvement and participation of the faithful diminished progressively as the professionals officially monopolised each of the charisms and developed privileges that were later protected by canon law. This is an essential element of clericalism that could be remedied simply and directly by any pope.

Decision 3: Shortage of priests.

Just as the care of the needy was the characteristic activity of the churches, the celebration of the Lord's supper was the defining ritual that unified them. Allow me to repeat myself: 'It was reasonable, respectful, and necessary for the responsible authorities, the 'overseers', to introduce some regulation and standardisation to a celebration that was at once sociable and sacred'. Since the third or fourth century, they have ordained selected men to preside, since the thirteenth century, these men have been required to be celibate, and since the sixteenth century they have been required to undergo six years or more of tightly specified seminary training the object of which is 'formation'. The celebration of Mass has thus become the privilege of a highly standardised professional elite.

That elite is now shrinking at an alarming rate. Instead of providing priests to help the bishop, sacramental ordination has now become an obstruction preventing many Catholic faithful from obeying the foundational commandment to "Do This" (or

---

[91] The idea that each of two things can be in the other is counter-intuitive, but we are dealing here with the interface between the human and the divine, between the finite and the infinite. And nothing is impossible with God.

[92] See Romans 12:6-13

even 'attend at' this) with appropriate frequency and making it difficult for many to access "the source and summit" of the spiritual life for long periods of time. This is particularly true in mission areas or in countries where the institutional church is being persecuted.

The continuing decline in vocations has exacerbated a shortage which was already of deep concern to Pope Pius XII as far back as 1950[93] and was officially identified at Vatican II. Since about 1970, the profession has been visibly headed towards extinction. It is a management problem calling for decisions which the papacy has been unable or unwilling to make. The bishops are acutely aware of sacramental famine, but their hands are tied.[94] They are controlled in their responses by Canon law. As a bureaucracy made up of similar professionals with identical training, the curia is incapable of considering, let alone adopting, policies that might impinge on the current prestige, privileges, traditions, or prerogatives of their profession. (In Chapter 1 we discussed the idiosyncrasies of homogeneous groups).

Furthermore, the rigorous control structure inhibits creative solutions and the amount of pseudo-infallible teaching foisted on the faithful during the past 150 years leaves little room for manoeuvre. Any significant change risks the scandal of a 'doctrine' that has become untrue or can no longer be labelled essential for salvation.

The bureaucracy dismisses every solution proposed and often chastises the proposers. It offloads some of the responsibility for the scarcity on to the laity[95] by exhorting them to further prayer for vocations.[96] It urges a Catholic young man to be generous and make a lifelong commitment while its own commitment to him can be ended at any time if he should fall in love and 'attempt to marry'. He then stands to lose his profession and livelihood when he needs them most. He may even see himself replaced in the parish by an Anglican convert with wife and children. The inconsistency reveals the central management as prioritising the wrong things. It appears to be silly, incapable, and heartless and makes the life-long commitment demanded for ordination unnecessarily risky for potential candidates. For those who are not contemplating priesthood, the evident irrationality creates a temptation to dismiss the church authorities as out of touch and irrelevant.

---

[93] "[T]he number of priests, both in Catholic areas and in missionary territories, is for the most part unequal to the ever increasing needs"—See Pope Pius XII, apostolic exhortation *"Menti Nostrae"* (AAS 42 (1950),

[94] Bishop Morris was fired for suggesting some remedies for the Eucharistic famine in his diocese of Toowoomba. (See Chapter 9)

[95] "The task of fostering vocations devolves on the whole Christian community"— Vatican II, decree on Priestly Formation (§2)

[96] Coincidentally, while working on this section, I went to Mass and the priest led the congregation in prayer for vocations, using the phrase *"so that the Mass can continue"*!

As the Church starts into its third millennium without any serious action to change the conditions or reverse the trend, the bureaucracy seems to be calmly contemplating, as though it were part of an obscure Divine plan, that the Eucharist will come to an end, (and thus the Church), when the profession finally peters out. The needs of the bureaucracy are now directly at odds with the mission of the Church. "He who loves his life will lose it". The bureaucracy is now seen to be more concerned with its reputation for inerrancy and continuity than about its mandated objectives. They are unable to see that authority to manage a lighthouse does not extend to letting the light go out permanently or turning it down so low that it cannot be seen in a storm.

Decision 4: Wasted missionary effort

Dedicated Catholic missionaries have endured hardship and travel to preach the faith and bring converts into the Church by Baptism. They have been successful. They set up mission stations but, due to the huge areas involved, they can only get back to say Mass a few times in the year. Thus, for centuries a significant proportion of the new believers have been denied reasonable access to nourishment in the faith, denied the 'source and summit' of their spiritual life and the opportunity to worship in the unifying liturgy of the Eucharist as Jesus instructed them. In mission areas it has been customary for catechists to be appointed to teach the Catholic community and lead prayer services in the absence of the priest.

Fr Raymond Hickey OSA suggested in a book published in 1980 that these catechists should be ordained as auxiliary priests. He offered an estimate of 54,000 trained catechists in Africa alone at the time of publication.[97] They could easily be taught to lead the community in the celebration of Mass, as St Paul would have done. They could bring regular Sunday Mass to congregations aggregating perhaps another 5-10 Million souls. With Mass now being celebrated in the vernacular, with the availability of printed missalettes, with the Internet, YouTube, mobile phones, and widespread literacy this would be entirely practical today and could be implemented at short notice. Only the rules stand in the way. Ordaining thousands of catechists or letting the congregation celebrate, however, would impact the status and mystique of the priesthood and it is the priestly profession that would have to open the doors.

St John Chrysostom would have ordained the catechists. In the fourth century, he expressed the view that administering the sacraments can be entrusted to relatively uneducated priests, but that the proclamation of the word had to be restricted to 'wise and educated clergy'.[98] Current missionary practice reverses this and is contrary to reason. Ordaining the catechist, however, might upset some of the existing priests. It

---

[97] Fr. Raymond Hickey OSA, *Africa, The Case for an Auxiliary Priesthood,* London, Geoffrey Chapman,1980. Fr Hickey presents the case for in-service training of catechists cogently and with wide theological scholarship.

[98] . —Edward Schillebeeckx, *The Church with a Human Face*, New York, Crossroad Publishing Co., 1985, p 141.

appears that the Roman *magisterium* has for long been prioritising the ordained professionals above the commandment of Jesus that they were ordained to serve.

Decision 5: Clericalism combines with complacency

Recognising in 1988 that the shortage of priests is not confined to the foreign missions, the Congregation of Divine Worship issued a Directory for Sunday celebrations in the absence of a priest. This document lays great stress on the importance of the traditional Sunday assembly simply as an assembly, even without the Mass, but as something that in itself can give witness to the faith and promote a sense of community.

To emphasise the importance in tradition of the assembly *just as an assembly* the directory quotes St Justin's letter to the Emperor and Senators (c. 160 AD):

> "And on the day called Sunday, all [Christians] who live in cities or in the country gather together to one place …"

The excerpt is cut short in mid-sentence. This is misleading. Justin's letter immediately goes on to describe exactly what takes place at these gatherings—the Lord's Supper! So, the emphasis on the historical assembly for its own sake irrespective of the Mass is a deliberate fabrication.[99] The bureaucracy is ready to use misrepresentation to cover up its self-centred obstruction of Christ's only liturgical commandment: "Do This". "How ingeniously you get round the commandments of God in order to preserve your own tradition". (Matthew: 7:9, Jerusalem Bible).

The *Directory for the Sunday Celebration in the absence of a Priest* admitted that in 1988 the absence of a priest was *normal* for many congregations and anticipated that this was likely to continue. It described how some priests had to celebrate Mass several times in widely spread locations while some parishes had no Sunday Mass at all. It comments serenely that "this practice is regarded as not always satisfactory either to the parishes lacking their own pastor or to the priests involved". Wow! How's that for complacency?

That is more than thirty years ago and none of the proposed strategies for increasing their number has been implemented.

The document accepts that the cause is the shortage of priests but leaves that problem to one side as if the Congregation of Divine Worship had no function in the matter. Instead it sets norms, in more than six thousand words, for Sunday prayer gatherings led by a lay person, with or without the distribution of pre-consecrated Holy Communion. The norms, apparently, take precedence over Christ's commandment. He told us what to do. So, church management, that makes so much of the virtue of obedience, here mandates something different. As a gesture towards Christ's instructions, they say that preferably the Sunday assembly should be scheduled to

---

[99] Here I am not denying the importance of frequent assembly. ("Wherever two or three are gathered … ") I am decrying the practice of cutting short a crucial quotation to mislead the reader as to its meaning. As we will see in Chapter 12, this is not a unique occurrence.

coincide with a Mass being celebrated somewhere nearby and the pre-consecrated hosts should come from another Mass celebrated on the same day!

These *desiderata,* however inessential, will become increasingly difficult if not impossible as the availability of priests declines further. The remaining priests will presumably have to consecrate larger and larger numbers of hosts for distribution by courier over widening areas. Where does this end? If the hosts were to be packaged and labelled before consecration, the packing and addressing could be done at the factory by un-consecrated hands. Without breaching canon law, the hosts could be consecrated efficiently without taking them off the truck, provided a little wine and water is consecrated at the same time. Would this be 'faithful to the example of the Lord Jesus'?

Rome can lecture the faithful on the importance of preserving the integrity of every single marriage act, while the integrity of the Lord's Supper can be sacrificed to protect the traditional prerogatives of the profession. Very few of the pastors that I have known would want the perpetuation of their professional privileges to take prec-edence over the timely celebration of the Lord's Supper. This situation, however, is perpetuated by Canon Law as drafted by the bureaucracy and the power to remedy it rests, in Canon Law, with the papacy.

Moreover, one of the reasons advanced for denying inter-communion to Protestants is that they understand the Eucharist as a memorial meal but not as a symbolic sacramental sacrifice. Much is made of the distinction when unity is being opposed, yet the *Directory for the Sunday Celebration in the absence of a Priest* allows Catholics to fulfil their Sunday obligation by attending a memorial meal without any symbolic offering and immolation, which constitute the essence of the sacrifice. Is the *Directory* not demanding in practice what the Church rejects as error on the part of the Protestants?

Decision 6: Outdated response to a new problem

Participation in Sunday Mass is often taken as the touchstone of Catholic practice. In regions where it is securely established, the Church considers attendance at Sunday Mass to be so important that to miss it without grave reason is deemed a mortal sin.[100] Does this not create an equally grave responsibility on the management to provide parish Mass with appropriate frequency and accessibility, so as not to lead people into temptation? And further, to plan for its continued provision into the future? The current policy of 'clustering' parishes and closing churches is a short-term stopgap that allows fewer priests and fewer Masses to meet the obligation of more thinly spread (and dwindling) congregations. It cannot go on forever. Further-more, closing churches tends to break up Christian communities and distance the remaining faithful from their pastors and from one another. The task of building the community that was so important to St Paul is reversed as congregations are drawn

---

[100] Catechism of the Catholic Church, Dublin, Veritas, 1994, §2181

from further and further afield. The social value of the assembly is further eroded. In the United States there have been many examples of congregations demonstrating against the closing of churches and parishes and the loss of community. . Why not let educated, capable communities run their own parishes?[101]

The current policy accommodates the Mass to the system and seems to reflect the same inversion of priorities. The priestly bureaucracy is afraid to make changes affecting the priestly profession.

Decision 7: New rules needed for doing what Jesus told us to do.

Vatican II wished that "Through a proper appreciation of the rites and prayers they [the faithful] should participate knowingly, devoutly and actively". Unfortunately, fear of revisiting the Council of Trent creates problems here. Trent laid down rules for the preparation of candidates for ordination. It conceived the seminary system to meet the needs of its own day when Europe was awash with priests, many of them inadequately educated. We now face precisely the opposite problem with a grave shortage of priests and many highly educated men and women in the congregation. It seems that even the practical arrangements of the Council of Trent, cannot be modified, if the faithful are aware of them. They have become tainted with pseudo-infallibility.[102] The regulations intended to improve the ordained priesthood at the time, now threaten its very existence. The Church authorities should revert to the arrangement prior to Trent when bishops made the judgement as to how many priests were needed and could be afforded in their dioceses and then selected suitable people to ordain.

If the papacy cannot find the courage to permit the ordination of women or married men, why not authorise some lay volunteers to celebrate … while there is still a congregation from which to select them? We have ample precedent from apostolic and post-apostolic times. Many dedicated priests to whom I have spoken see the need for radical action and would prioritise the Eucharist and the needs of the faithful ahead of their own status. Strangely, the bishops at the Synod on Amazonia, having discussed the urgent need, could only bring themselves to recommend the ordination of existing married deacons. Pope Francis rightly dismissed this proposal. It would have added nothing to the total number of ministers. It would have been a gesture rather than a solution and would have had initiated a domino effect far beyond the Amazon area.

The point has been made since then that a Synod focused on a specific region is not the proper forum to address a worldwide church problem. Regrettably, the

---

[101] The St William Parish in Louisville, Kentucky has developed this way under lay leadership since 2002 with notable success as a lively Catholic community, with only a 'drop-in' priest for Sunday Mass, baptisms, and confession. This has allowed the faithful to grow in responsibility, ministering to one another under the guidance of the Spirit without being pushy or encroaching on anybody's turf.

[102] The term 'pseudo-infallible' is used to describe fallible human teaching that masquerades as infallible or that is treated as such, explicitly or implicitly. We define it on page 117

proper forum has been silenced. The College of Bishops as proposed at Vatican II was legislated into impotence by the papacy in the 1983 revision of the Code of Canon Law, continuing a thousand-year tradition of prioritising papal power.

The papacy disapproves of discussion among the faithful of female, temporary or non-celibate celebrants. Is this because they know their present policies are indefensible? Are they afraid of the reaction of the existing priests who have endured celibacy (or irregular unions) as the price of continuing in ministry? Or of the ire of those who have done the honourable thing and married the girl at the cost of their ministry and their livelihood?

Why is the papacy so bent on safeguarding the distinction between the priesthood of the ordained and that of the people? Pope Benedict XVI expressed concern about this several times without explaining why he considered it so important. The difference is described as ontological. But since nobody knows exactly what that difference is—except for the odd idea of a 'character or mark' on a soul—it is hard to deduce what it should enable or prevent. Maybe it is because there is not much difference at all, except that of legal authorisation to preside[103]. But that would not be ontological. Maybe, like celibacy, there are underlying considerations that must not be spoken of, let alone admitted. Volunteer clergy, as suggested, could be non-stipendiary, but they would be harder to control and besides, the Anglicans and some Protestant churches have taken that step already. If we were seen to be taking our cue from them, it might imply that they responded to the prompting of the Holy Spirit ahead of us. And that could never be or, at least, it could never be admitted by the papacy.

If the problem here is not simply pride, it probably boils down to a question of personnel management. The organisation is accustomed to celibate staff with vowed obedience for life. They can be treated with less consideration than volunteers or part-timers who might have wives and children.

"Do this" is both a command and an authorisation. Without denying that a person needs ordination to offer the Eucharist individually, it seems that the People of God, by virtue of baptism and the command, have a binding duty to celebrate in his memory with appropriate frequency. They are a priestly people. Jesus is present among them. The assembled congregation is recognised as the Church in microcosm, so the duty and right applies to the group, without need of any further sacrament. Canon law should be revised to permit a congregation that lacks an ordained priest to celebrate a Community Mass together, without an individual 'celebrant', as the Christian churches did for the first few centuries. If the clergy recoils in horror at this suggestion, it will simply prove that the liturgical prerogatives of the profession are

---

[103] 'In the letters of St Paul and the Gospels that followed, there is no hint of "clergy" and "laity" as we know them today'. Those who continually beat the drum about a difference of kind, and not merely of degree, between the general priesthood of the faithful and the ministerial priesthood of the ordained are really only defending the institution while claiming to defend the faith'.—Paul Lakeland, *Catholicism at the Crossroads: How the laity can save the church,* New York, Continuum, 2007,

being prioritised ahead of the commandment. Of course, whenever an ordained person would be available, he or she could preach and celebrate *in persona Christi* in the conventional way and offer the Mass on behalf of the congregation.

Since the shortage of priests impacts the essential sacrament, it is an existential problem for the Church. This has been evident for half a century and more, yet central management has failed to come up with a solution.[104] Nor has it allowed the responsible bishops to experiment. Solving such a long-outstanding problem and opening new possibilities for community involvement would require a major change in attitude in the bureaucracy and a readiness to drop a number of pseudo-infallible teachings. Exaggerated infallibility and pride are at the heart of the paralysis. "Pride is the queen and mother of all the vices".[105]

Decision 8: Ex Opere Operato.

Roman paganism was not greatly concerned with motivation or personal sanctity. It was the exact performance of the prescribed actions that could turn away the wrath of the gods. This attitude may have influenced the Christian response to the Donatist heretics who were claiming that the efficacy of the sacraments depended on the moral character of the minister.[106] Such a teaching would have threatened the standing of the Church as the dispenser of the grace merited by Christ. It could have been used to undermine the status of any individual priest or bishop. The heresy was rejected by Pope Melchiades and later by the Council of Arles (314 AD).[107] The position has been maintained ever since by Catholics and subsequently by Anglicans that "the sacraments act *ex opere operato* (literally: ('by the very fact of the action's being performed')[108]. At a practical level, the reasoning was that the faithful were entitled to certainty in relation to the validity of the sacraments, most particularly baptism, which, at times, was taught to be essential for salvation. St Thomas offered a more principled reason in the thirteenth century: "The sacrament is not wrought by the righteousness of either the celebrant or the recipient, but by the power of God"[109].

The Donatist schism hinged around the treatment of priests and bishops who had fallen away under persecution. It continued long after the persecutions had ended. Holiness is attractive, however, and powerfully evangelising. If we think of the young priest who is ordained by the pope or of the parents whose child is baptised by the bishop during the Easter Vigil or of people who travelled long distances to make their

---

[104] Since the Council, the number of priests per 100,000 Catholics in the USA has dropped from 121 to less than 50 while the average age has gone up from 44 to more than 65. We consider the implications of this on page 216.

[105] No 22 from a list of maxims drawn up by Angelo Roncalli as a seminarian. (The original is attributed to Aquinas)

[106] —*A Catholic Dictionary Ninth* Edition h, Virtue & Co, 1925. p 286

[107] *Ibid.*

[108] Catechism of the Catholic Church, 1128.

[109] St Thomas Aquinas, Summ, Theol, III, 60, 3, quoted in Catechism of the Catholic Church.

confessions with the Curé d'Ars, we can see why being baptised, absolved, or ordained by a very holy pastor can be instinctively prized by pious Christians. So, the Donatist heresy was attractive and continued to find some adherents for the best part of 500 years.

In the meantime, the principle of '*ex opere operato*' avoided ongoing difficulties for church management and denied the busybodies an excuse for prying into the moral behaviour of their clergy. However, it also provided a hostage to fortune which we will come to with the issue of ordaining women in Chapter 12.

Decision 9: Extraordinary Ministers

Prior to Vatican II the distribution of Holy Communion was reserved to the consecrated hands of the ordained. Changes in the understanding of the liturgy at the Council made the appointment of lay ministers an arithmetic necessity. The curia resisted this intrusion into an area that was traditionally reserved to the profession and insisted on the official title in English of 'Extraordinary Minister of the Eucharist', despite strenuous opposition from the Hierarchy of England and Wales who favoured 'Special Minister'. The term 'extraordinary' had one obvious advantage over 'special'. It would facilitate a reversion to the previous arrangement, which the curia preferred, if an opportunity were to arise at a later stage.

Decision 10: Forgiveness of sins

The Gospel in general suggests that Jesus was always anxious to forgive sins.[110] He forgave gratuitously, even without being asked. He did so without a listing of sins, without judging and without any reference to 'temporal punishment' in Purgatory. He even forgave Peter for denying him, and the other apostles for running away. And his style was always to take the initiative. He died for us "while we were yet sinners".[111] Such magnanimity cannot be reconciled with the bureaucratic need to control. They cannot believe, or will not encourage the faithful to believe, how loving and magnanimous in this respect is our Father God.

Jesus went farther. Before he died, he delegated to his followers the right to forgive sins. "Receive the Holy Spirit. Whose sins you shall forgive, they are forgiven" was addressed to his disciples, not just to the Apostles.[112] The early Christians took him at his word. For most of the first millennium, any Christian, male or female, could exercise their royal priesthood responsibly and, on the authority of the Lord Jesus, forgive sins. In Ireland, the idea of spiritual direction was well developed. In the Irish language, we still have an expression that comes to us from antiquity: '*Anamcara*'. This

---

[110] Luke 11:17, Mark 3:25, Matthew 12:25

[111] Romans 5:8

[112] John 20:22. This occurred "in the room where the disciples were, for fear of the Jews". In the very next verse John makes specific reference to "the Twelve". He was keeping the distinction clear. By the word 'disciples' he meant the larger group of Christ's followers, which always included women.

translates effectively as 'soul-friend' or spiritual director. Private confession in Ireland is traceable from the fifth or sixth century.

Early in the second millennium the capacity to administer the sacrament of reconciliation was gradually withdrawn from the faithful and reserved to ordained priests.[113] Later, even ordination was not enough. For the sacrament to be 'valid', a priest had to be granted faculties for each specific diocese. The power of the Church depended on its ability to open and close the gates of heaven and consequently of hell for the faithful. This would be vitiated if forgiveness were too readily available. In the thirteenth century, Canon 60 of the Fourth Lateran Council, made it mandatory for every Catholic to confess their sins at least once a year *to their own [parish] priest.* If they had good reason, they could ask his permission to confess to another priest! Without such permission, the confession would be invalid. Severe punishments were attached to failure to comply with Canon 60. "[T]hey shall be barred from entering a church during their lifetime and they shall be denied a Christian burial at death". In simple terms, they would be consigned to hell, leaving God with no discretion in the matter. This is in marked contrast to Christ's way of doing things. But the papacy was at the height of its powers under Pope Innocent III and much of that power stemmed, directly or indirectly, from the perceived ability to confer or deny salvation.

In such a situation, of course, the definition of new sins, or upgrading of the gravity of established ones, has the effect of enhancing control. However, respect for the very concept of morality and the binding power of conscience is bound to be eroded if sins appear to be created arbitrarily by human edict. [114]

Even now the papacy is remarkably parsimonious about the astonishing gift of forgiveness. It strongly discourages the bishops from permitting the use of the third official rite of penance, general absolution, although this could help to reconcile some people to the Lord. It is superficial to dismiss general absolution and even aural confession as 'cheap grace'. This overlooks the fact that all grace is a gift from God and that his magnanimity knows no bounds. If church authorities were being 'faithful to the example of the Lord Jesus', they would make the first move. The reassurance that they have been reconciled to Jesus, that past transgressions are not being held against them, would encourage some people to try to amend their ways and be more faithful disciples in future. Forgiveness generates love. Jesus explained the relationship when he was dining with the Pharisee:

---

[113] In our present sacramental discipline, only a priest can hear confessions. Up to the fourth Lateran Council early in the thirteenth century it was permissible to confess to an un-ordained person. —Nicholas Peter Harvey, *Safeguarding What,* in The Furrow, March 2012, p 143

[114] For the majority of Catholics who think that Rome is wrong or acting on prejudice against the ordination of women, a recent declaration upgrading their ordination to a more serious sin is more likely to confirm than change those opinions. Moreover, it trivialises the concept of morality.

"I tell you that her sins, her many sins, must have been forgiven her, or she would not have shown such great love. It is the man who has been forgiven little who shows little love"[115]

Decision 11: Purgatory and temporal punishment.

Beyond the issues of who administers the sacrament and when, where, and how, there is the issue of what the papacy or the profession has done with the concept of forgiveness itself. When Christ said 'forgiven', he undoubtedly meant forgiven. The introduction of purgatory and the 'temporal punishment due to sin' is a reversion to pre-Christian ideas of vengeful[116] and vindictive gods. It mutilates the concept of forgiveness. It contradicts the Gospel message that God loves us. It is as if the Governor of Alcatraz were to tell the prisoner: "The good news is that you have been granted a presidential pardon, but the bad news is that it has been decided that you must serve out your full sentence anyway".

In fact, purgatory was put into the mainstream of Christian teaching by Pope Gregory the Great (590-604 AD) for a relatively benign reason; to solve a theological problem. In those days, sacramental forgiveness was provisional to start with and only became absolute on completing the penance (satisfaction) imposed. Penances were often lengthy affairs, and the question arose as to what should happen to the soul of one who died before completion. If he were to be allowed entry to heaven with a debit balance on the satisfaction ledger, so to speak, it would be unfair to others who had balanced their accounts before death.[117] Hence purgatory. God, who is infinitely just, would allow the penitent serve out the balance of his sentence there. Unfortunately, Gregory overlooked the parable of the workers who were all given the same reward although some had only worked a few hours in the vineyard.

Purgatory was not Gregory's idea. Several important saints, Ambrose, Jerome, and Augustine, who corresponded with one another and were writing at the end of the fourth century or beginning of the fifth, were in agreement on the need for an intermediate stage between earth and heaven. Origen, an influential theologian with an enormous output who was unfairly listed as a heretic, and who died 100 years before Augustine was born, may have been their common inspiration. He relied on the passage in I Corinthians 3:11-15, which modern exegetes do not accept as being a direct reference to purgatory. This led him to the conclusion that there had to be a place where the dead who did not deserve to go to hell were purified before they could be presented in the sight of God. In one of his homilies, he used a metaphor, familiar in the Old Testament, of purification by fire:

---

[115] Jerusalem Bible, Luke 7:47 This verse was mistranslated, even in the Douay-Rheims Bible, leading Catholics to see forgiveness dependent on love where the context demands the reverse.

[116] The Catechism of the Catholic Church specifically says that it should 'not be conceived of as a kind of vengeance' (§1472). Whatever it is, it besmirches the image of a loving, merciful Father God.

[117] —Colish, quoted in Peter Watson, *History of Ideas*, London, Phoenix, 2006, paperback, p 316.

> All, therefore, must come to the fire; all must come to the melting furnace, for the Lord sits and melts down and purifies the sons of Juda. But when one comes to that place, if he brings many good works and very little iniquity, that little is separated by fire like lead and is purified and the whole is left pure gold.[118]

The three saints saw a further need for such a place. It was considered a 'holy and wholesome thought to pray for the dead that they may be loosed from their sins'. But such prayers would be superfluous if the soul was already in heaven and unavailing if resident in the other place. They needed a holding area of some sort if prayers for the dead were to be efficacious. For Augustine, it was more than a metaphor. It would be a place, or interim state, of intense expiatory suffering. " … yet will that fire be more grievous than anything that man can suffer in this life whatsoever".[119]   The implication of that would be that Christ's sufferings fell short of what was necessary for the forgiveness of sins! Another implication (or explanation) is that God's infinite sense of justice forces him to prioritise law and retribution over compassion and love. Is this the message of the Gospel? It is strange that churchmen who can usually find wriggle room around their own regulations, cannot credit God with a similar capacity.

What one pope, three saints and one 'heretic' theologian failed to appreciate was that the sequences of cause and effect and the structure of time, space, energy and matter are earthly limitations that cannot be assumed to govern God and the afterlife. Kierkegaard put it more elegantly, calling attention to the "infinite qualitative distinction between time and eternity".[120] For the dying sinner, God can respond to prayers as yet unsaid. God can, and sometimes does, answer our prayers before we say them.

If Christianity had been preaching a God of love and of a forgiveness that evokes love in return, we might have done better in making disciples of all the nations. But the doctrine of purgatory, [121] where souls are purified by a process of suffering lasting for years or centuries, delivered a lot more power and control to a papacy which claimed to be the steward and sole dispenser of the grace 'merited' by Christ. It opened the way to a whole economy of calculated time remissions attached to certain meritorious actions or devotional exercises that could only be specified by the pope and had to be taken on trust. In time, these remissions, became known as 'indulgences', and came to be granted in return for donations, giving rise to a new papal revenue stream. Corruption became institutionalised.

Decision 12: The response to reform

500 years ago, Rome was selling indulgences on an international scale. These could be interpreted as licences to sin while escaping the related 'temporal punishment due to sin' in purgatory. The proportion of the money that finally found its way back to Rome was going towards the construction of a new St Peter's Basilica. The end was

---

[118] *https://www.scribd.com/document/344026065/Origen-homilies-on-genesis-and-exodus-pdf*

[119] —St Augustine, Ennarration on Psalm 37.

[120] —Harvey Cox, *The Secular City,* New York, 1965, The Macmillan Company.

[121] Defined at the 2nd Council of Lyon in 1274 which is no longer claimed as ecumenical.

obviously justifying the means. One of Christianity's most able theologians, Martin Luther, saw this as a corruption of the Gospel message and felt it his duty to challenge the abuse. While he was taking the significant risk of speaking out, he identified several other problems and made related suggestions for reform.

His action was attributed to intellectual pride. Ironically, the reaction of the papacy to Luther was governed by its own pride; by its obstinate claim to inerrancy[122]. He was questioning a papal authority that claimed that it had not erred and could never err under any circumstances. This claim inhibited the papacy, for four hundred years, from recognising merit in any of Luther's proposals. Several of these were adopted when the bishops at Vatican II were given the freedom to speak their minds.

Luther was excommunicated in 1520 by the Bull *Exsurge Domine,* of Pope Leo X, which summarised 41 teachings (some out of context) and condemned them on the basis of papal inerrancy. Some of them would rank low in any hierarchy of truths. One of the "errors" condemned was the statement: "That heretics be burned, is against the will of the Spirit"! Luther was also condemned for maintaining that giving the laity Holy Communion under both species was *not* a heresy. The papacy at that point insisted it was, echoing the earlier Council of Constance. The papacy was too proud and too vulnerable to listen or engage in dialogue, so what started out as a genuine search for truth and reform ended up in a split that is still with us.

Some Catholic are beginning to accept that God permitted the Reformation to happen in the course of fulfilling the Promise. He writes the screenplay. Martin Luther, Calvin, and others could all have died in infancy, and who would have been the wiser? God had not abandoned the Promise, he is always fulfilling it. Apparently, there were gifts that the Latin Church was incapable of receiving—nourishment that it could not bring to the faithful—for whatever reason. God found another route.

> Michael Ramsey, Archbishop of Canterbury from 1961 to 1974, argued against seeing Anglicanism as an end in itself and in favour of understanding it as a product of disunity - but a providential one with a mission and a purpose lasting until, with disunity itself, it disappears.[123]

Decision 13: Baptism essential for salvation.

The theological arguments that rotate about original sin, sanctifying grace and death are interminable and beyond the scope of this book or the ken of the author. The most famous protagonists were St Augustine and Pelagius. While Augustine taught pessimistically that decadent man, born in a state of original sin, required baptism for salvation and sanctifying grace to enable him to do anything good, Pelagius took a more benign view. In his view, men and women are created good by

---

[122] See Papal Bull, *Exsurge Domine,* of Pope Leo X, 1520

[123] Mark Woodruff, Paper read at the *Receptive Ecumenism Conference III* – Fairfield University, July 2014
https://www.academia.edu/29233403/Anglicans_and_Catholics_in_Communion_Can_the_Ordinariates_represent_Christian_Unity?email_work_card=view-paper. Accessed 23 November 2019

God and therefore capable of good actions by virtue of their nature, without a further gift of grace. He was accused of saying that people could be saved by their own efforts alone. If we wanted to rehabilitate Pelagius, we might say that he saw some grace as a normal, natural endowment; with grace working through nature. Pelagius revised his line of reasoning several times but lost the argument in the end. His thinking seemed to imply that there was a gate to heaven other than the one for which the pope held the keys. Some people outside of the Church might be saved and this was a completely unacceptable idea during the first and most of the second millennium[124]. Pelagianism in general was condemned no less than three times; at two Synods of Orange (441 & 529) and again at the Council of Trent. This is not surprising. The Church was in charge of the sacraments and alone could dispense the grace 'merited' by Christ. Original Sin underpinned its power by making baptism essential for salvation. Not surprisingly, the Church authorities adopted St Augustine's view although it consigned a lot of innocent unbaptised babies to hell and called into question the loving nature of God.[125] In ordinary reasoning, the absurd conclusion should have led to a rejection or re-examination of the issue. This seems never to have happened. It might have led to a compromise, somewhere in between the two opinions.

Decision 14: The sacrament of marriage

In the eleventh century, the reasonable rule was introduced, that a marriage contract between Christians must have two witnesses. In the thirteenth century it was declared that a marriage is *invalid* unless solemnised in the presence of a priest. The eleventh century ruling made obvious sense. It removed uncertainty about the mutual commitment which distinguishes conjugal sex from fornication, and it helped to secure property rights. The thirteenth century ruling placed marriage under the control of the clergy. Natural marriage, by mutual commitment and co-habitation, which had been normal from time immemorial, became equivalent, for Catholics, to fornication. In 1611 the Inquisition formally declared all deliberate genital activity outside of marriage to be it a mortal sin, always and without any exception.

Decision 15: Papacy can invent sins, and attach sanctions to them

Canon Law developed slowly as separate decisions. It was promulgated as a code in 1917, providing, *inter alia,* a legal framework for the 1870 Dogma of universal papal jurisdiction. It specified powers to grant dispensations from the various laws according to different ranks in the ordained hierarchy. At its extreme, the Pope is deemed

---

[124] It was finally accepted at Vatican II.

[125] Oddly, God's infinite sense of justice could be used to establish the existence of purgatory but could be overlooked in deciding the fate of the innocent unbaptised infants. In 2007 Pope Benedict XVI announced that there are "reasons to hope that they may be saved". He avoided admitting any earlier error by stressing that the Limbo teaching had never been defined as a doctrine. In a church that relies heavily on tradition, that was a risky distinction to make.

to have the power to grant dispensations from the natural law which is believed to be written by God in the hearts of men and women[126]. Mercifully, the right to approve or incite murder has not been exercised for some centuries. Breaches of Canon Law, without appropriate dispensation, were declared to be grave sins. The right of members of the hierarchy to give graded levels of dispensation undoubtedly gave them power but it trivialised the entire concept of morality.

Decision 16: Appointment of bishops

The selection, appointment, retirement, and dismissal of Bishops was reserved to the papacy. This control became virtually absolute in the fifty years after Vatican I, strengthening the power of the papacy. The pious fiction that, whatever the method of selection, the choice is ultimately the work of the Holy Spirit, has taken a bit of a battering in recent decades. It cannot be claimed that secretive central selection by a curial committee has served the Church well.

Decision 17: Recognition of sanctity reserved to the pope

Canonisation is a declaration that a dead person is in heaven and that the ban on public veneration throughout the world has been lifted. The holiness and virtues of saints have always been identified initially by their own church communities because of their clear and obvious sanctity. Their cults flourished because of the efficacy of their intercession with God. Sites associated with very holy people could attract large numbers of pilgrims and could become significant commercial assets. Some regulation was needed.

Up to the twelfth century local bishops judged whether a cult should be approved or discouraged. Pope Alexander III, however, reserved this approval to the Holy See. Urban VIII (1623-44) forbade the veneration of the dead or representations of them as saints, unless authorised by Rome. This enhanced the power and control exercised by the papacy. Furthermore, bishops were to suppress spontaneous expressions of popular veneration. These could not affect the sanctity of the candidate posthumously, of course, but premature veneration might prejudice the options open to the authorities. Canon Law stipulated a complex, multi-layered procedure, much like a trial, for investigating the lives of candidates and scrutinising their writings for unorthodox ideas. Reported miracles were studied and verified. All participants in these activities were sworn to permanent secrecy and the proceedings of the various commissions were not published. This meant that the final judgement of the sanctity of the candidate could not be challenged, leaving the process subject to internal politics and other inappropriate influences as is evidenced by the unseemly haste in canonising John Paul II and the years of foot-dragging in the case of the martyred Oscar Romero. The ceremonial canonisation is reserved to the pope. Although not a

---

[126] At the top of the scale, the pope can dispense from Natural Law. —Cf. Dominic M. Prummer O.P., *Handbook of Moral Theology*, Cork, Mercier Press. 1956, Fifth (first English) edition, p434. (Original edition in German, 1921)

matter of faith or morals, this declaration is given the aura of infallibility. It is a perfect area for the exercise of pseudo-infallibility since it is impossible to establish independently whether a deceased candidate is or is not in heaven.

Decision 18: A smoother path to canonisation & enhanced influence.

The 1983 Code omitted the canonisation procedures from canon law entirely, replacing them instead with a set of 'pontifical laws' which were really regulations for the working of the Congregation of the Causes of Saints. These were promulgated on the same day as the new Code but with *immediate* effect. They would facilitate easier modification than the canons they replaced. They were described as streamlining an archaic process. Instead of using the procedure of a trial, the assessment of the evidence would be entrusted to a series of committees and experts working under conditions of secrecy, with the pope continuing to make the final decision. The new regulations maintained the nominal position of 'Promoter of the Faith', known more colloquially as the 'Devil's Advocate'. In effect, however, it abolished the office by stripping it of its responsibilities, authority, and power of veto. This removed the safeguards, previously considered essential, designed to avoid a situation where a canonised person might later turn out to have been unworthy, immoral, or heretical.

The Devil's Advocate had an important function in the bureaucracy, where peer pressures tend to inhibit opposition to a developing consensus or to the presumed preferences of the leadership. Under the earlier code, the Devil's Advocate had a canonical duty to bring forward anything in the life or writings of the candidate that could undermine the reputation for sanctity, so the appointed person was able do this without earning the disapproval of his colleagues and endangering his future career. With the trial-like structure abandoned and the Devil's Advocate stripped of his duties and powers, a crucial counterbalance to bureaucratic groupthink and possible corruption was removed. Moreover, things could move more quickly with fewer unforeseen obstructions or unwanted obstacles.[127] And they did.

By speeding up the procedures, the new regulations opened the door for canonisations on a scale never seen before. In the period 1900 to 1978, the average was just over one canonisation per annum.[128] In his time as pontiff, St John Paul II canonised no less than 480, an annual average of 18! Apparently, canonising was something he liked to do. The curial bureaucracy and the new regulations facilitated him by approving suitable candidates more expeditiously.

Ironically, the regulations introduced under Pope John Paul II facilitated his own canonisation. By long tradition, there had been a waiting period of fifty years to allow the emotional climate to settle before the process (known as the cause) could be

---

[127] They could also be slowed down or stopped if politically expedient as, for example, in the cause of the martyred St Oscar Romero which was stalled in Rome until Pope Francis set it in motion again. Cf. https://www.ucanews.com/news/oscar-romero-and-the-politics-of-canonization/72939

[128] 1.2 per annum. Source: http://www.unamsanctamcatholicam.com/history/79-history/351-devil-s-advocate.html

started. Pope John Paul II himself had reduced this to five years, but even this was waived in his case by Pope Benedict XVI, allowing the process to start more or less immediately. Benedict's decision in this conveyed his predilection to members of the bureaucracy, ensuring the proposal got an easy passage. The decision to canonise was made long before Church archives relating to the life of the dead pope would be generally available. And there was no effective Devil's Advocate. Without an official duty and responsibility, or right to access documents or power of veto, what member of the bureaucracy could press the case for the opposition? And there were prudential grounds at least for opposing the rush to canonisation with all that that implies.[129]

The issue is not about whether he is in heaven; few Christians would doubt it. The problem is that the canonised saint is put forward as a role model for the faithful and his or her opinions gain additional authority. This effect is particularly noticeable in the canonisation or beatification of any well-known historical figure who has left a significant body of writing. It can be used to make an opinion in a papal document virtually unchallengeable.

In recent decades, the process has been turned into a new way of exalting the papacy. Adding haloes to previous incumbents improves the authority of the office. This, as we have seen, is one of the standing objectives of the bureaucracy—that is, provided the pope is allowing himself to be managed by the system.

Canonising popes has echoes of the practice of the pagan religious bureaucracy in Rome of making gods of dead Emperors (and occasionally, live ones!). Here we must remember what they meant by a god, or more exactly, what they did not mean. They had many gods who were more akin to members of a spirit world, with ability to influence earthly events. Accordingly, they *had* to be respected, even to the point of ritual sacrifices or burning incense in their honour. The great advantage of deifying a dead emperor was that it gave the office of the reigning one additional prestige. Some of the aura rubbed off on to the current incumbent. If it could enhance an office then, why not now?

Decision 19: Papal primacy of Universal Jurisdiction

Vatican I turned the bureaucratic dream of dominance over every church and diocese in the world into a dogma. The claim to Universal Jurisdiction had been repeated by the Apostolic See for fifteen hundred years but was never conceded by the wider Church. As a dogma defined at an ecumenical council it is generally deemed to be irreformable. It was approved, however, at a Council from which non-Catholic Christians were excluded. It suits the papacy to treat Vatican I as an 'ecumenical' council. The recognition by Vatican II that the Spirit works in the other Christian Churches, however, calls for its status to be downgraded to that of a General Council of the Roman Catholic Church[130].

---

[129] The content of Chapters 12 and 16 will suggest some of these.
[130] As was done informally by Paul VI in the case of the Second Council of Lyons

This decision scarcely needs a comment to show that it could have been made by any secular bureaucracy without any spiritual inspiration. It was an open and direct power grab.

It was also an attack on the hierarchical system which we are forever being told is part of God's eternal plan for his Church. Its effect was not to dispense with bishops, but simply to leave them with their titles and strip them of the power to fulfil their responsibilities. A totalitarian regime is not a hierarchy. A regime that combines legislative, judicial, and executive functions and uses coercion to maintain full, supreme, ordinary, and immediate power at the centre is totalitarian. There is no evidence in the New Testament that Christ wanted his Church to be governed, *de facto,* by a powerful, permanent, unchanging central administration. He wanted to win the hearts and minds of all the people. There is unequivocal evidence that he wanted his followers to be united in serving him out of love for him and for one another. The full, supreme, ordinary, and immediate power centre of Roman Catholicism is, by its own admission, the greatest barrier to the unity Christ prayed for. If, as seems likely, the curia will never voluntarily relinquish the power that it has amassed, some pope should exercise his legal power and scrap it in its present form, decentralising it, subordinating it to a functioning College of Bishops, or both.[131]

Decision 20: Papal Infallibility

Papal infallibility was an ambition of Pope Pius IX from the earliest days of his pontificate.[132] He got it passed at Vatican I by manipulating the agenda and changing the voting rules, although it had been condemned by a predecessor as a "pestiferous doctrine" and a "work of the devil".[133] It has only been invoked once officially since then but has been widely abused to enhance the power of pope and curia.

Since the Dogmas of Infallibility and Universal Jurisdiction have shaped the Church for 150 years for better or for worse, we will devote the next chapter to the first Vatican Council.

AMBITION, THE COMMON ELEMENT IN TWENTY DECISIONS

The common characteristic of all the above decisions is that each one added to the power and influence of the pope and the central bureaucracy, which together make up the papacy. Each decision could have been expected from any large secular bureaucracy without any inspiration from the Holy Spirit. The group dynamic in the bureaucracy prioritises pride over humility, power over service, law over love, authority over conscience and obedience to its directives over every other virtue.

Many Roman policies, since Christianity became the State Religion of the Empire, have owed more to the bureaucratic need to perpetuate itself and enhance its power

---

[131] Of course, the Vatican, as a sovereign state will need to maintain a civil administration.

[132] Cf. Encyclical Letter of Pope Pius IX, *Qui Pluribus,* 9 Nov. 1846.

[133] Pope John XXII, Encyclical *Quia Quorundam,* 1324

than to the example of Jesus Christ. Instead of patiently bringing disciples to love, to stop thinking about self and care for others, by example and by evoking love of God by spreading God's forgiveness, Rome has concentrated on enhancing its power by frightening believers into compliance. This has continued into modern times, prompting Yves Congar to write, in a letter to his mother written from Rome:

> "It is clear to me that Rome has never looked for and even now does not look for anything but the affirmation of its own authority. Everything else interests it only as matter for the exercise of this authority. Except for a certain number of cases dealing with people of holiness and creativity, the whole history of Rome is about insisting on its own authority and the destruction of everything that cannot be—reduced to submission".[134]

From the time of the Council of Sardica the church in the East has been openly resisting Roman claims to total hegemony while the Latin Church supported it.

Rome can support its claim by quoting Christ's words to the disciples in Matthew and John and to the 72 in Luke:

> "I tell you solemnly, whatever you bind on earth shall be considered bound in heaven; whatever you loose on earth shall be considered loosed in heaven". (Mt. 18:18)

> After saying this he breathed on them and said: "receive the Holy Spirit. For those whose sins you forgive, they are forgiven; for those whose sins you retain, they are retained". (Jn. 20:22-23)

> "Anyone who listens to you, listens to me; anyone who rejects you rejects me, and those who reject me reject the one who sent me". (Lk.10:16)

This extraordinary power was given, not just to the apostles, but to all Christ's faithful followers. The context suggests that whoever may be exercising it, must always be acting conscientiously under the guidance of the Holy Spirit. As in the case of a civil judge who abuses his position, we may safely assume that God, who sees into the inmost heart, immediately suspends the power when it is being abused.

---

[134] —Yves Congar, Letter to his mother, September 1956 (quoted in the National Catholic Reporter, June 2, 2000, p 20 and reprinted in ARCC Light May-June 2000, Vol 22 No 4

Chapter 7

Infallibility and its genesis

I look with anxiety at the prospect of having to defend decisions which may not be difficult to my private judgement but may be most difficult to defend logically in the face of historical facts … When has definition of doctrine de fide been a luxury of devotion and not a stern painful necessity?

—Newman to Bishop Ullathorne, 28/1/1870

DEALING WITH DISAGREEMENTS

Confidence that the Holy Spirit is guiding the beliefs of the Church should not lead us to think that the early Christians shared the same opinions or understanding. There was little or no centrality, compared with today. Christianity was the Way, a movement rather than an organisation. When important issues arose, the emerging bishops discussed them with other leaders in local synods to resolve them. At the Council of Nicaea it was accepted that the best way of dealing with uncertainty about what the people of God believed was to bring together a large number of representatives who would witness to the belief of their churches—to the *sensus fidelium*—and try to articulate what was essential and common to all. If they could arrive at a morally unanimous understanding, this would motivate the small number that disagreed to rethink their positions. It would help to keep the church in peace.[135] The Emperor championed the importance of 'unanimity and concord' in deciding what the Church really believes and in maintaining unity.[136]

These councils were not without political dimensions. Nor were they without some less-than-edifying squabbling about the relative prestige and power of the various bishoprics and about their geographical boundaries. This should not surprise us. The Apostles had a propensity to argue about their own relative importance. The Bishop of Rome was unable to travel to Nicaea due to his advanced age but sent two presbyters.[137] From the Council of Constantinople on, the popes generally shrank from participating in the debate, emphasising their superiority by sending legates. This reinforced their authority and primacy and left the pope with the last word; the

---

[135] Vatican II stressed that infallible teaching is bounded by the extent of the deposit of faith and espoused the principle of the 'Hierarchy of Truths'. If adhered to, these two principles together can stop the proliferation of grounds for disunity.

[136] Theodoret, History of the church, from AD 322 to the Death of Theodore of Hopsuestra, AD 427 https://archive.org/stream/ahistorychurchf03walfgoog/ahistrychurchf03walfgoog_djvu.txt. Accessed 21/1/2019

[137] *Ibid.*

exercise of the Petrine prerogative of 'confirming the brethren'. This did not always settle the matter. An ecumenical council could claim to be the highest authority in the church, and the Council of Constance certainly did this. It did not, however, claim infallibility. Divergence and even contradictions between the teaching of one ecumenical council and another have demonstrated that, even for Councils, infallibility is a phantom. Faith is a virtue. It is not grounded in proof. In combination with the virtues of hope and humility, it allows us to trust that despite human frailty the pilgrim church of Christ of which we are members will not be allowed to go too far astray for too long on important issues.

No infallibility in post-apostolic times

St Irenaeus flourished before ecumenical councils were known. He carries great authority within the apostolic succession—in its original meaning, that is. During the second century Irenaeus taught that Christ's promise to be with us 'until the end of the age' (hereinafter, 'the Promise') would be meaningless if Christ were to allow the truth he had revealed to be forgotten or corrupted among his followers. This was not to say that his followers would always be of one mind. Irenaeus was very aware of the heresies dividing the church. He did not sit back and presume on the Promise, however, but argued cogently against the heretics of his time. Some of his writings survive.

He was a supporter of the primacy of the Roman See as the final arbiter for settling significant issues that could not be settled locally, the court of final appeal.

Primacy of jurisdiction was not an issue for him. That, in his day, was a characteristic of the *pagan* bureaucracy, headed by the *Pontifex Maximus,* which managed the polytheistic religious affairs of the Roman empire. The fact that the bureaucracy remained in Rome, however, when the imperial court moved away had immense significance for the later development of Christianity.

Irenaeus considered that Christ's promise was addressed to the church as a whole. He knew from experience that defining the content tends to be difficult. He would want us to trust that the beliefs of the whole church, what we might refer to today as the shared belief of Christianity, the *sensus fidelium,* is protected by the Promise and will continue to be until the end of the age. He was referring to basic apostolic faith.[138] He did not attach the same certainty to derived doctrines. We should not be too proud to admit that, as individuals, we frequently get things wrong and that different groups tend to have conflicting, even contradictory, perceptions on specific issues. Furthermore, the Promise cannot be expected to guarantee the right answers to all questions at every point in time. The bishops at Vatican II accepted this.[139]

---

[138] "The preaching of the Church truly continues without change and is everywhere the same. It has the testimony of the Prophets and Apostles and all their disciples."
—St Irenaeus, https://aleteia.org/2016/06/27/10-inspiring-quotes-from-saint-irenaeus/
[139] Vatican II, *Gaudium et Spes,* §33

It is important to dwell on Christ's promise for a moment and to make some distinctions that will condition our argument later. He did not promise to remove uncertainty. He did not specify when or how the promptings of the Spirit would be conveyed. The Spirit, being God, acts in total freedom. Equally, Christ never promised that the Spirit would prevent bad human decisions from having bad effects. On the contrary, he had indicated earlier that the cockle would be allowed to grow with the wheat until harvest time. While the Church would never want for guidance, Christ's followers would still be free to choose their actions, good or bad, wise, or foolish, responding to the Spirit or to the self.

Lumen Gentium grounds infallibility in the full agreement of all the members of the People of God.[140] It touches on the possibility of divergence between infallibility of the whole body of the faithful or the bishops and a possible declaration of dogma by the Roman Pontiff but dismisses this difficulty by reference to the fact that all are inspired by the same Holy Spirit. This is a romantic notion. It paints an idealised view of reality. It piously overlooks the human freedom of choice that popes and bishops enjoy and their option to ignore the promptings of the Spirit and pursue more earthly goals and ambitions—an option that is all too evident in the history of the papacy.

Whatever charism of infallibility is implicit in the Promise, it was given by Christ to the People of God when he gave them the mandate to go and teach all the nations and promised to be with them. For 18 centuries it sufficed. At Vatican I, an equivalent charism was conferred on Pope Pius IX and his successors after he had changed the voting rules to facilitate the decision. Since then Christians who wish to be in full communion with Rome are expected to believe that the Pope can speak infallibly under certain limited conditions. If, over a reasonable timescale however, papal teaching is seen to be at variance with the beliefs of the People of God, and if one has to make a choice, then it would seem prudent to rely on the original Promise. As with St Augustine and St John Henry Newman, we must relate *"Securus iudicat orbis terrarum"* to our own time and circumstances[141].

HOW THE POPES BECAME INFALLIBLE

Irenaeus did not consider the Bishop of Rome infallible. If that had formed part of the deposit of faith as he received it, or even if he could argue that it was implicit therein, he would certainly have invoked this against the heretics of his day. But he did not. A thousand years would pass before infallibility was forced onto the Papal agenda by a Franciscan, named Peter Olivi. He was anxious to prevent a subsequent pope from reversing a teaching of Pope Nicholas III that suited his branch of the Franciscans, the Spirituals. Pope John XXII saw the potential conflict between papal infallibility and sovereignty. Olivi's theory was a threat to papal freedom of action; an

---

[140] LG §25
[141] See 'The Promise and the message at the end of chapter 2.

attempt to tie his hands and those of future popes.[142] Styling it as a "pestiferous doctrine" and a "pernicious audacity", in the papal bull *Quia Quorundam (1324)* he condemned this "Franciscan doctrine of papal infallibility as the work of the devil"![143]

John XXII, however, was overlooking a very convenient corollary of the proposition he was so roundly condemning. The papacy later realised that infallibility could be used to enhance its power. An infallible pope could overlook the pronouncement of a predecessor, or could reinterpret it, or even rule authoritatively that it did not apply to the question at issue. And who in Christendom could challenge him? There were no Reformed churches in those days and the educated layman was aware that an accusation of heresy could bring torture and death and the expropriation of all his assets, enriching the Church, leaving his dependents penniless. It was wiser not to tangle with a bishop, particularly the bishop of Rome. In the nineteenth century, the papacy changed its policy. To make the pope legally infallible became a strategic objective. In just 70 years it went from being a minority opinion to being a doctrine, essential for salvation on a par with the Incarnation or Resurrection.[144]

Promoting a minority opinion

The papacy had been openly ambitious to make itself into a world power, in the temporal as well as the spiritual sphere, from the time of Pope Gregory VII (eleventh century). The papal bureaucracy could be expected to promote anything that would add to the prestige of its leader. It made sense to promote the claim of infallibility as part of its ongoing policy of strengthening itself. Despite continued claims, however, papal infallibility was never widely accepted by the Catholic, let alone by the universal, church.

In 1828, when the British authorities were considering legislation for Catholic Emancipation in Ireland, they would have been aware of the Ultramontane movement in France that was campaigning to strengthen the papacy. The Ultramontanes wanted a definition that an edict of a pope on *any* issue is right and true and must be followed by all Catholics if they want to escape hell. This would have had unsettling political implications. The British Government was concerned about the potential effect that a papal edict might have on their not-always-so-loyal Catholic subjects in Ireland. The Irish bishops were able to reassure the politicians that papal infallibility was not a doctrine of the Church, nor could it ever be so defined as it was not part of the deposit of faith handed on by the Apostles. (This was later confirmed by

---

[142] We saw this effect almost a thousand years later when Paul VI felt unable to change the teaching of Pius XI in *Casti Connubii*, although it was not infallible, and Pope Francis hesitated to reopen the possibility of ordaining women because John Paul II had ruled against it.

[143] Prof. Brian Tierney, *Origins of Papal Infallibility 1150-1350: A Study of the Concepts of Infallibility, Sovereignty and Tradition in the Middle Ages* (Leiden: E.J. Brill, 1972).

Quoted by Hasler, A. B., *How the Pope Became Infallible: Pius IX and the Politics of Persuasion* (Doubleday; Garden City, 1981 NY), pp 36–37

[144] It was the refusal of Ignaz Döllinger to accept this doctrine that led to his excommunication.

members of the German Bishops Conference, who expressed it in a pastoral letter intended to calm disquiet among the faithful. [145]

A 24-year programme.

The Irish Bishops were right in their analysis but wrong in their prediction. They reckoned without the determination of the future Pope Pius IX, who was then merely Giovanni, Archbishop of Spoleto. From the very beginning of his reign, Pius IX championed the infallibility of his office. He revealed it as a major priority for his pontificate within months, writing in his very first encyclical:

> "*And this living infallible authority is active only in that Church* which was built by Christ the Lord upon Peter, the head of the entire Church, leader and shepherd, whose faith He promised would never fail. This Church has had an unbroken line of succession from Peter himself; these legitimate pontiffs are the heirs and defenders of the same teaching, rank, office, and power. And the Church is where Peter is, and Peter speaks in the Roman Pontiff, living at all times in his successors and making judgment, providing the truth of the faith to those who seek it. *The divine words therefore mean what this Roman See of the most blessed Peter holds and has held*".[146]

The wording is deceptive. It reads as if it is a statement of Catholic doctrine. He would have known perfectly well that it was not a doctrine nor was it the mind of the Church. It was just another repetition of the unilateral Roman claim to inerrancy and total hegemony which had always been resisted and disputed by a significant body of the episcopate and their flocks. Cardinal Edward Manning, himself a leading supporter of the definition at Vatican I, later confirmed this as a fact, describing the infallibility of popes as:

> "a conflict which for centuries had troubled the peace of the Church"[147].

Preparatory strategy

Pius IX turned the conflict into a doctrine. Over the space of 24 years, he made a series of strategic moves that ultimately brought about the passing of the Dogmas of Infallibility and of Universal Primacy on 18th July 1870.

> 1. He jumped the gun. He declared the Dogma of the Immaculate Conception (8/12/1854) without mention of episcopal approbation[148]. To cite the witness of the bishops would have weakened the case for papal infallibility. "In effect, therefore, Pius by his action anticipated the definition of infallibility at the council and thereby gave comfort to those campaigning for it".[149] Cabinet ministers are familiar with this stratagem for enhancing personal power: First you

---

[145] Hasler, op. cit., P. 49.
[146] Pope Pius XI, *Qui Pluribus,* Nov. 9 1846, §10. (Emphasis added).
[147] Edward Manning, *The True Story of the Vatican Council,* London, Henry King, 1877, P143.
[148] J.N.D. Kelly, *Oxford Dictionary of Popes,* Oxford & New York, Updated 2005, P310
[149] John W. O'Malley, *Vatican I, the Council and the Making of the Ultramontane Church,* Cambridge MA, The Belknap Press of Harvard University Press, 2018, p 103

announce the decision, preferably something popular, this brings it to cabinet level. Rather than display disunity and risk unpopularity by reversing the decision, the cabinet approves, however grudgingly, and finds the necessary budget. If they do not pull the rug out from under you entirely, you emerge with your reputation for strength, leadership and influence enhanced.

2. Having thus prejudiced the issue of whether he was entitled as Pontiff acting alone to define a Dogma, Pius summoned cardinals and bishops from all over the world to be present for its promulgation. If a bishop felt that it should have been an invitation to discuss the proposed dogma rather than promulgate it and that the Pope had abused his position by acting *ultra vires*, there was little he could do individually, except to disobey the summons and pointedly stay away. This about eighty per cent of the bishops did. None the less, approval was communicated to the world in general by the presence of 206 cardinals and bishops at the promulgation of a dogma of faith based on the sole authority of their leader.[150]

Pio Nono was a nineteenth century Italian. He knew well that power burgeons with every successful manifestation. With the populace generally illiterate, rallies were an effective part of politics at the time in Italy. Large scale ones were used in 1859 in the towns and cities of Romagna to validate the annexation of papal territory as the unification of Italy progressed under King Victor Emmanuel II.

ADDRESS OF THE BISHOPS TO POPE PIUS IX

July 4th 1862

Long may you live, Holy Father, to rule the Catholic Church.
Go onward, as now, in defending it with your power,

guiding it with your prudence
and adorning it with your virtues.
Go before us, as the Good Shepherd,
by your example; feed the sheep and the lambs
with heavenly food refresh them with the
streams of heavenly wisdom.

For you are to us the teacher of sound doctrine, the centre of unity, the unfailing light to the nations kindled by divine wisdom. You are the Rock, the foundation of the Church against which the gates of hell shall not prevail. When you speak, we hear Peter's voice, when you decide, we obey the authority of Christ.

---

[150] Manning, Opus cit.

3. In 1862 Pius held another big rally in Rome. This time it was to mark the occasion of the Canonisation of the Japanese Martyrs. A more impressive 265 prelates of all descriptions responded to the summons and made the journey despite the unsettled state of Italy. (In 1861 the new Kingdom of Italy had declared Rome to be its capital city although it was not yet within its territory!) The bishops presented the Pope with an address so sycophantic that it must be read to be believed. (See box)

Pius IX was astute enough to know that these two great rallies would enhance his power and personal authority and help spread the notion of infallibility. Archbishop Manning confirmed their effect:

> "There can be little discernment in any man who cannot perceive how these two events brought out the infallibility of the Roman pontiff: that of 1854 in the defining of a dogma of faith, that of 1862 in matters which, though not dogmas of faith, are nevertheless in contact with his supreme office as 'teacher of all Christians.'"[151]

4. The earlier events had boosted the status and moral authority of the papacy, compensating in some way for the concurrent loss of most of his temporal power. In June 1866 Pius IX again summoned the bishops of the world to Rome, the occasion being the eighteenth centenary (29 June 1867) of the martyrdom of St Peter. Although St Paul shares the June 29 feast-day and suffered the same fate in the same persecution, he was all but airbrushed out. The focus was entirely on Peter for obvious reasons. This time 500 bishops attended along with thousands of pilgrims who joined in celebrating the life, death and special dignity and authority of Peter as Prince of the Apostles. The Pope delivered an allocution to the bishops on 26th June during which he announced his intention of calling an Ecumenical Council—without specifying the date or agenda.

5. Five days later, the assembled bishops addressed a response to the allocution. Cardinal Manning tells us that the bishops made very few changes to the draft of the formal address which had been prepared by Msgr. Haynald, the Archbishop of Kalocsa. From this Manning implies a high level of approval by the bishops. Significantly, however, among the changes that the bishops demanded was the removal of the word 'infallible' in several places[152]. This was done, Manning would have his readers believe, out of thoughtfulness, because they were conscious that the particular word had never been used previously in conciliar documents in reference to the successor of Peter, and "a new word" might offend sensitivities, particularly in the East, rather as had happened with 'filioque'.

---

[151] Cardinal Edward Manning, *The True Story of the Vatican Council*. London, Henry S. King. p 44

[152] It is doubtful if the word 'infallible' was Haynald's own choice. At Vatican I, only eighteen months later, he was prominent among the opponents of the definition.

Manning is being disingenuous here. What was at stake was not just a word or sensitivity. It was the concept. It was the disputed claim about the locus of the infallibility with which Christ endowed his church. It was a major coup for the Ultramontane agenda. They were drafting a formal statement by an exceptionally large assembly of bishops and in those days, bishops still carried significant teaching authority. It is more probable that those bishops who opposed papal infallibility, and there may have been hundreds of them, objected vociferously to an attempt to pre-empt a controversial matter without proper discussion—to create another dogma *en passant,* so to speak. They were shepherds, not sheep. Some must have been thinking ahead to the upcoming Council where the question of papal authority would surely be on the agenda. By that stage, the ambitions of pope and curia had been clearly signalled to all the bishops of the world. Rome wanted infallibility.

Manning saw the gathering as a major step[153] on the road to infallibility:

> "It is not too much to say that, of the proximate causes of the definition of the infallibility, the Centenary of St Peter's Martyrdom was the most powerful".[154]

Thus, Pius IX was still on course to turn the contentious statement of his first encyclical into a doctrine that would enhance his power and that of future popes.

6. The following year, when Pius IX summoned the first Vatican Council to meet on the 8th December 1869, the question of infallibility was omitted from the agenda. It might have been considered unseemly if the Pope were to make a proposal designed to enhance his own position. The expectation was that several bishops would raise the issue 'spontaneously', although the procedures laid down in advance precluded the Council from deciding its own agenda or procedures. This could be circumvented by the authorities if necessary, and they were. When the Council first assembled, the Pope maintained a pretence of neutrality on 'the question'. He abandoned this, however, when he learned the extent of the opposition. From then on, he promoted the idea vigorously, categorising those who opposed his wishes as being against the church.

7. When it became apparent that no definition acceptable to the pope was going to secure the virtually unanimous approval that has been traditional for decisions reflecting the mind of the church since the meeting at Jerusalem and at ecumenical councils since the first was held in the fourth century, Pius IX abandoned tradition to ensure his objective would be approved. He mandated

---

[153] Edward Manning, *The True Story of the Vatican Council,* Henry S. King, London, 1877, P62. Among others, the Pope released Manning, a leading infallibilist, from his oath of secrecy so he could counteract the negative European press reports on the proceedings of Vatican I, for which the sources could not be quoted. Furthermore, this allowed Manning to write a personal account of the Council, something not allowed to any opponent of the proposal.

[154] *Ibid.* p 45.

procedures allowing for decisions to be made by a simple majority! Bishop Strossmeyer immediately rose to object to the change of procedure. Not surprisingly, he was ruled out of order by the presiding cardinal. The minority lodged objections in writing, but these were ignored.

8. As the intolerably hot Roman summer drew nearer, and as the security situation deteriorated with the threat to Rome from the Kingdom of Italy and the drift towards war between France and Prussia threatened the withdrawal of the French garrison which had been defending Rome, he switched the order of the agenda. He interrupted the discussion on the Catholic Faith to bring forward a new chapter on the powers of the papacy, including his own infallibility and universal jurisdiction,[155] which had not been on the original agenda. This was done in response to a 'spontaneous' petition signed by 150 bishops, including Cardinal Manning. It meant that the papal position and status would be dealt with outside of the context of the episcopacy and the rest of the church. Three of the five Presidents opposed this agenda change but Pius overruled them. The two dogmas were now firmly on the agenda and with the changed voting rules, it became inevitable that the great ambition of the papacy of Pius IX would be achieved. This put the opposition in a quandary. The assumption at the time was that definitions by ecumenical councils were infallible and that the presence of Roman Catholic bishops from far and near made the gathering ecumenical. Acceptance of the proposition by a majority vote of the Council would mean that numerous bishops would suddenly have to believe (or at least profess) what they had previously judged to be untrue and what they had been vehemently opposing for months or years.

The pope's strategy and tactics succeeded, with no time to spare. The argument continued, and the final vote did not take place until July 18th. Rather than be seen to vote 'against the Pope', many of the opposing bishops had left Rome when it became evident that the opposition cause was lost. The excessive heat provided a convenient and plausible explanation for their withdrawal.

PROCEEDINGS AT THE FIRST VATICAN COUNCIL

Papal Infallibility was the most contentious and divisive issue in the Church at the time. Pius IX had started his own monthly magazine, *La Civiltá Cattolica,* in 1850. He commissioned the Jesuits to write and publish it but continued to control it. Editorially, it has always been known to be very close to the pope. In the run up to the Council (1869), it published an article suggesting that Papal Infallibility could be approved at the Council 'by acclamation'. This persisted as a rumour, or more than a rumour, as the Council proceeded. The minority of bishops who were against the

---

[155] Of the 51 decrees in the *schema* on the Catholic Faith, only 6 had come before the Council. The other 45 had not been addressed when the discussion was suspended and so they were never debated. Moreover, the bishops had been invited to submit items that they felt needed attention. Not one of the 400 issues they suggested was brought forward for discussion.

definition (20-25 per cent) were very perturbed because it could have been used to drown out their opposition entirely. At one stage, four bishops (Kenrick, Carroll and Fitzgerald from America and Moriarty from Ireland) were aware of enough evidence that this was being planned that, despite their oaths of secrecy, they wrote to the Presidents of the Council giving notice that if such a thing were intended, they would leave the Council without permission and tell the world why they had done so. The Presidents denied it officially, asserting that only madmen *(insensati)* could envisage such a thing. It will never be known for sure what had been intended, but the intervention by the four bishops made adoption by acclamation impossible.

As the debate proceeded, Pius did not hesitate to pressurise those who disagreed with what he wanted, or who looked to modify it. When Cardinal Guidi, who was one of the majority, proposed a conditional formula that could have commanded general agreement,[156] and restored the unity of the Council[157], the pope took it as a personal affront. He summoned Guidi and gave him a dressing down. He upbraided him, as a bishop of the Pontifical States and as a cardinal, for opposing him. Guidi was surprised and said he had maintained only that bishops are witnesses of tradition. 'Witnesses of tradition?' said Pius; 'there's only one; that's me'.[158]

Basing himself on the work of Bellarmine, Guidi had suggested that "a condition of infallibility was that it should not be exercised rashly *(temere)*, and the pope was bound to use ordinary human diligence in arriving at a right judgement, as prayer, consultation, study; and that the normal means was consultation with a greater or less number of bishops, according to the circumstances, the bishops being the witnesses to the belief of their churches".[159] This was a constructive compromise but Pius would have none of it. For him, the requirement for consultation was probably the sticking point. How could someone in his position, infallible and with *plenitudo potestatis,* be required to consult?

Tragically, the failure to listen to Guidi's proposal facilitated another credibility disaster for the papacy a century later, when *Ordinatio Sacerdotalis* was drafted secretly with inadequate prayer, study and consultation and scant regard for logic. We revert to this in Chapter 12.

---

[156] O'Malley, *Vatican I,* p 212

[157] It would also have made infallibility a little less objectionable to Protestants and Anglicans.

[158] There were no witnesses. The report of this extraordinary statement is taken from the private journal of Bishop Felix Dupanloup of Orleans who was "in a position to know". —Butler, p 98. Moreover, O'Malley states that a large number of bishops , including Schwarzenberg and Dupanloup went to congratulate Guidi that evening and were shocked to learn what had happened.

[159] Dom Cuthbert Butler O.S.B., *The Vatican Council 1869-1870,* Collins and Harvill Press. London 1962 pp 353/4. I have made extensive use of this book. The Council participants were sworn to secrecy for life, ensuring no unauthorised reports could be published. Butler's book, which appeared 60 years later, was made possible because Dom Butler had access, *inter alia,* to a meticulous diary of the Council kept by Bishop William Ullathorne of Birmingham and to his correspondence.

Guidi's suggestion had been well received by others in the Council hall. While the above interview was going on, leaders of the majority and of the minority met and agreed that Guidi's proposal could form the basis of a definition that both sides might be able to support. This good news was conveyed to Cardinal de Luca, one of the Presidents, who would have consulted the pope about it. It was never brought forward for discussion. Thus, the opportunity to reach a virtually unanimous decision foundered on the uncompromising ambition of Pius IX.

The scolding that Cardinal Guidi got from the Pope figures in John W. O'Malley's response to the doubts of Newman and others about the freedom of Vatican I. O'Malley also mentions the 'blatant partisanship of the pope' and Cardinal Bilio's 'reprimand to Manning and Senestréy that their manoeuvring was inappropriate for a council' and continues:

> "Moreover, there is something almost predetermined in a meeting about the scope the authority of the CEO that takes place in his headquarters, that is prepared and organised by his staff, that is presided over by his appointees, and that is carried out under his immediate scrutiny".[160]

He claims rightly that the minority had freedom of speech and quotes opinions from Cuthbert Butler and Roger Aubert that the council had enough freedom. Both were priests, writing sixty and ninety-four years after the Council respectively. He dismisses August Hasler's challenge to their assessment on the grounds that Hasler 'won few disciples'. Given the activities of the CDF this is not surprising. While O'Malley's research is impeccable, his judgement on this point is scarcely justified by the evidence he presents.

The Decision becomes a foregone conclusion

The final vote was analogous to the final voting at a presidential nomination convention in the USA, where it is the penultimate vote that really decides the selection. In the final vote, the entire party must be seen to unite enthusiastically behind the selected candidate. The bishops were in a similar position. The result had been decided by the change in voting rules. Infallibility was about to become a dogma which they would not be able to deny. Many left before the final vote. Once dispersed back home, the opposing minority lost cohesion. One by one, they bowed to Roman pressure to conform and duly promulgated the definition in their dioceses.

Divine Delight or Divine Disgust?

A violent thunderstorm over St Peter's coincided with the final ceremonial vote. Although it was mid-day, it became so dark that a burning taper had to be brought to enable the names to be read out for the final vote. Cardinal Manning quotes the graphic description by *The Times* correspondent in Rome.

---

[160] O'Malley, *Vatican I,* p 231

The Placets of the fathers struggled through the storm, while the thunder pealed above and the lightning flashed in at every window, and down through the dome and every smaller cupola. " Placet! " shouted his eminence or his grace, and a loud clap of thunder followed in response, and then the lightning darted about the Baldacchino and every part of the church and Conciliar Hall, as if announcing the response. So, it continued for nearly one hour and a half, during which time the roll was being called, and a more effective scene I never witnessed. Had all the decorators and all the getters-up of ceremonies in Rome been employed, nothing approaching to the solemn grandeur of the storm could have been prepared, and never will those who saw it and felt it forget the promulgation of the first dogma of the Church.[161]

Manning interprets the storm as an indication of divine approval of what was being done although most people feel threatened or frightened by thunder and lightning. For those who thought that the definition was a good thing, it could be interpreted as a celestial fireworks display. The opposition, on the other hand, could see it as a mark of disapproval, arguing that ambition was influencing doctrine.

Manning himself admits, that it could also be seen in this light or, perhaps, this lack of light:

"Other critics saw in this thunderstorm an articulate voice of divine indignation against the definition".

He searches the scriptures selectively to refute this view. He goes back to the Book of Exodus: "They forgot Sinai and the Ten Commandments". He himself had to 'forget' several New Testament passages with which, as an archbishop and a one-time Protestant, he would have been quite familiar. Like the earthquake that marked the death of Jesus when "the sun was darkened" (Luke 23:45), St John's description of Jesus as "the light that darkness could not overpower" and Jesus' self-description as the light of the world.[162] Similarly, in St John's first epistle[163] we find:

"God is light; there is no darkness in him at all. If we say that we are in union with God while we are living in darkness, we are lying because we are not living the truth. But if we live our lives in the light, as he is in the light, we are in union with one another, and the blood of Jesus, his Son, purifies us from all sin".

There is a record of an interesting symposium held at Istanbul in 2009 which discussed light, as both scientific and spiritual phenomena:

It is certainly so that in all the world's religions light has served as a metaphor for ultimate reality. The Abrahamic faiths, in particular, associate God with uncreated, primal light and the creation itself with the (first) divine command: "Fiat lux." But the link between divinity and light also exists in archaic Greek

---

[161] Cardinal Ed. Manning, *The True Story of the Vatican Council*, p 145
[162] Jn 1:4. 1:5. 1:8, 1:9 and Jn 8:12. "I am the light of the world; anyone who follows me will not be walking in the dark; he will have the light of life".
[163] 1 Jn 1:5

> literature where gods glowed with brightness. In Plato's cave, goodness enters the material realm "as sunlight enters darkness." [164]

We should not be too surprised that the message of the thunderstorm is unclear or ambiguous. God does not force our assent or overwhelm our freedom of choice with too clear a revelation of himself. Perhaps the real message of the thunder and lightning at that important moment is that God wishes us to ponder the matter and figure it out as part of our life-long search for him. "Man, he made to serve him wittily, in the tangle of his mind" [165]

WINNERS AND LOSERS

For the Ultramontanes, the victory was tinged with defeat. They had campaigned for an untrammelled infallibility, a sort of permanent miraculous intervention that would put an end to uncertainty and allow a pope to answer any question definitively,[166] thus obviating the need for future Councils, or indeed for scholarship or discussion. What they got was limited to issues of faith and morals—and, to make it worse, there were conditions attached.

For Pius IX and the bureaucracy, however, the limitations mattered little. The title itself conveyed the power. With Universal Jurisdiction added, the papacy can ignore the conditions. In an oath-bound hierarchical organisation with no separation of powers, there is no provision for challenge the leader or his immediate staff.

For many bishops who had hoped that Vatican I would be used to heal the divisions in the church, there was disappointment. Far from trying to heal the wounds, the Council knowingly created two new 'irreformable' barriers[167] to unity.

Moreover, on the one occasion that papal infallibility has been officially invoked, it raised yet another barrier. The Assumption was already accepted by the Catholic faithful. It had been part of the Rosary for centuries. They did not need a definition. Protestants did not generally share the belief, so it created yet another obstacle to unity. They would have to profess it on the basis of papal authority alone, even if they honestly thought it improbable for lack of biblical evidence or considered it irrelevant to salvation. The papacy prioritised a discretionary honour for Our Lady over Christ's prayer for unity and made this faulty sense of priorities permanent.

The repercussions of Vatican I on the life of the Church, however, were more immediate and dramatic.

---

[164] Report of the symposium 'Light from Light' sponsored by the Templeton Foundation, April 2009, Istanbul. —http://humbleapproach.templeton.org/LightFromLight/ Accessed 3/3/2018

[165] —attributed to St Thomas More by Robert Bolt in his play, *A Man for All Seasons*.

[166] Like Fionn Mac Cumhail in Celtic mythology. While cooking the Salmon of Knowledge, he sucked his thumb having burnt it on the hot fish. Thereafter, whenever he needed to know something, he only had to suck his thumb and, magically, he had the answer!

[167] In Chapter 17, we outline several formulas that would enable the irreformable to be reformed.

Chapter 8

The fruits of Vatican 1: External

"But though Jesus is always present to his disciples with his love and his healing patience, they do not always respond with their attention to him. They are absent minded, still partially the prisoners of their own plans and desires. When, in the evening, Jesus asks them, 'What were you arguing about on the way?' they keep silence 'because on the way, they had been discussing who was the greatest'.

—Bernard Häring

CIVIL AUTHORITIES REACT TO HEIGHTENED PAPAL POWER.

The two dogmas adopted at Vatican I gave the maximalist understanding of papal power a legal basis and made assent to it essential to salvation for Catholics. This immense power has permeated and influenced everything in the subsequent history of the Church, for better or for worse. While there were countless other factors at work, O'Malley sees them as the crucial factor that resulted in the current situation.[168]

Universal Jurisdiction

The first dogma, which establishes universal jurisdiction, had been resisted by other dioceses for more than 1500 years. It had its beginnings in second century Rome. Pope Victor I (189-198) has been described as "a striking example … of a pope claiming the right to interfere in other churches".[169] The key event, however, came in 380 AD when the pagan religious bureaucracy abruptly became Christian with the Bishop of Rome as its new leader. It continued to exercise full civil authority on religious standards and administration throughout the entire empire which then comprised most of the known world. It enjoyed a hundred-year-long regime of complete jurisdiction over the Christianised State Church, only to be limited by the collapse of the Western Empire. The later bureaucratic determination to re-assert its authority was the principle cause of the division of the Church between the Latin and the Orthodox and still is. When enacted as dogma in 1870, it hardened the division. It enabled and shaped the codification of Canon Law (1917) and facilitated the further growth of central power.

The power garnered by the papacy in 1870 has enabled the curia to shape itself into the permanent *de facto* government that writes its own rules. It has created a structure that guards its power and independence in perpetuity. Theoretically, the pope is superior, but popes are managed by the curia and are mortal while

---

[168] O'Malley, *Vatican I,* p 242
[169] J.N.D. Kelly, *The Oxford Dictionary of Popes,* Oxford (Updated) 2005, p 12

the bureaucracy persists, maintaining its ethos by controlling recruitment and promotions. In theory also, the college of bishops is superior, but the curia selects every member of the college and has legislated to ensure, as far as possible, that it will never meet without curial approval. Under Canon Law, the College of Bishops can only meet when called together by the pope, who is normally under the control of the curia. In this way, the curia, which would be unable to control the deliberations of the College, can normally prevent it from meeting. The intervals between Lateran V, the Council of Trent and Vatican 1 were three centuries each. Between Vatican I and Vatican II was only ninety-two years because Pope John XXIII outfoxed the bureaucracy. He caught the curia off guard with a surprise announcement without prior consultation. He knew what he was doing. Once the Pope had made a public commitment, the curia had no choice but to show unity, get into line and proceed, however reluctantly.

Papal Infallibility

The second claim, that of papal infallibility, had been around in various undefined forms since the thirteenth century when it was condemned by Pope John XXII as a 'pestiferous doctrine.[170] In the fifty years before Vatican I, it was promoted vigorously by the Ultramontane movement (which also had a political dimension) and by Pope Pius IX from the start of his pontificate. It has been used officially only once since being defined, but abused repeatedly, there being no mechanism in canon law for challenging abuse. Together the two doctrines shaped the development of the Church during the next century or more.

Opinion is still divided as to whether these two dogmas were the inspiration and gift of the Holy Spirit or the realisation of a long-established secular ambition to maximise the power of the leader and thus of the bureaucracy. Judging by the fruits, the definition of the two dogmas was a papal power grab that initiated a century-long obsession with its own status at the expense of its mission.

Civil authorities react to infallibility as a potential threat

The Ultramontane campaign to make the pope infallible had created great apprehension among European governments, pitting them strongly against the Church in advance of the Council. The infallibility they feared was the totally untrammelled variety that was being promoted by the Ultramontanes. It had made the British politicians nervous in the run-up to Catholic Emancipation fifty years earlier. Rome had been slow to shed its distrust of democratic systems and was linked to powerful monarchist pressure groups in many European states. They supported the Royalists in

---

[170] Pope John XXII condemned "infallibility as a "pestiferous doctrine" and a "pernicious audacity."— James A. Brundage, Department of History, University of Wisconsin-Milwaukee in a book review in *The Jurist, 69 (1973)*
http://www.canonlawcentre.com/2015/01/30/canon-lawyers-and-papal-infallibility-in-the-middle-ages-prof-tierneys-study-revisited/ Accessed October 2016

France and were generally against (ill-defined) 'liberalism' elsewhere, during a time when liberal ideas relating to popular sovereignty were gaining support. Governments feared that one rash edict from an infallible pope could galvanise Catholics into actions that might destabilise a government or even a nation. Civil powers are understandably leery of religions that can command overriding loyalties. Joseph Görres, a leading although moderate Ultramontane in Germany, had warned the Prussians not to take the collective power of the Catholics in Germany too lightly.[171] Prior to the definition, Chancellor Bismarck had said that a papacy armed with infallibility would have an absolute power exceeding that of any monarchy.[172] He had predicted an 'open fight' against Catholicism. Prince Clodwig zu Hohenlohe had expressed the view that papal infallibility would elevate the power of the pope above that of princes and people, "to the detriment of both". The Pope and curia would not have considered such an outcome as undesirable, quite the reverse. Widespread temporal dominance had long been a Roman ambition and increased international political influence would have been a partial compensation for the ongoing territorial loss of the Papal States.

Papal Infallibility had been omitted from the agenda of the council although it was the hot-button issue that obviously needed to be discussed. This invited suspicion of a hidden agenda as did the oaths of secrecy, although these could not be enforced. The decision not to invite rulers or heads of state to participate was noted by governments as they considered how to respond to the vague invitation to cooperate. For the first time in the history of councils there would be no lay participants[173]. The reason offered for this break with tradition was the widespread political instability. This was unconvincing, in that it had not prevented the calling of the council itself. The real reason may have been that catholic lay leaders of the day were likely to be less accommodating than bishops to papal preferences. The scope for rumours and conspiracy theories did nothing to allay the anxieties of civil authorities.

The Dogma of Infallibility was defined with a much more limited extent than the campaigners had been looking for and the German Bishops Conference issued an interpretive statement playing down the changes. Pius IX endorsed this publicly, but this did not allay the fears. German politicians, with a substantial Catholic population reacted strongly. Governments at that stage could not know that the dogma would only be invoked officially once in a hundred and fifty years, and then only to define a Marian doctrine that had no direct political implications.

Although it was a watered-down version of infallibility, the definition in July 1870 gave Bismarck the political climate to unleash the battle he had predicted. Evidently, he had been waiting for the opportune moment to initiate the 'open fight'. Over the next six years, Germany introduced a litany of laws that amounted to persecution of

---

[171] O'Malley, *Vatican I,* p 72

[172] For this period, I have relied heavily on Frank J. Coppa's, *The Modern Papacy since 1789,* New York, Addison Wesley Longman, Ltd, 1998, *p*113

[173] O'Malley, *Vatican I,* p 114.

the Catholic church. The epoch is known as the Kulturkampf. Schools and hospitals were appropriated by the state, impossible conditions were imposed on clergy and many went to jail or were deported. First the Jesuits were dissolved and expelled, then the law was extended to cover other congregations including the Redemptorists and the Holy Ghost Fathers. These laws even transferred internal Church administration into the hands of the state.

The death of Pius IX in 1878 and the election of the more pragmatic Leo XIII coincided with a change in Bismarck's political agenda. He realised that the anti-church legislation had backfired, strengthening his opponents, the Centre Party, which was predominantly Catholic. He was also nervous of the socialists. Starting in 1880 the laws were gradually softened or repealed and in May 1887 Leo XIII was able to declare that the struggle was over. The Church in Germany, however, had lost a great deal of cultural and institutional influence and many traditional privileges.

Similar reactions to the definition of infallibility, with similar but much less extreme effects on the Church, were encountered in Italy, Switzerland, Russia, Austria, and the USA. Venezuela confiscated Church property as did Colombia.

When the President of France, Emile Loubet, was in Italy in 1905 and wished to visit the Pope, Pius X declined to receive him because he had visited Victor Emmanuel III, of the Kingdom of Italy which had annexed the remnant of the Papal States thirty-five years previously. Refusal to talk to somebody because he had spoken to your enemy was strange behaviour for one who claimed to be the Vicar of Christ! Although subsequently judged to be a saint, he showed no forgiveness, in this case not for an enemy but for someone who had spoken to an enemy. It was not even good diplomacy. The Pope turned down an opportunity to improve relations with France at a critical juncture. Amid controversy later that year, the French enacted the laïcité laws which severed any state relationship with the churches, including the Roman Catholic Church and has tended to further secularise French society.

Leo XIII blamed the enemies of the Church and in particular the Freemasons. Cardinal Manning blamed the 'liberals' in some countries[174]. Neither could acknowledge that the undiluted Ultramontane demands would have given the pope a level of control over Catholic populations with the potential to threaten temporal powers. Apparently, neither the pope nor the curia could see that it was their own ambitions that had generated genuine grounds for anxiety and provoked a backlash. The political consequences were probably foreseen by the highly sophisticated papal diplomatic corps but their warnings, if any, were ignored. Ignored also was a memorandum to the pope from 70 per cent of the German bishops that stressed the extreme danger of a definition at that time.[175]

---

[174] Cardinal Manning, The True Story of the Vatican Council, Henry S. King, London, 1877,
[175] Hasler, op. cit., P49

It was no use afterwards telling the politicians that the dogma as ultimately defined carried limitations and conditions. Politicians know better than most that authority can ignore the small print; all the more easily in the case of the Roman Catholic Church where the functions of legislator, judge and executive are combined and there is no mechanism of appeal.

For Pope Pius IX and the bureaucracy, the focus of Vatican I had been on getting the two dogmas approved. Having created a situation where they were legally in complete charge – the pope for his lifetime and the curia forever – they were determined to turn the legal position into a reality ... for the greater glory of God, of course. The next stage was to demonstrate the leader's infallibility and authority and make them felt. Power grows with every successful exercise. The involvement of infallibility meant that the bureaucratic intolerance of potentially competing power centres now applied in the intellectual sphere. Differences of opinion could not be countenanced, particularly if they were cogently expressed or tended to find a following. An infallible and all-powerful papacy had to be seen to deal decisively with dissent or independence. The days when the papacy looked to the great universities for advice were over. Now the universities should look to the pope. Dissension, whether superficial or profound, had to be silenced, or stamped out and necessity would decide the means.

The tradition of *church* infallibility, with the People of God trusting that Christ would honour the Promise in his own good time on important issues through the workings of the Spirit, had been replaced by an authoritarian system of legally unchallengeable propositions that were not open to question or disagreement.

The modern world becomes the enemy

There were perceptive voices within the clergy and laity, who were trying to make the teaching of the Church relevant to a more educated society and reconcile it with new knowledge in the sciences and better methods of research in historical and biblical studies. But this challenged the aura of generalised infallibility being promoted by the papacy. Like the prophets of old, the thinkers were treated as enemies. Their ideas were clustered under abstract labels, the more easily to be condemned. Rationalism, Liberalism, Americanism and Modernism all shared the loose title of Modernism.[176] It was almost impossible to defend oneself from an accusation of one of these 'isms' because they covered such a potpourri of ideas. Moreover, just as it is today, the prosecutors were ultimately the judges and they were under obedience in an authoritarian structure that does not admit to error.

Professor David Tracy, a past president of the Catholic Theological Society of America has commented:

> History alone should remind us of certain salient facts: the tragic experience of
> the modernist and Americanist crises earlier in the century are there for all to

---

[176] We revert to the Modernist crisis in Chapter 15.

see. What should have been an intellectual argument became an institutional coercion—and with a price to intellectual integrity that we are all still paying.[177]

Not unusually in CDF practice now as then, the verdict precedes the defence, and the CDF demands a clarification or recantation from the defendant in terms that the CDF knows he cannot in conscience provide. The objective is to get a paper record that vindicates the authority of the Congregation. The intellectual integrity and conscience of the victim are of little consequence and can be dismissed, after the manner of the military, as collateral damage.

BARRIERS AGAINST PROTESTANTS AND ANGLICAN CHURCHES REINFORCED

The opportunity to heal some of the divisions in Christianity. was squandered. As we have seen, the Pope and curia were focussed on the enhancement of their powers, so the Council ended up doing the opposite. It introduced the new dogmas, in the clear knowledge that they would be unacceptable to the other denominations. An arrogant papacy did not recognise them as part of the Church of Christ. The repeated warnings that the definitions would create new barriers to unity were ignored. The warnings were well founded. With the insights of Vatican II, even the papacy can now admit to some responsibility for the two great break-ups and to recognise itself currently as" the greatest obstacle to Christian unity".

The Anglican Communion and Apostolicae Curae

The Anglican Communion is closer to the Roman Catholic Church in doctrine and practice than are the other mainstream Churches of the Reformation. Among them, it is the most likely candidate for closer unity with Rome. Any such development at an official level would be vetoed by the curia because it would involve some modification of the legally unlimited power of the papacy. The Anglicans, who continue to practice synodal governance, are unlikely to agree to the unchallengeable role of the pope, much less the unchanging Roman curia. With the tensions that led Henry VIII to break with Rome no longer relevant, the principle obstacles to unity are now the dogmas of Papal Infallibility and Universal Jurisdiction, the Marian dogmas, the issues of Women's Ordination and of sexual morality in general with attitudes to homosexuality in particular. The papacy created the first four and can remedy them. The last two might move closer to agreement if the papacy were to initiate the review of moral theology which the Council mandated and recommended as a suitable area for ecumenical dialogue.

The Papal Bull, *Apostolicae Curae* on the validity of Anglican orders was part of the post-Vatican I campaign. It was issued on 15th September 1896 during the papacy of Leo XIII. While it opened with the words 'Apostolic care', its content was in fact devastating for the Anglican community. It describes at length the thorough studies undertaken in its preparation and the worthy people consulted. It goes back to a letter

---

[177] David Tracy, *On hope as a Theological Virtue in American Catholic Theology,* in Swidler & Küng (eds), The Church in Anguish, San Francisco, Harper & Row, 1987, *p271*

of 1554 from Pope Julius III to his legate, Cardinal Reginald Pole. The supporting arguments while cogent are narrowly legalistic, being limited to Roman Catholic sacramental theology and, Church law.

There is no pastoral dimension to the document except for the patronising and dubious opening phrases which asserted that the papacy had dedicated "no small portion of the Apostolic care and charity" … "to the welfare of the noble English nation"[178] and that "obeying the dictates of apostolic charity, [We] have considered that nothing should be left untried that might in any way tend to preserve souls from injury or procure their advantage". Would that all this were true! It then goes on to entirely subvert the Eucharist as celebrated among Anglicans for hundreds of years.

There is no Biblical dimension apart from a repeated assertion that Christ instituted the sacrament of ordination, for which no supporting details are offered.

It affirms that sacraments are composed of 'matter and form' enacted with the "intention of doing what the Church intends". Matter, in the case of ordination being the laying on of hands, is dismissed in a sentence as being too unspecific to count. The prayers are the 'form'. The assumption throughout the document is that the ordination prayers are automatically answered by God, precisely as petitioned. If the wording is imperfect, the sacrament is invalid. There is no recognition that God in responding can make up for the inadequacy of human prayer, or indeed that he has any continuing part, or discretion, in the matter of sacramental grace.

In the sacrament of ordination as administered by Anglicans for a period of a hundred years, the 'form' of words (the Edwardine Ordinal) lacked any reference to sacrifice, consecration, and priesthood. Since this omission deliberately reflected the Reformers opinions, the necessary "intention of doing what the Church [silently equated with Rome] intends" is obviously missing.[179] The faulty wording was amended in 1662 and might technically have remedied the 'form' but by that time it was too late; there were no validly consecrated bishops left to ordain new ministers. The Apostolic Succession of consecrating and consecrated bishops going back to the Apostles had thus been broken.[180]

The Apostolic Succession of the consecrating bishop is not part of the matter nor the form of the sacrament, so it is difficult to see how its absence can invalidate the sacrament. The Donatist heresy led to a clear teaching that the efficacy of a sacrament arises *ex opere operato*, ('by the very fact of the action's being performed'). Yet, Leo considered Apostolic Succession essential and this led him to the stark conclusion:

---

[178] Papal Bull of Leo XIII, *Apostolicae Curae* Sept 15th 1896.

[179] (The Church here is identified with the Roman Catholic Church. The acceptance since Vatican II that other churches and ecclesial bodies make up the Church of Christ, undermines the argument).

[180] "…it is a juridical narrowing of the concept to see apostolic succession primarily in a continuous chain of impositions of hands. As if such a chain of ordinations could supply by itself the apostolic spirit!" —Hans Küng, *Concilium 1968*

"We pronounce and declare that ordinations carried out according to the Anglican rite have been, and are, absolutely null and utterly void".

Having assumed the absolute need for the apostolic succession[181] of the consecrating bishops, the Bull establishes that the Anglicans have lost it. This was deeply upsetting for many Anglicans who see themselves as being very much part of the great tradition of the Catholic, albeit not the Roman Catholic, church.[182]

The Bull does not look back any further than Henry VIII. If it had ventured into the institution of the Eucharist or into the development of sacramental ordination for priests in the fourth century, it might have been less glib in its conclusions. Nor does it refer to the teaching (see Decision 8, Chapter 6) that the sacrament is effective *ex opere operato*. If it is not invalidated by the moral depravity of the minister, how can we believe that it is invalidated by some breach in the chain of Apostolic Succession. Leo XIII is conscious that the church is the dispenser of grace but avoids any reference to the essential part that God plays in every sacrament.[183]

Can God compensate for human deficiencies?

Christ founded the Eucharist at the Last Supper. It is unthinkable that he would lie. Therefore, his statement, "This is my body" is true, although a mystery to his followers. Similarly, with "This is my blood". We will never know how the mystery is accomplished. When he followed up by saying "Do this in commemoration of me", the word "this" implies the inclusion of the same mystery. Christians humbly accept that it is beyond human explanation, but none-the-less true. With rather less humility, we impiously fight about the mechanics of the mystery. Words like 'transubstantiation' and 'consubstantiation' were specially coined for the argument. They work better as slogans and denominational identifiers than as clarifiers of the mystery. Yet for all our differences we share the belief that whatever Christ intended happens *somehow*. Christ keeps his word. He asks us to believe what we cannot see or prove. It is unthinkable that, where two or three believers are gathered in the name of Jesus for the purpose of obeying his instructions, he would betray their trust and refrain from accomplishing the mystery because of some legal flaw in the distant past, or because the wording was liturgically imperfect.

---

[181] If God created the mysterious effect of apostolic succession, what could stop God from mending it when it gets broken? Incidentally, I have never seen a claim that the apostolic lineage of the consecrating bishop is part of the matter or of the form or how it comes to be necessary… other than in church discipline. The argument from tradition is weakened by the change in meaning of 'apostolic succession' from the original 'succession of teachers going back to the apostles' to 'a continuous chain of consecration as bishop with official authorisation to ordain and consecrate others'.

[182] The climate of ecumenical relations at the time ruled out any possible offer, in charity, to remedy this deficiency. Subsequently, the Old Catholics, who can trace their apostolic succession back as far as anyone else, generously provided bishops as co-consecrators to re-establish the apostolic succession in Anglicanism and reassure those who think it important.

[183] "The sacrament is not wrought by…the celebrant or the recipient, but by the power of God".— St Thomas Aquinas, S.T., III, 60, 3.

Apostolicae Curae conveniently disregards the fundamentals: Christ's institution of the Eucharist at the Last Supper and the question of who would have been with him to celebrate his last Passover.

Although not stated explicitly, the implications of *Apostolicae Curae* cut the Anglican communion down to size. The flawed intention of centuries back is deemed to invalidate everything. Anglican ministers are thus ordinary laity. Pope Leo XIII implies that the Eucharist as celebrated among the Anglican communities has been and is now meaningless, a 'sham'.[184] For Rome to deny that implication would be to accept that ordination is not necessary for a valid celebration of the Eucharist.

Leo XIII would have us believe that despite the faith and trust in Jesus Christ of generations of Anglican congregations, the bread and wine are nothing more than, well, bread and wine? What does this sophistry make of Jesus?

An ignoble Christ?

The Bull unwittingly, and pseudo-infallibly, cuts Jesus down to size also; making him out to be something less than an honourable person. By saying: "Do This", "This Is My Body" and "This Is My Blood", he gave a command, and made two statements. While there are various ways of understanding and defining the mystery, Christians accept that Jesus' statements are true. He made a commitment that we cannot fully understand or test. He asks us to believe and to trust him. "Blessed are those who have not seen but have believed". He accomplishes whatever transformation is necessary. It is unthinkable that Jesus whispered under his breath: "Terms and conditions apply", or "Provided the baker uses wheaten flour containing not less than $x\%$ of gluten", or worst of all: "Provided that the person who says the words has been duly authorised and consecrated for the purpose in accordance with canon law and in an unbroken line of succession of consecrator and consecrated going back to the apostles". If we believe that Jesus is God and that he said what is reported in the gospels, we simply must believe that he keeps his word. An honourable person will be the more punctilious about keeping a promise when the beneficiary has no opportunity of checking up on it. It is an outrage to suggest that Jesus would break his promise … that Jesus would deceive those who trust him when they gather in his name to commemorate his life and offer themselves with him.

"For where two or three are gathered together in my name, there am I in the midst of them" is unambiguous.[185] It certainly does not exclude believers who call themselves Anglicans and meet together in good faith. Thomas O'Loughlin has reminded

---

[184] 'Sham' was the word Archbishop Desmond Connell used when he faulted the President of Ireland, Mary McAleese, a committed Catholic, for taking Holy Communion at an Anglican service.

[185] Tertullian who is sometimes quoted as a patristic authority in Roman magisterial documents, claims that in cases of necessity even a layman (sic) might preside. 'Where three are, there is the church, even if they are laymen'—Tertullian, *De Exhort. Cast. 7.3,* quoted in Paul Bradshaw, *Liturgical Presidency in the Early Church,* Bramcote, Notts., 1983, Grove Books. (Grove Liturgical Study 36) p27.

us of the real presence of Jesus in every congregation even before anyone says the words of consecration.[186] What sort of a God would fail to fulfil his promise to a group of people who are trying to worship him in the way he instructed them?

Is this the kind of God that Roman Catholics are supposed to believe in? According to Leo XIII, it seems so. It is just a high-level instance of presenting as infallible something which is wrong. A cast-iron example of pseudo-infallibility and of prioritising legalities over faith. Or even of elevating the predispositions of the bureaucracy into Church teaching when there is an opportunity to knock the competition.

An Anglican minister may lack the 'dignity' of Roman Catholic Ordination, or the vaunted ontological change, but if he does what Jesus commanded, representing a community of the Christians or leading them in doing it together, we can be confident that Jesus does not fail in his part, but accomplishes the mystery. The sacrament is wrought through the power of God. It is efficacious *ex opere operato.* If we can trust Jesus to tell the truth, then it can be argued that Leo XIII has established officially that a valid ordination is not necessary for a valid Eucharist. The papacy should stop telling God what he may and may not do. Jesus is not subject to canon law.

I am not alone in challenging this example of pseudo-infallibility. At least two Cardinals, Cocopalmieri and Hume, have broken ranks to express doubts as to whether *Apostolica Curae* can be taken literally today. That is about as far as a Cardinal can go in disagreeing with pseudo-infallibility. But we can go farther.

One of Leo XIII's reasons for dismissing Anglican ordination is that by not mentioning the word 'sacrifice' in the ritual the ordaining bishop failed to intend in detail what the church intends in the sacrament. By 'church' here, he was referring to the teaching authorities in Rome. But Vatican II later defined the churches that are not in full communion with Rome as being part of the Christian Church. Therefore, whatever the intention of the Anglicans was, it can now be deemed in a general way to be what a significant part of the church intended. So, that line of argument loses whatever validity it may once have had.

And finally, when disaffection over women priests created the possibility that entire Anglican parishes, with their pastors, would make their submission to Rome, Pope Benedict XVI issued an Apostolic Constitution, *Anglicanorum Coetibus,* which swept away obstacles in a way that has never been done (and could yet be done) to promote the work of the foreign missions. The Roman flexibility surprised many, but not those who saw it in terms of a large bureaucracy being tempted to score over a competing power centre.

---

[186] In a webinar organised by the American reform group, Future Church, 11th July 2018

Chapter 9

The fruits of Vatican I: Internal

INTERNAL EFFECTS OF THE DOGMAS

Internal opposition

Vatican 1 caused another lasting schism. A substantial number of educated and committed Catholics were unable in conscience to believe or profess the new dogmas which were being promulgated as binding on the Catholic conscience. Consequently, entire congregations and many academics found themselves defined out of full communion with Rome. They were mainly in Germany. They linked up with the long-established Old Catholics of the Netherlands who had bishops who could claim valid ordination in the 'apostolic succession with the imposition of hands'. They formed a breakaway church with the consecration of their own bishop in 1873, adopting the title of 'Old Catholic Communion'.

The intellectual leader of the campaign opposing infallibility had been one of the foremost church historians of the day, Dr Ignaz Döllinger, a theology professor in Munich. Döllinger, although he had been excommunicated by the archbishop of Munich in the meantime, declined to become a member of what he considered to be as a schismatic church. Until his death, he piously and obediently refrained from administering or receiving the sacraments; believing that he would be vindicated in the ultimate court of appeal. "Convinced that the sentence decreed against me is unjust and legally null," he wrote, "I persist in regarding myself as a member of the great Catholic Church; and it is the church herself, through her Holy Fathers, tells me that such an excommunication cannot harm my soul."[187]

He maintained, in a letter to the archbishop of Mainz, that the two dogmas had come into being through force and coercion, and predicted that they would require force and corruption to support them into the future.

Another great historian, the famous Lord Acton, had been a pupil of Döllinger and was also prominent in opposing the definition. He was fluent in four European languages plus Latin and Greek and had first-hand knowledge of the church archives in many of the great ecclesiastical centres. He was familiar with the many forgeries that had been used to support papal claims to power, both civil and ecclesiastical. He insisted, that it was idle to pretend ignorance of the wilful falsehood and fraud upon which the theory of infallibility was based. He expressed the view that the papal

---

[187] —Thomas Albert Howard, *A Question of Conscience, The Excommunication of Ignaz von Döllinger,* Commonweal, September 29, 2014

despotism was maintained by the same insidious arts with which it was first won.[188] Acton was in Rome during Vatican 1 at the age of 36. Despite his relative youth, his language skills and encyclopaedic knowledge of church history enabled him to help coordinate the bishops who were opposing the definition. Afterwards, he expressed disappointment at what he saw as their lack of consistency and courage.

Acton was a very committed Catholic and would have been deeply distressed if he too had been excommunicated. His public standing in England, however, and his scholarly skills enabled him to outmanoeuvre Cardinal Manning in this regard.

Abuse of infallibility

After Vatican I, the papacy abused the dogmas by governing as if the infallibility conferred on the pope was unconditional and applied to virtually everything. The popes had been claiming *Plenitudo Potestatis* since the twelfth century at least, so nobody within the Roman system, could demur. Papal Encyclicals have never been claimed as infallible because that contention would be too easily rebutted, but the bureaucracy gives selected parts of them unquestionable, irrevocable and irreformable status. This enhances central power. Fr Yves Congar commented:

> "On the one hand the popes proclaim that Scripture and Tradition constitute the source and rule of everything and that all they do is to guard and protect it. But, on the other hand they behave, and they want everyone to behave—and they do all that they can, with implacable power, to make sure that everyone does behave—as if the popes themselves were the source".[189]

Congar has also complained that in the preparation of documents for Vatican II, with some of the key officials, an encyclical could take precedence over a clear text of scripture This should not surprise us. God leaves us freedom to choose, whereas universal papal jurisdiction is enforced by a powerful and vigilant bureaucracy.

The twin dogmas of Vatican I have allowed the papacy to pretend that legacy regulations and practices in regard to the sacraments of Order and Eucharist are irreformable and most of the faithful have been led to believe that these cannot be changed. In consequence, the conditions for the spread of sacramental famine have now become standardised in virtually every diocese in the world, the notable exception being Rome itself, and the management is precluded by its own pretence from doing anything about it—other than calling the faithful to more prayer for vocations. The process is at different stages in different areas, but the trend has been discernible for fifty years. It is only a question of timing. The threat of Eucharistic famine is as real as climate change but, as with climate change, the people who can do something about it will be the last to suffer its impact.

---

[188] Gertrude Himmelfarb, Review of Roland Hills biography of Lord Acton (Yale University Press), in *The New Criterion*, Vol. 18, No. 10, June 2000. http://www.anthonyflood.com/himmelfreviewhillacton.htm

[189] —Yves Congar OP, *My Journal of the Council*, Liturgical Press, Minnesota, 2012, p 48

The Authority of bishops undermined

During the debates at the First Vatican Council, some speakers had warned that to make the pope infallible and give him universal jurisdiction would be to reduce the influence of the bishops in their own dioceses. This has happened and the effect has intensified as authority has become ever more centralised and the scope of pseudo-infallibility has been expanded. While centralism has strengthened the papacy, it has weakened the organisation globally.

Improved communications have been used more to enhance control than extend consultation, forcing bishops to toe the line and to stay quiet on issues until Rome has reached a decision. The bishops are left with the responsibility for sacramental life and the 'powers' necessary to resolve the famine but are denied the permission to use those powers to meet their responsibilities.

A bishop's primary job is to sanctify the faithful, by praying, preaching[190] and providing the sacraments and liturgy. Progress in electronics made the elevated pulpit obsolete but now compensates by providing the immense potential of Radio, TV, Email, Twitter, Facebook, and Instagram. Not that every word of every bishop will be perfectly chosen or will always be well understood by his listeners. The Promise reassures us that the body of the faithful will not go far astray over time. Exaggerated papal infallibility and modern surveillance, however, have inhibited the bishops in heart-to-heart communications and brought in an era of legally precise orthodoxy and conformity with official opinion. The bishop now must be much too careful—much too circumspect about orthodox niceties—to be convincing to his listeners. Even the admission of a few inconvenient historical facts can attract the undesirable attention of the CDF.

In the distant past, when a bishop made a mistake or a misjudgement, it could be corrected by his peers, by theologians, even by the faithful or by all these combined at a local synod. The *sensus fidelium* was gradually formed in discourse, under the guidance of the Spirit, because discourse was then permitted. Thus, the *sensus fidelium* could develop; unfettered by the necessity of being legally and infallibly correct at every step. The bond of Christian unity rested in love for one another, in care for the needy, in the shared beliefs of the Creeds, in the shared Eucharist and in a patient, humble, trust in the Spirit to blow where he wills, when he wills.

Enforcing restrictions on discussion and opinions is an affront to the dignity, freedom, rationality, and integrity of humanity. Furthermore, it inhibits the development of knowledge and understanding, and obstructs the identification of error. As a policy in Church management it stifles the *sensus fidelium* and reveals a remarkable lack of trust in the Holy Spirit.

Now, the rare courageous Roman Catholic bishop who speaks his mind to his flock on issues of doctrine, or even of discipline, can expect chastisement, if some

---

[190] Acts 6:4

people in the curia do not like what he is reported as saying or how or where he says it—or if he is seen to be more compassionate than headquarters towards the marginalised or those who hold that criminal law should not be designed to enforce Catholic moral standards on the population at large.

Archbishop Hunthausen of Seattle is a case in point. He was side-lined on the basis of inaccurate delations (complaints) made to Rome and had to be re-instated when the issues were properly examined. Bishop William Morris of Toowoomba was fired by Pope Benedict XVI for airing some ideas about how the Eucharistic famine in his diocese might be addressed. He is said to have had some difficulties with the Vatican for four or five years previously. When he touched on the prerogatives of the Catholic priesthood, however, the reaction was swift and draconian. In theory, as a bishop, he had been selected by the Holy Spirit and was officially responsible to God for the provision of the sacraments in his diocese. He could see that a resolution of the problems would require a change in some traditional practices and prejudices. Unfortunately, he was touching at once on pseudo-infallibilities and the privileges of the profession. He was never given an opportunity to defend his ideas or relate them to the manifest needs of his diocese.

This is not the way Jesus said his church should be managed. The treatment of Bishop Morris probably had a chilling effect on other bishops. There must be many of them who struggle to reconcile their responsibility to their flocks with the limitations imposed by the centralised regulators. Some have dared to call for a reversal of the trend to ever-greater rigidity and centralisation.

The church is the visible manifestation of the mysterious, interior, and spiritual relationship with Jesus Christ and with one another that unites the diverse People of God. If it is going to be effective in evangelising the world, it is to that spiritual and mystical relationship the church must give visibility or witness. This happens all the time at local level as the lives of the People of God permeate society. The local church membership is the evangelising interface *par excellence,* and it must be visible, alive, and vibrant, if it is to respond to the needs and opportunities of the times and culture. Central management should not get in the way.

Greater unity is crucial for better evangelisation, but greater unity should not be confused with uniformity or equated with more effective central control. The objective of the papacy should be to empower the local church under its bishop. If embracing Christianity demands freedom, so too does spreading it. Church management should be decentralised, placing much greater reliance on bishops and other local leaders. The Promise would still apply but in ways that could be more sensitive to changing times and diverse cultures. A decentralised management would be less bureaucratic and might be more responsive to the promptings of the Spirit, or to the needs of the faithful.

Appointment of bishops monopolised

When the elders and overseers appointed by the apostles and other itinerant preachers died off, the selection of replacements was made by the relevant church communities. Pope Leo the Great said "Nobody should be bishop anywhere whom the people do not want as their bishop". When the overseers developed into consecrated bishops, nearby churches had some input on the suitability of a candidate because three bishops were traditionally required for the consecration. Between the Edict of Thessalonica in 380, and the collapse of the Western empire in 476 AD, the Roman religious bureaucracy, as the key part of the imperial civil service, was in charge of all episcopal appointments.[191] 1500 years later, it tried to re-establish the equivalent level of central control. The appointment of bishops from above may be accepted passively by the faithful. But passivity is not what Jesus epitomised. If vibrant, enthusiastic communities are what is desired, the faithful should select their bishops and the bishops should be free to lead.

The office of bishop has been covetable. It generally brought wealth, comfort, and influence that extended even into civil affairs. Recognising this, monarchs sought and secured privileges in relation to episcopal appointments, rights of appointment, consultation, or confirmation of candidates. In feudal times, Rome was often the only countervailing force since the faithful were all subjects of the monarchy. In establishing its universal jurisdiction after Vatican I, the papacy concentrated on ending these privileges and was largely successful.[192] The code of Canon Law in 1917 reserved the appointment of bishops to the pope absolutely.[193] Some dignitaries and civil governments are still allowed the privilege of proposing, presenting, or designating a candidate but the appointment rests with the Roman Pontiff who is advised by the relevant papal nuncio and a homogeneous committee within the curia.

In contrast to the patristic precedents of popular election, the process of selection is now highly secretive; the pastors have a cosmetic input and the faithful, none. The office of bishop is still coveted, and the secrecy of the selection process leaves it open to corruption. Bernard Häring commented "I know cases in which apostolic delegates accepted gifts, noticeable gifts, and that already tells me enough". He saw it as an "institutional temptation" that a small group of men should control the appointment of 4,000 bishops.[194] In an interview with the *Radharc* television team from Ireland, Fr Häring referred to the statement that Archbishop Jean Jadot saw fit to make on his appointment as apostolic delegate to the United States: "I come from a wealthy family but I live as simply as I can and everyone should know that the apostolic

---

[191] They were not above listening to local advice. St Augustine was selected by the clamour of the populace and, presumably, confirmed or tolerated by the Roman authorities.
[192] The emergence of a united Italy facilitated this process because several concordats that allowed rulers to nominate bishops ceased to have effect when the separate kingdoms were no more.
[193] CIC 1917, Canons 331,332.
[194] Joseph Dunn, *No Lions in the Hierarchy,* Dublin, The Columba Press, 1994, pp 306/7.

delegate does not need and does not accept any gift". It is a disgrace that he should have seen a need to make such a statement.

In the past, Church Councils have repeatedly condemned the buying and selling of sacred offices. Yet many popes have set a bad example, using appointments as a source of revenue to fund papal extravagance. The reassuring theory that the Holy Spirit influences the choice of bishops can only be realised to whatever extent the men who make the appointments listen to his promptings, and God never overrides our freedom to do things our own way.

No system of selection will guarantee perfect bishops. The fallout from the sexual abuse scandals has demonstrated, however, that the centralised system has been no exception to this rule. Moreover, being centralised ensures that its mistakes have consequences on a world scale.

INFALLIBILITY AND PSEUDO INFALLIBILITY

Doctrines are especially difficult to define, and some transcend human understanding and/or language. Over the centuries, the Holy See has always been taken very seriously by Christians as the final earthly court of appeal on disputed matters of doctrine and discipline. The primacy of the Bishop of Rome has always been widely acknowledged. Papal teaching has been treated with great respect although, like the Councils, popes often focused on condemning errors rather than elucidating truth.

The legislation that enabled the pope to make infallible definitions had the consequence of creating a new category; that of generally accepted doctrines that had never been formally defined as infallible. Not being legally infallible, they are legally fallible and thus in some way open to question. Vital, legally undefined doctrine on which all Christians agree, like the Incarnation, Death and Resurrection of Christ and the basic call to care for the least, were unwittingly downgraded into this category.[195]

Pope Benedict XVI was concerned about this anomaly yet took advantage of it when he changed the teaching on unbaptised infants, erasing Limbo from Catholic theology. To avoid admitting an error, he was able to say that the teaching had never been defined, so the teaching that he was rescinding had never really been taught! This despite 1500 years of telling distraught women who had just experienced a miscarriage or a stillbirth that the child would never see God and that canon law forbade a Christian burial (until 1983) because the unbaptised child would 'pollute' the consecrated graveyard.

---

[195] On one side are critics of "creeping infallibility," meaning a steady expansion of the set of church teachings that lie beyond debate. On the other are those, including Benedict, worried about "theological positivism," meaning that there is such a sharp emphasis on formal declarations of infallibility that all other teachings, no matter how constantly or emphatically they've been defined, seem up for grabs.—John L. Allen Jr. National Catholic Reporter, May 9, 2011

Was everything infallible?

While the definition of infallibility enhanced the power of the papacy, it was limited by conditions. The narrow and conditional nature of the definition, however, has not constrained the authorities. The papacy has been assiduously expanding the boundaries of 'infallibility' since then, except during the reign of John XXIII and that of the current Pope Francis.

As early as 1889, Margaret Anna Cusack, Foundress of the Congregation of St Joseph for Peace, complained of the trend:

> "In many cases Roman Catholic priests and superiors put obedience to themselves in place of obedience to God, and though they themselves do not and dare not teach a theory of personal infallibility, they act as if it were an article of faith, and make it a sin if obedience is not rendered to commands which are often wrong, because they are contrary to the true spirit of Christian charity."[196]

In the late 1940s, when I left one of the foremost Catholic secondary schools in Ireland, the students were still being taught that everything in the catechism was absolutely true and guaranteed by God. If there was *anything* you doubted, you were guilty of 'picking and choosing' and therefore, a heretic and destined for eternal damnation. It was better not to think about specifics and prudent not to concern yourself with inconsistencies. Being a Catholic had little to do with conviction or personal belief in the risen Christ; you just had to accept the whole package without question because you were born into a Catholic family.[197] As such, you were safe, personally, here and hereafter. If you questioned one teaching, you were said to be questioning them all. I distinctly remember one student asking for an explanation of an apparent contradiction only to be told "you should not ask questions like that".

In 1961, when Church Unity was listed for discussion at Vatican II, I was puzzled as to what use that might serve. What was there to discuss? The Roman Catholic Church was already in possession of all the truth. Church unity was simply a matter of getting other Christians, individually or collectively, to assent to Catholic teaching *en bloc* and return to the one fold and submit to the one shepherd. The people of today, who have never experienced the pre-Vatican II Catholic church, may find this hard to credit. They might wonder at my naïvety in accepting what I was being taught. Looking back, I wonder at it myself. But I was not alone; I was just one of the flock. That was what it meant to be a Catholic in Ireland then.

The belief that the Christ's promise to be with us to the end of the age would be meaningless if he were to allow his church to stray from what he had revealed goes

---

[196] —Margaret Anna Cusack, *The Nun of Kenmare*, 1889, Kenmare. Co. Kerry, quoted by Dan at , http://www.catholicdigest.com/books/201011-01the-nun-of-kenmare/ Accessed 21/1/2018. Emphasis added

[197] Chapter 4 of the other dogmatic constitution, *Dei Filius,* approved at that Council. While it declared that faith is a free act, it also ruled that once having embraced it, a person can never have "just cause for changing it or calling it into question". —Cf. O'Malley, *Vatican I,* pp 169/70

back at least as far as St Irenaeus in the second century. This gives the *sensus fidelium* of the universal church a teaching authority, although individuals and groups are likely to be in error on various points at times. Rome claims to articulate this teaching authoritatively under the inspiration of the Holy Spirit and therefore, infallibly. If God, however, never overrides our freedom then as humans, we always have the option of ignoring the prompting of the Spirit. Lord Acton was adverting to the papacy when he penned the words: *"There is no greater heresy than that the office sanctifies the holder of it"*.[198]

Spurious certainty

Rome has made its own magisterium infallible by identifying it with that of the entire church. In doing so it introduced a level of detail and specificness not found in the original and it developed gradually from authoritatively articulating the *sensus fidelium,* to legislating it. If people are to be persuaded to believe and profess on the basis of authority what they would doubt or reject on careful examination, then the independence, wisdom, fairness, justice, knowledge, honesty and competence of that authority must be beyond question. In recent decades, the evidence of the lies and secrecy employed to cover up sexual, financial, and judicial abuse, has impugned the integrity of the papacy on which so much of its authority has depended.

Vatican II teaches "This infallibility with which the Divine Redeemer willed his church to be endowed in defining a doctrine of faith and morals *extends as far as extends the deposit of divine revelation,* which must be religiously guarded and faithfully expounded" (LG, 25 with emphasis added). Guarding means protecting from both diminution and accretion. This is not to say that our understanding does not develop over time just as our understanding of the world and human nature develops.

Rome has not been averse to extending infallibility to include current teachings derived, or claimed to be derived, from the deposit of faith. Where interpretation involves bringing the deposit of faith to bear on some external knowledge or assumption, or *vice versa*, as is normally the case, this other knowledge or assumption does not have any claim to infallibility. It follows that derived teachings or interpretations should never be labelled as infallible, if only because the relevant external knowledge may change. The Galileo debacle is the best-known demonstration of this mistake, but it is not alone. Think of Darwin and evolution. Think of Aquinas' classifying the female as a defective male or the moral evaluation of masturbation before the contribution of female ovulation to procreation was proven. Nowhere has

---

[198] The great historian and deeply committed Catholic, Lord Acton, is frequently quoted on the corrupting effect of power. It is illuminating to set his famous assertion in context. It comes from his letter to Archbishop Creighton in the discussion on unfettered infallibility that preceded the first Vatican Council. "Power tends to corrupt and absolute power corrupts absolutely. Great men are almost always bad men, even when they exercise influence and not authority. There is no greater heresy than that the office sanctifies the holder of it."

the progress in human knowledge been greater than in the understanding of the female, discrediting the fear[199] and the determination to keep women in subjection.

The needed reform of some derived doctrines and interpretations is obstructed by the bureaucratic determination to avoid admission of error about almost anything. Exaggeration of its scope and precision undermines whatever infallibility is implicit in the Promise and brings it into disrepute. The boundaries of the deposit of faith as outlined by the Second Vatican Council should be respected scrupulously by Church authorities. Not only would this be the proper thing to do. It would be a small step towards removing the biggest barrier to Church unity.

Content of infallibility

Even if we believe that the ordinary magisterium of the universal church cannot err, we must accept that there has to be a boundary to what is included and some limit to the granularity to which it extends.

God has put us to live in an uncertain world and the recorded sayings of Jesus are often hard to understand. Jesus did not promise to attach an automatic guarantee of certainty to every detailed interpretation issued by the management. Rome would like the faithful to think he did. Rome generally behaves as if he did. It tries to control the faithful as if he did. It postures as if he did. It governs as if he did—at times with a heavy hand more redolent of a dictator than an evangelist.

In relating the deposit of faith to issues of everyday life, Church authorities have tended in modern times to rely on a broad assumption of infallibility which inhibits discussion of issues on their merits. This has divided the Catholic faithful into two groups: those who genuinely think that personal salvation depends on accepting without question everything that has emanated from Rome and those who tend to think critically and accept that the human leaders of our pilgrim church, including popes and bishops, have at times been mistaken, have done or tolerated morally indefensible things, and are not above getting their priorities confused. Teaching in recent generations supports the first group but history supports the second. For the first group, trivial issues can assume a disproportionate importance; any significant change threatens to undermine the basis of their belief and can be unsettling. No wonder that conservative polemicists are sometimes intemperate and aggressive.

Catholics have been taught for four generations that Mother Church (Rome) was custodian of all the truth and therefore nothing could change. With so much deemed to be unchangeable, pseudo-infallibility has achieved what Peter Olivi failed to do in the thirteenth century. It has subordinated reigning popes to any opinion or decision of a recent predecessors of which the faithful are cognizant.

---

[199] "From the moment that they become your fellows they will become your masters".—Cato, as quoted by Livy (Book 34.3)

Church teachings that have changed over time

Catholics have been led to believe that all the doctrines expounded by Rome over the centuries are divinely revealed and must be treated as infallible, even when not officially defined as such. The adage, *Roma locuta, causa finita est,* encapsulates that attitude. If it were true, doctrines could never change. Hence the cry we heard from some curial bishops and cardinals in relation to recent Synods on the Family: "Doctrine cannot change". Historically, however, many doctrines have changed, including some propounded in encyclicals or agreed by Ecumenical Councils.

The following list of fifty changes is certainly not comprehensive:

1. Papal Infallibility is a 'pestiferous doctrine' and 'the work of the devil' – Pope John XXII, *Quia Quorundam. (1324)*

2. For Salvation, all must be subject to the Roman Pontiff – Boniface VIII, *Unam Sanctam.* (1302)

3. Burning heretics is the will of the Holy Spirit. Leo X, *Exsurge Domine.* No. 33 (1520)

4. The Roman Pontiff can, and ought to, reconcile himself, and come to terms with progress, liberalism, and modern civilization. (Condemned by Pope Pius IX in the Syllabus of Errors, 80) (1864)

5. Charging interest on a loan is immoral.

6. It is sinful for Catholics to pray together with non-Catholics.[200]

7. Slavery and the buying and selling of enslaved people is morally acceptable.

8. The practice of torturing and burning witches is justified and recommended. (Encyclical, Pope Innocent IV)

9. The death penalty is morally acceptable.

10. Limbo. Existence erased from Catholic teaching by Benedict XVI after 1600 years (2007)

11. The Earth is flat, and Rome is the centre of the universe. (Galileo affair, 1633)

12. The Literal Truth of everything in the Bible.

13. The addition of Filioque to the creed.

---

[200] Christians of all kinds together with Jews and some Muslims and others have come to a realisation and indeed a belief that we all worship the same unchanging Creator— although we use different names for him and have very different ideas about him. This was the clear message when Pope John XXIII prayed at Assisi with the leaders of other churches. His action scandalised many Catholics who had been taught that it was sinful to join in prayer with someone who had erroneous ideas about God. As if their misconceptions somehow created a different God! One must ask: would it really upset a loving and infinite God if some of his finite children have different misconceptions about him?

14. It is not permissible to receive Holy Communion on the day after having sexual intercourse.

15. Forty days in the field fighting for the pope earns one an overriding papal guarantee of eternal salvation.

16. All Jews will go to hell. (Council of Florence, 1443)[201]

17. No parvity of matter in sixth and ninth Commandments. (Confirmed by the Inquisition in 1611 AD.) The rejection of this has not yet been admitted to the faithful.

18. No Salvation outside the Church. (The words may be the same, but the interpretation of this important phrase has changed several times.)

19. The Roman Catholic Church cannot possibly be reformed because it is not subject to any defect. (Pope Gregory XVI, 1831-46) *versus*. the Church is always in need of reform. (Vatican II)

20. Only a bishop has authority to confirm … under pain of excommunication. (Trent). The presbyter also can be the ordinary minister of confirmation (Vatican II).

21. Purgatory, an established idea among Jews and Pagans, was only imported into Christian teaching in the sixth century by Pope Gregory the Great and defined in 1324 AD (See page 73).

22. Cremation of the dead is sinful.

23. The Divine Right of Kings.

24. Torture of people suspected of heresy is morally acceptable.

25. Allowing the laity to share the chalice is heretical. (Council of Constance and Pope Leo X).

26. Bishops, once appointed, are 'married' to their diocese and should never move to another. (Council of Chalcedon, and several others)

27. Women may not sing in the church choir.

28. Castration, although a bodily mutilation, is morally justifiable if the intention is to improve the quality of liturgical music without admitting women to the choir. In this case the end was being invoked officially to justify the means.

29. The Gospel reference to 'two swords' gives the pope authority over all temporal rulers.

30. The pope has authority to depose and/or appoint kings and emperors and allocate territories to them.

---

[201] Rabbi Rivon Krygier, *La Croix,* 11th October 2018

31. The pope can dissolve contracts to which he is not a party and absolve subjects from oaths of fidelity to their sovereigns.

32. The state of virginity is superior to that of marriage.

33. The use of the 'safe period' for contraception is a mortal sin.

34. Primacy of Conscience.

35. Freedom of Religion.

36. Separation of Church and State.

37. The existence and political independence of the Papal States is essential to the life of the Church.

38. Those to be promoted Cardinals must be 'in the order of priesthood'. (This is a relatively recent change.)

39. Scholasticism is no longer the unique and essential philosophy of the Catholic Church. (Confirmed by John Paul II in direct contradiction of Pius IX. The great German scholar, Dr Ignaz Döllinger, was condemned for saying this.)

40. It is legitimate to use violence to achieve spiritual ends. (St Augustine)[202]

41. The Theory of Evolution is incompatible with the faith.

42. That love of God and neighbour implies care for the environment. (Pope Francis.)

43. That sexual intercourse is sinful except when procreation is the aim. (Here again, the old teaching used the ends to justify the means!)

44. That the Jews are guilty of Deicide and are to be held responsible for the death of Jesus. [203]

45. That the Protestant and Catholic understandings of Justification are not capable of being reconciled.[204]

46. Ecumenism was "a most grave error, by which the foundations of the Catholic faith are completely destroyed" according to the encyclical *Mortalium Animos,* of Pius XI in 1928. The bishops at Vatican II decided instead that it was a "movement, fostered by the grace of the Holy Spirit".[205] Note that the reversal of this encyclical teaching was made by the bishops, not the papacy.

---

[202] Hans Kung, *The Catholic Church,* Weidenfeld & Nicholson, London, 2001, *p*97

[203] This was part of the liturgy for centuries until changed by Pope John XXIII and the Second Vatican Council.

[204] Disproved by the ceremonial signing of the Joint Declaration on the Doctrine of Justification (JDDJ) at Augsburg, in November 1999.

[205] Second Vatican Council, *Unitatis Redintegratio* n1, 21 November 1964.

47. Priests must abstain from sexual intercourse the night before saying mass. (The celibacy discipline was influenced by this idea, but it is not taught today in relation to married Anglican priests who have converted.)

48. People born out of wedlock cannot be admitted to priestly ordination. This is no longer applied.

49. Only physically perfect men can be admitted to priestly ordination. In the past, a missing limb, or finger or even a limp ruled one out.

50. The Church does not feel authorised to ordain women. This was changed on the 22nd May 1994 by Pope John Paul II in the Apostolic Letter *Ordinatio Sacerdotalis* with the words: "I declare that the Church has no authority whatsoever to confer priestly ordination on women and that this judgment is to be definitively held by all the Church's faithful".

This last item in our list failed the three criteria specified by the definition of Papal Infallibility at Vatican I. However, a year or so later the Congregation of the Doctrine of the Faith started claiming that it was infallible.

In the 1980s I had asked Cardinal Tomás Ó Fiaich about women's ordination. I learned his response by heart:

> "There is no reason in Dogmatic Theology why women should not be priests. There is no reason in Biblical Studies why women should not be priests, but they won't be priests, Loughlin, because the body of men required to make that decision is incapable of making that decision"[206]

The greatest doctrinal changes have happened informally and slowly; 'by amnesia', as has been said. The difficulty about openly changing a teaching that still occupies the minds of the faithful is that it would undermine the Roman posture of never being wrong. Protecting the aura of infallibility gets prioritised in the curia over everything except its own power and authority, of which it forms an element. Change generally implies some degree of error or imperfection in the existing teaching.

For John Courtney Murray the question of how far change could be tolerated was "*the* issue under the issues"[207] throughout the whole of Vatican II. That issue will never be resolved while Rome accords an overriding priority to its own inerrancy and backs it up with *plenitudo potestatis*. The idols of the Old Testament were easier to recognise for what they are than the idols of the New.

Pseudo-infallibility

The steady expansion of the scope and granularity of infallibility since 1870, is frequently referred to as creeping infallibility. The polite adjective fails to convey its

---

[206] I was careful never to quote him on this during his lifetime. It would have impaired his influence in Rome. I would be interested to know if he expressed this view elsewhere, officially or in private.

[207] Cf. Robert Nugent, *Silence Speaks,* Paulist Press, 2011, Paperback P69

spurious nature. If a papal teaching does not meet the conditions of the definition, then it is not infallible at all. Even the most dyed-in-the-wool legalist must admit this. It is more accurate and truthful to name it 'pseudo-infallibility'.

The infallibility defined by Vatican I was limited to faith and morals and was subject to conditions, so it did not provide the unbounded authority that Pope Pius IX, the curia and the Ultramontane party had been looking for. In the circumstances, it is not surprising that pseudo-infallibility emerged as a working substitute and that new formulas have been produced to support Roman infallibility claims. As recently as May 1998, in *Ad Tuendam Fidem,* Pope John Paul II amended Canon Law to require that "each and everything set forth definitively by the Magisterium of the Church" (i.e. Rome) must be believed, just as if it were infallible.[208]

Pseudo-Infallibility has had a devastating effect on the faith. It has spawned deception of the faithful, and some notably unsuccessful attempts at deception that have impugned the integrity of some of the highest church authorities. It is widespread in Roman Catholic teaching and the loyalty oaths (and canon law) prevent bishops and pastors from identifying and challenging it. The official teaching in regard to papal encyclicals is that they are important expressions of faith and doctrine that deserve the utmost respect of the faithful but are not infallible. None the less, encyclicals and lesser magisterial documents are routinely quoted and treated as if they were infallible. And there is no avenue of appeal or forum where this can be questioned.

Pseudo-infallibility and universal jurisdiction have bred fear of admitting problems and have created specious limitations when it comes to solving them. The aura of infallibility and unquestionable universal authority bolsters groupthink and makes humble listening impossible. No totalitarian regime, temporal or spiritual, can tolerate criticism no matter how constructive or apposite.

The consequential neglect, or suppression of the rethink on moral theology called for by the Second Vatican Council has not prevented the development of the *sensus fidelium* in the meantime. The widening of the gap between it and the magisterium is impossible to measure but is obvious on issues such as women's ordination, capital punishment, contraception, pre-wedding cohabitation, original sin, hell, and indeed, infallibility itself.

Posturing to mislead is the antithesis of evangelisation. If Jesus is the Way, the Truth, and the Life, then evangelisation in his name must be scrupulously honest and must be seen to be so. Accordingly, nobody, bishop, priest, or lay person should be chastised for seeking responsibly to correct a distortion, however inconvenient this may be. All Church authorities, including the papacy, and the Congregation for the

---

[208] The amended canons were 750 & 1371 for the Latin Church and 598.1 and 1496. 2 for the Eastern Churches.

Doctrine of the Faith, should adopt an Overwhelming Option for the Truth. Nothing less is worthy of Jesus. If they baulk at this proposal, they will only be proving the need for it.

Unfortunately, pseudo-infallibility survived Vatican II. When he was questioned in 1995 about the teaching in the Apostolic Letter of John Paul II on the ordination of women, the Prefect of the CDF, then Cardinal Ratzinger, was reported to have responded simply: "The Pope is infallible". If that report is accurate, he was being disingenuous. The Cardinal was in a position to know that the Apostolic Letter in question fails all the stipulated requirements for papal infallibility. The CDF is still trying to classify it as infallible because the deception meets an institutional need. We revert to the reception, or rather the non-reception, of that Apostolic Letter by the faithful in Chapter 12.

Pseudo-infallibility has a high maintenance cost, involving deceit, obscurantism, and hypocrisy. The loyalty oath and coercion have thus become its essential supports. Ignaz Döllinger's prediction, referred to on page 105, has been more than vindicated by subsequent events.

Theologians may critique papal or curial pronouncements within their own pro-fessional circles, but they share their findings with the faithful at their peril.[209] The oath has put papal documents beyond reasoned reassessment, at least for hot-button issues that have the attention of the public. It has made thoughtful disagreement with the pope on non-infallible issues hazardous for clergy. It forces officials to treat good Catholics, who sincerely seek reform, as pariahs.[210] The doctrinaire refusal to consider the possibility of being wrong has made it impossible for the papacy to listen to the bishops and for the bishops to listen to the priests who maintain the everyday contact with the consciences of the faithful and who understand the obstacles to faith and better practice.

Pseudo infallibility is not concerned with truth. Pseudo-infallibility is about power, and the reputation and authority of the governing institution.

Exaggerated claims about the scope and precision of its own authority has been a characteristic of the Apostolic See throughout history, particularly since the eleventh century papacy of Gregory VII. Pseudo-infallibility boosted Roman power in the short term after 1870 but has left it vulnerable to the admission of one internal con-tradiction or apparent error. Even the introduction of disciplinary change has the potential to shake the confidence of the faithful in the teaching office of the papacy.

---

[209] See Tony Flannery, *A Question of Conscience, Dublin, Londubh Books* 2013, especially Chapters 6 and 7. Fr. Flannery could be one of many. He is unusual in that he had the courage to tell the story.

[210] Evidently, this treatment originates in the curia. It is not given to senior members of the curia itself. They appear to be free to contradict Pope Francis when they are unable to control him and want to resist his reforms.

This effect is already apparent and is probably a factor in the erosion of congregations. The solution is to avoid exaggeration, prioritise humility and truth and bear with the short-term cost of renouncing generalised infallibility.

As in any organisation, church membership ranges from conservative to progressive. If people tolerate one another, such tension can be creative. However, the multiplication of pseudo-infallibilities has created too many issues on which orthodoxy can be demanded. This creates division which, coupled with authoritarianism, has generated a current level of internal intolerance that ought to shame any Christian church. To promote progress in unity, both internal and external, the papacy will have to learn to deal more gracefully with diversity of opinion.

Making too many things 'infallible' is analogous to issuing too much currency; it tends to devalue what is already in existence. As with currency, moreover, a few counterfeit notes in circulation can make people look dubiously at the good ones.

Paralysing management.

The need to protect pseudo-infallible teaching imposes limits on the options available to management when it encounters problems in obeying the mandates. This is at the root of the paralysis that characterises the papacy and the bishops in dealing with the shortage of ministers, the sacramental famine, the dwindling congregations, inculturation and the revision of moral theology. Not only has it inhibited the authorities from listening to the Second Vatican Council. It makes them insensitive to the *sensus fidelium*. It impedes the development of the *sensus fidelium* itself by inhibiting the free exchange of ideas at all levels among the faithful, the theologians and the hierarchy.

For the curia, pseudo-infallible doctrines must be defended by all means and at whatever cost. They get a remarkably high priority, ahead even of truth. The failure to defend one tenet could threaten a domino effect, leading to a reduction of power and control. This process may be happening even now.[211] If a doctrine proves difficult to defend, the curia, instead of revising it or encouraging discussion among the faithful under the promised guidance of the Spirit, have resorted to options that are hard to reconcile with the teachings or example of Jesus. Some of these options:

1. Exhort the faithful to accept the illogicality as another mystery of religion.

2. Ban discussion of the subject among Catholics.

3. Castigate thinking Catholics who continue to seek the truth or explanations and accuse them of intellectual pride and/or disloyalty. Refuse permission for them to speak at meetings held on church property.

4. Treat the questioner as a heretic and excommunicate him.

---

[211] Cardinal Ladaria Ferrar recognised this in his article in Osservatore Romano on 29th May 2018.

5. If the questioner is a member of a religious congregation and is unable in conscience to conform or recant to the satisfaction of the CDF, force their congregation to expel them.

6. If the dissenter is ordained, remove him from public ministry, silence him and forbid him to admit the truth about his silencing, under a further threat of removal from the priestly state.

Historically, the attack has ranged all the way from accusations of arrogance and intellectual pride to torture and burning at the stake. Thankfully, the last two are no longer tolerated by the *sensus fidelium* but other forms of coercion are available and are still used, mostly in secret—particularly against vowed religious and/or those who feel bound by their loyalty oaths.[212]

APPROPRIATING AND EXAGGERATING THE PROMISE.

The Promise of Jesus was made to all his followers, to the People of God, along with his instruction to teach all nations. It must mean that Jesus, while respecting the freedom on which a person's capacity to love depends, will not let his followers as a body stray far from the truth he has revealed for a significant length of time. The first fiction is that this Promise provides a guarantee against any error in doctrinal detail at a given point in time. The second is that a similar guarantee applies to any subsection of his followers. The idea that the Roman Magisterium (teaching authority) is always a perfect, reflection and interpretation of the beliefs of the People of God is becoming harder to maintain in the information age as the chasm between the two becomes more evident. The *sensus fidelium* is notoriously difficult to define but divergence in detail and in emphasis between it and the official line is now palpable. This is confirmed by the repeated lamentations of conservative churchmen and by the "plethora of new documents, ordinances, admonitions and directives" emanating from the curia. In 1987 Hans King listed these as ranging

> "From decrees about heaven and hell to blatantly ideological refusal of the ordination of women; from the prohibition of lay preaching (now even lay theologians) to the prohibition of altar girls; from direct curial intervention in the larger orders (selection of the Jesuit general, regulation of the Carmelites, inquisitional inspection of the United States female orders) to the notorious proceedings to ban certain theologians from teaching".[213]

A century and a half of pseudo-infallibility in combination with the normal bureaucratic need to defend its hegemony makes it difficult now for the papacy to adjust its position, even on minor issues. The consequent need to manage the truth has given rise to spin, deceit, shoddy scholarship, injustice, silencing and police-state tactics, including prohibitions on discussion of certain issues by the faithful, by the

---

[212] Cf. Fr Tony Flannery, *A Question of Conscience,*

[213] Hans Küng, *Cardinal Ratzinger, Pope Wojtyla, and Fear at the Vatican,* in Hans Küng and Leonard Swidler, (eds) *The Church in Anguish,* San Francisco, Harper & Row, 1987, p 68.

theologians and even by the bishops assembled at Vatican II and at synods. All this in the name of Jesus Christ! Is this a harsh judgement? I think not. It explains how a bureaucracy of talented and mostly excellent, prayerful, and dedicated men has managed to lead the organisational church into its present state. The dynamic of a homogeneous group and the bureaucratic lust for power, have together created a body of controlling regulations and 'irreformable' doctrines that have become an obstacle to faith for many Christians, an obstruction to evangelisation of unbelievers and a straitjacket for church leadership which finds itself constrained by inessentials that it is afraid to change. Much of the problem derives from giving pseudo-infallible status to papal opinions, traditional practice, or legacy management choices. Papal documents tend to be lengthy and detailed; such that only a tiny proportion of the faithful will ever study them. Thus, extracts or headlines can easily acquire a pseudo-infallible status.

With little respect for their personal integrity clerics have been bound by oaths of loyalty to speak and act as if most of Church teaching and discipline is irreformable, even infallible. Correcting the distortion in the minds of the faithful after three or four generations is bound to be upsetting and cause scandal for many in the short term. Scandal, as we have seen, comes with exposure of the deception. Postponing exposure is not the answer. Ending the deception is.

Governing and acting as if many things are infallible

Since the definition, popes, with one exception, have taught without invoking infallibility. The bureaucracy, however, has consciously or unconsciously confused pseudo-infallibility with the real thing. It has been taken in by its own propaganda. The policy of acting and speaking as if encyclicals and other papal documents are infallible or pseudo-infallible and thus not open to discussion, has had disastrous effects on the credibility of the leadership and the institutional Church.

Some examples:

1. The *Humanae Vitae* debacle is a case in point. It started as an objective study by a Papal Commission of the morality of contraception within marriage. While the study was in progress, the Second Vatican Council agreed that moral theology as a whole needed a rethink, "more thoroughly nourished by scriptural teaching".[214] Nobody on the commission was able to find cogent grounds for the teaching of Pope Pius XI that contraception was 'intrinsically evil'. Since this was a non-infallible teaching, the commission, in a secret report to the pope, recommended that it be changed. (In this they were virtually unanimous, 94 per cent concurring.) The curia, led by Cardinal Ottaviani, Secretary of State, opposed the change. The ruling, that contraception was 'intrinsically evil' and merited eternal damnation had been presented, like so many other things, as

---

[214] Second Vatican Council, *Optatam Totius* §16

infallible and could not be changed without affecting papal authority. This would have revealed pseudo-infallibility for what it was.

It took two years for Pope Paul to make up his mind. In the end the curial strategy prevailed, and he confirmed the pseudo-infallibility; again relying solely on papal authority. In the meantime, however, the secret report of the Commission had been leaked. It was published in full by the *National Catholic Reporter* in Kansas and *The Tablet* in London and discussed at length in many religious and secular publications. Bishops, priests, theologians and attentive Catholics learned that a high-powered papal expert group, handpicked for their orthodoxy and working objectively and in freedom, had failed to find any reason why contraception should be deemed 'intrinsically evil'. For many, this made sense. They could practice responsible parenthood in good conscience' It accorded with their instinct of the faith and they welcomed it. Many had made up their minds long before *Humanae Vitae* was published. At its launch, it was described as not being infallible so there was little reason for the faithful to change their minds or practice.

Paradoxically, the worst fears of the curia were realised. In recommending that the faithful be kept in the dark, the so-called Minority Report had expressed the fear of admitting an error:

> "If the Church could err in such a way, the authority of the ordinary magisterium in moral matters would be thrown into question. The faithful could not put their trust in the magisterium's presentation of moral teaching especially in sexual matters."

Here deception of the faithful is being recommended with a view to preserving their trust in the magisterium! In consequence, the aura of papal authority, which they had prioritised over telling the truth, suffered its greatest set-back since the Reformation.

When the encyclical was issued, the loyalty oath prevented the bishops from discussing the morality of contraception thoroughly with the faithful.[215] They could not engage in the lively debate that ensued. They had to express their disagreement with the teaching obliquely. Some episcopal conferences interpreted the encyclical for their flocks in ways that relativized the teaching, and some stressed that people should follow their consciences. All were duly chastised the following year at a hastily summoned Synod in Rome. But the damage was already done to the authority and credibility of both the papacy and the bishops. The attempt to deceive the faithful on an issue of morality failed.

2. Pope Leo XIII's papal bull *Apostolicae Curae* (1896) is another instance. In it he declared "that ordinations carried out according to the Anglican rite have been, and are, absolutely null and utterly void". This was never an infallible

---

[215] They could not even categorise it as a venial sin. It had something to do with sex and therefore had to be considered 'mortal' in all circumstances.

statement and would surely not be heard today. Yet, in a conversation with Dr Geoffrey Rowell, the Anglican Bishop in Europe, Cardinal Joseph Ratzinger, Prefect of the Congregation for the Doctrine of the Faith gave the bull pseudo-infallible status by treating it as irreformable:

> In discussions about Anglican Orders, Pope Benedict [then Cardinal Ratzinger] admitted to him [Dr Rowell]: "We cannot do anything about Leo XIII's words".[216]

Of course, we can. We can repudiate them as wrong, misguided, erroneous, inadequate, or uncharitable. But the bureaucracy would fear this might erode papal authority further. (Paradoxically, at this stage a humble admission of an error or two from that quarter might well have just the opposite effect.) The faithful can treat Leo's words, quite properly and legally, as being erroneous and therefore open to rejection.

3. Very recently the CDF demanded that the Irish priest Fr Tony Flannery, C.SS.R., sign up to four Doctrinal Propositions and remain silent on them in future, before it would 'gradually' lift the suspension of his ministry as a priest. None of the propositions is essential to salvation or the faith. All four issues need examination and synodal discussion by clergy and laity. On two of the issues—'the reservation of priesthood to men alone' and 'gender theory'—Jesus said absolutely nothing. Church understanding of the other two—'the moral liceity of homosexual practices' and 'same-sex marriage'— is likely to be refined significantly if the review of moral theology recommended by Vatican II, is ever allowed to proceed. This is unlikely to happen. It would require a synodal approach and synodality cannot co-exist with centralised infallibility.

4. To support the refusal of ordination to women, several attempts have been made to persuade Catholics that the Apostolic Letter *Ordinatio Sacerdotalis* of Pope John Paul II on the issue is infallible. That is simply untrue. It did not fulfil the conditions for infallibility and was quickly rejected by the faithful. Study after study has shown that, far from being received by the People of God, the teaching is widely rejected. Chapter 12 below proves that it is an example of pseudo-infallibility and the rejection is well deserved.[217]

5. Episcopal consecration gives the bishops the 'power' to ordain priests, but current discipline prevents them from using it to fulfil their responsibility for the availability of the sacraments in their dioceses. Furthermore, they are forbidden[218] from discussing the main factors contributing to the sacramental

---

[216] https://www.churchtimes.co.uk/articles/2017/30-june/gazette/obituaries/obituary-the-rt-revd-dr-douglas-geoffrey-rowell, accessed 5/2/2018

[217] Here we are not being disrespectful of a canonised saint. Canonisation is an assurance by the pope that a person is in heaven and a declaration that the papal ban on his public veneration by the worldwide church is, from that moment on, officially lifted. It does not mean that a saint was never in error, mistaken or biased. Moreover, apart from Mary, all saints are deemed to have been sinners.

[218] As an exception, discussion was allowed in preparation for and during the Synod on Amazonia.

famine; celibacy, life-long commitment, the reservation of ordination to males and the limiting of Eucharistic celebration to the ordained. None of these factors is traceable to Jesus or the apostles. Open discussion would reveal the weak grounds of the regulations that now conflict with the two mandates of Jesus. The problem does not lie in the regulations but in giving them pseudo-infallible status as part of a supposed divine plan. Furthermore, any change would touch on the privileges of the profession.

Bishop Morris was not questioning traditional belief, but traditional practice which has consistently prioritised the prerogatives of the profession over the provision of the sacraments, the latter being the bishop's responsibility in his own diocese. Instead of answering his questions or addressing the problem he raised, Rome instituted an Apostolic Visitation to his diocese by Archbishop Chaput. Morris was never told the outcome or allowed to defend himself against what must have been a very damaging report, given that it led to his removal. The report has not been published and he has never been allowed to see it. Archbishop Chaput was required to destroy his own copy after he had submitted it to the curia.

The Church preaches love and justice for all but is seen as hypocritical when top management abandons both to condemn someone who raises relevant questions that point to its own inadequacies.

Recapitulation

Thus, the fruits of Vatican I have not been nourishing nor its leaves medicinal.

- The popes became infallible. The infallibility defined was narrow and conditional; such that it has only been exercised once. The title alone, however, delivered power which has been abused by gradually extending its scope far beyond the definition. This has been called creeping infallibility, but we have named it pseudo-infallibility because that is what it is.

- Internally, both dogmas enhanced the power of the popes and consequently the curia.

- Externally, the dogma of infallibility caused apprehension among civil rulers and triggered a backlash from several countries, especially Germany where it was costly and had lasting effects.

- The Council weakened the episcopate. Thousands of dedicated and educated bishops, who could have been leaders in a vibrant evangelising church, were reduced in status and denied the authority to match their responsibilities.

- The appointment of bishops was monopolised and centralised. This introduced standardised selection criteria although dioceses tend to have differing needs. In the pontificates of John Paul II and Benedict XVI, the criteria were so narrow that it could be questioned whether they could witness to the beliefs of their flocks. The episcopacy is potentially a substantial resource which is currently constrained and underutilised.

- The Council reinforced the barriers against other Christian denominations and led to further alienation of the Anglicans.

- It caused a schism with some who considered the new dogma false.

- It gave rise to the Modernist Crisis, a large-scale, misjudged campaign that pitted authority and power against scholarship and intellectual integrity.

Pseudo-infallibility is insidious. It sometimes claims its infallibility in words, but more often, it does so indirectly, through attitudes and actions. Catholics were led to believe that their religion had the right answers to all the questions;[219] That the Church (meaning Rome) mediated Christ's Promise as well as his merits. It was the conduit of truth and was wise beyond compare. Good Catholics accepted everything without examination. The pervading atmosphere of infallibility put everything safely beyond question.

While the Second Vatican Council undid some fictions. The *Humanae Vitae* debacle and the sex abuse scandals shook the confidence of some and the faith of others.

But all of this has had limited effect on the curia. It is too well protected from outside forces. This leaves it chronically ill-prepared to deal with a changing world. Legal infallibility enhanced the power of the papacy initially. Exaggerated since then, it has become a weakness, a straitjacket. The need to protect the aura of infallibility causes paralysis. The curia has gathered virtually all the power and authority to the centre and yet finds itself unable to cope with some very long-standing problems. Fear of having to admit to any error or imperfection limits initiative and adaptability and makes subsidiarity unworkable. The promise, which could embolden Christians to 'launch out into the deep'[220] has been turned on its head as pseudo-infallibilities combine to inhibit creativity and limit management options. The curia cannot [221]risk changing its position on anything, so it cannot listen to reason—even when the Pope favours a change.

The lesson is clear. If you must paint yourself into a corner, don't use infallible paint. It never dries!

---

[219] The bishops at Vatican II felt the need to lay this canard to rest. *Gaudium et Spes §33*

[220] When He had stopped speaking, He said to Simon, "Launch out into the deep and let down your nets for a catch. (Luke 5:4, New King James Version)

[221] Hasler, opus cit. P. 16.

Chapter 10

Deceit, coercion, and hypocrisy

"And know that I am with you always; yes, even to the end of time".

—Matthew 28:20

CURIAL MANOEUVRES

The Birth Control Commission was an innovation by Pope John XXIII. It was the first formal enquiry in the history of the Church into the morality of contraception that had freedom to study and report without being constrained by existing law or teaching. Paul VI had shown his commitment to the search for truth by appointing both progressive and conservative members and by strengthening the commission when it had little progress to report. He increased its budget and encouraged it to work with "complete objectivity and liberty of spirit" instructing the secretary, Fr. de Riedmatten, to "Press on".[222]

Later, if he had *acted* on the advice of the Commission, or made a modest exercise in collegiality during the two years when he was agonising over the decision, he would have avoided the great disaster of twentieth century Catholic teaching. During that time, the curial officials conspired to keep Cardinal Suenens and the other members of the Papal Commission on Birth Control away from him lest they influence him. In contrast, Cardinal Ottaviani and Fr John C. Ford S.J., who were against telling the faithful the truth, had ready access, with Fr Ford in particular playing on the Pope's need for loyalty to a predecessor.[223] As we have seen, the Papal Commission had studied the issue objectively for more than three years but accepting its conclusions would mean correcting the teaching of Pius XI in *Casti Connubii*. The curia feared that this would undermine the authority of the papacy, although Pius XII had modified *Casti Connubii* without any ill-effects in 1951, when he approved the use of the rhythm method which, up to then, had been taught to be a grave sin, meriting eternal damnation for Catholics. Moreover, Vatican II had reversed a teaching of Pius XI on

---

[222] The story of how *Humanae Vitae* took shape may be found in Robert Blair Kaiser, *The Politics of Sex and Religion*, Kansas City, Leaven Press, 1985. The quoted phrases are from pages 97 & 100. Cardinal Suenens never wrote the story himself but vouched for the accuracy of Kaiser's account.

[223] Fr Ford himself explained on receiving the first Cardinal O'Boyle Award: "During an interview with Pope Paul, he and I were discussing the positions being proposed in the Commission. The Pope was calm and composed while we talked about these … But when I said to Pope Paul, "Are you ready to say that *Casti Connubii* can be changed?" Paul came alive and spoke with vehemence: "*No!*" he said. He reacted exactly as though I was calling him a traitor to his Catholic belief. I have never before told that story publicly. Perhaps you interpret his reaction the way I did and do".

127

ecumenism without upsetting the faithful. The *sensus fidelium* had accepted that new teaching without demur. It was consistent with gospel values.

On the question of contraception, however, the entire commission of seventy, made up of cardinals, bishops, theologians, experts, and lay people hand-picked for orthodoxy and strengthened in numbers several times as they wrestled with the problem, had been unable to find any grounds in natural law, scripture or reasoning why contraception should be considered 'intrinsically evil'. This was an opinion from an authoritative source on an issue that immediately affected the personal lives of the faithful. When their report was leaked, it added to a debate that had been going on since the possibility of a change in teaching had been flagged at a Vatican press conference on 29th October 1964. Thus, the married faithful and their bishops had had nearly four years to consider the matter before *Humanae Vitae* was published on the 25th July 1968. By then, many had already made up their own minds. Many had reached the same conclusion as the Papal Commission. Others followed its judgement as they were fully entitled to do since 'one is not bound by a doubtful law'. The demographic evidence is that the proportion that revised their behaviour in the light of *Humanae Vitae* was small. A much larger proportion simply ignored it. From dismissing papal teaching on contraception, it was a small step for people to start questioning teaching on other aspects of sexual morality and for some, on the Church's moral teaching in general. The *'Because I Say So'* school of moral theology was crumbling, because the papacy was less than honest.

By resorting to manipulation and attempting to deceive the faithful, the papacy diminished the very authority it was trying to safeguard. This may not be as big a disaster as at first appears. Unmasking pseudo-infallibilities can only be good for the Church in the long run. Side-tracked by concern for its own needs, the bureaucracy has managed to create a chasm between marital morality as understood by the People of God and as legislated by the papacy. Two, or is it three, *Synods on the Family* have failed to bridge the gap. They might have done better if they had not been restricted in their discussion.

DECEIT

Church authorities are tolerating a continuing deception of the faithful on another profoundly influential element of its teaching on sexual morality. On the authority of a confirmation issued by the Holy Office of the Inquisition on the 4th April 1611[224] Roman Catholics have been taught that every sin against the sixth or ninth commandment is *ipso facto* a mortal sin. For breaches of these commandments, the technical phrase is that 'there can be no parvity of matter'. This was groundless theology then and it is groundless theology now. I have been told by someone in a position to know that nobody at a significant level in moral theology now holds that

---

[224] Uta Ranke-Heinemann, *Eunuchs for the Kingdom,* New York, Penguin Books, paperback, *p*256

there is 'no parvity of matter'[225]. It was taught to all Catholics, however, until the 1970s at least and it has never been rescinded. The papacy may be hoping it will be forgotten. In the meantime, however, dutiful priests are required to apply it in the confessional. It still bedevils high level discussions on access to the Eucharist for divorced and remarried Catholics. It is one of the things that would surely have been dealt with if the rethinking of Moral Theology suggested at Vatican II had been allowed to proceed. The bureaucratic policy in the meantime, is to keep the truth from the faithful.

Pragmatic deceptions

Deceptions and half-truths are tolerated in the bureaucracy. Maintaining the facade of blanket infallibility, makes this practice almost inevitable. Some examples:

1. During Vatican II, Archbishop Hélder Câmera held well-attended press conferences to let journalists know the truth. [226] He could see that the protection of the institution from "disedifying" insights was being used to justify "pious fibs". After the Council, when he had become something of a celebrity, with speaking engagements all over the world, the curia told him, mendaciously, that Pope Paul VI disapproved of his widespread speaking engagements and would prefer if he stayed in his own diocese. He started to cancel forward engagements. When the media guessed that he had been grounded, the curia, with consistent disregard for truth, denied it. They then blocked him from visiting the Pope to clarify the matter. But only for a time. When he finally manoeuvred an appointment to see Paul VI, who was an old friend, he learned that the Pope actually approved his travels and advocacy on behalf of the poor[227]. He knew then that the curia had been lying. Fr David Regan C.S.Sp., who was close to Hélder, describes the scene:

> When ... Hélder went in for what would be his last meeting with Paul, the audience was moving, the Pope not letting go of Hélder's hand as he told him that he had had *saudades* for him (a Portuguese word much used in Brazil, meaning deep and nostalgic longing) ... Paul VI handed Hélder a chalice, saying, "Dom Hélder, I have said Mass using this chalice, and am giving it to you to use during your evangelizing journeys around the world, as a sign that I am with you"—yet another powerful gesture, well in the Montini diplomatic style, and disauthorising so many curial messages ... Paul VI added the heartrending admission: "Dom Hélder, you have become 'the voice of those who have no voice'. Do you know who is the one with least voice in the Church of God at the moment?"

---

[225] I shall not identify my source. It could initiate another silencing. The possibility of 'parvity of matter' in sins against the 6th and 9th commandment is one of the things that can be agreed among theologians but must not be shared with the faithful.

[226] David Regan C.S.Sp., *Why are they poor?- Hélder Câmera in pastoral perspective,* LIT Verlag, Münster, Undated (actually 2003), p 88

[227] *Ibid.* pp 104-5

And, after a dramatic pause, Paul pointed at himself, slowly repeating the gesture twice.

Thus, the top officials are ready to lie about the pope's wishes or decisions and then block the access that could confirm or correct. They can conspire to make a request for confirmation itself look like disaffection. Monarchies and dictatorship are particularly prone to such abuses of power. They should not be a feature of church management. Regrettably, Hélder Câmera's case is not unique.

2. The sex abuse scandals have demonstrated that the abuse of truth, in the form of spin, mental reservations and downright lies, can be tolerated at the highest level in the church administration, if it serves the immediate interests of the papacy. The bureaucracy gives top priority to the protection of its own power, reputation, and personnel. It tries to cover up the contradictions and/or the abject failure of headquarters to practice what it preaches. One might have hoped that for all its homogeneity, a group of dedicated, Christian clergy would rise above such venality and human frailty.

3. The reason given in *Humanae Vitae* for dismissing the advice of the Papal Commission was that their report was not unanimous. This was a deception. They *were* unanimous on the issue that counted. The disagreement was only on the wisdom of sharing this truth with the faithful, which would mean a change of teaching. Four members of the commission, a minority of just 6 per cent, advised against this on the grounds that revealing the truth to the faithful could damage the authority of the papacy![228]

4. In 2010 Pope Benedict XVI addressed a Pastoral Letter to the people of Ireland on the revelations of child sexual abuse by clergy and the cover ups that had gone on for decades. He blamed some of the Irish bishops for failing "at times grievously, to apply the long-established norms of canon law" and wrote that "grave errors of judgement were made, and failures of leadership occurred". Pope Benedict XVI made a grave error of judgement himself by avoiding the acceptance of any blame or failing on the part of the Roman authorities, system, or structure. In particular, he refrained from mentioning that all bishops were bound by their oaths of loyalty to the Pope to maintain pontifical secrecy about all cases of clerical sexual abuse. Rome knew, as far back as 1922 with formal confirmation in 1974, from the number of complaints being handled, that something had to be done about the problem. Instead of doing something about the problem, however, its response had been to bind the bishops of the world to secrecy under pain of excommunication. That meant that they were forbidden from reporting such crimes to the civil

---

[228] The working papers of the Papal commission have been locked away and never been made available for study.

authorities.[229] Benedict was blaming the Irish bishops for following the repeated authoritative instructions from Rome.

Irish people understand that their bishops have been selected and appointed exclusively by Rome for the past century or more and that most of them tend to follow Roman policies and procedures meticulously. Furthermore, Irish people had learned by the time the Pastoral Letter was issued that bishops in several other countries had adhered to the identical procedure; moving the alleged offender to the other end of the diocese and binding the victims and their advocates to silence lest they cause harm to Holy Mother Church. In some instances, they had allowed the alleged perpetrators to move to a foreign diocese without alerting the new bishop to the problem. The similarity in the response indicated that they were following the same instructions from headquarters; the object being to protect the reputation of the institution. While accusing some Irish bishops of cover-up, Pope Benedict was himself attempting to cover up the essential roles played by popes and curial officials over a period of 80 years or more. The obvious absence of any humble admission of wrong-doing, neglect, complicity, or failure on the part of anyone in Rome undermined the authenticity of the letter and the sincerity of the writer. That letter would have been better never written.

The Irish Church has always been loyal to Rome since the time of St Patrick and so the unfairness in the pastoral letter evoked a pained resignation rather than a remonstration or an outcry. Nevertheless, the Pope had insulted the intelligence of the Irish faithful and his authority was weakened when he was seen to be less than honest in allocating blame and proposing remedies.

HYPOCRISY

"Faithful to the example of the Lord Jesus" is a new prescription for Catholic behaviour, dating from 1976. Unexceptionable in itself, it has been used just once; to justify a discriminatory practice. It makes a virtue out of following a distorted example based on a misrepresented verse of scripture. In 1976, after the Pontifical Biblical Commission had been unable to find a New Testament basis for refusing to ordain women the CDF manufactured one. A deliberate misrepresentation of scripture was required to create the example to which they were claiming to be faithful! This is dealt with in detail in chapter 12. Here it is enough to say that it is dishonest to misrepresent scripture and hypocritical to enunciate a principle and then apply it only when it happens to suit your preference or prejudice.

---

[229] This has been changed twice. For a time, they could report the alleged crimes to civil authorities in countries where this is legally required i.e. where failure to do so would provoke sanctions against the bishop or the Church itself. Later (December 2019) Pope Francis removed sex abuse cases from the ambit of Pontifical Secrecy.

The Church would be unrecognisable if the principle were to be applied across the board. We will list some positive examples first. The more amusing negative ones come later. on b

Positive examples that deserve fidelity

1. Jesus celebrated the Eucharist, oth occasions, in the context of a meal, one formal and one informal. The second occasion was within a few days of the first. It was with two people who had apparently given up on him and his message. They had abandoned the community of the disciples and were getting out of Jerusalem. They had rejected the good news of the Resurrection. Yet "they recognised him in the breaking of bread". This implies that they had been present on the earlier occasion, the Last Supper, although they were not apostles. They immediately headed back to find the other disciples, in effect, to rejoin the 'church'. We can learn much from the order of events. Jesus made the first move, going over the scriptures with them as they walked, until their hearts were burning within them. Then they had a meal together and Jesus shared the Eucharist with them. Repentance, faith, and unity *followed*. If we genuinely want to be 'faithful to the example of the Lord Jesus', we should begin by sharing the Word and the Eucharist with 'misguided' fellow Christians instead of finding reasons why not. If sharing the sacrament signifies the unity we are seeking, in time, the sacrament will achieve what it signifies.

2. Jesus was prepared to sacrifice everything, including himself. If we, who claim to be his followers, were faithful to this example the whole world would have been redeemed by now.

3. Jesus generally makes the first move unilaterally; "While we were yet sinners, Christ died for us". His gift of grace comes first. He takes the initiative.

4. When he was celebrating the Eucharist, all those present were invited to share the bread and the cup. Jesus did not make reception conditional on an orthodox understanding of the mystery, on acceptance of the governance of Peter, on marital status in accord with canon law, or even on baptism.

5. In addition to the mere fact of dining together, the sacrament symbolised unity, although individual understanding of what was being done must have been rudimentary and varied at that time. Sharing a cup was, and is, counter cultural. Churchmen of several denominations have been finding reasons to ignore Christ's example and instruction on this point ever since. At one stage, only the ordained could share the cup. Giving it to the laity was officially deemed heretical by Pope Leo X.

6. Jesus accorded women a status above that given by the civil society of his time. Church management today does the opposite.

7. He forgave gratuitously. He was magnanimous. He did not demand a listing of sins in advance or satisfaction (penance) afterwards. (Canossa was a profoundly un-Christlike event.) His approach was to forgive first and reassure, and so draw into love. By making a judicial function out of his gift and limiting it to the profession, church authorities ignored his example but gained immense power over the faithful. Only the clergy could save the sinner from hell and new sins could be defined where real ones were lacking. In contrast to his magnanimity, Rome is remarkably parsimonious about the use of the third rite of penance, general absolution. We have discussed this on page 72.

8. He defined his disciples exclusively in terms of love.

9. He made it clear that 'all the law and the prophets', are dependent on love of God and of neighbour; a relationship that should imbue *every tenet* of Christly Moral Theology.

10. He sent the 72 out to preach and he appointed the Twelve without making the appointments dependent on oaths of fidelity. "Only in freedom can man direct himself toward goodness"[230]. They served in freedom because they loved. Judas clearly prioritised money over love but, in the process, he proved just how free the apostles were.

11. He sent a woman, Mary of Magdala, to announce the Good News of the Resurrection. St Thomas Aquinas was not jesting when he called her[231] the 'apostle to the apostles', but her significance has been eclipsed by fake news, denigrating her as a former prostitute. Recently Pope Francis has made amends by giving her a special feast day Mass in the liturgical calendar.

12. Jesus revealed to the Samaritan woman that he was the Christ. She believed. Leaving her bucket at the well, she hurried back to her town to share the news with her neighbours. She did not know it, but she too was an apostle, she too was sent to preach the good news—although it was among her neighbours rather than as an itinerant preacher.

13. It was in conversation with a woman, Mary of Bethany, that Jesus confirmed for us the promise of resurrection and eternal life, an issue disputed among the Jews until then.

14. He became a man like us, born of a woman, so that he could communicate with us and so that the example of his life would be relevant to ours. In contrast, John Paul II writes: "The sacerdotal ministry in a sense separates bishops and ordained priests from the members of the People of God who

---

[230] Gaudium et Spes, N17

[231] Aquinas is popularly credited with saying this. He may have, but I have not been able to find where he said it.

only share in the general priesthood".[232] To the extent that hierarchs stress their ontological difference (whatever it means), their titles of honour, status, special clothing or their distinctive role at Mass as separating them from the faithful, they are reversing the example of Jesus who "emptied himself" to become one of us.

15. He liked women and valued their company and their contribution to his mission.

Negative examples that might give us thought.

16. He did not distinguish between official and unofficial ministries. "as long as you did it to one of these my least brethren, you did it to me" was addressed to all.

17. Jesus never excommunicated anybody, not even St Thomas who refused to believe in the resurrection, or Peter who denied him thrice, or the two disciples who had given up on him. They were lapsed Christians and, as we have noted, were getting out of Jerusalem having rejected the news of his resurrection.

18. Unlike Pope Benedict XVI, Christ did not employ a butler, nor did he take anyone to court for publishing embarrassing truths.

19. Jesus did not raise a hand or a weapon in self-defence, even though he demonstrated that he could do so at the time of his arrest when "they all went backward and fell down". (John 18:6). He told Peter specifically to sheathe his sword. The early Christians were faithful to that example, many martyrs going serenely and unresisting to their deaths.

20. He never wore red shoes or slippers or a ring as a symbol of office.

21. He never expected anyone to kiss his feet or ring or to wear special clothes in his presence.

22. He never wore a triple tiara although he had grounds for the symbolism; "All power has been given me in heaven and upon earth".

23. Jesus did not ride aloft on a *Sedia Gestatoria,* borne by eight underlings. For his triumphal entry into Jerusalem, he chose a donkey.

24. He did not attempt to coerce those who disagreed with him.

25. He never collaborated in the burning of a heretic.

26. He never raised an army, nor did he guarantee eternal salvation in return for forty days of military service on his behalf.

---

[232]—Karol Wojtyla, *Sources of Renewal, The Implementation of Vatican II,* San Francisco, Harper & Row, 1980, p228, quoted by Ronald Modras in Hans Kung and Leonard Swidler, *The Church in Anguish,* same publishers, 1987. Emphasis added.

27. He never absolved from an oath, although he disapproved of oaths and vows in general.

28. He never ordained a priest, male or female.

29. He never described or treated people of homosexual orientation as being intrinsically disordered.

30. He never abducted a Jewish child because of an alleged secret baptism.

31.He did not make the ministry of the apostles' conditional on celibacy or vows of chastity.

32. He never ranked virginity over marriage. He said remarkably little about sex or gender.

33. He was never deceptive although often necessarily obscure.

34. He did not condemn the Samaritan woman who had had four husbands and was then living with a man who was not her husband. Instead, he promised her living water, an obscure prediction of the Eucharist.

35. He did not condemn the woman taken in adultery but saved her from those who were invoking the law to kill her.

36. He was not ambitious for political or temporal power.

37. He never incited his followers to kill anyone, much less their civil ruler.

38. He did not claim to be infallible, although he could have.

This list illustrates the hypocrisy of making 'fidelity to the example of the Lord Jesus' into a virtue for one selected issue; particularly an issue on which prejudice had already been amply demonstrated. It is especially hypocritical to parade this as 'fidelity' while making it impossible for many communities to keep Christ's clearly expressed commandment, "Do This", with appropriate frequency.

We have noted earlier that one of the few things that evokes condemnation from Jesus is religious hypocrisy. The above list demonstrates, however, that 'fidelity to the example of the Lord Jesus' has not always been a guiding priority among the leaders of the Roman Catholic Church. It was presented as a virtue in 1976 when no honest scriptural or theological grounds could be found to justify a long-established discrimination against the ordination women. To make it relevant even then, scripture had to be artfully misrepresented to create the 'example' to be followed. (See Chap. 12). The accompanying expression of sadness at encountering this "grave new obstacle" on the path of reconciliation was doubly hypocritical. Firstly, it tried to shift the blame onto the Anglicans even though the obstacle was being created by the Roman refusal to consider women's ordination as being "within a diversity of legitimate traditions". Secondly, the new obstacle was more likely to bring joy than sadness to the bureaucracy whose hegemony would be threatened by ecumenism.

Hypocrisy degenerated into mendacity in 1994 when the curia prepared the Apostolic Letter which tried to make a doctrine out of the same issue on the authority of the pope and the bishops. The reference to the bishops was a lie. They had not been consulted. The lie was challenged and removed just before publication. At the time, the loyalty oath prevented the bishops from discussing the new doctrine and 'pontifical secrecy' kept the faithful in the dark about the attempt to deceive them. Hypocrisy, apparently, knows no bounds; curial officers were prepared to *lie* in an Apostolic Letter so that a questionable teaching could be passed off as *irreformable*. Despite the hypocrisy, or perhaps because they sense it, the faithful have rejected the doctrine and continue, overwhelmingly, to believe that women can, and should, be priests.

Bishops' Conferences

Contradicting the value accorded to them by Vatican II, the CDF denies that Episcopal Conferences have any authority, on the grounds of protecting the divinely willed authority of the bishop in his own diocese. Since Vatican I, however, the papacy has not hesitated to enhance its own power by appropriating and overriding the same authority of the individual bishop. The bureaucratic principle underlies the hypocrisy; alternative power centres must be controlled or eliminated. The curia can always bully the dispersed bishops individually but fears them in uncontrolled groups.

SHODDY SCHOLARSHIP

Pseudo-infallible authority makes genuine scholarly search for truth difficult if not impossible. Later we will see how the CDF let its Prefect use an irrelevant footnote to lend spurious authority to a statement ruling out women's ordination. and how a verse from the gospel was misrepresented in one magisterial document and truncated in another in an effort to justify the same denial.

In Chapter 16 we discuss *Ut Unum Sint.* The original draft of this encyclical on Christian Unity was done by a leading ecumenical theologian, Fr. J.M. Tillard. In its final form it establishes beyond all doubt that the present disunity is contrary to the will of Christ. It admitted that the papacy is the gravest obstacle to ecumenism but goes on to lay down conditions that make that obstacle as permanent as possible.

In Chapter 13 we will see how, in a similar way, the papal encyclical, *Veritatis Splendor,* gives the impression of building on *Gaudium et Spes* by referencing it in a multiplicity of footnotes. However, while the footnotes generally relate to similar subject matter, the drift of the argument is frequently in the opposite direction. Overall, and at tedious length, *Veritatis Splendor* tries to elevate 'law and precept' over the primacy of conscience which is a key teaching in *Gaudium et Spes.* It surreptitiously reverses one of the remarkable re-discoveries of Vatican II.

Own goals

Pride, we are told is the greatest of the seven deadly sins. So papal insistence on its own inerrancy and infallibility would be clearly immoral were it not for the theory that the successors of Peter always have divine assistance and the pious assumption that the papacy always listens. Not everyone who shares the theory shares the assumption.

We have noted above how the treatment of dissenting theologians, has frequently backfired and given their ideas more publicity. Unfortunately, the reputation of Rome for injustice generally suffers from the publicity.

The 2008 visitation of the Leadership Conference of Women Religious was an attack on the American nuns who have tended to avoid condemnations and chosen instead to be true disciples, caring for the marginalised in a non-judgemental way and ministering to the needy. It reflected badly on Roman leadership. In scale, in dedication and in quality, the work of the nuns is the outstanding tangible evidence of Christ's love in the USA today. The nuns maintained their patience and dignity throughout the ordeal until Pope Francis quietly put an end to it.

Among these sisters are many highly educated and qualified women, committed to a better understanding of the faith, the world, and their vocation. The Vatican seems chronically short of scholars who can engage with them at their own level.

Together, the persecution of theologians and the 'visitation' of the American nuns can only discourage new recruitment to the profession and the convents. How does the papacy expect the Church of the future to fulfil its mission without courageous theologians and unselfish nuns?

Two common elements underly these own goals. The bureaucracy has forgotten that Christianity is a way of living characterised by active loving care for others. It has focused instead on policing a set of rules and propositions of which several support its own position of authority and some are indefensible. It ignores the Council teaching on the hierarchy of truths. It acts as if the truths of the faith depend on the teaching authority and any disagreement, however trivial, is a challenge to the authority itself. Accordingly, they must guard against any new ideas or understanding. Even a minor correction might threaten the fiction that the papacy has never erred and can never err. Pride in this fiction underpinned Pope Leo X's condemnation of Martin Luther's writings[233] in 1520 and led to widespread excommunications. It turned a good theologian's well-grounded call for reform into a division that has lasted 500 years.

---

[233] Encyclical of Pope Leo X, *Exsurge Domine,* 1520. This supports the fiction of inerrancy by appealing to Matthew 28:20 "I will be with you to the consummation of the world". This Promise would be meaningless if Jesus were to allow the People of God to go significantly astray in understanding his revelation for a significant period. It is an extravagant interpretation, however, for the encyclical to claim that it means Church management cannot be wrong on any detail at a given point in time. Ironically, it is now apparent that the encyclical disproved its own contention by being categorically wrong on at least two points. It condemned as heretical two teachings which are now accepted by the universal church: heretics should not be burnt (Item 16) and the faithful may be permitted to communicate under both species (Art 33).

In drafting the definition of conditional papal infallibility at Vatican I, Cardinal Cullen was careful not to include inerrancy. The widespread application of pseudo-infallibility, however, has re-introduced the idea at an operational level since then.

COERCION

The CDF, as successor of the Inquisition, still resorts routinely to coercion of one kind or another, to silence any member of the clergy who dares to question dubious doctrines or to share with the faithful the uncertainties admitted among theologians. Even the admission of inconvenient historical facts can provoke such reactions. This attempt to block the search for truth, to stifle the *sensus fidelium,* betrays a practical and deplorable lack of trust in the Holy Spirit. The most un-Christ-like actions are used to defend dubious doctrines, and to protect authority against those who dare to disagree or seek reform, no matter how cogent the argument or how indisputable the scholarship.

This extraordinary justification of means by reference to ends reached its height in the Inquisition and some of it is still with us in the Congregation for the Doctrine of the Faith, after two changes of name. It is beyond the scope of this or any one book to deal with the slaughter of alleged heretics and witches. Even today, the merciless treatment given to priests and theologians who refuse to profess what they do not believe, is a virtual martyrdom suffered at the hands of fellow Christians. They pay dearly for their integrity.

Coercion is the necessary guardian of pseudo-infallibility.

Apart altogether from the immorality, sooner or later the staff of the CDF will wake up to the futility of their methods in this age of instant communication. By turning honest theologians into celebrity victims of rank injustice, and by excluding them from the official teaching structures of the church rather than correcting them by reasoned argument, the curial authorities have often gifted them with notoriety, enhanced their reputations and broadened their following, inside and outside of Roman Catholicism. This has encouraged learned Catholic theologians to take up employment in non-Catholic institutions; allowing them to write in freedom and to bring reasoned theology to a greatly increased audience. The net effect has been to reduce confidence in the Roman magisterium while improving theology in other denominations.

Chapter 11

Authority over the sacraments

"The sacrament is not wrought by the righteousness of the celebrant or the recipient, but by the power of God"

— St Thomas Aquinas, *S.T., III, 60, 3.*

THE COUNCIL OF TRENT

The Council of Trent settled the number of sacraments at seven, noting that in excellence the Eucharist is above the rest. It taught that the Church has authority in relation to them provided the substance is not changed.

> "In the Church there has always existed this power, that in the administration of the sacraments, provided that their substance remains unaltered, she can lay down or modify what she considers more fitting either for the benefit of those who receive them or for respect towards those same sacraments, according to varying circumstances, times or places"[234]

Authority as exercised in the past.

Taking the most important sacrament as an example, we find the authorities have been ready to initiate or tolerate a remarkable variety of changes in its celebration since apostolic times.

1. Christ gave us the liturgy of the Eucharist in the fellowship of the Passover meal. He repeated it when he dined casually with two travelling companions at the inn at Emmaus, thus indicating that he did not intend it to be an annual affair. Early Christians celebrated it weekly, on the Lord's day. In later practice, the Eucharist was separated from the *agape* meal and thus lost most of its social value; the bonding and mutual strengthening in the faith, the learning from one another, the absorption of tradition, etc. The *agape* meal on its own lacked its essential liturgical and religious focus. In time it was forgotten. Since then the Eucharist has always been celebrated separately.

2. Holy Communion was long considered a reward for those deemed sufficiently righteous; the judgement often being made by their confessors. Approaching the altar thus developed implications of moral superiority. Humble people stayed at the back of the church … with the 'tax collector and sinners'.

3. The habit of reception by the faithful of Holy Communion was discouraged in the first millennium to the point where, by 1215, it became necessary to introduce an *obligation* to receive once a year.

---

[234] The Council of Trent, Session 21, chap. 2: Denzinger-Schönmetzer, *Enchiridion Symbolorum* 1728.

139

4. A social event in the evening where brothers and sisters in Christ broke bread together in the context of a memorial meal, was changed to a morning obligation for individuals to attend, where conversation and social intercourse were frowned upon. Reception of the sacrament became a relatively hurried morning event –conditional on fasting from the previous midnight. After many centuries, the fast was shortened to one nominal hour.

5. After individual men were ordained as priests, the priesthood of the community was quietly forgotten for 1500 years. On being rediscovered at the Second Vatican Council, its exercise was negated by the continued legislation allowing only an ordained priest to celebrate,[235] with no provision for substitution in case of need. This is Church discipline, not a divine commandment. In relation to the liturgy, the Council agreed on "the primary principle of enabling the faithful to participate intelligently, actively, and easily".[236] Yet the laity and deacons are *forbidden* to say the Eucharistic prayers along with the priest or to make the gestures *proper* to him.[237] Is there some anxiety that, by saying the prayers together, they might begin to see themselves as a priestly people again? They might begin to realise that the sacrament is wrought by the power of God' rather than that of the priest. The faithful are still encouraged, however, to join in the prayer with an assenting and affirmative "Amen" at the end.

6. The limitation to ordained, celibate, priests inevitably led to larger and larger gatherings where the intimacy in which the faith is caught was further diluted.

7. The gathering around the table was changed. The table became an altar, as among the Jews and Roman pagans of the time. Only the celebrant is at this table and he is isolated and elevated by a specified number of steps. with the 'laity' banned from the sanctuary, *i.e.* the area immediately around the table.

8. An ornate barrier to prevent trespass by the un-ordained became standard church furniture until the late twentieth century.

9. In the early church the Lord's Supper was not an obligation. It was a gathering of people who believed in Jesus and came together to commemorate and give thanks for his life and sacrifice. This dimension has been almost completely lost. It is now necessary to remind Catholics that the word Eucharist derives from the Greek word for thanksgiving.

10. From the thirteenth century, obligatory celibacy was imposed on celebrants and this limitation persists today (with exceptions, of course, for Evangelical and Anglican converts and priests in many of the Eastern Catholic Churches) although there is no natural or sacramental logic and there is an acute shortage of priests. Worship of the tradition of celibacy is the only explanation.

---

[235] Canon 900
[236] *Sacrosanctum Concilium,* §79
[237] Canon 907

11. The symbolic 'breaking of bread' which gave its name to the ceremony for generations, has been reduced to a token 'fraction' of one large wafer in the Mass. The significance of this is not understood by the congregation. It has never been explained to the congregation in my lifetime experience of attending Mass and listening to homilies.

12. The sharing of the cup with all who are present, an important and counter-cultural symbol of unity, which Jesus enjoined on his followers, has by times been denied them entirely, omitted, ignored and declared heretical by a pope who claimed he could not err.[238] It is currently tolerated in limited circumstances.[239]

13. For several centuries, some churches used water where we now use wine. They were not considered heretics at that time.[240] Wine is considered essential today. An exception is allowed for priests who are recovering alcoholics. They are permitted to use unfermented grape juice, called *mustum*. Conveniently, this is not deemed to be part of the 'substance' or to invalidate the sacrament.

14. The reception of Holy Communion was restricted to those who had reached ten, twelve or fourteen years of age and who had been confirmed. This was changed[241] to 'about seven' and allowed to precede confirmation.

15. If the priest at Mass were really playing the role of Christ, he would be sharing the table with his friends having washed their feet or whatever would be the equivalent humble service today. The washing of feet is now omitted, except for a token gesture of remembrance once a year. The rule until quite recently was that only male feet could be washed.

16. The loaf, which was of such symbolic importance to St Paul, was replaced by the more convenient wafer. Provided it is not gluten free, (it must have 20 ppm) it is canonically valid. It has no natural resemblance to bread. As a representative symbol or icon, a female person, made in the image of God, has a much greater resemblance to Jesus Christ than the wafer has to a loaf of bread.

17. The faithful had to receive Holy Communion on the tongue. Letting unworthy, un-consecrated, hands touch the host or the sacred vessels without a dispensation is no longer considered to be a sin.

18. When I was an altar server the reception of Holy Communion more than once in a day was forbidden even if you served Mass two or three times. Now, full participation is seen as including reception and is encouraged for anyone attending additional Masses.

---

[238] Pope Leo X, *Exsurge Domine,* Rome, 1520, Condemnation No 16.

[239] In the distant past, infants who were too small to manage the host, were given the sacrament under the species of wine only.

[240] Thomas O'Loughlin, writing in *The Furrow.*

[241] Encyclical Letter, Pius X, *Quam Singulari,* August 1910

19. Prior to Vatican II, concelebration was restricted to Ordination Masses. At parish level it was virtually unknown, except at High Mass where the Celebrant was assisted by a Deacon and Sub-deacon (usually priests playing the subordinate roles). Concelebration is now approved.

20. The 1988 *Directory for the Sunday Celebration in the Absence of a Priest* recommends a kind of pseudo-eucharist in which consecrated hosts are imported from another parish. This was already happening in the Netherlands at that time. Edward Schillebeeckx describes it as a trivialisation of the eucharist. It is certainly not what Jesus told us to do. It is, however, recommended in the circumstances by the Congregation for Divine Worship. The alternative would have required the leadership of the profession to decide to share their distinguishing prerogative with outsiders. Not the sort of unselfish gesture that one can expect from a bureaucracy, particularly a homogeneous one, as discussed in Chapter 1.

No longer a social gathering

Unfortunately, the first ten of the above changes had the cumulative effect of changing the Lord's Supper from an attractive social celebration into an obligation for individual Catholics under pain of mortal sin and eternal damnation. This was a significant loss with immeasurable downstream effects.

> "We experience and demonstrate the love of God in a community, the people of God, which is the source of our encounter with God; and it is in the context of the community that we encounter the neighbour we are called upon to love as well, either as someone inside or outside the community".[242]

All these significant changes, which the Church was able to adopt without specific divine authorisation, make nonsense of the teaching introduced in 1994 that "the Church has no authority whatsoever to confer priestly ordination on women". We have noted earlier that popes have claimed that the instruction, "feed my lambs and my sheep", applies very specifically to themselves as successors of St Peter and can be interpreted as giving them 'universal jurisdiction' over all the faithful. But before that authority can be derived from the instruction, a duty and responsibility must be admitted: to do whatever is necessary to ensure that the sheep get fed at appropriate intervals. The Church tradition is that Christians should celebrate the Lord's Supper weekly on the Lord's Day. By their own claims as successors of Peter, popes have an immediate personal duty to make this happen. They have a parallel responsibility, therefore, to use that universal jurisdiction and plenitude of power to abolish any rule or practice that make it impossible, or unnecessarily difficult, regardless of any opposition and whatever the cost.

---

[242] Joseph A. Selling in Joseph A. Selling and Jan Jans (Eds), *Splendor of Accuracy,* William B Eerdmans, Michigan ,1995, P. 55

Even if the papacy were to bring itself to change the rules about eligibility for ordination, however, it would be decades before the numbers of priests would be available to provide the sacraments to all who are entitled to them. Famine demands immediate action. As a matter of urgency and obedience, therefore, Canon Law should be changed to allow any congregation that normally lacks the services of a priest to say mass together as a community, just as the early Christians did for the first three or four hundred years. The Community Mass could give way to a personally celebrated Mass whenever an ordained priest or bishop would come to visit and preach.

After seventy or a hundred years of a spreading Eucharistic famine, the authorities should ask themselves where they got the authority for a blanket refusal of ordination to women who make up more than half the members of the Church. The next chapter examines how this prejudiced practice of long standing was elevated into a pseudo-infallible teaching.

Chapter 12

The priestly ordination of women

The Roman Pontiff and the bishops, in view of their office and of the importance of the matter, strive painstakingly and by appropriate means to enquire properly into that revelation and to give apt expression to its contents. But they do not allow that there could be any new revelation pertaining to the divine deposit of faith.

—Lumen Gentium § 25.

CAREFUL READING PRESUPPOSES CAREFUL WRITING.

The current teaching on the issue of women's ordination as set out in the Apostolic Letter of John Paul II, *Ordinatio Sacerdotalis,* in 1994 is probably the most clearly documented example of pseudo-infallibility to date. It is also an example of remarkably weak scholarship. It seems, however, to be shaping up as a possible example of how the *sensus fidelium* can discern prejudice and error and reject both,[243] although this is a process that normally takes a long time.

When asked whether the denial of ordination to women would last forever, Pope Francis has supported the negative attitude by referring to this Apostolic Letter. He did not say it was infallible but was reported (2 November 2016) as saying that we should read it carefully: "it goes in that direction". The Letter, however, does not withstand the 'careful reading' he recommended.[244] Whatever its direction, it does not bring the careful reader with it.

The saint was ill-served by those who drafted it for him. It depends heavily on an earlier Declaration (1976) on the same subject from the Congregation for the Doctrine of the Faith (hereinafter CDF) entitled *Inter Insigniores.* It recites the signs of the times only to dismiss them, displaying faulty logic and truncating a verse of scripture to suit its thesis. It introduces a new doctrine in an effort to maintain a discredited practice. It has been falsely described as infallible.[245] Both documents treat of the subject of women's ordination without any reference to the institution of the Eucharist or

---

[243] Cf. International Theological Commission, *Sensus fidei in the life of the Church (2014)* §2, http://www.vatican.va/roman_curia/congregations/cfaith/cti_documents/rc

[244] I am interpreting the Pope's suggestion that we read it carefully as an easing of the disapproval of further public discussion by Catholics that is implicit in the Apostolic Letter, *Ordinatio Sacerdotalis.* Moreover, the publication of an article on the subject in *Osservatore Romano* (29/5/2018) by the Prefect of the CDF appears to have re-opened the subject for discussion.

[245] The Congregation for the Doctrine of the Faith, affirms that it is part of the deposit of faith in *Responsum ad Propositum Dubium,* October 1995. Moreover, Pope Benedict XVI, at the Chrism Mass on 5th April 2012, asserted that it had been "declared in an irrevocable manner".

of the sacrament of Order itself, while giving scant attention to the greatest command-ment on which depend all the law and the prophets.

In the interval between the Declaration and the Apostolic Letter there was a lively debate, with new arguments supporting the ban being produced by the curia as each one was refuted. As one respected conservative ordained Irish theologian observed in my presence,[246] "they all proved bankrupt".

The discussion had been going on since April 1971 when a meeting in Canada between 65 bishops and 60 women had called (with one dissenting vote) for the up-coming Synod in Rome to strike out all the Canon Law discrimination against women and approve the ordination of suitable women in the future. The Synod responded by calling for a profound study of the issue of women's place in the Church by a mixed commission of men and women, religious and lay. Eighteen months later, the curia set up such a commission, but issued a secret letter commanding that the ordination of women was not to be discussed! The secret leaked out, of course, revealing the determination within the curia to stifle the *sensus fidelium* on the issue.

We need not rehearse the detailed arguments here. The Pontifical Biblical Com-mission searched the New Testament at the request of Pope Paul VI and could find nothing to prevent the ordination of women. Fr Eric Doyle O.F.M. dealt with all the main issues when he presented a paper on the state of the question in the Roman Catholic Church at a meeting of the Anglican Roman Catholic International Commis-sion (ARCIC) in Assisi (10-14 Nov. 1975). He had been selected to prepare the paper by the Vatican Secretariat for the Promotion of Christian Unity. The finding of his dispassionate and scholarly review [247] was clear. There was no theological objection to the ordination of women.

The strongest theological argument against change had been that the priest in offering Mass acts *in persona Christi* and symbolises Christ and that a female cannot be a satisfactory symbol for Christ since he was a man. This argument requires a strong emphasis on Christ's maleness whereas the important thing about the Incarnation is that God became one of us, a human being. Fr Doyle, however, refuted this argument decisively by pointing to the generally accepted principle that all the sacra-ments are the work of Christ and that the minister of a sacrament always acts *in persona Christi*. Husbands and wives administer the sacrament of matrimony to one another and lay men and women can baptise. Therefore, females can act and have acted *in persona Christi*. The natural resemblance required for a symbol does not demand a physical likeness.

Fr Doyle carried too much weight as a theologian and a media personality to be ignored even when dead and the ARCIC meeting at Assisi was too important to be forgotten. When Msgr. Desmond Connell, Professor of Metaphysics at University

---

[246] He shall remain anonymous.

[247] The essence of his paper can be found in Eric Daly O.F.M. 'The Question of Women Priests and the Argument *In Persona Christi*', in *The Irish Theological Quarterly,* vol. 50, (1983-84).

College, Dublin read a paper on 'Women Priests' to the Canon Law Society of Great Britain and Ireland. on 21st May 1976, he attempted to undermine Fr Doyle's conclusions, referencing his work several times. In a footnote he even faulted Fr Doyle for failing to 'appreciate the ambiguity in the phrase *in persona Christi'*. In contrast, his paper, creates the ambiguity and exploits it to find a new reason for denying ordination to women. For all its weakness, his paper seems to have met with approval in Rome. The following year Msgr. Connell was named as the new Archbishop of Dublin. The paper was published in *Briefing*, a periodical that circulates among members of the Bishops Conference of England and Wales and which, regrettably, is not subject to peer review. [248]

Msgr. Connell's reasoning, in over 6,000 words, is difficult to summarise because he is not above equivocation, a classical error of reasoning where the meaning of a word or phrase changes within the argument. Relying on the Latin phrase *in persona Christi,* he allows that a woman acts *in the person of Christ* for marriage and baptism but for the Eucharist he translates the same Latin phrase differently. It is now: *in the person of Christ, the head and shepherd of the Church.* He contends that symbolising this is beyond a woman … and is even beyond the Church itself. Although the Church is one with Christ, apparently this does not include his functions as "head and shepherd". While the Church is identified with Christ at an earlier point in the argument, here Christ transcends it "in an order of priority" and the Church must transcend itself to offer the sacrifice. It does this by creating "the sacramental identification between the ordained priest and Christ".

He contends that a priest is symbolically configured more closely to Christ than is the Church itself because it does not include "the head and shepherd". Here he is equivocating between the Church as the Mystical Body of Christ and as the visible organisation which does not include its head. But the priest, he contends, symbolises Christ fully. "The ordained priesthood has a sublime excellence". Here, he is carrying the exaltation of the profession he shared to an extraordinary level.

If, however, the sacrament of ordination has this wondrous power for a man, surely it could work equally for a woman. Msgr. Connell does not think so:

> "The reason why a woman cannot be ordained has essentially to do with that priority, which enters into the symbolism, the sacramental mode of significance, of the eucharist".

If this means anything, it means that the papal teaching that a female cannot symbolise Christ simply because he is a male has been abandoned, but replaced by saying that she still cannot celebrate the Eucharist because she cannot symbolise Christ in his capacity as head and shepherd. But surely, it is the redemptive life of Christ and his sacrifice that we commemorate in the Mass not his capacity as head of his own

---

[248] *Briefing*, Vol 18, No13, 24 June 1988. It is not widely available. My copy was a gift from a friendly theologian.

body. Moreover, this argument is still fatally dependent on the presumed lack of eminence of womankind.

Msgr. Connell maintains that the Church itself is inadequate to offer Christ's sacrifice symbolically in the Mass because it does not include "the head and shepherd". It must transcend itself by ordaining the priest who is thus so configured to Christ that he can truly say "this is my body" and "this is my blood". Here he is equivocating again, this time on the extent to which the earthly church can be identified with Christ.

Five difficulties arise:

1. In theorising that the Church must transcend itself, Msgr. Connell seems to be confusing the Mystical Body of Christ with the visible organisation.

2. The implication is that, while ordination creates a "sacramental identification between the ordained priest and Christ" it would not have the same effect with a woman. This implication begs the question—another classic logical fallacy. Moreover, the idea that the sacramental symbolism works for a man and not for a woman seems to be confusing symbolism with reality or confusing the sacramental with the biological.

3. When the priest says "this is my body" in the Latin Rite Mass, he is not referring to himself but is narrating part of what Jesus said and did at the Last Supper. Moreover, we do not know at what point in the ceremony the transformation takes place. There is an opinion among theologians that it takes place earlier, when the priest invokes a blessing on the offerings and prays that they "may become for us the Body and Blood of your most beloved Son, our Lord Jesus Christ". In the Latin Mass, this prayer immediately precedes the Last Supper narrative.[249]

4. The contention that the Church must 'transcend itself' to offer Mass contradicts the institution narrative and ignores Christ's mandate, "Do This", which conveyed a duty, a right, and the necessary authorisation without any conditions. In avoiding any detailed reference to the institution of the Eucharist or the origins of ordination for priests of any sex, Msgr. Connell was following the strategy of the CDF in *Inter Insigniores* and of Pope John Paul II in *Ordinatio Sacerdotalis*. Evidently the area is too treacherous for exploration.

5. The contention that the Church must "transcend itself in the ordained priest" if it is to celebrate the Eucharist must be erroneous. It would invalidate the celebration of the Lord's Supper and Holy Communion for the first few hundred years in the life of the Church, before individual ordained priests were introduced.

---

[249] The Anaphora of Addai and Mari, the rite traditional in the Assyrian Church of the East does not contain the words of consecration, "This is my body" and "This is my blood" at all, but it is accepted by the Holy See as a genuine celebration of the Eucharist.

New teaching for old.

The papacy had to fall back on raw authority when their reasoning had failed to justify a long-standing discrimination. And they overstrained that authority when they claimed that the exclusion of women because they are not men is not discrimination on the grounds of sex when, in the ordinary meaning of the words, and in the palpable attitudes and actions of Church authorities, that is exactly what it is[250].

In Catholicism, since 1870, a new doctrine or the reinterpretation of an old one must either stand on infallibility or on its cogency. In either case it is ultimately dependent on its reception by the faithful. "The body of the faithful as a whole, anointed as they are by the Holy One (cf. Jn. 20:20,27) cannot err in matters of belief" (LG §12).

The Apostolic Letter was occasioned by the manifest failure of the faithful, including many pastors and theologians, to 'receive' the views of the earlier Declaration which had been issued in 1976 with the approval of Pope Paul VI. It had concluded:

> " … the Sacred Congregation for the Doctrine of the Faith judges it necessary to recall that the Church, in fidelity to the example of the Lord, does not consider herself authorized to admit women to priestly ordination".

This was a statement of fact that left open the possibility that a later administration might take a different view, as did those who were rejecting the document. For instance, they might give priority to Christ's Eucharistic command, "Do This" over 'fidelity to the example' of something he did not do on a specific occasion. Or they might judge that while women from the fourth to thirteenth century were considered lacking in the status, education, or 'eminence' appropriate to the exalted dignity of priest or bishop, the twentieth century church could not take these alleged deficiencies seriously.

Finally, they might rely on the principle that a mandate to do something implies authority to do whatever seems conducive to achieving it, short of breaking the law. The Church accepts this principle.[251] It also accepts that it has insufficient ordained celibate males to discharge the mandate with the appropriate frequency now and into the foreseeable future. It therefore has, not only the authority, but *the duty* to find, train and authorise enough other people to fulfil the mandate. If that requires ordination, then the Church has the necessary authority to ordain other people. If the management cannot bring itself to allow the bishops to ordain enough people, then it has *a*

---

[250] In the 13th century, St Thomas Aquinas wrote without apology: "Accordingly, since it is not possible in the female sex to signify eminence of degree, for a woman is in the state of subjection, it follows that she cannot receive the sacrament of Order . . ." (Summa Theologica Suppl. qu. 39 art. 1.). In the 21st Century, at the 2018 Synod in Rome, unordained male heads of religious orders were permitted to vote while female heads were denied. What was this except discrimination on the grounds of sex?

[251] This principle is recognised in Canon Law.§138: "Ordinary executive power and power delegated for all cases are to be interpreted widely; any other power is to be interpreted strictly. *Delegation of power to a person is understood to include everything necessary for the exercise of that power.* (Emphasis added)

duty to scrap the regulation that limits celebration to the ordained which is preventing the mandate from being fulfilled.

Despite losing the debate for 18 years, the papacy was still implacably against ordaining women. In his Apostolic Letter, Pope John Paul II formulated a new doctrine which, if it were to be received by the faithful, would transfer the issue from the arena of rational discussion into the realm of the divinely revealed eternal plan, thereby tying the hands of future popes. Providentially and demonstrably, the new doctrine has not been received. It reads:

> "Wherefore, in order that all doubt may be removed regarding a matter of great importance, a matter which pertains to the Church's divine constitution itself, in virtue of my ministry of confirming the brethren (cf. Luke 22:32), I declare that the Church has no authority whatsoever to confer priestly ordination on women and that this judgment is to be definitively held by all the Church's faithful".

It is right to refer to this as a new doctrine. It cannot be described as a development of the earlier position. There is a theological chasm between the two. One is a statement of fact about the people in authority in the Church at a given time. They did not feel that their authority stretched to the ordination of women. The second is an attempt to force a new doctrine on the faithful who wish to stay in full communion with Rome. It is a 'judgement … to be held definitively'. It does not concern faith or morals and does not seem necessary for salvation, but it is an unnecessary burden on the conscience of the many Catholics who would wish to remain in full communion but would honestly rate the papal judgement to be a product of misogyny, clericalism, patriarchalism, and prejudice combined with pride in inerrancy and/or the fear of change.

Furthermore, if divine Revelation did in fact leave the church with "no authority whatsoever" in this regard, how come the doctrinal experts of the CDF were unaware of such a convenient limitation in 1976 when they were charged with finding arguments to support Pope Paul's rejection of women's ordination, as expressed in his letter to Dr Donald Coggan, Archbishop of Canterbury, of 30th November 1975?[252] If it was a doctrine "already possessed by the Church", it would have suited their assignment exactly. How could they have overlooked it? They did not advert to it because it did not exist. If the experts could not find it in the deposit of faith in 1976, how could it be there in 1994? Manifestly, we are dealing here with a new doctrine, although it relates to a very long-established exclusion.

---

[252] In a further exchange of letters, Dr Coggan (10/2/1976) suggested that the desired Church unity could be "manifested within a diversity of legitimate traditions". The Pope 23/3/1976) did not accept this, (although, for example, Rome considers the married priesthood in Eastern Churches to be a legitimate diversity) and mentioned "the measure of the sadness with which we encounter so grave a new obstacle and threat on that path" [to unity]. The correspondence can be read at http://www.womenpriests.org/church/cant1.asp

Is it infallible?

The first thing to note is that the Letter is not an exercise of papal infallibility although Pope Francis seems to be treating it as currently beyond re-assessment. The teaching fails all three requirements as defined by Vatican I:

1. The Pope was not addressing the universal church, but Catholics through their bishops.
2. It is not a matter of faith or morals.
3. It was not declared *ex cathedra*. It did not include a claim to be infallible.

Furthermore, it goes beyond the boundaries of infallible teaching as set down by Vatican II:

> This infallibility with which the divine Redeemer willed His Church to be endowed in defining a doctrine of faith and morals extends as far as extends the deposit of divine revelation, which must be religiously guarded and faithfully expounded (LG §25).

The responsibility of guarding the deposit of revelation must surely demand that the faithful resist accretions as firmly as reductions. Intelligent Catholics have a duty to look critically at novelties, whatever the source and to openly 'receive' (accept and believe) or reject what they find. The failure of a substantial proportion of Catholics, and virtually all Christians of other denominations to receive this doctrine has been so obvious and widespread, despite attempts to stifle discussion, that the curia has been trying to find ways to classify it as infallible ever since. A subsequent assertion that something is infallible does not make it so. There has been a succession of such claims starting with one from the CDF[253] which appeared the following year. This was followed by a letter from the Prefect, Cardinal Joseph Ratzinger[254] in which he writes "In this case, an act of the ordinary Papal Magisterium, in itself not infallible, witnesses to the infallibility of the teaching of a doctrine already possessed by the Church". Here he is proposing a new formula for making a papal teaching infallible whenever a pope declines, or is unable, to meet the conditions laid down by Vatican I. A pope just witnesses, fallibly, to the fact that the doctrine has always been there, infallibly! *Quod Erat Demonstrandum*. It's a wonder nobody thought of that one before. It would have saved the bother of having all those Ecumenical Councils!

Here the Cardinal is telling us that the Pope, in exercising his responsibility of confirming the brethren, is telling us, non-infallibly, that the Church has always possessed this doctrine infallibly. There are several difficulties in all this. First, there is reason to believe that the Pope might have been wrong in the fallible statement; the studies he was relying on are faulty if not dishonest, as we demonstrate later in this chapter. Second, he was not confirming the brethren in their opinions; the curia was

---

[253] The CDF should know this, so they were being either deceitful or culpably ignorant. Let us call it disingenuous.

[254] Joseph Cardinal Ratzinger, Prefect, Congregation for the Doctrine of the Faith, *Concerning the CDF Reply* Regarding Ordinatio Sacerdotalis, 28 October 1995.

determined not to consult the bishops or the faithful at large. The document had been drafted in secret, forestalling any uninvited observations. Third, it is simply not credible that a teaching "already possessed by the Church" could have been overlooked in the research by the CDF prior to issuing *Inter Insigniores*, a magisterial document of 6,500 words in 1976.

When he became Pope Benedict XVI, Joseph Ratzinger acquired the legal authority to review his predecessors' work and make a formal statement that would fulfil the infallibility criteria of Vatican I but he was unwilling or unable to do so. Towards the end of his pontificate, however, at the Chrism Mass on 5th April 2012, he was still promoting the teaching of *Ordinatio Sacerdotalis,* as if it were infallible,[255] although he avoided using the word, asserting instead that it had been "declared in an irrevocable manner".

Beating the drum

Neither of the two magisterial documents succeeded in settling the issue. Popes have continued to repeat the teaching at intervals responding in various ways to the challenges.

On the 15th August 1988 Pope John Paul II published his Apostolic Letter, *Dignitatis Mulieris,* on the dignity of women. In §26 he repeated the ideas of *Inter Insigniores* and added an argument based on the supposedly limited attendance at the Last Supper. We will revert to this below.

John Paul II repeated the teaching of *Inter Insigniores* again as part of his Apostolic Exhortation after the Synod on the Laity (1988), although discussion of women's ordination had been banned during the Synod itself.

> "In her participation in the life and mission of the Church a woman cannot receive the Sacrament of Orders, and therefore, cannot fulfil the proper function of the ministerial priesthood. This is a practice that the Church has always found in the expressed will of Christ, totally free and sovereign, who called only men to be his apostles".

Note that he relies here on the *practice* of the Church. It would be a further six years before he would expound a supporting doctrine which Cardinal Ratzinger would have Catholics believe, was always "possessed" by the Church as part of the deposit of faith transmitted to us by the apostles … even though the apostles never ordained a priest, male or female. Note also the phrase *"expressed will of Christ".* This is nonsense. His will on the matter is merely implied, as we shall see below, from a misrepresentation of St Mark's account of the appointment of the apostles.

Christ could not have expressed a view on ordination at that time. The apostles were being appointed to be sent out to preach the kingdom. Celebration of the

---

[255]http://w2.vatican.va/content/benedict-xvi/en/homilies/2012/documents/hf_ben-xvi_hom_20120405_messa-crismale.html

Eucharist could not have been part of their special remit. It would be some time before it would be instituted, and Christian priesthood was yet unknown.

Moreover, the Exhortation quoted above unwittingly completes another classic logical fallacy, the circular argument. It explains that "a woman cannot receive the Sacrament of Orders, *and therefore, cannot fulfil the proper function of the ministerial priesthood*". But this reverses the cause and effect as taught in *Inter Insigniores,* which the pope relies on. Here, a female is described as incapable of offering Mass *and therefore cannot receive the Sacrament of Orders!* All the authority and infallibility in the world cannot make a fallacious argument convincing.

Since all these official statements have not been enough to convince the faithful of the new doctrine, yet another formula for establishing infallibility was proposed (or restated) in the article in *Osservatore Romano* (29 May 2018) by Archbishop Luis Ladaria, the current Prefect of the CDF. He acknowledges that there are still doubts and "grave confusion among the faithful" about the definitive nature of *Ordinatio Sacerdotalis* and he is concerned that this may create wider doubts "with regards to the Ordinary Magisterium that can teach Catholic doctrine in an infallible manner". He must surely be right in this, although perhaps a generation too late.

For many twentieth century Catholics, faith in the person of Jesus Christ was conflated with an aura of certainty surrounding the papacy. The open split in the curia between opponents and supporters of Pope Francis' reform agenda together with the continuing cover-up of the papacy's contribution to the worldwide problem of clerical sexual abuse and episcopal cover-ups have shaken the unquestioning confidence in the probity of the papacy[256]. For many Catholics, there is now a tension between faith in Jesus Christ and trust in Rome. The distinction has been forced upon them. Some have formally left the Church, others especially the younger generations consider its leadership largely irrelevant. Vocations in the developed world have all but dried up and the authority of the papacy has tanked. Pope Francis is trying to deal with the causes but is opposed by powerful group self-interest within the bureaucracy.

In the circumstances the CDF sees a danger of yet more scandal if they were to admit to even one papal misjudgement. Yet by continuing to insist on a doubtful infallibility when the faithful have already rejected the teaching, they risk dividing the

---

[256] Other contributing factors have included the sudden mid-stream suspension of a Vatican Audit by PwC in April 2016, and the abrupt resignation of Libero Milone, the Vatican's first Auditor-General, in June 2017. He had been appointed by the Pope to clean up the IOR (Vatican Bank). He was to report directly to the Pope but was forced out of office by the Under-Secretary of State and denied access to the Pope at the time. In Ireland in particular, the resignation of Marie Collins from the Pontifical Commission for the Protection of Minors on the grounds of non-cooperation by Vatican Dicasteries was damaging, as were Pope Benedict's Pastoral Letter to the Irish, and the unjust and disgusting treatment of three Irish priests, Frs Fagan, Flannery, and O'Connor, to which we revert in Chapter 15. For those who knew them, these dedicated pastors were seen as prophets, their persecution only serving to confirm that status.

Church and losing more authority as time goes on. In a sinful world, the truth may reveal the scandal of deceit but is the only way to end it.

Archbishop Ladaria's article seems to admit the failure of the earlier claims for infallibility by advancing yet another formula:

> "It is important to reaffirm that infallibility does not only pertain to solemn pronouncements of a Council or of the Supreme Pontiff when he speaks *ex cathedra*, but also to the universal and ordinary teaching of bishops dispersed throughout the world, when they propose, in communion among themselves and with the Pope, the Catholic doctrine to be held definitively".

Newman would not agree. He pointed to the fact that it was the faithful and their priests who preserved the faith during the Arian heresy. *Lumen Gentium* (§12), quoting St Augustine, would only agree with the suggested formula if the unanimous assent of the faithful were to be established. Furthermore, in defining the conditions for exercise of Papal Infallibility outside of a Council, Vatican I made no provision for substituting the agreement of the dispersed episcopate. Finally, the formula does not apply regarding *Ordinatio Sacerdotalis*. The bishops did not "propose [the teaching] in communion among themselves with the Pope". It was the papacy that proposed the doctrine. Not only were the bishops not consulted, their uninvited opinions were precluded by keeping the preparation of the document a closely guarded secret. After it would be signed, the oath of loyalty to the Pope could be depended on to inhibit any free expression of contrary views by a bishop.

The curia attempted to lie about the lack of consultation with the bishops by substituting the assent of the Presidents of the Episcopal Conferences but these, at the time, refused to speak for their bishops without consulting them. This article in *Osservatore Romano* informs us now for the first time, twenty-four years later, that these presidents all agreed to the doctrine! Even if it could still be corroborated, this would be poor evidence on which to ground an argument, let alone a claim to infallibility. And it would not make the slightest difference anyway, because the agreement of presidents is not part of the Cardinals suggested formula.

Moreover, if the presidents had been able to speak for their episcopal conferences, which they were not, it would have added nothing. The conferences "have no theological basis",[257] according to Cardinal Joseph Ratzinger when Prefect of the CDF. In his opinion: "Bishops' conferences do not have any teaching authority".[258] *A fortiori,* the conference presidents would have less.

It has been something of a mantra that 'doctrine cannot be decided by majority vote'. However, because of the definition in *Lumen Gentium* quoted above, no doctrine

---

[257] "We must not forget that the episcopal conferences have no theological basis, they do not belong to the structure of the Church, as willed by Christ, that cannot be eliminated".
—Excerpts from the Ratzinger Report, Ignatius Press, accessed May 2018.
https://www.ignatius.com/promotions/benedictxvibooks/excerptRR.html
[258] Church, Ecumenism and Politics: *New Essays in Ecclesiology* (New York: Crossroad, 1988)

can be considered infallible in the face of disagreement by a significant minority. Many surveys in many countries have shown that a substantial and growing majority of Roman Catholics, not to mention virtually all the Christians of other denominations, simply do not believe the current papal teaching on women's ordination. The decision by the Prefect of the CDF to publish an article in May 2018 suggests that the Congregation is aware of this inconvenient fact.

The merits of the magisterial teaching

Since the Apostolic Letter, *Ordinatio Sacerdotalis,* has no credible claim to infallibility, we must take it on its merits. This means reading it carefully, as Pope Francis has suggested, in tandem with the 1976 Declaration, *Inter Insigniores,* on which it depends. Separately or together, they are unable to stand up to careful reading.

ORDINATIO SACERDOTALIS: SECTION 1

The Letter begins with an ambiguous statement; that priestly ordination has been reserved to men alone 'from the beginning'. Does this refer to the beginning of the Church or the beginning of ordination? The difference has a crucial bearing on the conclusions. The status of *priest* only began to appear among the Christians around about the third century and then only gradually. The eminence of the individual priest, who sacrificed and mediated on behalf of those present, was long established among the Jews and Roman pagans. St Paul was familiar with both, but only uses the term 'priest' in relation to the community. The believers understood themselves to be a priestly people. Even before they had designated elders or organisers,[259] when the community of men and women assembled on the Lord's Day to commemorate Christ's life and sacrifice at a memorial meal they joined themselves spiritually with his self-offering as St Paul had taught them. Baptized into the body of Christ, they did not need a priest to mediate between them and God. The individual ordained priest came some hundreds of years later. On page 34 we quoted Fr Robert Taft S.J:

> "From the fourth century we see a growing consciousness that presbyters celebrating the eucharist together with the bishop are doing something that the laity cannot do, something only they have the mandate to perform".[260]

It was only after the elders and overseers had assumed the dignity of priests and bishops that the rest, men and women alike, were excluded from doing what Christ had commanded, and what the apostles had taught them to do in his memory.[261] Leaving aside the problems of changing terminology and variations of time and place, it is evident that the arrangements developed and changed during the fourth and fifth

---

[259] Titus 1:5 makes it clear that Paul had established groups of believers in several towns but had not got around to appointing elders or overseers before he left. Titus was to do this. In the meantime, the people celebrated the Lord's Supper with one of themselves presiding.

[260] Robert Taft S.J., Ex Oriente Lux, Some Reflections on Eucharistic Celebrations, *Worship 54 (1980),* quoted in Paul Bradshaw, *Liturgical Presidency in the Early Church,* Bramcote, Notts, Grove Books, 1983, p 27

[261] Canon Law continues the ban to this day in the ordinary uncritical interpretation of Cn 900.

centuries. At the upper levels of hierarchy, they continued to change after that. If they could change then, for whatever reason, why not change now to enable the mandate to be followed?

The Apostolic Letter repeats the three 'fundamental reasons' given by Paul VI why women may not be ordained while leaving open the possibility of falling back on others:

1. Faithfulness to the example of Jesus in choosing only men as his apostles,

2. The constant practice of the Church and

3. The teaching authority of the Church which has constantly held that the exclusion of women is "part of God's plan for his Church".

The second and third 'fundamental reasons' depend on the first and only add a claim to long-term consistency.

ORDINATIO SACERDOTALIS, SECTION 2

The Letter repeats the conclusion of the Declaration and invokes the Gospels and Acts to support the idea that Jesus, in choosing only men as apostles (apostle = one who is sent), was giving us an implied blueprint of 'God's eternal plan'.[262] To do this, it has to misrepresent scripture, it draws logically false conclusions and it quotes some sources that, when followed up and examined, yield little or no support to the point being made.

Cultural taboos

In stressing that Jesus chose freely in selecting only male apostles, it relies heavily on Mark 3, verse 13 and the first part of verse 14. It carefully omits the second part where Mark provides a clear explanation for Jesus's choice on that occasion: "they were to be with him *and to be sent out to preach*".[263] Mark does not need to say so, but being an itinerant preacher was no job for a woman in the Palestine of his day.

The authors of the 1976 Declaration had the same need to interpret the omission of women on that occasion as implying a Divine policy decision valid for all time. They were also relying on the passage from Mark 3. To avoid the second half of verse 14, which presented the same difficulty for them, they had paraphrased the verse, but not for the sake of clarity. They changed the meaning of the part that did not suit their remit. This is how it appears:

(Mk 3:14): they are to represent Jesus to the people and carry on his work.

For the un-careful reader, this reads as if it were an excerpt from the gospel. Although quotation marks are not used, the colon after the reference leads the reader to

---

[262] "In fact, the Gospels and the Acts of the Apostles attest that this call was made in accordance with God's eternal plan;" —*Ordinatio Sacerdotalis,* Section 2

[263] Jerusalem Bible, London, Darton, Longman and Todd 1966. gives "they were to be his companions and to be sent out to preach".

believe that they are quoting the gospel.[264] But it is purposefully different from what the evangelist wrote.

The Internet offers convenient access to 26 translations of the verse and none of them reads like this. The apostles were to be with him and *to be sent*; "to preach", in 24 translations, "to spread the Good News", in one, and "to proclaim His Message", in another. So, let us go back to the Greek. It does not present any translation problems. A word for word translation reads:

And - he - appointed - twelve - ones - and - apostles - he - called - [them] - that - they-might - be - with - him - and - that - he - might - send - them - to - preach.

So, the CDF officials were faced with a clash between scripture and the conclusion they were expected to reach. They did not quote any advanced biblical scholarship that would change the ordinary meaning of the words. Instead, the authors of the Declaration stooped to misrepresentation. When faced with the same difficulty eighteen years later, John Paul II chose instead to omit the inconvenient part of the verse. Little evidence here of striving "painstakingly and by appropriate means to enquire properly into that revelation and to give apt expression to its contents".[265] In fact, quite the reverse. And these are the key documents of the magisterium on the subject.

It must be acknowledged that modern methodology in Biblical studies has changed, and is changing, our understanding of many gospel passages. However, if the papacy wishes to be 'faithful to the example of the Lord Jesus', the officials should be restrained from misrepresenting a sacred text to support a predetermined conclusion. The instinct of the faithful, the *sensus fidelium*, would seem to be right in rejecting their conclusion.

It is argued that, because Jesus had elsewhere risen above the cultural taboos of his time and the prejudices about women, he was free to ignore them in this instance and since his choice of men was not culturally constrained it should be interpreted as a divine preference or norm for all time. But this is barking up the wrong (cultural) tree. Jesus was dealing with reality. The taboos and prejudices that shaped the selection of the apostles were not those of Jesus himself but of the tribes and cultures to whom he was proposing to send his preachers. He wanted those he was sending to be listened to. Apart from everything else, a woman's evidence was considered worthless—a prejudice shared across the entire Roman empire and even by the apostles

---

[264] Less than two years earlier, John Paul II had been able to quote the verses fully and accurately: "And he went up on the mountain and called to him those whom he desired; and they came to him. | And he appointed twelve, to be with him, and to be sent out to preach | and have authority to cast out demons" (Mk. 3:13-15).—Post Synodal Apostolic Exhortation, *Pastores Dabo Vobis*, (25/3/1992).

[265] *Lumen Gentium* §25

themselves.[266] The cultural prejudices about women that Jesus was coping with survived in some societies into the twentieth century.

Women certainly formed an important part of Christ's support group, but they were not itinerant preachers. Christ had indeed shown a readiness to override cultural taboos on previous occasions but only when it made sense.[267] On this occasion, however, he was avoiding what would have been an idiotic choice. To use this example to justify excluding women from ordained offices in general is irrational and a capitulation to the same kind of prejudice. The many exclusions suffered by women over the centuries that followed is not unconnected with the widespread taboos about women, to which Christian leaders were in no way immune.

By omitting the job description and thus suppressing the reason for his choice of men, the authors make it almost plausible to infer that Jesus considered women unsuited to ecclesiastical office. If one reads the verse as the evangelist wrote it, however, one can see that Jesus, and Mark, considered an assignment as itinerant preacher inappropriate for a woman.

The distortion of this bit of scripture is a twentieth century phenomenon. It was unknown in apostolic and patristic times, so it could not have been the reason for the gradual exclusion of women from offices in the Church. It supports the view that Church authorities were unable or unwilling to follow the example of the Lord Jesus and rise above the cultural taboos and prejudices of their times and societies.

The exclusion of women makes even less sense now. The *official successors* of the apostles, the bishops, are no longer itinerant preachers, but are required by canon law to reside in their own dioceses and women are now widely accepted as fully rational, responsible human beings. Their evidence is now every bit as acceptable as that of a man.

Why the distortion of scripture?

Why then did the curial officials truncate and misrepresent Mark 3:14 so as to present the exclusion of women on this occasion as an expression of God's 'eternal plan'? There are two obvious explanations. First, it was the job of those who drafted the document to find some scriptural basis for an historic practice that was beginning to be recognised as sexist, discriminatory and at odds with the overall gospel

---

[266] They would not believe Mary of Magdala when she was sent (apostle to the apostles) to bring them the good news of the resurrection. Jesus later reproached the eleven for their 'incredulity and obstinacy'. The successors of the apostles still seem to have some difficulty in listening to what the faithful, particularly the women, are trying to tell them.

[267] His first, albeit obscure, promise of the Eucharist was to the woman at the well who was known to be in a canonically irregular relationship. Not only did he talk to her, which was taboo in any case, but he made her his first *de facto* missionary, prompting her to hurry off to tell her neighbours the good news of who Jesus was.

message. [268] To avoid change, the bureaucracy had to find some reason for overriding the normal principles in this case. Secondly, and maybe more decisively, their immediate assignment was to find scriptural support for the refusal by Pope Paul VI, in correspondence with Dr Coggan, to reconsider the Catholic position on women's ordination. [269] Instead, the Pope had, with "sadness", installed it as a further obstacle to Christian unity. It was Paul VI himself who mandated their work[270] and the conclusion he expected them to reach, having prejudiced the issue, or prejudged it, in the correspondence.

Earlier, he had asked the Pontifical Biblical Commission to study the issue. [271] The commission had been unable to find any scriptural support for his position and had been faced with the problem of how to say "No" to the pope. In April 1976, the Commission had done so, diplomatically concluding in its official response:

> "It does not seem that the New Testament by itself alone will permit us to settle in a clear way and once and for all the problem of the possible accession of women to the presbyterate".[272]

This raises interesting problems about the relationship between authority, scripture, and theology. Crucially however, the Pope did not wait for the official response. He dismissed Dr Coggan's suggestions in a letter dated 23rd March 1976. Rather than draft another letter in which the Pope would revise his decision, the CDF, treated the papal opinion as pseudo-infallible giving it precedence over the gospel. As we have seen, they misrepresented Mark 3:14 to create a pseudo-scriptural argument in support. (The curia did not share the Pope's "sadness". Ecumenism was moving forward at the time and the bureaucracy had every reason to welcome a further obstruction to Christian unity.)

---

[268]One is reminded of Antonio in *The Merchant of Venice:* "The devil can cite Scripture for his purpose". (Act 1, Sn. 3). A more apt quotation in this instance comes from St Irenaeus: "I carefully noticed the passages which they garble from the Scriptures, with the view of adapting them to their own fiction". *Against Heresies, Book II,* Preface, §1.

[269] The papacy defines the vocation of the theologian as one of finding convincing arguments to support current Vatican teaching. See the Instruction of the CDF, *Donum Veritatis,* 1990. Furthermore, "*Veritatis Splendor* has reworked the role of the moral theologian into a disseminator of magisterial teaching only" —Dr Mary Elsbernd O.S.F, Director of the Institute of Pastoral Studies, Loyola University, Chicago, writing in *Horizons,* Vol 29, No. 2, p 226.

[270] *Inter Insigniores* itself describes the assignment: "For these reasons, in execution of a mandate received from the Holy Father and echoing the declaration which he himself made in his letter of 30 November 1975",—Sacred Congregation for the Doctrine of the Faith, Declaration: *Inter Insigniores,* 15/10/1976, Introduction

[271] It should be noted that most of the members of the Pontifical Biblical Commission are acknowledged experts in Biblical studies, appointed for periods of five years. They are in a position to resist the group dynamic of the bureaucracy

[272] Indirect source: http://www.wijngaardsinstitute.com/magisterium-ignores-theology/, accessed 1/3/2017. It would have been preferable to quote the Pontifical Biblical Commission directly. While their website provides access to official documents going back to 1905 this one is not included.

If the Pontifical Biblical Commission had given more thought to Mary of Magdala as the bearer of the ultimate Good News, they would have been able to settle the question on the basis of the New Testament, but it would not have been the answer the Pope or the curia wanted. As if to correct in advance the false interpretation of Mark 3:13-14, Jesus, when the circumstances permitted, chose to send a woman as an apostle. He could as easily have sent a man or an angel.

There is a further lesson to be learned from Mary of Magdala. It directly opposes the withholding of all authority in the Church from women. Mary was entrusted with the additional job of telling the apostles exactly what Jesus wanted them to do in the changed situation. They were to make their way to Galilee where he would meet them. Thus, a woman was chosen to convey the next step of the divine plan to the College of the Apostles.[273] And yet, to this day, church authorities generally deny women executive and preaching authority on the grounds that they are not ordained.

Expanding the exclusion

It gets worse. The Letter uses the same grounds to justify excluding women from the entire 'ministerial priesthood', the elite group exclusively allowed to 'confect' the Eucharist; a category, like the laity, unknown to Jesus or the apostles, or indeed to Christianity, until centuries later. Thus, from a misrepresentation of something Jesus did not do, the Roman magisterium infers a further extension to the 'eternal plan', this time to exclude women from offices that Jesus never spoke about. The reasoning is so far-fetched that the argument must fail.

The document concludes that since women were not chosen as apostles they cannot be ordained as priests. The term 'apostle' at one point indicates the unique status of the Twelve and at another is taken to encompass the entire priestly ministry. There are two classic logical fallacies at work here; the *non sequitur* and/or the *equivocation*. The faulty logic destroys the validity and credibility of the conclusion.[274]

What then did Jesus mean when he named them 'apostles' in Mark 3:13-14? If 'apostle' relates to the unique twelve, (and the 'foundations' in Rev. 21:14 would support this view) then we must look elsewhere for the origins of what we know as the priestly ministry. If 'apostle' on that occasion, however, was meant to encompass the entire ministry, then Jesus' failure to appoint any priests, deacons or sub-deacons must carry the same force as his failure to appoint any women. If it is counter-argued that priests, deacons and sub-deacons are merely 'helpers' for the bishops (and this poses

---

[273] However, things are changing. On June 16, 2017, the Vatican raised the memorial of St. Mary of Magdala to the rank of liturgical feast and published a new preface for her, characterizing her as "the apostle of the apostles". This decision by Pope Francis has several ramifications which are not yet fully appreciated.

[274] "As, however, an unsound proof is worse than no proof at all, discrediting the truth that depends on it when itself discredited…" H.W.Fowler, *Modern English Usage*, Oxford at the Clarendon Press, (Who and whom)

difficulties since they are deemed to share the same ordination), then we must go back to Genesis for a precedent as to the gender of the first helper!

The faulty reasoning leaves the reader looking for some hidden or subconscious motive for the exclusion. No need to look very far. The Declaration itself is revealing. It admits: "in the writings of the Fathers, one will find the undeniable influence of prejudices unfavourable to woman". It follows this splendid understatement with a bland dismissal "these prejudices had hardly any influences on their [the Fathers] pastoral activity, and still less on their spiritual direction". How can the curia be so sure? How could anybody know this? This unsupportable claim indicates that some of the ancient prejudices may still be shared in some quarters. Prejudice does not recognise itself. Shared prejudices defy group discernment.

Worse again, the Church has excluded, and still excludes, women, and men who are not ordained, from all offices of authority or decision making. For centuries, the churches had *presbyteri* and *episcopi*, following the pattern that Jewish[275] and, to a lesser extent, Roman converts were accustomed to. They were normally male, but not always. These Greek words originally meant elders and overseer/organisers. Later, they were applied to priests and bishops, respectively. It took time, however, probably about the fourth century, before these officers monopolized the distinctly priestly functions of sacrifice and mediation, and this doubtless happened at different times in different places. The records are sparse.

There were other recognised charisms and ministries in the early church. The First Letter to Timothy indicates that widows had some distinct ministry for which they were 'enrolled'. St Paul recommends that young widows should not be enrolled[276] because if they should remarry, they would be faulted for revoking their earlier pledge. This implies a formal commitment to an order or office of some kind which was suppressed or phased out later. Why was this apostolic precedent ignored?

In writing about the character of those being selected to become deacons, Paul makes specific reference to the qualities needed in the women. (1 Tm 3)The context indicates clearly that he was talking about deaconesses. Verse 11 reads: "Similarly, the women must be respectable, not gossips[277], but sober and wholly reliable". This is sandwiched between two verses describing the qualities required in the men. This posed a difficulty for translators in centuries after the office of deaconess had been suppressed and long forgotten. Many of them followed the King James version and translated 'women' as 'wives'. but this is not justified by the Greek text or the context.

As time went on the priestly elite absorbed or phased out all the minor orders and ministries that St Paul considered essential to the life and growth of the church. Even the diaconate and sub-diaconate were effectively absorbed by being reserved to those

---

[275] See: Num. XI, 16-18

[276] 1 Tm 5:11-12

[277] 'Gossips' is a delicate translation. It the Greek it is 'slanderers'.

who were on the verge of being ordained priests. Vatican II revived the permanent diaconate and instituted 'extraordinary' ministers of the Eucharist.

The earliest surviving rite that approximates in any way to ordination is found in the writings of Hippolytus.[278] Dating from the early third century, it makes no mention of priestly powers or of the Lord's Supper and was probably a benediction used for the induction of an elder or overseer. It would have been quite natural to have some ceremony to mark such an appointment so that that the chosen person and all the community would be clear about the new responsibilities being taken on. Acts 14:23 describes how Paul and Barnabas "In each of these churches they appointed elders, and with prayer and fasting they committed them to the Lord". The idea of ordaining or of conferring power to confect the Eucharist came much later. The earliest surviving rite that mentions *priestly powers*— the 'transformation of the body and blood of the Son'—is in the *Gelasian Sacramentary* which dates from the late seventh or early eighth century.

Prejudice is like alcoholism; To overcome it, one must first admit it.

While the evidence is clear that Jesus could and did rise above the cultural taboos of his time and place, there is no evidence that the clergy of centuries (or millennia) later have miraculously shared the same capability. Or that they were able to recognise prejudices for what they were.

Over the centuries, however, women religious eroded some of the prejudices and gradually came to exercise non-liturgical ministries in education, health care and other forms of social care. That they should attempt to do so without ordained male supervision was often a source of contention.

The exclusion of women from the exercise of priestly functions, wherever and whenever it occurred, cannot but have been influenced, perhaps unconsciously, by the cultural, theological and philosophical perception of women as inferior, incapable and unreliable, and as a source of temptation. The church rejects this perception now. It should also reject its legacy. Unfortunately, to do so now would undermine the façade of inerrancy and would admit to some misjudgements in the past.

Paul's argument that 'woman cannot be the head of a man' must have been a very persuasive metaphor in the context of his time and place.[279] However, it carries no weight in the world of Angela Merkel, Mary Robinson and Christine Lagarde, or where girls frequently win the Young Scientist Competition or outperform the boys in the GCE. In Autumn 2017 Oxford University admitted more women

---

[278] The earliest extant rubrics and prayers for presbyteral ordination are in the Apostolic Tradition of Hippolytus c, 217 AD. At that time presbyter still meant elder or overseer. Cf. John Bligh S.J. *Ordination to the Priesthood*, London and New York, 1956, Sheed & Ward, *p*31.

[279] Cf. E. Schillebeeckx, O.P., *Marriage in the Old and New Testament*, Sheed and Ward, New York, 1965, p 196 ff.

undergraduates than men. Such trends may have been in Cardinal Martini's mind when he made that famous deathbed assertion: "The Church is two hundred years out of date".

Fidelity to the example of the Lord Jesus?

In *Ordinatio Sacerdotalis* emphasis is given to the fact that:

> "In calling only men as his Apostles, Christ acted in a completely free and sovereign[280] manner . . . without conforming to the prevailing customs and to the traditions sanctioned by the legislation of the time".[281]

This is a Janus argument. It looks whichever way you want it to. The Pope can use it to justify doing exactly what Jesus did even when the time, place and circumstances are different. However, precisely because he is making a virtue of 'fidelity to the example of the Lord Jesus', then the Church is equally entitled to act 'in a completely free and sovereign manner' to solve the problem of the day, without needing to conform to the 'prevailing customs' or 'the legislation of the time'. If the second option were to be followed, it would remove the conflict with the direct command of Jesus at the Last Supper and allow a more complete fidelity to the example of what he did and commanded.

Can God be stupid?

God brings infinite love and imagination to bear as he works in history to build the kingdom, while respecting the freedom of choice and action that enables his children to love him in return. If God is unchanging, then his overall will for his people certainly does not change. But any plan for how something is to be achieved must relate to the existing situation and build from there. One of the classic signs of stupidity is the refusal to reconsider one's answer when the question has changed, or to revise one's strategy and tactics when presented with a new situation. The idea that the details of God's plan can never change will always be comforting to those who find the *status quo* satisfactory and fulfilling. But God, being infinitely intelligent, does not share their irrationality.

The perception of women

Even if the exclusion of women were justified in apostolic times, it would not be so now. It is claimed that the celebrant at Mass must act *in persona Christi,* that is 'in the role of Christ' and that the symbolisms of the sacraments must be natural and meaningful to those in attendance.[282] Women, it is argued cannot be a symbol or 'icon'

---

[280] We have dealt above with the question of whose taboos were relevant in the choice of men as apostles.

[281] Here John Paul II is quoting from his own Apostolic Letter, *Mulieris Dignitatem* (1988).

[282] I must confess to a difficulty about *in persona Christi.* (as per Aquinas) The Catechism of the Catholic Church has added the word *Capitis* (the Head) and goes on in §1548: 'In the ecclesial service of the ordained minister, it is Christ himself who is present to his church". The symbolism is

of Christ because Christ was a man.[283] But symbols communicate only if their meaning is understood. They are thus culture-dependent. In the cultures of the past, the perception of women could have made this difficult, maybe impossible for some. Even the great St Thomas Aquinas was misled by the lack of eminence and state of subjection that was 'natural' for women in his day.

An icon is a sign or representative symbol that can lead one to the reality. A good icon shares some distinctive characteristic that suggests the reality. Christ has many extraordinary and distinguishing characteristics, but his maleness is not one of them. To be one of us, to be a convincing example for us, Christ had to be either male or female, not hermaphrodite. The extraordinary thing about the Incarnation is that the Word was 'made flesh'—that the Creator became a human being, not that he became a man. A picture can act as an icon for him, or a person, but not a dog or a locomotive. Who could say now that Teresa of Avila, Catherine of Sienna, Theresa of Calcutta, Thérèse of Lisieux, Jeanne d'Arc, Brigid of Kildare, or Dorothy Day did not icon Jesus Christ to those around them, each in her own distinctive way?

Far from being part of some unexpressed eternal plan, God may well have been prepared to *tolerate* the exclusion of women while churchmen thought, and taught, that she was not made in his image, while mankind was still blind to the subtle and remarkable gifts, the intuition, the 'genius' and the rich humanity and management skills with which the Creator has so wondrously endowed womankind.

While outdated prejudices against women still survive in some cultures, Christians in the developed world cannot plead that blindness now. Such attitudes should not shape policy or doctrine. The perception of 'woman' has developed, and most rapidly in recent centuries. The reality of being a woman has changed. Her place, education, options, leadership potential, and expectations have changed. She is now accepted as being made, just like her brothers, in the image of God. Imagine that! She is made in the image of God. She is a part of the mystical body of Christ. She lives in Christ and Christ in her. Yet we are being told she cannot be an icon of Christ. Can we not allow the words to have their meaning?

The Oxford Dictionary includes a definition of an 'icon' as: "a sign which has a characteristic in common with the thing it signifies". St Paul says that Christ is all and lives in each of us without discrimination and we live in him. "They are the ones he chose … and intended to become true images of his Son" (Rom. 8:29). Christ became

---

inappropriate. We are being told that the priest coming out on to the altar is making Christ present to his church. What does that say about our faith in the reality of Christ already present where *'two or three are gathered in my name'*?

[283] *Inter Insigniores,* Section 5. Footnote 18 reads: "For since a sacrament is a sign, there is required in the things that are done in the sacraments not only the 'res' but the signification of the 'res'". It recalls Saint Thomas, precisely in order to reject the ordination of women: *In IV Sent.*, dist. 25, q. 2 art. 1, quaestiuncula 1a. corp."

a human being. A baptised woman is a human being who has "put on a new self ... renewed in the image of its creator and in that image there is no room for distinction between Greek and Jew ... slave and free man" (Col. 3:10-11). Thus, if a man can act as an icon of Christ, then today's woman can do so just as well. To borrow a phrase from John Paul II "the analogy implies a likeness, while at the same time leaving ample room for non-likeness"[284].

The question: "Can a woman be ordained?" is a different question now because our understanding of what it is to be a woman has changed radically. So, we should accept that God's plan for this world of matter, energy, space, and time can respond to the signs of the times. We should trust in the Holy Spirit and honestly address the new question: "Can Third Millennium Women be admitted to priestly ordination? The answer is manifestly "Yes". Banning discussion of the question only betrays a fear of the rational answer.

Traditional beliefs and traditional practices

The second and third of the 'fundamental reasons' given in *Ordinatio Sacerdotalis*, are the constant tradition of Church practice and of Church teaching. We will start with practice.

The attempt to justify the limitation of priestly ordination to men based on tradition fails for two reasons. First, the tradition of ordination itself does not go back far enough. It was the Christian community, the priestly people, who commemorates Christ and offered themselves with him when they celebrated the Lord's Supper during the first two or three centuries. We have discussed this in Chapter 4. Second, the argument relies on traditional behaviour not traditional belief.

Catholicism teaches that Christ's revelation, which ended with the apostles, has been passed down to us through scripture and tradition. There is room, of course, for development in the expression of doctrine and in our understanding of how it affects, or ought to affect, our lives. The Spirit is leading us to 'all truth'. The traditional beliefs of the universal church are therefore a reliable channel of revelation. Not so with traditional practices, however, since we are all sinners, and churchmen are no exception. *Inter Insigniores* is blind to this inconvenient fact when it makes the extraordinary statement: "The practice of the Church therefore has a normative character".

God forbid! If that were true, the Church would still be torturing suspected heretics and witches, burning the convicted ones (including an odd saint or mystic) and expropriating their property, not to mention abducting Jewish children who were alleged to have been secretly baptised. Popes would still be raising armies to regain control of 'holy' places and selling indulgences to boost the building fund. They would be, wearing red shoes and the triple tiara, riding the *sedia gestatoria* and appointing young nephews as Cardinals.

---

[284] John Paul II, Mulieris Dignitatem §25

The argument that "The practice of the Church therefore has a normative character" cannot be taken seriously. It would mean that there can never be any change.

Furthermore, even the practice which is presented here as normative and claimed to go back in an unbroken tradition, does not go back far enough and there is ample historical evidence of women being ordained during the first millennium.

As regards teaching authority, the writings of several saints in the second millennium can be quoted as they advance various reasons why women are not ordained. They were writing in defence of an ongoing Church practice which apparently needed some defending even then. If they had taken a different view they would never have been canonised as saints. Quite the reverse; for more than a millennium, they would have risked being burned at the stake. Counter-cultural thinkers were wiser to keep their opinions to themselves.

Flaky footnotes

The Apostolic Letter was issued in 1994. It has footnotes that refer the reader to existing magisterial documents that support the exclusion of women as "the *constant* practice of the Church". On examination, however, one discovers that all the referenced documents originated in the previous twenty years!

Lest the careful reader might get the impression that the tradition is of relatively recent origin, however, there is a reference in the Declaration to the writings of 'the Fathers'. Here, it is not always clear whether traditional belief or practice is at issue:

> "A few heretical sects in the first centuries, especially Gnostic ones, entrusted the exercise of the priestly ministry to women: This innovation was immediately noted and condemned by the Fathers, who considered it as unacceptable in the Church". (7)—*Inter Insigniores*

On checking footnote 7, however, it turns out they are relying on five Fathers, one, Epiphanius, from the end of the fourth century and three from the third. The fifth, Irenaeus, is at the end of the second century. There are no citations from apostolic or post-apostolic times. There cannot be, because the Christians had not yet adopted the Jewish pattern of having representative priests[285] to act on behalf of the faithful.

The references offer poor support. Epiphanius shows clear and strong opposition to the priestly ordination of women but he displays such an extravagant misogyny that it discredits any contribution he might make on the subject. The third century writers, Tertullian, Origen and Firmilian were all deemed to be heretical in some respects or were excommunicated or both. Probably unjustly. Tertullian and Origen were men of extraordinary learning, each with such a prodigious output that they were bound to

---

[285] By 'Representative Priest' I mean an individual who is authorised to performs the priestly function of sacrifice on behalf of the followers and who acts as a mediator between them and the deity. Christians do not need such. They are a priestly people "and there is only one mediator between God and mankind, himself a man, Christ Jesus". (1 Tm 2:5). Christians are members of Christ's body. (1 Cor. 12, Eph. 5)

be wrong on some points, and the third century was a time of many great controversies over discipline and doctrine. It also included Pope Stephen I (254-257) who had a special penchant for excommunication. These three Fathers all base their comments on the ontological inferiority of women. This doctrine is now reprobated by the Church, so conclusions based on it should not be cited as Church teaching. Thus, the attempt to root the *teaching* in the patristic fathers fails.

The fifth, St Irenaeus, was writing at the end of the second century. In the cited work, he was not writing about women priests or even about the Lord's Supper but about a charlatan called Marcus, a magician who performed magic tricks and presented them as miracles wrought by Charis or Grace. He is described as deceiving gullible women and ordering them to "give thanks" over a small cup of wine. This then magically increases to fill a larger one to overflowing. St Irenaeus may well have been against women's ordination for all we know, but in the reference cited he is simply denouncing an idolatrous ritual which would have earned his condemnation equally whether performed by men or women, gullible or sensible. The appeal to St Irenaeus to support the exclusion fails because the reference is found to be irrelevant.

The key passage in *Inter Insigniores* that links Church practice to the example of Jesus reads:

> "that by calling only men to the priestly Order and ministry in its true sense, the Church intends to remain faithful to the type of ordained ministry willed by the Lord Jesus Christ and carefully maintained by the Apostles".

We have already shown that this statement cannot stand up to 'careful reading'. Whatever "priestly Order and ministry in its true sense" is intended to mean here, however, it is inappropriate to confound it with the unique status of the Twelve who are presented in Revelation 21:14 as the foundations of the entire edifice.

The footnote to the quoted paragraph cites three patristic references to justify its contention. Two of these are closely related collections of documents; the fourth Century *Constitutiones Apostolicae* being largely based on the *Didascalia Apostolorum* which dates from the middle of the third century. They both depend, to a great extent, on the natural inferiority of women, a belief generally accepted then but, as we have said, now rejected by the Catholic Church. The third reference is to St John Chrysostom, *De Sacerdotio 2,* 2: PG 48,633. This may be a mistake. "The citation makes no appeal to the example of Christ and the desire to remain faithful to it".[286] These references are examined in detail by John H. Wright S.J. and can be consulted easily on the Internet.[287] Fr Wright concludes:

---

[286] John H. Wright, S.J., Patristic Testimony on Women's Ordination in Inter Insigniores, in *Theological Studies 58 (1997),* P524

[287] In the above, I have drawn freely on John H. Wright, S.J. *Patristic Testimony on Women's Ordination in Inter Insigniores,* in Theological Studies 58 (1997),
 www. http://theologicalstudies.net/readers/download-past-articles/

"It seems to me that if the examples cited by the CDF as the testimony of the Church Fathers are at all representative of what tradition has to offer, we must acknowledge that their testimony offers meagre support for the claim that the tradition of not ordaining women was motivated primarily by the Church's intention to remain faithful to the will of Christ".

Where then did the exclusion come from? From the cultural environment of the Mediterranean, the Roman Empire and even the invading barbarians. Professional ambition probably played a part. Culturally, the inclusion of women would have impacted negatively on the developing dignity of priests and bishops.

Incidentally, Tertullian, Firmillion, the *Didascalia Apostolorum*[288] and *Constitutiones Apostolicae*[289], are unanimous in condemnation of women baptising, but this evidence of belief from the same sources can be brushed aside as culturally conditioned and given no binding force today.

Some church practices are deemed to be 'normative'. Some precedents are binding while others apparently can be ignored.[290] Disagreement over the historicity of a precedent can be used to stop a sensible modern initiative. The categorisation appears to be arbitrary and seems to depend on convenience, or the preference or, dare we say it, the prejudice of the management team of the day.

Both the Declaration and the Apostolic Letter deal with the issue as a peripheral one and neither attempts to relate its teaching to the fundamentals of the faith: the incarnation, death and resurrection of Jesus, the Gospel message of love, feeding the hungry, salvation, the institution of the Eucharist or even the origins of ordination as a sacrament. There is no attempt to show how the exclusion of women from the priesthood serves either of the basic mandates. Furthermore, the documents refer to the issue as "this important problem" and as "a matter of great importance" respectively, yet leave the reader wondering why it should be so important. Any Christian can see the importance of celebrating the Lord's Supper as commanded by Jesus but the issue of who presides seems secondary or trivial by comparison. The priorities appear to have been prejudiced by the practice.

Fundamental reasons 2 and 3 above are thus seen to be flawed. They depend essentially on a readiness to confuse traditional beliefs which are protected by the Holy Spirit with traditional practices which have been governed by sinful man. The history of Church management is not without corruption, ambition, greed, prejudice, murder, forgery, simony, sycophancy, arrogance, discrimination, injustice, dishonesty, and

---

[288] "Women to baptise . . . for it is a transgression of the commandment" —*Didascalia Apostolorum*, trans. R, Hugh Connolly, Oxford, Clarendon Press, 1929, 3.6.133.

[289] *Constitutiones Apostolicae*, Book III, c. 9.

[290] For Example: Acts 1:24-26 gives a useful precedent for resisting simony in the appointment of bishops. In the selection of the first 'successor of the apostles', Matthias was selected by lot from a short list after a prayer for guidance. But now the choice of bishop seems to be too important to be left to the Holy Spirit unaided!

repression of independent thinking. Christians should not accept traditional practices as a guide to doctrine or morality.

Contradiction between magisterial documents.

Regarding the sacraments generally, Inter Insigniores asserts that the Church has "power down the centuries in order to determine their signs and the conditions of their administration" but has "no power over the substance".

It quotes an early eighteenth-century document, which contains the teaching of the Council of Trent[291] which we referred to in the previous chapter:

> "In the Church there has always existed this power, that in the administration of the sacraments, provided that their substance remains unaltered, she can lay down or modify what she considers more fitting either for the benefit of those who receive them or for respect towards those same sacraments, according to varying circumstances, times or places."

This places the issue squarely in the category of Church discipline and management. It stands in direct contradiction to the new doctrine of the Apostolic Letter: *"that the Church has no authority whatsoever to confer priestly ordination on women",* unless of course one can prove that the gender of the recipient forms part of the substance of the sacrament. I don't think this has been done or can be done. The Apostolic Letter does not define what the substance of the sacrament is, nor does it attempt to deal with the contradiction.

In a letter to the *Irish Times* (16 April 2018), Fr Vincent Twomey, S.V.D., Professor Emeritus of Moral Theology, Maynooth University took the present writer to task for raising this issue. He wrote[292] that "the sacraments are symbolic by nature" and thus *"it would seem,* the male gender is part of the substance of the sacrament of ordination".[293] He did not offer any support or proof for this strange opinion. Gender does not symbolise the recipient of a sacrament, it is a reality.

Six weeks later, Archbishop Ladaria took up the same issue. He asserted that "the Church recognizes that the impossibility of ordaining women belongs to the 'substance of the sacrament' of Orders".[294] In support, he refers the reader to Denzinger-Hünermann, §1728. This is spurious and misleading. The reference offers no support whatsoever to the point he is making. It leads the reader to the same sentence from the sixteenth century Council of Trent that we have already reproduced above, and which says or implies absolutely nothing about women or of what constitutes the 'substance' of a sacrament. This is presumably the best that the experts in the CDF could find by way of support, and it offers none.

---

[291] Council of Trent, Session 21

[292] In response to an op-ed piece by this author in the Irish Times a week earlier.

[293] Emphasis added

[294] Pius XII confirmed that 'the Church has no power over the substance of a sacraments' in his Apostolic Constitution on priestly ordination, *Sacramentum Ordinis,* 13th November 1947. He did not identify gender as being part of the substance

The Council of Trent did not feel the need to clarify or define what it meant here by the term 'substance', so we can presume the ordinary meaning of the word is intended. In this context, the common meaning of substance is the 'essentials that make something what it is'. In the case of the sacraments these are: the matter, the form, and the intention of the conferrer. Even for these, Church tradition allows some flexibility. For instance, in the form, the formula of words or the language may vary provided they are substantially identical in meaning. The gender of the recipient has not been shown to be of the substance. Thus, the Prefect's contention has no foundation in Catholic doctrine and *Ordinatio Sacerdotalis* still stands in direct contradiction to the Council of Trent. One or other must be erroneous.

Substance of the sacrament?

The sacraments are composed of matter and form together with the intention of the minister of doing what the Church does or what Christ wills. The Church has taught since the time of the Donatist heresy (Chapter 6) that the efficacy of a sacrament is not dependent on the moral character of the minister. After decades of discussion, the verdict of the Church was that the sacraments are effective *ex opere operato*. The Anglicans retained this teaching, specifically in Article XXVI of the Thirty-Nine Articles which reads: "*Of the unworthiness of ministers which hinders not the effect of the Sacrament*".

The ruling, *ex opere operato,* put an end to the idea that the minister of a sacrament had to be like Jesus. It clearly excluded the quality of the celebrant from the substance of the sacrament. The church teaches that the predisposition of the recipient limits the grace he or she receives but has never taught that it invalidates the sacrament. Therefore, neither celebrant nor recipient is part of the substance and the Church can 'lay down or modify what she considers more fitting'. The claim to *Plenitudo Potestatis* gives a pope arbitrary but legal authority to permit or forbid almost anything. It does not, however, entitle him, or the curial bureaucracy, to create a new doctrine or to bend scripture and logic to dress a new claim up as an old one, or to tie the hands of future generations who may not share the current questionable pontifical priorities.

The sacraments have been consistently regarded as imparting divine grace. They have been variously defined over the centuries. St Augustine saw them as "the visible form of an invisible grace". The current Catechism of the Catholic Church describes them as "efficacious signs of grace instituted by Christ and entrusted to the Church, by which divine life is dispensed to us".[295] St Thomas Aquinas teaches:

> "Therefore, a sacrament is a sign that commemorates what precedes it – Christ's Passion; demonstrates what is accomplished in us through Christ's Passion –grace; and prefigures what that Passion pledges to us –future glory.[296]

---

[295] CCC 1130.
[296] S. TH. III, 60, 3 as reproduced in CCC 1130.

While every sacrament has one who administers it and one who receives, there is nothing in any of the above definitions that would remotely suggest that either minister or recipient forms part of the substance of the sacrament, much less that his or her gender does. If the recipient were of the substance of the sacrament, then it would be a different sacrament when administered to each different candidate.

Finally, how can the recipient be the substance of the gift or grace that he or she is about to receive?

Exaggerated infallibility and management paralysis

The pretence that the Church has no authority to ordain women is a smokescreen to cover fear of change and the enduring curial prejudice against women.

The general authority of the mandate was enough to permit the changes in the Eucharist listed in the previous chapter without any specific divine authorisation. Authorising a woman to preside would be trivial in comparison. The problem, of course, is the carefully built aura of general infallibility. The papacy has invested a great deal in the denial of ordination to women and into minimising the priesthood of the laity. Any change would involve a climb down, and an admission of recent error. This would affect authority, power, and pride.

If the authorities want us to understand 'substance' in a very loose way, then some of the changes in the Eucharist listed in the previous chapter would seem much closer to the substance of the sacrament than the gender of the recipient is to ordination, which should be deemed of little consequence unless proven otherwise. The maxim to be applied here, however, would be: in essentials, unity; in doubtful matters, liberty; in all things, charity.[297]

It was Church authority that stopped women from concelebrating as part of the congregation in or about the third century or later, as individual ordained priests became available in sufficient numbers. It is only canon law that forbids women now … and individual priests are an endangered species.

The Eucharist without a priest?

Some Catholic women and men believe that Christ's command, "Do This", was addressed to all his disciples and they feel they can rely on Christ's assurance about two or three who are gathered in his name. They celebrate the Eucharist together, generally in small groups in their homes – privately to avoid provocation. If present trends continue, this will once again become a normal way for Roman Catholics to celebrate the memorial sacrifice. For many it may be the only way. Will it be valid? The teaching is that the effect of the sacraments occurs *ex opere operato*. They will be breaking canon law in their efforts to continue as a Christian community. Canon 900 will probably be an anachronism long before it is repealed by the authorities.

---

[297] Quoted with approval by Pope John XXIII, *Ad Petri Cathedram*, Encyclical on Truth, Unity and Peace, in a Spirit of Charity. June 29, 1959.

If the Church can include a ban in canon law, the Church can remove it. Surely *plenitudo potestatis* can stretch that far? The Catechism of the Catholic Church tells us that the pope "as pastor of the entire Church has full, supreme and universal power over the whole Church, a power he can always exercise unhindered" (§882). Elsewhere, (§937) it teaches: "The pope, enjoys by divine institution, 'supreme, full, immediate and universal power in the care of souls'". It is strange that successive popes have used this power to deny reasonable access, for literally millions of Catholics, to the form of worship and the nourishing sacrament instituted by Christ. Is that what is meant by 'the care of souls'?

The Catechism of the Catholic Church was published in 1994, in the same year *Ordinatio Sacerdotalis* was defining the doctrine that the pope has 'no authority whatsoever' to admit women to priestly ordination. How strange that the many experts who prepared, checked, and authorised the Catechism did not know about this unique limitation on papal power "already possessed by the Church". Elsewhere the Catechism refers to a limitation, stating in §1125 that "even the supreme authority in the Church may not change the liturgy *arbitrarily*" (emphasis added). The concern there, however, is with the 'what' of the liturgy, not the 'who'. Furthermore, *arbitrarily* is meaningless in a situation where nobody can judge the pope's actions.

Who was authorised?

If it were to be accepted that the 'fundamental' reasons given for excluding women can no longer be sustained, we can expect the revival of another argument, based on the improbable theory that only men were present at the Last Supper.[298]

Jesus had many women disciples. Many of them had come up to Jerusalem with him. (Mk 15:41) It is not surprising that their presence was not mentioned, (women did not count in those days) but it does seem uncharacteristic of Jesus that he would have excluded them from his last meal before he died,[299] the more so since it was the Passover meal which is normally a family or inter family celebration. If he did, it is stranger still that such uncharacteristic behaviour would not have been recorded or commented on by any evangelist. We know that Peter and John negotiated the use of the room, but they are described as "arriving" in the evening with Jesus (Mk 14:18). Were the people who prepared the meal in the meantime then excluded? Was that a job for men only? Would Christ have slighted the women who had travelled with him and ministered to his needs?

The Gospel record is of 'disciples' being present. The 'apostles' or the 'twelve' are only distinguished from the others at one point in the narrative. They are at table with Jesus and he is telling them that one of them—his specially chosen twelve— is about to betray him. (Mark 14:20, Luke 22:14). Yet Catholics have been led to believe, if

---

[298] Pope John Paul II floated this idea in *Mulieris Dignitatem,* §26, in 1988. It was one of many supporting arguments that proved indefensible, leading the papacy ultimately to resort to authority and pseudo-infallibility in 1994.

[299] (Luke 22:15): 'I have longed to eat this Passover with you before I suffer'.

only by the many artists who have depicted the scene, that only the apostles were present,[300] and this has been used to justify the exclusion of women from the ordained priesthood which was instituted centuries later. Moreover, it has been used to suggest that the instruction "Do This" was only addressed to the apostles who passed on their implied 'powers' to their successors the bishops. But what about priests? They are not successors of the apostles. They somehow qualify to confect the Eucharist as the bishops' helpers. Are we forgetting that St Paul had helpers of both genders?

If their alleged absence from the Last Supper is accepted as good enough grounds for ruling that women cannot confect the Eucharist, why then do we allow women to receive Holy Communion? The glib answer would be 'apostolic practice'; the apostles, who could best interpret Christ's wishes, allowed women to receive. But the apostles also allowed women to concelebrate the Lord's Supper alongside the men of the community and this arrangement continued until *all* the un-ordained in the community, men, women and children alike, were categorised as laity and excluded. This happened gradually, starting about two centuries or more after all the apostles were dead. There was no precedent in Christian tradition for the exclusion. Nor was it based on doctrine. The limited guidance available from scripture would favour inclusiveness.

Charisms and offices

Writing to the Corinthians, St Paul lists the gifts and services that together build up the body of Christ:

- preaching with wisdom,
- preaching instructions,
- transmitting the faith,
- healing,
- the power of miracles,
- prophecy,
- discerning spirits,
- the gift of tongues,
- the interpretation of tongues,

"All these are the work of one and the same Spirit, who distributes different gifts to different people just as he chooses"[301]. In Ephesians he gives another list:[302]

---

[300] In the great works of art from the 15th to 17th Century, Jesus is shown with the twelve. Most depict the dramatic moment when Jesus is predicting his betrayal. A painting by Polish artist, Bohdan Piasecki showing a mixed attendance of men and women got a mixed reception when published in Dublin in the 1990s. Copies can be viewed and bought online at http://wearechurchireland.ie/last-supper/

[301] 1 Cor 12: 8-11

[302] Ep 4:11-12

- And to some his gift was that they should be apostles,
- to some prophets,
- to some evangelists,
- to some pastors and teachers,
- so that the saints together make a unity in the work of service.

In these lists Paul does not mention praying or offering the sacrifice of the Lord's Supper. These were the basic activities of every Christian. They were not differentiating gifts. In the Pauline Church, women were equal to men when it came to celebrating the Lord's Supper, and there is no trace of a ban on their presiding. The ban on celebrating, when it came centuries later, applied equally to men and women who had been reduced to the status of laity when the elders and/or overseers had assumed the dignity of priests and, for some, the greater dignity of being bishops.

The multi-rung hierarchical ladder developed from there, the new rungs being added by those already on it. The addition of lower levels had the effect of raising the upper ones. Catholics are expected to respect each added rung as an expression of God's eternal plan for his Church as if the apostolic obsession with being the greatest never existed. In the early church, women could not be great, let alone be the greatest. Culturally, they were less than human and had no place on any ladder. But they could be full disciples of the Lord.

ORDINATIO SACERDOTALIS: SECTION 3

On a 'careful reading' Section 3 in *Ordinatio Sacerdotalis* proves to be largely irrelevant or at best a distraction. There is a preoccupation with dignity. Once again, a binding precedent is to be derived from something that was *not* done. Once again, no attempt is made to explain why.

Dignity and titles

Without changing the title of presbyter, the elders (including overseers) became representative priests and bishops. They, or their flocks, gradually cultivated their dignity. Here, as we have seen, they were following the pattern of the Jews and Romans of their time. The Christian congregations may well have wished their leaders to have a matching dignity in the wider community. The dignity of the clergy seems to have become disproportionately important, at least to the clergy themselves.[303] St Alphonsus Liguori (1696-1787) quotes more than 20 saints (most of them priests) effusing about the dignity and grandeur of the priesthood. Among them Alphonsus quotes St Bernardine of Sienna, and comments approvingly:

> "Holy Virgin, excuse me, for I speak not against thee: the Lord has raised the priesthood above thee". The saint assigns the reason of the superiority of the

---

[303] St Paul saw fit to warn Timothy about the danger that an appointment as presbyter might go to a person's head. (Tim 3:6)

priesthood over Mary; she conceived Jesus Christ only once: but by consecrating the Eucharist, the priest, as it were, conceives him as often as he wishes, so that if the person of the Redeemer had not as yet been in the world, the priest, by pronouncing the words of consecration would produce this great person of a Man-God.[304]

Alphonsus then quotes St Augustine:

"O wonderful dignity of the priests. In their hands, as in the womb of the Blessed Virgin, the Son of God becomes incarnate".[305]

Dignity and women

The preoccupation with rank and dignity is a distraction. Women are reassured that the denial of priestly ordination does not imply any reduction in their dignity, because Mary, whose dignity outranks us all, was not admitted to apostolic office among the initial twelve or even when Mathias was selected to fill the vacancy[306]. This is pious nonsense. Dignity has nothing to do with the case; being an apostle was still a question of service as an itinerant preacher. It was still no job for a woman. Mary was by then fifty years of age or more, quite elderly for the time, and twenty-five or thirty years older than most of the apostles, as far as one can guess. She was not on the short list. As far as we know, she was not even considered.

Mary had already fulfilled her mission by bringing Jesus into the world and raising him. By saying 'Yes' to the angel, she had courageously surrendered herself totally and without reservation to the will of God, prefiguring Christ's self-sacrifice. She had suffered a vicarious martyrdom 'as she stood by the cross of Jesus'. Mary was the first of the priestly people, albeit with no hierarchical title, offering her own total self-sacrifice with that of her Son. She was never ordained; she did not need to be. She had been given, as mother, to all who would be Christ's followers. She was destined to draw people towards her Son until the end of time. Priestly ordination or episcopal consecration, if it had been known at the time, would have been something of a reduction in her status. It would have added nothing to *her* dignity, although some of the saints quoted by St Alphonsus seemed to think it should. On any scale of dignity, if Mary were to be a bishop, she would certainly have to be pope!

The papal assurance that the refusal of ordination to women does not impugn their dignity is disingenuous or displays unwitting ignorance. As we have noted in a footnote on page 148 above, St Thomas gave lack of dignity as the very reason women could not be ordained: "since it is not possible in the female sex to signify eminence of degree, for a woman is in the state of subjection". Women are no longer in a natural

---

[304] St Alphonsus de Ligouri. *The Dignity and Duties of the Priest* or *Selva,* edited by Rev Eugene Grimm, C.SS.R., Brooklyn, Redemptorist Fathers, 1927.p 32. Both saints are surprisingly unaware of Christ's presence in the congregation before the priest appears on the altar.

[305] *Ibid.* p 32

[306] The reference to Mathias comes from *Inter Insigniores,* (end of Section 2 and start of Section 3) which is incorporated into *Ordinatio Sacerdotalis.*

state of subjection and have achieved degrees of eminence in a myriad of different ways. Applying thirteenth century standards to them is certainly an affront to their dignity.

Those who prepared the text of *Ordinatio Sacerdotalis* seem to be a lot more obsessed with dignity than are today's proponents of women's ordination. The women that I have heard speak and whose writings I have read on the issue are not asking for the dignity of office. They want to answer what they experience as a call from God. Instead of carefully appraising the authenticity of each call, the authorities apply a blanket gender exclusion based on canon law. The women are looking for an opportunity to provide a vital service in a situation of dire need that conflicts with a clearly expressed divine commandment. They reject the patriarchal notion that God created them inadequate.[307] They are looking only to be treated as fully human beings … as Jesus did during his lifetime.

Section 3 goes on to recognise, rather patronisingly, women's presence, roles and contribution in the Church as true disciples; "women who—faithful to the Gospel— have shared in every age in the apostolic mission" of the whole People of God. But it offers no convincing grounds for excluding such women from the official apostolic mission. The Declaration lists St Clare, St Teresa of Avila, and St Catherine of Sienna as exemplars of the outstanding contribution of women and reminds us that the last two have left "writings so rich in spiritual doctrine that Pope Paul VI has included them among the Doctors of the Church". It does not explain why their gender should have excluded them and others with such remarkable spiritual gifts from authoritative teaching and preaching offices; an exclusion that can only have left the People of God spiritually poorer than it might otherwise have been. Imagine for a moment the effect of St Teresa preaching.

Furthermore, the section rules women out of the governance, by saying: "The pastoral charge in the Church is normally linked to the sacrament of Order". This is just another form of the argument from traditional behaviour and savours of arguing in a circle. Why should ordained people[308] monopolise management functions as well? Why should management monopolise liturgical leadership as well? A greater variety or mix of people might do a better job. Recent news reports suggest that the Vatican could use a few more professional accountants, auditors, and communicators.

This section ends with the claim: "Moreover, it is to the holiness of the faithful that the hierarchical structure of the Church is totally ordered". One would wish that

---

[307] St John Chrysostom considered that *no woman and few men* were up to the job of bishop. He lived too early to appreciate the management skills of Jeanne d'Arc or the Great Teresa.

[308] It was not thus in the Island of Saints and Scholars. "Bishops there were still, of course, since the ecclesiastical dignities and sacramental functions of the bishop could never be dispensed with. But his administrative jurisdiction was apparently a thing of the past; that now rested in the hands of the abbot." —Dáibhí Ó Cróinín, *Early Medieval Ireland,* Longman/Pearson, Harlow, 1995, p147. (See also Ch. 8 above)

that were true. The inclusion of holy women in the hierarchical structure might well promote the holiness of the people and indeed of the hierarchical structure itself. Now *that* would be worth a try. But in a pseudo-infallible Church, documents like these tend to obstruct the way of creativity, experimentation, and adaptation.

SIGNIFICANT OMISSIONS

Surprisingly, Christ's Eucharistic commandment, "Do This" is not mentioned in either document, although it is foundational. Nor do they face up to the crisis in the supply of priests or dare to visit the origins of sacramental ordination itself. This would have raised the question as to when and where the Church got the authority to ordain males as mediating, representative, individual priests. They also avoid the question of the response of God to the Lord's Supper when celebrated by the unordained in the early centuries, or those not properly ordained. (See Chapter 8 for discussion of this in relation to Anglican orders). Furthermore, they fail to deal with the fact that there were no Christian priests (or bishops as we know them now) in apostolic or immediate post apostolic times.

The Apostolic Letter makes no attempt to reconcile the potential conflict between new teaching, that "the Church has no authority whatsoever to admit women to priestly ordination" with the broad general authority implicit in the mandates, "Do This" and "Make disciples". A mandate authorises whatever is conducive and proportionate to its achievement unless limits are specified. (Moral or legal constraints may be implicit). The need for decorum in the celebration of the sacred rites may have caused the overseers, *episcopii* or bishops to insist on suitably trained or qualified leaders, beginning in the third or fourth century. As we have seen, the Roman emphasis on law and their obsession with detailed precision in pagan rituals, would have introduced this trend or accelerated it after 380 AD, when Catholicism became the state religion and the bureaucracy had to hurriedly retrain the entire religious staff throughout the empire. The requirement of a trained leader must have been enforced gradually as qualified personnel became available. Otherwise it would have negated the mandate itself. Qualification ceremonies for trained personnel may have become the sacrament of ordination. And ordination became the *sine qua non* of liturgical leadership. This was a tolerable regulation for as long as there were enough ordained personnel to fulfil the mandate with appropriate frequency. But this has not been the case for some time. History created this situation. The management has the responsibility and the authority to deal with it.

The Apostolic Letter does not explain where the authority to ordain male priests comes from, other than by implication from the mandate, "Do This". But the mandate was and is addressed to all Christ's disciples, male and female, and is fundamental. The papacy has "no authority whatsoever" to exclude half the faithful by reference to a distorted example from Christ's life that depends on misrepresenting a verse from scripture. But the need to manufacture a scriptural basis to support Pope Paul's ill-considered response to Dr Coggan took priority over academic integrity and honesty. Once again, the inability of the papacy to admit the possibility of error or wrongdoing contributes to Christian disunity

The attempt to create a new 'defined' doctrine was an abuse of papal power. It met a need of the papacy. It avoided having to admit to a prejudice of long standing. However, "thanks to a supernatural instinct of faith which characterizes the people as a whole", the People of God, including more than 70 per cent of the Catholic faithful, have clearly rejected the new doctrine.

Apostles were not priests

The apostles themselves were not priests, in that they did not interpose themselves as mediators between the Christians and their God, nor was it their job to offer sacrifice on behalf of the assembly as the Jewish and Roman priests did. They did not consider themselves to be *in persona Christi*. (They had known Christ. I think they would have rejected such a claim in horror as utterly arrogant and impertinent.) On the contrary they taught the faithful to offer themselves along with Christ to God in the fellowship of the memorial meal. The apostles understood their calling as one of preaching and praying. This is clear from the account of the institution of the ministry of deacons:

> A problem had arisen regarding the daily distribution of food. The Twelve called a full meeting of the disciples and addressed them. 'It would not be right for us to neglect the word of God so as to give out food: you, brothers, must select from among yourselves, seven men of good reputation, filled with the Spirit and with wisdom; we will hand over this duty to them, and continue to devote ourselves to prayer and to the service of the word. The whole assembly approved of this proposal and elected … " (Acts 6: 2-5).

This proves that the apostles were not priests, run off their feet on Sundays trying to reach all the new groups of Christians. Their duty was to pray and preach. Preaching included teaching. 'In the beginning', among Christians there were no individual, representative priests, offering sacrifice and mediating.

A different blueprint

But we can learn more than one lesson from this account. A problem was identified. The apostles made a proposal to establish a ministry that would meet the need, and the full assembly of the disciples made what could be described as a unanimous democratic decision. They did not look for a precedent. They responded to the need. The plan was approved and implemented. But it was interpreted flexibly. While the ministry was set up initially to manage the distribution of food, the duties were allowed to extend as needs arose so that in time deacons were administering baptism, marriages and funerals and taking Holy Communion to the faithful who could not attend.

The fourth century Liberian Catalogue, in recording Pope Fabian's division of Rome into seven ecclesiastical districts, tells us that the major orders of deacon and sub-deacon were in existence. We may assume that the junior assistants referred to would be equivalent to what were later known as minor orders, such as lectors, acolytes etc. If there was any established tradition of individual priests at the time, Fabian would have had to specify where they fitted in to the new structure or why he was not including them. Would they be above or below the deacons? The deacons were in charge. Evidently, up to 350 AD the Bishop of Rome knew nothing of individual ordained Catholic priests and was making no provision for such.

The first group of deacons were all men, and their job was the daily distribution of food. We even know their names. Their selection and duties were not frozen as part of some eternal plan or rigid precedent. In time their duties were expanded radically, as needs arose, from physical services to spiritual. The ministry was extended to women. Regrettably, this did not last. They were phased out and, like the priesthood of the laity, quietly erased from Tradition. However, the existence of deaconesses in the early church can no longer be denied. A good deal of evidence survives of the later existence of women priests and rather less of an *episcopa*. The best source on this is the Wijngaards Institute Most of the institute's research has been ignored by the authorities. Some has been disputed, but very little refuted.

If the successors of the apostles, who so often act as prisoners of precedent, could take the general precedent of creating a ministry to fill an identified need,[309] they could get on with resolving many of the problems currently besetting the Church. The authority is there, implicit in the mandate addressed to all his followers: "Make disciples of all the nations" and backed up by the Promise "I am with you always".

The management team (wherever located) could make proposals. The College of Bishops would make the decisions since it is no longer practical to have a full meeting of the disciples. For this to work, however, the bishops would have to represent their flocks to headquarters, as well as representing headquarters to their flocks. The management team would have to allow the College of Bishops to function. They would also have to accept that the College would not always approve the proposals as presented. If, as at Vatican II, they eschewed infallibility, the diocesan bishops would be free to experiment and modify decisions in the light of experience. Given Christ's promise, and provided they tried to follow the promptings of the Holy Spirit, they would not go far astray for long. Mistakes would be limited to a few dioceses and could be remedied when they became apparent.

The supreme authority of the College of Bishops, when acting with the Pope, is already fully agreed. Only the legal machinery is missing.

Failure to reconcile with general gospel values.

There is a remarkable failure in *Ordinatio Sacerdotalis* to set the new teaching in the general context of the gospel or to reconcile it with other specific pointers:

---

[309] As they notably failed to do at the Amazonian Synod

1. The woman at the well was an unlikely candidate for orders, being a woman and a Samaritan and having had five partners, not all of them husbands.[310] Yet Jesus revealed himself to her as the Christ and made her into a preacher, causing her to announce the good news of his presence to the people of her own city. This drew some of them to him and he stayed in their city for two days. If the sending of the twelve as itinerant preachers can be interpreted as instituting the sacrament of Order, then, by turning the woman into a harbinger of the Messiah for the people of her town, Jesus created the precedent of including a woman in the same sacrament today.

2. In the parable of the talents, Jesus faults the servant who failed to trade the talent for fear of unspecified disapproval from his master. He knew what he was supposed to do but let assumptions about his master's *possible* displeasure divert him from getting on with the job he had been given.

3. Jesus said to his disciples, "The harvest is rich, but the labourers are few, so ask the Lord of the harvest to send labourers into his harvest". Church leadership has accepted for more than fifty years that there is a chronic and acute shortage of priests and keeps on exhorting the faithful to pray for more vocations. When and where did the people currently employed in the vineyard get the authority to turn away even one female volunteer, let alone all of them? Where did they get the authority to expel competent experienced vinedressers who do the honourable thing and marry the girl? By giving overriding priority (=worship?) to celibacy and maleness, Rome reduces the labour force in the vineyard to a fraction of what it might be—in direct conflict with the *expressed* wishes of Jesus.

4. We will be judged, Jesus teaches us, on one criterion only: "I was hungry, and you gave me to eat, naked and you clothed me'. The leaders have created laws that ensure that vast numbers of Catholics are denied reasonable access to Mass and the Eucharist; 'the source and summit of our spiritual lives'. If the hunger is for the grace of God, how can it be right to deny the faithful the sacramental means? The Roman curia behaves as if it does not believe in the efficacy of the sacrament.

5. The papacy, with a stroke of a pen, can change canon law. To do so on hot-button issues, however, would invite questions about blanket infallibility, and this would conflict with one of the top priorities of the bureaucracy. If the priorities are inspired by the group dynamic of selfishness, how will popes and curial leaders and indeed bishops, explain their paralysis in face of sacramental famine? For those in a position to change it, quoting canon law will be a poor

---

[310] At a symbolic level, the five partners have been taken to stand for the false gods of the five pagan groups assimilated by the Samaritans. But, if we are to read the passage symbolically, Jesus' sending of the woman becomes even more significant and more forceful.

defence. Misquoting scripture, as in the case of *Ordinatio Sacerdotalis* and *Inter Insigniores,* may not be much better.

FUNDAMENTAL CONSTITUTION

In *Ordinatio Sacerdotalis,* John Paul II quotes Paul VI approvingly as he explains:

> "The *real reason*[311] is that, in giving the Church her fundamental constitution, her theological anthropology … *Christ established things in this way*."[312]

Could anyone of lesser status than a pope get away with making such an historically contentious statement without adducing supporting evidence? In relation to the ordination of priests, the *real reason* cannot be that Christ 'established things in this way'. Christ never ordained a priest, male or female. What then *is* the real reason?

Constitution

Whatever shape the 'fundamental constitution' may have taken over the centuries, Christ did not give it to the Church. He gave the Twelve a mandate to make disciples of all the nations and left it to them and their successors to work out the practical details in changing circumstances down through the centuries. From an early post-apostolic stage, the structure was one of dispersed local communities with locally selected overseers gradually developing into diocesan bishops. It was characterised by mutual monitoring and accountability, co-operation and synodal deliberations, unified by faith in the risen Christ and by the celebration of the Eucharist. This has been changed into a highly centralised organisation, governed by a powerful, secretive, self-perpetuating bureaucracy, which also traditionally controls access to its head. Can this be what Christ gave his Church? We will revert to the question of the legal constitution of the Church in Chapter 13.

Neither Pope Paul VI nor Pope John Paul II offers any explanation of why the denial of priestly ordination to women should be 'fundamental'. To those who have survived seven years of seminary training, it may *seem* fundamental. To those steeped in the traditions of the Roman curia, where women have done only menial jobs for centuries, it is subconsciously self-evident. To the rest of the faithful, however, it appears to be an organisational issue which might well vary with time or place, with a legitimate diversity in a Church that spans many cultures and centuries and has varying needs. Christ never mentioned priestly ordination.[313] St Paul knew nothing of it except that in his understanding all the baptised shared and exercised Christ's priesthood; And indeed, this seems to be implicit in "Do This".

Among Christians, a study of the fundamentals cannot overlook the principal mandates:

---

[311] Emphasis added.

[312] Paul VI, Address on the Role of Women in the Plan of Salvation (January 30, 1977):

[313] Jesus often referred to the chief priests and high priests who were opposing his mission. His only recorded mention of a priest was a disparaging remark about the one who passed on the other side of the road to Jericho.

"Do this in commemoration of me" (Luke 22:19)

"Go, therefore, make disciples of all the nations … and teach them to observe all the commands I gave you. And know that I am with you always; yes, to the end of time". (Matthew 28:19-20

"By this shall all men know that you are my disciples, if you have love one for another"

"As long as you did this to one of these, my least ones you did it unto me".

Nor can one pretend that a fundamental statement from St Paul on equal filiation has no relevance in this context:

"All baptised in Christ, you have all clothed yourselves in Christ and there is no more distinction between Jew and Greek, slave and free, male and female, but all of you are one in Christ Jesus". (Gal 3:27-28)

Nor can we ignore, Jesus' answer to the question 'Master, which is the greatest commandment of the law? Jesus responded:

"You must love the Lord your God with all your heart, with all your soul, and with all your mind. This is the greatest and first commandment. The second resembles it: You must love your neighbour as yourself. On these two commandments hang the whole Law and the Prophets also". (Mat 22:35-40)

Yet, there is no attempt in *Ordinatio Sacerdotalis* or *Inter Insigniores* to harmonise the exclusion of women with *any* of these fundamentals. For those who take Christ at his word, the failure to link it to love of God and love of neighbour is a crucial weakness. From a theological point of view, the failure to relate it to the institution of the Eucharist is probably fatal.

HOW THIS PSEUDO-INFALLIBLE DOCTRINE WAS CRAFTED.

The production and publication of *Ordinatio Sacerdotalis* involved a conspiracy of deception which remained a secret for a decade, thanks to the oaths of loyalty of those prelates who were in the know.

The Presidents of all the Bishops Conferences of the world were summoned to Rome early in 1994 without being told the reason. There they were presented with the Apostolic Letter, *Ordinatio Sacerdotalis*, ready for publication. It contained a statement to the effect that it had been prepared "having heard the views of the bishops", which was untrue. Pontifical secrecy had ensured that their views would not be heard. The bishops had not been consulted or even informed that a review of the issue was being undertaken. The Presidents were asked to approve it on behalf of their bishops. They refused on the grounds that they would have to consult their bishops first. If they were to approve it without consulting their bishops, and without the revisions necessitated by the response, the statement would be a lie. Had the Presidents not been strong enough as a group to stop them, the curia personnel were prepared to issue an Apostolic Letter in the name of His Holiness that contained a deliberate falsehood! What is possibly worse, the letter included the term 'irreformable', which in Rome-speak implies infallibility. Had the letter been issued, the bishops of the world, whose views had *not* been sought, would have had to break their oaths of loyalty if they wished to correct the falsehood.

When the Presidents refused, the curia personnel had the option at that stage of circulating the draft letter, openly or *sub secreto pontifico*, for comment by the bishops, but they were no more willing to risk an uncontrolled survey of the bishops then than when the document was in preparation. From the trend of the discussion over the previous eighteen years, the curial officials were in a position to guess what the result would be if the bishops got a hint that the issue was being reviewed in Rome and that they were free to express their honest opinions. Most of the bishops were coping daily with a worsening shortage of priests and the ordination of women would open the way to a partial solution. The misogyny of the seminary may flourish in Rome, but it does not always survive the experience of running a modern diocese. The more practical bishops would have favoured any solution. Some of the more academically minded might have called their colleagues attention to the faulty reasoning or the ignoble footnotes.

After eighteen years of debate in the Church, the curia had good reason to fear they would get the 'wrong' answer from many bishops. So, they appeared to concede the point that the Presidents were making, and promised to make two deletions from the Letter:

1. the mendacious phrase about hearing the views of the bishops of the world,

2. the word 'irreformable' with its implication of infallibility.

However, about a year later, the doctrinal watchdog of the curia reneged on the second promise and put the irreformable bit back in again. Despite the assurance that had been given to the Presidents, the CDF issued a declaration affirming that the doctrine was "infallible".[314] The CDF knew that this did not make it infallible, but undoubtedly this double deception caused some of the faithful to believe that it was.

Not one bishop demurred at this bit of curial sleight-of-hand. The loyalty oath held. Only a retired bishop felt justified in telling what happened, and that more than ten years later.[315]

---

[314] Peter Burns S.J has an extensive consideration of this at: arcc-catholic-rights.net/burns.htm

[315] Bishop Geoffrey Robinson says as much in more diplomatic language: "In the twenty years I worked as an active bishop I can remember very few occasions when the pope consulted the body of bishops and none when the pope asked the bishops to vote on an issue. We were not asked to vote before the publication of the document on the ordination of women, not even when the Cardinal prefect of the Congregation for the Doctrine of the Faith spoke of this teaching as 'infallible', with the pope doing nothing to contradict him. If bishops are not asked their opinion even when the word 'infallible' is in the air, the college of bishops would seem to have no practical importance in the church, and the statement of the Second Vatican Council that this college is a co-holder of supreme power would seem to have little meaning. No explanation was given as to why the bishops were not consulted, but one may surely ask whether the reason was that some people close to the pope were afraid that the bishops would not give this teaching the near-unanimous endorsement that alone would have given

The clash illustrates the fragility of the power of the bureaucracy, which depends on keeping the bishops from acting in concert and explains why the papacy omitted practical structures for the exercise of Collegiality from the 1983 revision of canon law. It also illustrates how the needs of the bureaucracy can be prioritised to permit deception, even to the point of accretions to the deposit of faith.

The second promise was broken in Archbishop Ladaria's article which has been referred to above. The article stresses the importance that Pope John Paul II attached to consultation. This might lead the unwary reader to think that the bishops were consulted whereas, on the contrary, they had been carefully kept in the dark.

Structured weakness

How can a group of intelligent, educated, dedicated people tolerate this kind of deception in their name and in the name of Jesus Christ? The fault is not in the people, it is in the system they have inherited. In Chapter 1 above we quoted Jerry Pournelle's 'Iron Law of Bureaucracy': The people who are dedicated to the goals get over-whelmed while the people who are dedicated to the bureaucracy itself "will always gain control of the organization and will always write the rules under which the organization functions".

All organizations resist reform, but the curial culture has a special strength in this regard. It identifies the details of the religious *status quo* as God's plan. Thus, if one faults it, one is faulting God. It pretends that the teachings of the Roman Magisterium reflect exactly the Divinely protected beliefs of the People of God. Nobody teaches that the Holy Spirit works exclusively through the papacy, but the bureaucracy acts as if she does, treats theologians as if she does, treats bishops, pastors and faithful as if she does, and promotes the idea that, by some miraculous standing arrangement, Roman interpretations are right even when the thought processes have been shown to be wrong or even when the context of the question has changed.

This attitude was confirmed officially by the CDF in *Donum Veritatis* (1990) which defines the job of the theologian as that of producing better arguments in support of current Roman teaching. Like Lord Denning, people working in that bureaucracy are unable to contemplate the 'appalling vista' of the organisation they have given their lives to being undermined by an admission of contemporary error, deception, or corruption. It is better to let the deception continue than make futile efforts to correct it and be the one to trigger the scandal. Scandal, as we have observed, occurs as deception is unmasked. In a large bureaucracy, if a dedicated individual reckons that he has no chance of successfully challenging the system, what can he do but settle for doing his own job as dutifully as possible? And the loyalty oath absolves his conscience.

---

credence to the use of the word 'infallible' in speaking of it. —Bishop Geoffrey Robinson, *Confronting Power and Sex in the Catholic Church,* Dublin, The Columba Press, 2007, p125.

Conclusion from a careful reading

Current Church policy has been shaped by the reluctance of the papal bureaucracy to admit that *any* well-known post-1870 pronouncement by a pope can be wrong. The *traditional* defence of the long-established practice of excluding women from ordination has relied on the now discredited ontological inferiority of women and must fail. The *scriptural* defence—that Christ's selection of men only as apostles is part of a divine plan that cannot change to suit the time or circumstance, relies on a prejudiced interpretation of Mark 3 verses 13-14, that requires verse 14 to be misrepresented, truncated, and/or mistranslated.

Current Church teaching on the ordination of women is based on two remarkably inadequate magisterial documents which fall apart on careful reading. At one key point they contradict one another. The Congregation for the Doctrine of the Faith has tried to compensate for their weakness by mendaciously declaring the latest one infallible. The faithful are entitled to the truth from their leaders.

Chapter 13

Unwinding a Council

"For the authoritarian defensive stance of Vatican one,
Vatican two substitutes the posture of friendliness, self-criticism, and adaptability."

—Cardinal Avery Dulles

Papal Infallibility as defined at Vatican I was limited and conditional to the point where it has only been invoked properly once since then. It was a disappointment to the Ultramontanes who had hoped for a broad unlimited infallibility that would make future Councils or even discussion superfluous. They wanted a pope who, by virtue of a standing supernatural intervention, could give an infallible answer to any question that might be asked.[316]

The curia was more sanguine, however, realising that conditions and limitations can be circumvented. The title of infallible alone was enough to deliver immense authority. For the rest of the nineteenth century and the first half of the twentieth, the papacy ignored the limitations and acted as if nothing could be questioned. In teaching documents, it quoted excerpts from papal pronouncements as if they formed part of revelation[317] and the Inquisition/Holy Office/CDF used coercion to repress disagreement. At the same time, Universal Jurisdiction safeguarded the curia by burdening the pope with detailed responsibilities on such a scale as to make him totally dependent on the bureaucracy.

Curial anxiety

In such a situation, the unexpected announcement by Pope John XXIII of his intention of summoning a Council caused alarm in the bureaucracy. Most of the curia's power had been gained at the expense of the bishops. Any meeting of the world's bishops would be impossible to control and potentially damaging. But a Council focused on ecumenism could realise the worst fears of the bureaucracy. Any movement in that direction would threaten the absolute and arbitrary powers of the papacy that had been established at Vatican I. They had looked at the issue two or three times already in the twentieth century. Rome had stayed aloof from the Mission Conference at Edinburgh in 1910 and rudely declined an invitation to the follow-up

---

[316] "Again, on February 20, impatient at the slow progress of the Council, Veuillot [editor of the strongly Ultramontane French Catholic daily newspaper, *l'Universe*] exhorted the Fathers to hasten on to the definition, because once this was achieved affairs could proceed much faster, as pontifical acts could take the place of conciliar deliberations".—Dom Cuthbert Butler, *The Vatican Council 1869-1870*, Collins and Harvill Press. London 1962, *p292-294*

[317] Cf. Yves Congar O.P., *My Journal of the Council*, 2012, p48 §3

conference in 1927. The encyclical *Mortalium Animus* in 1928 had been designed to prevent the development of any movement at grass-roots level towards unity by declaring ecumenism to be … "a most grave error, by which the foundations of the Catholic faith are completely destroyed" and furthermore by ruling "nor is it any way lawful for Catholics either to support or to work for such enterprises".

Aware of the danger from the proposed Council, the curia immediately went into damage limitation mode and has stayed there for most of the time since then.

John XXIII intended Vatican II to focus on ecumenism and he offered a brave and warm welcome to other churches in his original announcement. He spoke of the "friendly and renewed invitation to our brothers of the separated Christian Churches to share with us in this banquet of grace and brotherhood". In the first indication of opposition, the authorised version of his speech issued by the curia changed what the Pope had said. His reference to them as Christian Churches was altered to read 'separated communities' and the invitation to 'a banquet of grace and brotherhood' became a call to 'follow Us … in this search for unity and grace'. Where John XXIII was deliberately opening a door to ecumenism, the curia dishonestly recast him as pursuing reunionism.[318] Furthermore, the warmth that characterised Pope John's way of expressing himself was toned down and the hint that the other churches might participate fully as churches was carefully edited out.[319]

Later, the Pope was persuaded to appoint the prefects of the relevant curial Congregations as leaders of the various preparatory commissions. He had been against this "but there was a veritable siege of the Pope, conducted by the personnel of the Curia"[320] and he had finally given way. Congar regretted that the overall objective of Christian unity, which should have imbued each one of the preparatory documents from the outset, had been generally disregarded.[321] In the event, the Council, with the approval of the Pope, set a new course and took a different direction from that proposed by the preparatory commissions but by that time it was too late for such a pivotal concept to permeate all the Council documents.

Curial obstruction

Congar writes in his journal: "It must be acknowledged that, since the beginning, throughout the whole preparatory period, and since the opening of the Council, there has been an ongoing conflict between the *Ecclesia* and the curia" … "The curia people

---

[318] 'Reunionism' is a convenient term to indicate a Christian unity achieved by having the other denominations simply return to the fold by submitting to the universal jurisdiction and infallibility of the pope and accepting Catholic teaching as a package. It was the only route to unity recognised by Rome until Vatican II reversed the teaching on Ecumenism.

[319] Cf. Hebblethwaite, Peter and Margaret, *John XXIII, Pope of the Century,* Continuum, London and New York, 2000, p 163, quoting Hales, E.E.Y., *Pope John and his Revolution,* Eyre and Spottiswoode, London, 1965, p 98.

[320] Yves Congar O.P., *My Journal of the Council,* 2012, p 515

[321] Congar called the attention of Pope John XXIII to this situation in a letter dated 12th July 1961. Cf. Yves Congar O.P., *My Journal of the Council,* 2012, p45 Footnote 5.

(Ottaviani, Browne, Staffa, Carli …) are doing EVERYTHING to prevent the episcopate from recovering the rights which have been stolen from it".[322] "These events, these past days are contributing to the maintenance of a kind of distrust with respect to the people of the curia, who are felt to be trying to sabotage the Council".[323]

Vatican II was not in the business of defining dogmas. It was reflecting about the faith and about the Church, how it sees itself, its teaching, liturgy, and organisation and how it relates or should relate to the modern world and the other Christian churches. In contrast to Vatican I, there was room in its documents for a variety of opinions. There was a large majority in favour of change, but it was appropriate that the views of the those opposed to change be heard and recorded. The criticism that the documents are ambivalent and self-contradictory in places is thus misplaced although it is true that they are open to different interpretations, depending on what is selected or emphasised. This is as it should be. The Church is the People of God, not an ideological monolith. Faith precedes membership of the Church. (It is presumed on behalf of the baptised infant by parents and godparents.) The faith that St Paul looked for was belief in the Risen Christ. This criterion has been replaced by acceptance, or profession, of belief in a bundle of doctrines—to a greater or lesser extent unexamined by the candidate for baptism. This does more honour to the authority of the church than to truth.

For a hundred years of pseudo-infallibility, the faithful were (mis)led to believe that the Church was perfect in all respects and divinely inspired in every detail of its teaching. For Catholics who accepted this piously, it logically precluded change. For the attending bishops, Vatican II offered the first opportunity to think outside the box and they grasped it. The possibility of change was described by John Courtney Murray as the issue that underlay every issue at the Council.

The non-curial bishops and cardinals at the Second Vatican Council and the members of papal commissions were free to pursue the truth unconstrained by oaths. They were not afraid to revise some explicit and implicit pseudo-infallibilities which had long been taken for granted in Roman Catholicism. In relation to Biblical studies alone, the Council defended the use of 'historical-critical' methods.[324] Catholic Bible scholars were encouraged to use all the tools of modern science to uncover what the authors of the Old and New Testaments were trying to convey in the language, culture and historical circumstances of their times. This was posing a threat to pseudo-infallibility since such studies tended to produce new insights and interpretations.

The CDF was faced with the daunting task of coping with the changed perspectives of the Council while not admitting to any imperfection in what had gone before. Within a year the CDF, under Cardinal Ottaviani, issued a letter which, had the effect

---

[322] Yves Congar O.P., *My Journal of the Council*, 2012, p 425. (Emphasis is in the original)
[323] Yves Congar O.P., *My Journal of the Council*, 2012, p 618
[324] See Georg Shelbert, *Defaming the Historical-Critical Method*, in Hans Kung & Leonard Swidler, eds, The Church in Anguish, San Francisco, Harper and Row, 1987, pp 106-124.

of undermining the Council. It was issued as a secret letter, but subsequently had to be made public.[325] It complained of misuses in the interpretation of the Council and made reference to scholars who were putting aside Tradition in their examination of the meaning of scripture. New methods of biblical scholarship had been encouraged, but Cardinal Ottaviani was not prepared to tolerate any new understanding. Later, under Cardinal Joseph Ratzinger, the CDF seemed to believe that some scholars had destructive intentions. What should have been normal scholarly disagreements in the search for truth became very divisive issues with participants failing to respect one another. Moreover, for the Catholics who had been led to believe that everything that emanated from Rome had a divine seal of eternal veracity, any significant doubt about one teaching threatened a knock-on effect, leading to great anxiety about the foundation of their beliefs.

When they were permitted freedom of debate the bishops at Vatican II changed the face of the church despite the best efforts of the curia to maintain the *status quo*. Paradoxically however, the theoretically supreme authority found itself lacking in immediate power. Some important issues were kept from its agenda and these still haunt the Church today. These are the very issues that have damaged the credibility of Rome in the second half of the twentieth century, and that have made Rome look irrational, prejudiced, untruthful, out-of-date, merciless, unloving, autocratic and, for many, irrelevant. They are the ordination of women, celibacy, and contraception.

On one issue of the greatest importance, the Council was outmanoeuvred between sessions. Having developed the idea of Collegiality, the bishops saw the need for a legal structure to make it effective on an ongoing basis. The plan was to address this in the fourth session. The curia forestalled them, however, by getting Paul VI to announce a Synod of Bishops that would be limited to an advisory role and be strictly under curial control. He did this in his opening address to the fourth session of the Council (14 September 1965). His Motu Proprio, *Apostolica Sollicitudo*, instituting the Synod of Bishops was published one day later. It was a *fait accompli*. Although the bishops were assembled in an Ecumenical Council, they were not consulted. They were bypassed completely. They were deprived of any opportunity to discuss a document that created a new permanent Church institution that had arisen out of the Council's own deliberations. In effect, it negated the most significant vision of the Council by preventing the bishops from setting up an effective structure to implement Collegiality. While the text claims that it was Paul's own idea,[326] this is probably untrue. Its creation and detailed constitution clearly involved enormous effort by sections of the curia working with unaccustomed urgency to complete it in the interval between Council sessions. *Cui bono?* The bureaucracy, of course, was the beneficiary;

---

[325] Shelbert, *Op. Cit.*

[326] Pope Paul VI expressed the hope that the Synod would become be a stronger institution in the future. If it really was his own creation, however, he could have given it deliberative power from the outset … or at least allowed the Council to decide its form, powers, and constitution.

the creation of an overriding power centre to which it would have been subject, was successfully nipped in the bud. The speed with which it was prepared indicates that it was a priority project within the curia. Paul VI was notoriously slow in making decisions.

On several other issues, the Council's decisions have been ignored or reversed. Immediate power can override authority where there is no appeal to an independent judiciary or if the authority is prevented by procedural rules from following up on its decisions.

FAILURES IN IMPLEMENTING THE DECREES

The curia of its nature is resistant to change, yet the job of implementing the Council decrees was left to it. This was inappropriate, since the curia had formed the core of the minority that had been overwhelmed time and again in the debate and by the consensus of the assembled bishops.

Consequently, while Vatican pronouncements during the past 50 years invariably paid lip service to the Second Vatican Council, the bureaucracy has been seen to ignore, obstruct or reverse many of the teachings and decisions of the supreme authority in the Church. This has had to be done piecemeal and surreptitiously lest it undermine the general authority of the papacy so sedulously built up over the previous century. This is not something they are ready to admit, but the record on the implementation of the Council speaks for itself.

Collegiality

Collegiality was the outstanding vision of the Council and Church governance by the College of Bishops with the Pope was its overarching proposal. Giving structure to the authority of the bishops, however, would have threatened the governing functions of the bureaucracy and reduced its remit to that of administration. Collegiality was effectively legislated into impotence by the curia when it drafted the 1983 revision of the Code of Canon Law. The former President of Ireland, Mary McAleese, herself a civil and canon lawyer, examines this issue in scholarly detail in her book, *Quo Vadis?*[327]

When Pope John XXIII announced his intention of calling the Second Vatican Council, he also announced a reform of the Code of Canon Law. It was understood from the outset that the deliberations of the Council would be incorporated in the revision. The responsibility for the revision fell to the curia although, as we have noted, it had formed the core of a remarkably small minority opposition on many issues during the debates. It took an inordinate 18 years[328] to complete the revision. This suggests extended infighting as to what should or should not be included, but

---

[327] Mary McAleese, *Quo Vadis* Dublin, 2012, Columba Press.
[328] The 1917 Code which followed Vatican I took 47 years to create but the task then was much more complex. It was codifying the canons of nearly two millennia and must have involved an enormous amount of research.

there are other possible explanations. They may have been waiting for Paul VI to die and make way for the possible election of a pope with a less conciliar mindset? Or were they waiting for the excitement and widespread interest in the Council initiatives to fade from public memory? In the end, although "the Bishops and the Bishops' Conferences were invited to associate themselves with the work",[329] the provision for the working of the College of Bishops ensured that the immediate threat to curial hegemony was removed.

Ecumenism:

The unity of the Church was Pope John's principal objective in calling the Council and the Council committed Catholicism unequivocally to the ecumenical process. This quickly led the church organisations to establish friendly and cooperative relationships. In this they were only catching up on the tolerant relationships that had existed between their members individually for generations.

Pope Paul VI was deeply committed to the Council and under his leadership the Christian faithful rejoiced in the Ecumenical spring. The curia, however, had reason to believe that any agreement on structural unity would lead to constitutional limits on its own power. In the following two pontificates (not counting that of John Paul 1) pre-conciliar attitudes reasserted themselves in Rome and an Ecumenical winter set in. Although the frost was palpable, Pope John Paul II signalled his approval of Ecumenism several times. He is said to have personally approved the celebration at Augsburg on 31st October 1999 that marked the signing of the Joint Declaration on the Doctrine of Justification (JDDJ) by Catholic and Lutheran representatives. This important doctrinal reconciliation has since been endorsed by the World Methodist Council (2006) and the World Communion of Reformed Churches (2017). The declaration was the fruit of Catholic-Lutheran contacts initiated during the Council and carried forward by the Secretariat for Promoting Christian Unity. Pope John Paul II had encouraged its work in 1988 by elevating the Secretariat into a Pontifical Council. Later he issued the encyclical, *Ut Unum Sint,* that identifies ecumenism as the will of Christ for his church but included some contradictory pre-conditions. We revert to this in Chapter 16 below.

Moral Theology

The Council expressed dissatisfaction about the discipline of Moral Theology and called for a re-think more grounded in biblical values. This work should have been initiated right away, continuing the Conciliar freedom of expression. It might have been better done in tandem with the eighteen-year long revision of the Code of Canon Law.

In view of the overwhelming importance in Christianity of personal conduct, the failure to generate an appropriate consultation and widespread discussion on this

---

[329] Apostolic Constitution of Pope John Paul II, *Sacrae Disiplinae Leges,* 25th January 1983

crucially important subject is nothing short of a disgrace. Theologians who took the initiative and made a start should have been facilitated and encouraged; instead, they were persecuted and silenced. The bishops of the world assembled in Council with the Pope, saw the need for a review, but any resultant change would risk undermining some of the pseudo-infallibilities, particularly those promoted since 1870. So, power trumped authority again and the protection of the papacy got prioritised over the search for truth. What's new? That a church founded by Christ would fail to pursue the truth fearlessly, points to a breakdown in governance or of trust in the Promise. Or both. We will have reason to revert to the issue of Moral Theology in more detail in Chapters 13 and 14.

Religious freedom

There should be no coercion in religious matters. The Council stated this unequivocally, yet the Congregation for the Doctrine of the Faith, representing the top management of the Church itself, continues routinely to ignore the principle and to behave as if the ends it serves can justify the means it uses. Since the CDF is itself the authority on doctrine and is still (at the time of writing) the dominant dicastery in the curia, nobody can challenge it effectively.

Episcopal Conferences

The importance of Episcopal Conferences was stressed by the Council and reiterated by Pope Paul VI in the motu proprio, *Ecclesiae Sanctae*. Cardinal Ratzinger, as prefect of the CDF, however, invoked the will of Christ to deny the Conferences any authority.[330] In another motu proprio, *Apostolos Suos* (1998) John Paul II had reinforced the procedural rules for the conferences in a way that effectively put the limited doctrinal and disciplinary decisions they were allowed to make back under Roman control. Decisions would have to be submitted to the Apostolic See for approval *unless they had been agreed by absolute unanimity.*[331] The chances of getting total unanimity on anything worth discussing among a group of up to 300 bishops are more remote than winning the Lotto. This stratagem reflects the curia's fear of bishops in groups and its capacity to control them as individuals. In practice, if one bishop can be found to disagree, then the decision reverts to the curia[332].

The submission of decisions to Rome protects pseudo-infallibility, by preventing the conferences from expressing different views or proposing different solutions

---

[330] "We must not forget that the episcopal conferences have no theological basis, they do not belong to the structure of the Church, as willed by Christ, that cannot be eliminated". —Excerpts from the Ratzinger Report, Ignatius Press, accessed May 2018.
https://ww.ignatius.com/promotions/benedictxvibooks/excerptRR.html

[331] Absolute unanimity here contrasts with the majority vote deemed adequate for dogmas in 1870.

[332] It is ironic that this rule was introduced during the reign of a pope from Poland where the 17th Century *sejm* (parliament) required unanimity for all decisions. Since all nobility were considered equal, none could be overridden. Thus, every member had a veto. This allowed Poland's aggressive neighbours to make its parliament ineffective by influencing one member of the *sejm* to use his veto.

when problems arise. It also obstructs discussion in general and hinders the development of the *sensus fidelium*.

The Hierarchy of truths.

The Council recommended that theologians participating in ecumenical dialogue "should remember that in Catholic doctrine there exists a "hierarchy" of truths, since they vary in their relation to the fundamental Christian faith".[333] This was more of an authorisation than a reminder and has significance for Christian life far beyond ecumenism. Catholic theologians were aware of the principle already but had not been allowed to admit as much. The idea allows a Christian to discriminate between the doctrines or disciplines that are important and those that are trivial. Authoritarian superiors, however, cannot brook the idea that inferiors should be entitled to make such judgements for themselves. Obedience is obedience. For the martinet mentality, obedience becomes an end in itself. Disobedience on a trivial matter can be seen to give greater offence, simply because the matter is trivial. Not surprisingly, the curia has downplayed the hierarchy of truths ever since. It does not fit well with a system based on domination and subordination.

There is a tension between freedom of opinion and authoritarianism. Is it possible to share a unity of love and purpose with people who do not profess *all* the same beliefs? Should they be seen to tolerate and cooperate with people who are deemed by official Catholic standards to be 'in error' on specific issues? An insidious purity ethic can interfere here, by prioritising one's own veneer of perfection; or through fear of being seen to dine with sinners. For example, it has stopped some bishops from openly supporting Amnesty International in its outstanding and vital work of love for neighbour, because one Amnesty policy, that on abortion, does not align with that of the Church. Given a Christly sense of values, and the Church tradition of ransoming prisoners, one would have expected today's Church to be a lively and committed participant in the effective work of Amnesty for prisoners of conscience.

Liturgy in the vernacular

The constitution, *Sacrosanctum Concilium*, of the Second Vatican Council approved the use of the vernacular in the liturgy and expressed the desire that "all the faithful should be led to that fully conscious, and active participation in liturgical celebrations". The Council decided that the translation of the liturgy into the vernacular should be the responsibility of the relevant bishops. This decision has been reversed by a congregation in the curia which had no authority and no right to override a Council decision. Unfortunately, it had the power and there was no avenue of appeal.

The constitution had recommended that "both texts and rites should be drawn up so that they express *more clearly* the holy things which they signify; the Christian people, so far as possible, should be enabled to understand them with ease and ... *that*

---

[333] *Unitatis Redintegratio*, §11

they be given new vigour to meet the circumstances and needs of modern times". In preventing this from happening, the curia catered for certain preferences in the Vatican but hastened the erosion of congregations and the loss of the younger generations.

The International Commission for English in the Liturgy (ICEL) had been set up by the bishops of the English-speaking world while the Council was still in progress to coordinate their response to the challenge of translation. Ensuring that meanings would not be distorted, required great sensitivity and cooperation by the best biblical, liturgical, linguistic, and musical scholarship available. Complications due to variant usage of language, both geographically and historically, needed to be resolved. The cooperation of scholars from other denominations was welcomed as befitted the ecumenical climate prevailing at the time the work was undertaken. A vast amount of careful study and consultation among experts went on quietly for decades with drafts and comments being exchanged openly for critical review. The results were submitted to the curia for *recognitio* (which normally means confirmation) in 1998.

As an international activity, ICEL had demonstrated that Catholic bishops could work together on creative pastoral work without detailed supervision by Rome. This turned out to be fatally provocative; such independent achievement could not be countenanced by the bureaucracy. A cluster of bishops working together independently might form a power centre that could get out of control. They had to be reined in. After almost forty years, and with the advent of different leadership in the Vatican, the days of ICEL were numbered. The Congregation for Divine Worship (CDW) went on the warpath, relying on power while declining to dialogue with the ICEL leadership about its concerns.

The CDW insisted on changes in the theory and objectives that had been guiding the work of the ICEL.

> "Instead of conveying an equivalence of meaning between the Latin and English texts, as had been ICEL's practice hitherto [approved twice by the pope], the congregation now wanted translations that conveyed an equivalence of individual Latin words".[334]

Furthermore, they banned the use of gender inclusive language which ICEL had judged to be more acceptable to twentieth century congregations. The developing cooperation with other denominations in the adoption of common texts was forbidden. This had given rise to some shared translations of scripture and prayers and was pointing in the direction of a common lectionary at some time in the future. The curia could not tolerate either trend. It fears anything that might make little of the differences between men and women because of the weakness of its case against women's ordination. It needs to maximise the differences also between Catholicism

---

[334] Excerpt from: John Wilkins, former editor of The Tablet, *Lost in Translation, The Bishops, the Vatican & the English Liturgy,* from *Commonweal,* November 28, 2005. I have used this well-informed source in relation to the topic, but the speculations are mine.

and the other Christian denominations. The barriers must be maintained. They know that Ecumenical progress can only reduce the bureaucracy's power and control.

In March 2001, the instruction, *Liturgiam Authenticam,* was issued by the Congregation for Divine Worship. It overturned the entire basis on which ICEL's work had rested'. In July of the same year a supervisory committee of Cardinals was imposed on ICEL. Both moves reversed the specific decision of the Second Vatican Council which had put the bishops who shared vernacular languages in charge of the translations. In overturning the decision of a Council, the Congregation was acting beyond its authority. But it had the power to enforce its preferences. ICEL, which legally belonged to the bishops was given a new structure that allowed it to be hijacked by the curia. All its long-serving, key personnel were fired and its careful work to make the liturgy more edifying and more meaningful for the modern Catholic congregation was set aside. (And secularism is still being blamed for the shrinking congregations!)

New translations were hurriedly produced under the supervision of people for whom English was not their mother tongue. They prioritised faithfulness to the Latin words and syntax in place of communicating the meaning. The outcome, for the English-speaking world, has been a liturgical language that commends itself to lovers of Latin but divorces the liturgy (and maybe religion) from the everyday life of the congregation. It had to be forced on a reluctant clergy and an un-consulted laity. Not only does it fail to speak to the faithful in understandable language, but it also gives the impression that the Church is out of date by several centuries, confirming Cardinal Martini's comment. This has been especially off-putting for the younger generations. Is it any wonder that the age profile of the faithful attending the liturgy is getting older while the congregations get smaller?

Why change something that was working?

It is hard to believe that Latin equivalence and syntax should have been prioritised over the accessibility of the liturgy for the faithful. That may not have been the real reason. Another explanation is more plausible. Had it more to do with bureaucratic fears than with the liturgy? The work of scholarship and translation had been proceeding without fanfare or controversary for several decades under the English-speaking bishops, working together without the intervention of Rome. The group of bishops and scholars, including a few who belonged to other churches, had been cooperating harmoniously, creatively, and openly on the work given them by the Council. They had produced hundreds of elegant texts in modern English, some of them quite beautiful and inspiring. If a group of independent bishops were seen to make a good success of this effort together, whatever might they think of doing next? Further liturgical cooperation with other denominations? An initiative to meet the need for additional ministers?

In this we can see a direct reversal of decisions of Vatican II, with power overriding proper authority, driven by curial fear of Ecumenism and of bishops acting collectively. ICEL was doing a good job, but too independently. The guiding principle of large secular bureaucracies was applied; what cannot be eliminated must be con-trolled—what cannot be controlled must be eliminated.

The whole sorry story has recently been published in book form by two of the most eminent and best qualified commentators in the Church.[335]

Episcopal teaching

The occasional serious commentaries of the US Conference of Catholic Bishops on issues of public policy and socioeconomics have ceased. According to Archbishop Rembert Weakland, Pope John Paul II disapproved of these because they were based on widespread consultation and research rather than top down authoritative instruc-tion,[336] which of course would normally come from the centre. For a papacy, or a magisterium that claims a broad infallibility, the idea of consulting the faithful is much too dangerous, and the very idea of a lesser body showing the way was anathema.[337] Only God knows what that might lead to! The US bishops' thoughtful documents were intended to make a Catholic contribution to current thinking about important moral issues. They tended, however, to put the USCCB in a position of leadership, not limited to the USA, taking the initiative in response to world problems and the signs of the times. They were thus encroaching on pontifical turf, tending to upstage the papacy. The USCCB could not be eliminated, of course. Instead they were brought under control. We may presume that pontifical displeasure was communi-cated. The policy of appointing more docile and compliant men to fill vacant sees ensured that the unwelcome initiatives came to an end and the standing of the U.S. Catholic bishops was weakened with consequences still being felt to the present day.

Primacy of conscience versus primacy of law

The Pastoral Constitution on the Church in the Modern World, *Gaudium et Spes,* had not been foreseen or prepared in advance of the Council but arose from the floor on the initiative of Cardinal Suenens. It grew out of the experience of the Council and expressed its maturing spirit. It looked to how the church could be of service to humanity. Rather than concentrating on its own culture, it saw its message, the mes-sage of Christ giving witness to the truth, and promoting love of neighbour, as being able to contribute to every culture. It saw the human being as a unity that could only exist in society, with all the consequent social and moral implications. It was able to see good in every culture. It recognised the sanctity of conscience in everyone, even the misinformed. Unfortunately, the confident, outward looking, positive, spirit of *Gaudium et Spes* with its readiness to take account of the signs of the times, was never fully shared by the curia. They had too much to fear, too much to lose.

---

[335] Gerald O'Collins, S.J with John Wilkins, *Lost in Translation,* Liturgical Press, United States, 2017.

[336] "He [John Paul II] totally disagreed, if not with the content, with the process of widespread consultation that went into the writing of the letters on peace and the economy, seeing that process as a democratization of authority and a serious threat to his exercise of centralized autocratic leadership". —John J. McNeill S.J in a review of Archbishop Weakland's memoirs.

[337] Our recently canonised saint, John Henry Newman, got into lots of trouble for initiating the idea.

Veritatis Splendor

The 1993 encyclical letter of John Paul II, *Veritatis Splendor* was a major attempt to unwind an important teaching of the Council, buried in 175 pages. It is in three chapters, but the evidence of the text is that Chapter 2 is by the hand of another or others.[338] It is with this chapter that we will mainly be concerned.

The encyclical presents itself as building on the Council document, *Gaudium et Spes,* but actually reinterprets it and changes its emphasis. Where *Gaudium et Spes* elevates obedience to the moral conscience as 'the very dignity of man' at the point where he is 'alone with God, whose voice echoes in his depths', the encyclical tries to elevate 'law and precept'. The papacy, of course, claims *plenitudo potestatis* in making 'law and precept', so this is not entirely surprising. *Veritatis Splendor* has not been received without some serious criticism. Six leading professional theologians from five universities have contributed to an 'examination' of its assertions in a book entitled *Splendor of Accuracy*.[339] It is probably fair to say that the encyclical fails the examination. Regrettably, however, under current practice, selected phrases can be given pseudo-infallible status in future documents.

Mary Elsbernd, Director of the Institute of Pastoral Studies, Loyola University, Chicago has pointed out that, while the frequent references in *Veritatis Splendor* to *Gaudium et Spes* might lead the reader to assume a continuity of thought between the two documents, the reverse would be nearer the truth.[340] What appears initially to be a reiteration turns out to be a re-interpretation in three significant areas.

> "First, the theological anthropology of *Gaudium et Spes* has been recast in a dualistic and individualistic concept in *Veritatis Splendor.*
>
> Second, Veritatis Splendor has recontextualised quotations from *Gaudium et Spes* on change, conscience, dialogue with modern culture, human autonomy, and social institutions by placing them into paragraphs stressing law and precepts.
>
> Third, relying on selective wording of *Gaudium et Spes, Veritatis Splendor* has reworked the role of the moral theologian into a disseminator of magisterial teaching only".[341]

The Council determined from the outset that none of its documents would be infallible. Thus, anybody, including a pope, may disagree with them. The pretence of continuity, however, while attempting to undermine the Council's important teaching on the primacy of conscience is disingenuous, if not dishonest. It reflects the Roman

---

[338] Cf. Joseph A. Selling, *The Context and Arguments of Veritatis Splendor,* in Joseph A. Selling & Jan Jans (eds), The Splendor of Accuracy, Grand Rapids, MN, William B. Eerdmans Publishing Company, 1995

[339] Joseph A Selling and Jan Jans (eds) *Splendor of Accuracy,* Grand Rapids, Michigan, William B. Eerdmans Publishing Company, 1995

[340] Cf. Sr Mary Elsbernd, O.S.F., *The reinterpretation of Gaudium et spes in Veritatis Splendor,* in HORIZONS, Villanova University, Philadelphia. Vol 29, Fall 2002, pp 225-239.

[341] Ibid. p226

need to protect the aura of generalised infallibility while it backtracks on a teaching that could reduce the impact of authoritarian papal pronouncements.

One cannot but recall Newman's remark:[342]

> "Certainly, if I am obliged to bring religion into after-dinner toasts, (which indeed does not seem quite the thing) I shall drink—to the Pope, if you please,—still, to Conscience first, and to the Pope afterwards".

The academic quality of *Veritatis Splendor* has been referred to in Chapter 10. and will emerge again in Chapter 14 in relation to the rethinking of Moral Theology.

A Constitution for the Church

Despite the Roman predilection for law, the Church has never had a 'fundamental constitution' in the legal sense. The nearest we have got is the description in *Lumen Gentium* where the twelve apostles with Peter at their head are given as the model and precedent for their successors, the College of Bishops who, with the Pope, govern the Church. If that is the constitutional structure, however, it currently stands suspended by the 1983 revision of the Code of Canon Law (CIC), which was written by the curia and reflects the fear of bishops acting in concert. As an active College, the bishops could be expected to regain some of the powers which, in Congar's words[343] were stolen from them over the centuries.[344] The 1983 Code makes the College as ineffectual as possible by denying it a legal way to meet except when summoned by the papacy in a procedure akin to that for a full ecumenical council.[345]

The vision of the College of Bishops led by the Pope governing the Church and modelled on the Apostles with Peter, has not been realised. The 1983 Code was drafted by the bureaucracy to keep its own hegemony intact. The bishops are not allowed to govern. The vision will remain a vision as long as the bishops are denied the right to meet except when summoned by the papacy (in effect, by the curia), and even then, told what they may or may not discuss. To govern, they must be free to meet when they see fit, decide their agenda, speak openly, and ensure that the executive implements their policies.

The model has been distorted. The first Council of the church met in Jerusalem on the initiative of the disciples in Antioch, the periphery and not by Peter at the centre. The agenda was set by Paul and Barnabas. The subsequent Councils were summoned and chaired by Emperors. The apostles were free to travel, preach, meet, and speak without seeking permission from Peter. Moreover, there was nobody in a position to prevent them from talking to Peter when they so wished.

---

[342] Newman's *Letter to the Duke of Norfolk,* 1874

[343] Cf. Yves Congar O.P., *My Journal of the Council,* 2012, p425

[344] At each of the Councils of Constance, Vatican 1 and Vatican II, the bishops recognised a need for them to meet at approximately 10-year intervals. The idea was tried once after Constance and ignored after Vatican I. At Vatican II it was forestalled by announcing a system of curia-controlled synods devoid of deliberative powers.

[345] Cf. Mary McAleese, *Quo Vadis,*

During the Second Vatican Council,[346] Pope Paul VI called for a written constitution to be created and the subsequent revision of Canon Law offered a perfect opportunity. A Constitution would have defined basic rights and responsibilities and introduced checks and balances, but these would have implied limits to the exercise of power, particularly by the curia. The idea of a separate Constitution died at some point in the seventeen-year gestation period but a few of the rights of members of the church that would have been in such a Constitution can be found scattered within the 1983 Code.[347]

Fr Andrew Greeley, in his foreword to Leonard Swidler's book on the subject,[348] has pointed out that the curia included a "bill of rights" for the faithful in the 1983 Revision of Canon Law but kept quiet about it. He comments that "those who revised the code wanted lay people to have rights but did not want them to know they had rights". There are 1752 Canons in the revised code, so not many members of the laity are aware of its contents. An attempt to publish the "bill of rights" in a separate booklet was blocked. Furthermore, the code does not include any procedures for vindicating these rights. Swidler's book discusses what a Catholic Constitution should encompass and includes discussion drafts of constitutions for the Church, for a Diocese and for a Parish. It is regrettable that the fiction of inerrancy makes it impossible for the curia to listen to the faithful and their pastors even when, as in this case, the project was put on the agenda by the Pope himself.

The existence of a written Constitution would help clarify the needed changes when the will to greater structural unity between the churches finally takes hold. Constitutions that endure tend to avoid detailed legislation but focus on fundamental principles and objectives. These Christ has left to us with adequate clarity. They are listed in Chapter 2 of this book, but Christians everywhere know them.

The resistance of the curia to the Council has continued despite denials and lip service. It has become more obvious, however, as Pope Francis pursues policies that better reflect the spirit of the Council. Moreover, he is reading the signs of the times by taking a moral stance on our care for the planet. At times important sections of the curia, whose *raison d'être* is to assist the Pope, are seen to be working against him.

---

[346] Pope Paul first suggested it in a briefing to the Commission for the Revision of the Code of Canon Law, (20 Nov. 1965) —Peter Hebblethwaite, *Paul VI, the First Modern Pope,* London, Harper-Collins, 1993, P572.

[347] Leonard Swidler, *Toward a Catholic Constitution,* New York, Crossroad Publishing Co., 1996

[348] Preface by Andrew Greeley to Leonard Swidler, *Toward a Catholic Constitution,* New York, Crossroad Publishing Company, 1996.

Chapter 14

Rethinking Moral Theology

Original Sin is not doing what God wants you to do.
—Hildegarde of Bingen, Doctor of the Church.

DOES MORALITY CHANGE?

The Second Vatican Council looked to the future, taking a positive attitude towards the world and the place of the Church in the world. One must read between the lines to find the implied criticism of past or present. The narrow, static, and abstract view of the world typical of scholastic theology was challenged in the Pastoral Constitution on the Church in the Modern World:

> "In pastoral care, appropriate use must be made not only of theological principles, but also of the findings of the secular sciences, especially of the findings of psychology and sociology. Thus the faithful can be brought to live the faith in a more thorough and mature way".—*Gaudium et Spes*, §62

Here they are calling for Revelation to be interpreted in the light of modern bible scholarship and the growing knowledge of the world and humanity so that the faithful can live the faith more fully.

The weakness of Catholic Moral Theology was identified directly as a current failing and inspired one of the most important and courageous demands of the Council:

> "Other theological disciplines should also be renewed by livelier contact with the mystery of Christ and the history of salvation. *Special attention needs to be given to the development of Moral Theology. Its scientific exposition should be more thoroughly nourished by scriptural teaching.* It should show the nobility of the Christian vocation of the Faithful and their obligation to bring forth fruit in charity for the life of the world."—*Optatam Totius,* (§16). (Emphasis added)

This was a diplomatic way of saying that the present state of moral theology does not adequately reflect the message of Jesus under modern conditions.[349] It was an extraordinary admission, implying a major challenge for the Church—a challenge that merited a response with a very high priority. It implied a threat, however, to the *status quo* and to an unpredictable amount of pseudo-infallible teaching. In the years following the Council, the papacy pointedly turned its 'special attention' elsewhere.

---

[349] "But it is part of the tragic and irreducibly obscure historicity of the Church that in both theory and practice it used bad arguments to defend moral maxims based on problematic, historically conditioned pre-convictions, 'prejudices'—Karl Rahner, (Schriften zur Theologie [1978], vol 13, 99-100) quoted by Ute Ranke-Heinemann, *Eunuchs for the kingdom,* paperback p. 334.

Could the Churches Re-think Moral Theology Together?

Referring to Moral Theology in the context of its overall focus on Ecumenism, the Council recommended:

> "Hence, the ecumenical dialogue could start with discussions concerning the application of the gospel to moral questions".— *Unitatis Redintegratio* §23

The wisdom of this last suggestion has not yet been fully appreciated. The business of rethinking moral theology together, does not have to await progress in other aspects of unity. It could even pave the way for them if it settled on how far agreement needs to reach. It will take time and should have been prioritised. Even if we can agree on the principles, it will keep the theologians and pastors busy for some time. The details should be dealt with patiently and openly. The faithful of all denominations should be kept in the loop. They will need time to absorb any new approach and adjust to the consequent changes. Otherwise trivial details will be used to obstruct the main issue[350] in the future when improved structures, whether of unity, federation, or mutual recognition, are otherwise within grasp.

On moral questions, however, Rome has not been ready to dialogue with other Christian denominations. The current policy is to stifle open discussion on such issues, even within the Roman Catholic community itself. But the door for reconsideration was authoritatively opened by the Council with the three extracts quoted above and cannot now be closed. Those who would use the power of their offices to prevent the renewal are being unfaithful to the supreme authority of the Church.

The overall objective of the Council was Ecumenism. In the third extract quoted above, the Council saw that the road to unity must include inter-church discussions on morals. The bishops were clearly unhappy with the current state of Roman Catholic Moral Theology. They called for revision. It would be a pity if we were to allow something that we know to be imperfect to keep us apart.

Catholicism now finds itself teaching a Moral Theology that it has already agreed is inadequate; that it knows is a step removed from Jesus. The admission of imperfection has been made. Sooner or later, Rome will have to tackle the renewal. This offers a rare opportunity to dispose of a significant obstacle to unity. Papal authorities concerned with unity should initiate an open and extended interdenominational debate on the renewal of Christly moral theology 'more thoroughly nourished by scriptural teaching' and in the context of the hierarchy of truths. Catholic participants will need a safe conduct, so nobody gets chastised or side-lined for expressing an honestly held opinion. Up to now the curia has been aggressively negative on the issue which, if pursued, it would inevitably lead to change.

Some Catholic theologians made a start on the re-think of moral theology, which had been mandated[351] only to be persecuted or silenced by the Congregation for the Doctrine of the Faith, which should instead have been fostering the debate. They

---

[350] See *Doctrinal Convergence* on page 282.
[351] Second Vatican Council, *Optatam Totius* §16.

included respected scholars such as Alfons Auer, Franz Böckle, Charles Curran, Joseph Fuchs, Karl Rahner, Bernard Häring, and Eduard Schillebeeckx. Incidentally, Bernard Häring was spared further attention from the CDF for his book *The Law of Christ* after Pope John XXIII wrote a warm and admiring letter about it and Pope Paul VI echoed the same sentiments![352]

Church officials have been understandably fearful of listening to those who have taken up the subject. Every change raises questions about pseudo-infallibilities. This has exacerbated the normal tension between the magisterium and academic theology to the point of serious divergence.

In 1993, Pope John Paul II issued an encyclical, *Veritatis Splendor,* which sought to enhance the importance of 'law and precept' at the expense of conscience. The encyclical was as weak as it was lengthy (175+ pages). It appeared superficially to be in continuity with *Gaudium et Spes,* but it wasn't. It fired a shot across the bows of un-named but identifiable theologians. The intimidation was not confined to them and has obstructed the debate on a renewal mandated by the supreme authority of the Church.

A side effect of this has been noted in the U.S. Young Americans who are still committed to the faith tend to be conservative and even anti-liberal in their ideas and are less inclined to pursue third-level studies in theology, with the consequence that the survival of departments of theology in a number of U.S. universities is in doubt.[353] With the dearth of vocations, this becomes a problem that the Church and academic theologians can only hope to solve in co-operation.

How Important is it?

Moral Theology is at the core of Catholicism because authentic Christianity is more a way of life than a compendium of beliefs. 'It is not those who say to me, "Lord, Lord", who will enter the kingdom of heaven, but the person who does the will of my Father in heaven'. (Matt. 7:21). It is not essentially about church membership *per se* but about being disciples of Christ according to his definition. In apostolic times, the Christians were known as followers of the *Way.*

Of course, we need our parents, teachers, pastors, and the organisational Church, to show us the way and guide and encourage us in this adventure. As the eunuch said to Philip: "How can I [understand], unless someone guides me?" (Acts 8:31)

Church authorities, however, like any good teacher, should start where the pupils are. The modern educated person thinks for himself or herself and is open to guidance provided it is coherent and convincing. We are bombarded with ideas, information, and issues. To be useful, guidance on moral issues should relate the general gospel message to mankind's current experience, understanding and developing knowledge of itself and of the world. Catholicism owes a great debt to feminist

---

[352] Fr Joseph Dunn, *No Lions in the Hierarchy,* Dublin, The Columba Press, 1994, p 301.
[353] See Massimo Faggioli, *A Wake-up Call to Liberal Theologians,* in *Commonweal,* May 16th 2018.

theologians for helping to focus attention on the relevance of human experience in articulating moral theology.[354] In a changing world, the conclusions and implications must be open to modification while principles remain constant. The principles of his moral theology are set down by Jesus in the Great Commandment and in his description of how his disciples will be recognised. If ever it is formulated, a Christly moral theology will be one of relationality, virtue, and motivation rather than a listing of bad actions to be avoided. It will have more emphasis on love than law. It will respect the primacy of conscience.

Since the late 1960s, starting with the long delay in issuing *Humanae Vitae* and its subsequent rejection by the faithful, confidence in Church ability to offer guidance on sexual morality has waned among the faithful. Furthermore, we have been assured that the papacy was not aware of the lasting injury being inflicted on victims by clergy sex abuse. This may be true or false. Either way, it leaves the centralised claim to teaching authority in tatters.

The teaching from the Holy Office of the Inquisition in 1611, that every sin against the sixth or ninth Commandment is a mortal sin, combined ill-considered theology with carelessly expressed legislation. It completely overlooked the significance of mutual commitment in the moral implication of sexual activity. It discerned no difference between fornication and pre-wedding intimacy. It saw God's beautiful gift of attraction between the sexes as essentially a source of sin, unless, and unless, and unless. It burdened the consciences of Catholics for almost 400 years and cast God in the role of a tyrant. By positing the same draconian punishment for teenage masturbation, contraception or pre-wedding intercourse as for gang rape, murder, or military aggression, the Inquisition turned our loving, forgiving Father into a crude and undiscerning disciplinarian, a vengeful martinet with as little sense of proportion as they had themselves, who would consign good people to eternal damnation for minor infringements … unless, of course, they went to confession very frequently, which may have been a reason for creating all those 'mortal' sins in the first place.

Experts in moral theology now reject the doctrine that there can be 'no parvity of matter' in sins against the sixth and ninth Commandments, although few want to profess this publicly. If the sins are not all automatically 'mortal' the faithful are entitled to know. This is something which should be conveyed officially and carefully by Rome lest it be misinterpreted as starting an 'open season'. It would immediately raise the question of where one should draw the line between parvity and gravity. It would call attention to the deplorable neglect of the demand of Vatican II for moral theology to be 'renewed by livelier contact with the mystery of Christ and the history of salvation'. The change in teaching will not come as too much of a shock to the faithful. The faithful may be ahead of Rome in this regard, but Rome cannot afford

---

[354] For example: Margaret Farley, *Just Love: A Framework for Christian Sexual Ethics,* London, 2008, Bloomsbury Academic/Continuum.

to listen. Many good-living Christians have already rejected or ignored official teaching. By now, however, it has acquired pseudo-infallible status in the curi, and it would take great courage for any official to raise the matter for discussion.

Roadblocks

It soon became apparent that the development of a moral theology 'more thoroughly nourished by scriptural teaching' could not be limited to minor adjustments. Once the relevance of scripture is admitted, the need for a New Testament foundation for moral life becomes an inescapable consequence of the Incarnation. Thus, the 'development' has become a 'revision'[355]. This has posed, and threatens to pose, multiple challenges to the Roman posture of total inerrancy and infallibility and to the hegemony which depends on both. Furthermore, conflict is unavoidable between a moral theology rooted in gospel principles—or indeed in any principles—and the current discipline, that is so heavily dependent on centuries of *ad hoc* legislation. To make matters worse, many of the canons enacted over the centuries had been formulated specifically to safeguard or enhance the power and dignity of the clergy.

A Christly moral theology

Without trying to anticipate the detailed outcome, it can safely be predicted that the more Christly moral theology arising from the debate will be quite different from that of the manuals which we have inherited. It is likely to lead to further interpretation of the Ten Commandments more influenced by the Great Commandment. From this a moral theology based on relationships rather than listed actions would naturally emerge. The focus would be on concern for others, individually and collectively, rather than on the avoidance of personal punishment in eternity. The element of selfishness in the pursuit of perfection would be reduced. The goal of self-denial would be to enable one to be more generous in relation to others. The main challenge would be that of loving and living unselfishly rather than striving to secure a better seat for oneself at the eternal banquet,

If the renewal of moral theology were to apply Christly principles to current knowledge of humanity and the world, and to people's life experience and circumstances, it would make morality more understandable and might encourage more people to take it seriously. It might find its expression in a positive call to habits of thoughtful, responsible, virtuous behaviour rather than in an endless, but never quite exhaustive, list of possible sins.

Sex and the desire for sex and intimacy are wonderful gifts in which God shares his work of creation with us. They involve powerful forces, with capacity to generate sublime human relationships or unspeakable unhappiness. Nowhere has the need for a careful reappraisal of moral theology been more clearly demonstrated than in regard to sexual relations. The Church has struggled to maintain coherence on issues around marriage, the family, and homosexuality. A rethink could bring forward

---

[355] Joseph A. Selling, Op. Cit. *p*12

the moral significance of life-long commitment and of concern for the well-being and happiness of one's partner (or potential partner) rather than oneself.

Some of the revised insights and guidance might be found to apply equally to same-sex relationships. Homosexual couples also form bonds, the sundering of which can be just as devastating as with heterosexual ones. LGBTQ people also are called to be disciples. Apart from demanding life-long continence, moral guidance for lesbian and gay Christians has been inadequate and neglected. The priests and nuns who have taken the initiative in ministering to the LGBTQ community should be listened to by top management rather than persecuted. Their work and their treatment confirm the urgent need to rethink Catholic moral theology.

The current talk of adding some ecological sins to the Catechism of the Catholic Church is misguided. Instead, the Church should teach ecological living as a virtue, a great way to express love for our neighbour, even the unborn generations. There are a thousand possible ways for people to lighten their own ecological footprints. The options vary, depending on one's circumstances. The Church should encourage the faithful to choose their own ways voluntarily to do their bit in their own situation. For the well-to-do, it might be to drive a smaller car. For the less wealthy it might be to cycle to work, eat less meat, or spend less time in the hot shower. Imagine the impact, if 2.3 Billion Christians were to habitually consider the environment in which humanity must live and lighten their personal footprint, while growing in the virtue of charity with everyday decisions.

I would hope that the renewal would produce a moral theology that is positive, promoting the virtues rather than focusing on sin. When Lord Baden-Powell wrote the scout law, he encapsulated Christianity in ten positive and challenging ideals. Knowing that habits of virtue and piety were a hard sell to teenage boys, he packaged the same habits into the ideals of scouting. People, particularly young people, respond to an idealistic challenge. Scouting and Guiding have helped inculcate good character and virtue in more than 2 Billion young people in the century since its foundation. Membership, leadership and adherence to the principles, promise and law have been entirely voluntary.

Perhaps Church authorities could learn from the international scout movement, which is served by a bureaucracy, but one that is accountable ultimately to the voluntary members worldwide.[356]

I would hope that, as a consequence of the renewal, vice and virtue will be understood as opposite ends of a gradation; replacing the concept of a state of grace or lack of same that assumes crucial importance at the moment of death. Our positions

---

[356] Like the Church, scouting can be used as a means of access to young people. My personal experience of scouting in Ireland was that abuse was never mentioned directly but was guarded against in camping standards and in the system of warrants for leaders and chaplains issued by headquarters. For example, Fr Brendan Smith was refused a warrant by headquarters and barred from any contact with Catholic scouting, years before the Church took any action against him.

on the scale will be grounded on the good or harm we have tried to do, or risked doing, to others, individually or collectively. Our lives will be judged on love in action. To whatever extent my eternal destination depends on me, it will depend on my habitual behaviour towards others. It will no longer hinge on whether I get knocked off my bike on the way to confession or on the way home![357]

As we have learned from St Thomas Aquinas, Christ would have had few quarrels with Aristotle's *Ethics*. But Christ asks so much more of his followers. Everything he did exemplifies a moral theology of love. He wants our actions to be guided by love of God and by caring love for one another. *"On this depends all the law and the prophets"*. Please forgive the repetition. But this extraordinary statement deserves repetition. In Christ's system, morality is bound up with relationships. Morality relates less to the specific actions than to the priorities that I allow to guide my choice of action—specifically and habitually. Even a cup of water in his name will not go unrewarded.

But what about those who have never known his name? I like to think that the cup of water in the name of love will not go without the promised reward. They too build the kingdom. Karl Rahner and Pope Francis would seem to agree. There was love and virtue in the world before Jesus was born. He kept saying that the kingdom was nearer than people might think. If love is the identifying quality of his disciples, then those who lived and loved generously before the incarnation were his disciples too. They were not known as Christians, but they were part of the kingdom of God.

A renewed moral theology will not be all new, but more likely a re-evaluation of the sources. Most of the implementation rules will remain the same. It won't change the ten commandments, although it might well improve our understanding of them. It won't make fornication virtuous although it might define it more perceptively. It will produce a change of emphasis, a re-ordering of priorities. It is a development of doctrine towards which, dare I say it, the *sensus fidelium* of the People of God may already be leading the authorities.

A wide-ranging review of morality will have to deal convincingly with immorality. A Christly approach might define it as a self-centred disregard of the bad effect, or the potentially bad effect, of my action and example, on myself, my neighbour or on society in general. It would be the inappropriate prioritising of self, whether the self is an individual or a group. Hopefully, it would include proportionality.

Loving my neighbour as myself implies some self-love. Love is about generous self-giving, from the smallest everyday thoughtfulness even to the point of inconvenience—or beyond. "Selfishness is the opposite of the Spirit". (Gal. 5:17)

---

[357] This is a fair caricature of the Irish understanding before Vatican II. I remember that when the Korean war started in June 1950, it was feared it would escalate into a nuclear holocaust. The rush for confession at Clarendon Street Church in Dublin created a queue that filled the church and stretched out into Johnson's Court and almost onto Grafton Street.

Being Wrong is not immoral

We have been taught that if you think that something is a sin and you do it anyway, you commit a sin. The obverse must be equally true. If you really feel in conscience that something is good and proper in the circumstances, then doing it is virtuous. If you serve God under a misapprehension, you still serve God. Jesus says we are children of God. If we are his children, then our heavenly Father understands our misunderstandings.

God, who is infinite, invented the finite. He invented time just as he invented cause and effect, the distinction between things, and the concept of number. When we turn our minds towards him, we are finite beings trying to grasp the infinite; a task for which we are woefully ill-equipped. He met this difficulty by becoming one of us. He became a person so we could relate to him personally and directly, with no need for a go-between or mediator. The Incarnation is what turns us into a priestly people.

If you worship God, serving him or praising him under another name, attributing to him whatever characteristics, powers, attitudes and forms you think are his, then you are worshipping the true God. We know that he understands our inadequacies and forgives the shortfalls in our understanding. He does not ask us to be inerrant, he asks us to love. The demand for inerrancy is the offspring of pride.

The Cathars[358] who accepted to die at the hands of the Albigensian Crusaders rather than abjure what they believed—although their beliefs were unquestionably heretical—worshipped God in their supreme sacrifice and should be counted among the martyrs. Paradoxically, the bishops who encompassed their public executions may also have been saved, assuming that they were convinced they were doing the will of God. Today, however, we would judge them, together with Pope Innocent III who sent them and St Bernard who urged them on, to have been gravely misguided. As Christians, they should have been exemplars of caring love and witnesses of the truth, rather than pitiless enforcers of doctrine and of clerical power.

Freedom is fundamental

Since Vatican II, the Church preaches the primacy of conscience and freedom of religion. The latter should apply not only as between governments and religions bodies but within the churches themselves. Those who are united by belief in the essentials, should afford one another a respectful freedom of study and opinion on the secondary and less important issues. Respect for human dignity and primacy of conscience demand as much. Obsession with office and authority opposes.

If Christ's disciples are to love unselfishly, they must remain free to choose. Sometimes they will choose to do good, sometimes bad. Ultimately, it must be up to them. In the process, their free choice will often involve some self-denial. Not mortification as the price of a better reward later, not fasting enjoined and enforced with threats of

---

[358] Cf. Stephen O'Shea, *The Perfect Heresy,* London, 2000, Profile Books

damnation, but *self*-denial and *self*-control so that we can love more generously. If love of other calls for self-denial, it also makes it easier. Freedom, habit, and the ability to love are inextricably entwined.

At all times we have the option of loving ourselves more and our neighbour less. For God to override our freedom of decision-making would run counter, it seems, to the entire objective of our existence and, indeed, of the Incarnation.

The guidance Christ promised has been with us all down through the ages in the promptings of the infinitely patient Holy Spirit. All Christ's followers, whatever their calling, are free to accept or reject those promptings in choosing their actions. Those who love and habitually accept the promptings build the kingdom. They are the saints. Those who prioritise individual self-interest or group ambition can ravage it, even if they hold high ecclesial office. *"There is no greater heresy than that the office sanctifies the holder of it"*.

Chapter 15

Top management in the Church

"The citizen who criticizes his country is paying it an implied tribute."

—Senator J. William Fulbright

THE CURIA IS RESPONSIBLE.

Peter Drucker, an early leader in management studies, admired the theoretically flat management structure of the Roman Catholic church, in which the bishops run their diocese and report to the head bishop in Rome. He would have been less enthusiastic had he been aware of the extent to which the practice diverges from the theory. In 1870, Vatican I made belief in the universal jurisdiction of the pope essential for salvation. This accelerated the transition of the curia from an administrative body into a layer of governance that now comes between the bishops and the pope. The independent authority and discretion that had characterised the episcopate for centuries was weakened, and bishops gradually came to be more like area managers under the direction of the curia, despite protestations to the contrary. They still report formally to the pope, of course, but at five yearly intervals while their working relationship is controlled by the curia. The curia also controls access to the pope. This leaves no avenue of appeal against curial decisions, lies or corruption as was shown above in the cases of Hélder Câmera and Libero Milone.[359] making the curia, as we have seen, the real government of the Church.

Accordingly, the curia cannot evade the historical responsibility for the state of the Church as we start the third millennium. With a mandate to make disciples of all the nations, Christianity numbers only one third of the current population of the world, or less than a fifth if we exclude those not in juridical communion with Rome. Moreover, liturgical participation and fidelity to the Roman magisterium are both in demonstrable decline among Roman Catholics themselves. This is a disappointing market penetration after two thousand years. Furthermore, we now have a divided church; a house divided, in more ways than one.

The management has been unable to accept the change in self-understanding articulated by the supreme authority in the Church, the pope and bishops assembled at Vatican II. In attempting to remedy this, Pope Francis has encountered significant pushback from the bureaucracy, some of which has become public knowledge. This presents the diocesan bishops with an invidious choice; to align themselves with a transient reforming pope or with the permanent bureaucracy. "If a house be divided against itself, that house cannot stand". There is work here for a succession of

---

[359] See page 130 and footnote on page 152

reforming popes, which places a heavy responsibility on future cardinals. They will have to resist the doom-laden predictions of their more bureaucratic colleagues and rely on the Promise, if the Church is to realise its potential or to progress in its mission.

In his approach to reform, Pope Francis clearly wants to be unifying rather than divisive. This will require a willingness on the part of the bureaucracy in Rome to admit to the need for change. Christ emptied himself for our salvation. (Phil. 2:8) If the Eucharist is a sacramental memorial of Christ's sacrifice, the top hierarchs, or oligarchs, must be ready to put everything on the altar, including their power, control, wealth, status, authority, certainties, and comforting traditions. They must be ready to see the papacy *as they currently understand it,* pass away to be replaced by a partnership among bishops and faithful, 'putting on Christ' in their magnanimity, generosity, love, and in their trust in the Holy Spirit.

Such a partnership would unleash the creativity of bishops and faithful alike. To make it work, bishops must be allowed to experiment and make mistakes. The curia must be ready to give magnanimously rather than negotiate or trade concessions. They must eschew selfishness, whether on behalf of themselves, their high offices, or the group. They must practice the virtue of humility. They must be ready to divest themselves of power or, at least, to share it generously. They must not let the essentially selfish nature of a bureaucracy overwhelm the promptings of the Spirit.

Unsuitably structured

The curia combines legislative, executive, and judicial powers in a structure that appears to be monarchical but is really oligarchical. It depends on oaths of fidelity and extreme deference to rank in a culture of secrecy. This inhibits creativity and makes it difficult to challenge bad decisions, dishonesty, or corruption. The Church preaches subsidiarity but the doctrine of universal jurisdiction and the need to protect the aura of infallibility together mean that most decisions must necessarily be reserved to a high level at the centre. Individual cases must be passed up the line to the point where a distant decision maker relies on second or third-hand information and may be quite unfamiliar with the context or culture.

Identification of the divine will with established practice further inhibits change, innovation and even problem solving. Legal wriggle room can be found, of course, when it is desired by the establishment. Bishops are routinely promoted to more important dioceses, although this practice fosters careerism and was repeatedly condemned at early ecumenical councils. Some are consecrated for non-existent dioceses to give them added prestige. Even the near worship of celibacy has been brushed aside to facilitate group recruitment of Anglicans. Married priests were approved by Pope Benedict XVI, ostensibly "to meet the needs of the Ordinariate", but far more than would meet those needs have actually been ordained, giving a ratio of one priest for every 60 converts! A similar derogation has never been made to meet the needs of thousands of congregations in mission areas who are unable to celebrate the Eucharist with meaningful frequency. Why treat Anglicans more flexibly? Does it reflect a bureaucratic wish to score over the competition?

A self-perpetuating curia resists reform

As a managing leader who has been charged with universal jurisdiction over 1.33 Billion Catholics, a pope would be unable to cope with his workload without the help and cooperation of a substantial administration. A pope also needs a cabinet of immediate helpers to advise him on decisions, manage his diary and correspondence and research his speeches. In managing him, they control him and control access to him, so it is essential that he should be able to rely implicitly on their personal loyalty. Their only right to exist is as helpers of the Bishop of Rome and it is always an abuse when they develop their own agenda. Pope John XXIII was driven to complain about the 'unspeakable manoeuvres' of the curia. He was amazed and pained by the disobedience of members of the First Section of the Secretariat of State who were pursuing alternative, very worldly, objectives.[360] Paul VI, as we noted in Chapter 10, described himself to Hélder Câmera as one who had no voice. He was only able to have that conversation because Hélder had outmanoeuvred the curia officers who had lied to him about the Pope's wishes and were conspiring to deny him access. Pope Francis is encountering overt resistance in the curia as he currently challenges the system.

Like any large bureaucracy, the curia is pathologically self-centred. It is unsuited to governing the Church organisation, whose function is to give visible institutional form to the Mystical Body. It has proved unable to reform itself and can easily circumvent the reform efforts of transient popes. The legal structure created by the same bureaucracy provides no way for it to be changed. Over the years, governance by the bureaucracy has gradually become unassailable.

The curia re-drafted Canon Law twice in the twentieth century, yet the papacy is still structured as a self-perpetuating oligarchy with many trappings of a medieval monarchy. In revising the 1983 Code, having dragged their feet until there was a new pope, they legislated the great vision of Vatican II—governance by the College of Bishops— into ineffectiveness. Furthermore, ignoring the signs of the times, they provided absolutely no way for the 1.33 Billion Catholics to influence how the visible church is structured or managed. They are making it unnecessarily difficult for people who have grown up in democratic societies to stay faithful, not to say committed, active, or enthusiastic. The faithful and their pastors can only watch as Christ's two foundational mandates, together with his call to love and his prayer for unity are treated as secondary issues, taking their place behind more earthly priorities—group self-interest, pride, celibacy, misogyny, precedent, pseudo-infallibility, hegemony, and professional dignity and privileges—when it comes down to decision-making and writing the rules.

---

[360] Peter and Margaret Hebblethwaite, *Pope of the Century,* abr. edition., London, 2000, p 249

Jesus continues to gently invite all to follow his way but never takes away anybody's freedom of decision. In contrast, the papacy does not hesitate to enforce its priorities by threats, coercion, and excommunication.

We are witnessing a large-scale demonstration of Pournelle's Iron Law of Bureaucracy, which we met in Chapter 1, with the difference being that in this case the bureaucracy is also the government. Like any civil totalitarian government, it has an insatiable appetite for power and has legislated to make any regime change virtually impossible. Providentially, however, change is possible, as we will see in the next chapter when we come to consider the call to put the Catholic house in order as a contribution to greater unity.

Management style

Pride in authority together with ambition replaced Christ's concept of leadership as a service of love with a domination/subordination model and helped to solidify the major schisms that have divided the Church.

Roman authoritarianism was a major factor in 1054. The theological differences now look like a proxy for the ongoing power struggle centred around the Apostolic See's claim of a right to dominate, and the competing rights of bishops and particularly the claim of the Archbishops of Constantinople to the title of 'Ecumenical Patriarch' with all that that could imply.

Large bureaucracies, however, are slow learners. By publishing his criticism and proposals, Martin Luther offended papal pride and authority. Stung by the validity of some of his criticism, unable to refute him theologically, and accustomed to the revenue from the sale of indulgences, the papacy angrily reasserted its divine authority and inerrancy, using spiritual and physical threats. Rome again relied on power and on threats of eternal damnation in its response. Again, these failed. What started off as reasoned criticism escalated into another schism because of the obsession of the Apostolic See with protecting its pre-eminence. Rome could not accept the idea of reform in the Church, much less reform in its management policies and practices. Ambition and angry pride[361] turned the theological criticism of papal policy into the Protestant Reformation. Of course, as was pointed out by Vatican II there was fault on both sides.[362]

Historically, it can scarcely be denied that arrogance, the will-to-power, anger and claims to inerrancy on the part of the Apostolic See played a crucial role in turning disagreements into the two schisms that have divided the Church to this day. Pride has helped to maintain the divisions. The instruction to love one another was not applied to the other denominations until John XXIII became pope.

---

[361] Readers who are in any doubt about the contribution of anger and pride should read Pope Leo X's Condemnation of Luther, *Exsurge Domine.* (1520).

[362] "often enough, men of both sides were to blame". *(Unitatis Redintegratio* §3). Note that even this admission blames 'men' not the papacy, not the institutional Church nor its management.

Coercion

The attitude of the Catholic Church to religious freedom changed radically during the Second Vatican Council but management has failed to apply the new teaching internally. They have been ready to ignore the change of policy called for in the Declaration on Religious Freedom:

> "The disciple is bound … to proclaim it [the truth] and vigorously defend it, never—be it understood—having recourse to means that are incompatible with the spirit of the gospel. At the same time, the charity of Christ urges him to act lovingly, prudently, and patiently in his dealings with those who are in error or in ignorance with regard to the faith".—*Dignitatis Humanae* §14

Despite this pointed criticism, the Congregation for the Doctrine of the Faith has reverted to persecuting and silencing Catholic theologians and religious whose scholarship it is unable to refute. This is particularly true for scholars who have had the temerity to address the issues of moral theology in areas where the *sensus fidelium* and the Roman magisterium are seen to be on diverging paths. In a manner redolent of its origins in the Inquisition, the CDF has treated these theologians and pastors in ways that mock morality of any description.[363] In a blatant abuse of the victims' vows of obedience, the Congregation has required some religious to withhold the truth about their own silencing and about the indefensible procedures experienced at the hands of the Congregation itself. Nobody outside of the CDF knows the extent of this persecution but even one instance is one too many. Does anyone believe that the enforced suppression of the *truth*, even if intended to protect the authority of the papacy, has any place in evangelisation in the name of Jesus Christ?

That this could continue for so long with so many men of great dedication and erudition has been made possible for generations of clergy since Trent, by standardised seminary training and 'formation' over a period of 6-8 years that:

• promoted the authority of the pope, and located the inspiration of the Holy Spirit exclusively in the hierarchical line of command,

• made obedience to one's superiors the virtue above all virtues, identifying it as the specific will of God for the subordinate,

• confused faith in Jesus with acceptance of a detailed list of doctrines,

• prioritised minutiae of the faith ahead of charity,

• tried to substitute the certainty of authority for the virtue of hope,

---

[363] Many of those theologians who were censured during the reign of John Paul II describe the processes as humiliating (Cornwell, 2001, pp. 210-214). Bernard Häring, the German moral theologian, for example, who was persecuted by the Nazis as a young man, said, after having been investigated and ultimately censured by the Catholic Church, "I would prefer Hitler's courts to another papal interrogation. Hitler's trials were more dangerous, but they were not an offence to my honour" (cited in Cornwell, p. 210). Haring was presumably not the only theologian who experienced such humiliation. —Marie Keenan, *Child Sexual Abuse and the Catholic Church*, Oxford University Press, p38

- postulated a divine origin for almost every traditional practice, good, bad, and irrelevant,
- substituted 'religious assent', whether mute or professed, in place of honest conviction or belief,
- characterised disagreement as disloyalty, dismissing it as a product of sinful intellectual pride, and
- imposed a vow of obedience that is taken in good faith at a young age but is open to later abuse in a different context by those exercising authority.

It is doubtful if the traditions of the Inquisition as found in the modern CDF could have survived were it not for some character traits of the officials and decision makers in the curia that arise from their shared formation. The effect is exacerbated by a lifelong commitment to working for the one organisation. A better mix of people with a wider variety of training and experience and with greater personal and intellectual freedom would give rise to more balanced decision making and more effective policies. In secular organisations, the involvement of several independent Directors at Board level is now considered essential in maintaining balance and in fighting corruption.

One implication is clear. If ever the papacy finds the courage to initiate a serious review of moral theology, the oversight of the project should not be assigned to the CDF or indeed to any narrowly homogeneous group.

Coercion, a continuing characteristic

As confidence in the reliability of the magisterium erodes, the curia has reverted to coercion to bolster its authority. And yet, even in this it seems unable it to learn by the mistakes of the past. Unable to learn from the modernist crisis, the CDF went on to persecute Yves Congar and John Courtney-Murray, only to see them, along with John Henry Newman, vindicated by the Second Vatican Council. Yet, since the Council, we have seen a litany of patently honest theologians, whose ideas the combined resources of the Congregation have been unable to refute, being abused and/or silenced for sharing what careful study has led them to believe, or for attempting to evangelise the people of today in their own language and culture.

The legal processes used owe more to the Roman Inquisition than to Roman Law or to Biblical standards of procedure or modern civilised jurisprudence, but the CDF is unable to move on from the traditions and procedures it has inherited. This is not surprising. The curia controls its own recruitment and only those who manifest unwavering commitment get promoted to positions of authority.

If it were not part of the papacy itself, the popes would have long ago condemned what the CDF does to people. Its practices would be deemed immoral even if it were dealing with the most dangerous heresies. Few of its modern victims have so much as been *accused* of heresy. The issues have ranged from questioning pseudo-infallibility to matters as trivial as publicly admitting to inconvenient historical facts or to differences of opinion among theologians. The severity of the CDF reaction seems to be related less to the significance of the issue and more to the inability of the Congregation to come up with a reasoned rebuttal. They react particularly strongly to issues relating to the origins or traditions of the ministry, hierarchical structures and 'apostolic succession', where the scriptural foundations are weak in the New Testament or in the record of apostolic times.

The names of post Vatican II victims that immediately spring to mind are internationally known and respected; de Chardin, Schillebeeckx (investigated and subjected to 'notifications' but never actually condemned), Dupuis, Küng, Häring, Gutiérrez, Boff, Curran and Sobrino. In the small island of Ireland and in our own time, we have listed Frs. Tony Flannery, C.SS.R., Seán Fagan, S.M. and Fergal O'Connor, O.P. These were silenced and ordered, under their vows of obedience, not to say they had been silenced; in effect, they were told to lie or dissimulate if asked directly. This was abuse by authority, of dedicated people and of vows taken in good faith. Some felt bound by their vows of obedience, and acquiesced. How many others were treated this way? Dozens or maybe hundreds? We shall never know. The answer is a secret, closely protected by – you guessed it – the oaths of loyalty to the papacy of their fellow churchmen.

Enough leaks out to inhibit other clergy from raising issues about inappropriate policies, procedures, and teaching. By the same token, the ill-treatment of the existing clergy must be contributing to the decline in vocations, although this of its nature cannot be quantified.

It would be foolhardy for the curia to let the ordinary faithful know the extent of coercion necessary to maintain the facade of total agreement among the clergy, particularly on the issues where the *sensus fidelium* seems furthest from the official line. If people knew how inconsequential and abstruse the theological differences on which some theologians or preachers have been carpeted, or the loss of time and probity involved, they might begin to think that what is at issue is not so much theology and truth as authority and control. For authoritarian systems, it is the mere challenge to obedience that counts, not the weight of the issue.

If coercion based on vows of obedience or oaths of loyalty proves insufficient, there are alternatives. Diocesan clergy who are on the payroll, so to speak, can be suspended, or removed from one assignment without being given another. Regular clergy who serve their Congregations or Orders under vows of poverty can be pressurised by threats that the congregation that they have loved and served for years will suffer the withdrawal of some traditional privileges or ongoing support. Finally, Rome may force the Congregation to expel them. At that stage, vows of poverty become something more than theoretical.

For as long as the papacy accords top priorities to its own hegemony and pseudo-infallibility and treats the lifelong celibacy of its exclusively male ministers as sacrosanct[364] and is afraid to compromise the privileges, prerogatives, powers, or conditions of service of the profession, the worship of God and the needs of the faithful for sacraments and truth must share subordinate places in their priority list.

SPECIFIC MANAGEMENT FAILINGS (SMF)

SMF 1: The Crisis in the Ministry

After the Synod in 1992, Pope John Paul II entitled his Apostolic Exhortation *Pastores dabo vobis* referring to the Old Testament[365] promise, "I will give you shepherds". He relied on this together with faith in "the constant activity of the Holy Spirit" to reassure the faithful "that there will never be a complete lack of sacred ministers in the Church". He mentioned "trusting abandonment". He raised hopes of an impending improvement by reporting an increase in vocations in some unidentified dioceses and by making little of the disastrous state of vocations generally. The shortage had been recognised twenty-five years earlier by Vatican II. Pope Pius XII had called attention to it in 1950. The Italian hierarchy had been aware of it since the 1920s. A century has passed since then, and no strategic remedial action has been taken. If the "constant activity of the Holy Spirit" has prompted any initiative during that period, the leadership has not been listening. There have been no significant policy changes to meet the situation, and experiments at diocesan level have not been permitted.

The combination of 'trusting abandonment' with a tribal denial of the trend seems to have sapped any sense of human responsibility in the matter during the pontificate of John Paul II and that of Benedict XVI. Arithmetically, of course, Pope John Paul was perfectly right. There will never be a 'complete lack' of sacred ministers as long as there is one member of the profession left to turn out the lights. By that stage, under present legislation ,there will be no Roman Catholic Eucharist and thus no Roman Catholic Church. This attitude on the part of management reveals an astounding level of complacency, or a state of management paralysis, or both. 'Trusting abandonment' may indicate great sanctity in a mystic. In an administrator, it is dereliction of duty. The group dynamic in Rome seems to inhibit acceptance of the scale of the problem that is developing.

Take the USA as an example. At the end of the Council, the US had 58,632 priests serving 48 million Catholics. Fifty years later, it was 37,192 priests for 80 million. Thus, the workload went from 826 Catholics per priest to just over 2,000. Bad enough. But the future will be much worse because of the age factor. In 1965 the average age of the priests was 44, which left them with 31 years to retirement at 75. By 2015, the average age was 62 with 13 working years remaining. From having a

---

[364] Except when facilitating Anglican group conversions)

[365] "I will give you shepherds after my own heart" (Jer. 3:15) and "I will set shepherds over them [my sheep] who will care for them, and they shall fear no more, nor be dismayed (Jer. 23.4).

resource of trained, ordained personnel capable of providing 1,818,000 man-years[366] of ministry, the US Church found itself in 2015 starting the next 50 years with a capacity of 483,000 man-years.[367] That is just over a quarter of the capacity, for a church that could grow to 130 million in the same period. And the bishops are not allowed to take any initiative to address the problem.

There is every reason to believe that the same calculations in respect of other areas would yield more or less similar results, except for some parts of Africa.[368]

Presumably, some department in the curia is doing projections of this kind. If so, top management is not listening. There are no strategic proposals emerging that begin to meet the scale of the challenge. The papacy was unable to listen in 1987, when the sociologist, Dean Hoge, published the results of several years of solid academic research on the priest shortage in the United States. He concluded firmly that the downturn in vocations evident since 1970 was not a random fluctuation but a long- term trend.

> The social pressures causing the downturn in vocations are pervasive and strong, and the Church is powerless to reverse them … The Church must be realistic about the new social context in which it finds itself today—which it cannot undo—and develop strategies for Christian mission in this setting.
>
> Since the prospects for a major increase in vocations is zero, responsible church leaders should look at other options for furnishing the best possible parish leadership in the future …
>
> The shortage of priests is an institutional problem, not a spiritual problem. This basic conclusion emerged from our 1983 research, and I am still certain it is true. Now I add a second part: . . .and it can be solved through institutional measures.[369]

To guide the institutional response, Hoge presents additional research among Catholic undergraduate students designed to discover what proportion have given thought to a religious vocation and their reasons for not choosing it. The study distinguished between those already involved in campus ministry and a random sample of students. "Not allowed to marry" emerged as the main deterrent. with "A life-long commitment is required" as the second most important. It should be noted that both

---

[366] $(58,632 \times 31 = 1,817,592)$

[367] $(37,192 \times 13 = 483,496)$ Note: By the time of writing, 2020, this total has dropped further by about 150,000. (The estimates do not allow for the fact that not all clergy will be able to retire at 75.)

[368] African clergy who volunteer to work in the more developed countries are surely to be welcomed. However, the importation of leaders across cultural and language barriers ignores human psychology and sociology. It is not the best way to build up the strength, enthusiasm, and commitment of established church communities. Who would have thought that the problem faced by the Synod on Amazonia would have its counterpart in Europe and the United States so soon?

[369] Dean Hoge, Ph.D., *The Future of Catholic Leadership, Responses to the Priest Shortage,* Kansas City, Sheed & Ward, 1987, p xii.

are matters of church discipline, under the direct control of the papacy but not of the bishops.

The survey included two hypothetical questions for men. 12% of the random sample indicated that they would be seriously interested in becoming a priest if the celibacy requirement were removed, 16% would be interested if there was an honourable discharge option after 10 or 15 years of ministry. Among those already involved in campus leadership 35% said "yes" to the first question, and 11% to the second. The hypothetical question for women assumed that they could be ordained. Of the random sample, 4% said they would be seriously interested and for those involved in campus ministry the proportion went up to 15%. The significance of these expressions of serious interest becomes clear when compared with the proportion of priests to the faithful which is currently one twentieth of one percent.

In 1987, while stressing that answers to hypothetical questions must be treated with caution, Hoge offered the opinion

> As a rough estimate, the number of young Catholic men who would be seriously interested in the priesthood under conditions of optional celibacy would increase fourfold or more from the present level.

It would take a sustained flood of vocations to catch up with present needs, let alone deal with the rapid extension of the problem that could be predicted from available data. He focuses on the need for parish leadership, both clerical and lay.

Hoge considered 11 options that would help to meet the problems identified in the research, including three that would present different levels of theological difficulty, namely ordaining women, utilising some retired priests as sacramental ministers, and instituting a term of service for the priesthood or an honourable discharge option. He estimated the impact of the first two of these on the shortage of priests as 'low' and the third as 'medium'. Of the eleven options only two would have 'high' impact. They were ordaining married as well as celibate men and expanding and developing lay ministries. This last would provide parish leadership but would only impact on sacramental famine to the extent that lay leaders would free the priests from non-sacramental duties.[370] This has been a trend in many dioceses since then but has been inhibited by the traditional link between ordination and management.

Already at the time of the study there were lay people, some of them nuns, running parishes with a priest coming to say Mass on Sundays. In some cases, the priest was coming every second Sunday and the sister was conducting a prayer service with distribution of Holy Communion on the intervening Sunday. The congregation were not allowed to follow Jesus' instructions. That would be in breach of canon law.

In the forty years since then, while bishops have expanded the role of the laity the papacy has been remarkably slow to recognise the value of their activity with a status, title, or office, particularly in the case of women. They are doing the work of deacons.

---

[370] Hoge, *op. cit.* p209

217

Pope Francis created a commission of experts to study the precedent, and to decide whether the deaconesses of the first millennium received a sacramental ordination as has always been assumed in the case of deacons. Nothing came from this because, as we were told, the commission was not unanimous in its (unpublished) findings.[371] This could have been predicted before the commission ever met. Is there any historical question worth asking on which 12 experts will be found unanimous? The real reason is that the papacy has been against the ordination of women since the issue arose with awareness of women's equality sometime after the Second World War. Whether this prejudice arises from fear of change or fear of women is irrelevant. It is prejudice. Moreover, we have all the precedent we need. The diaconal ministry was created to fill an evident need. It was decided by the faithful on the proposal of the apostles. We described this on page 177.

The worship of the ministry itself in its present form is at the heart of the challenge. A new paradigm of ministry and a new relationship between Church management and the faithful is needed. Unfortunately, the last people to recognise this will be the officials of the curia who are insulated from the problem and are all ordained ministers trained and nurtured in the existing system.

It is evident that the papacy, having arrogated all decision making to itself, is incapable of facing the problems, let alone solving them. Some long-established practices and pseudo-infallibilities are blocking the path. Moreover, the papacy would lose face if it were to authorise others to try where it is failing.

That a priestly people is short of priests results from an authoritarian centralism dominated by the leaders of the professional priesthood whose first concern is for the profession. Paradoxically, this team of celibate males is self-perpetuating. They select their own successors after an extended assessment over many years as the candidates work their way up through the system. So, the ethos does not change.

SMF 2: Eucharistic famine

But something must change. The growing shortage of priests can only mean a further extension of Eucharistic famine. There is more to the Eucharist than the reception of Holy Communion. The distribution of pre-consecrated hosts does not fulfil the mandate. It is not the Lord's Supper. It is not what Jesus told us to do to commemorate him. In obedience to him, something must change.

The option of changing canon law to re-admit married priests to the ministry has always been there but by the time it is exercised there will be too few of them left to make a difference, and it would open the door to the ordination of married men. There is no theological reason to prevent this. If precedent is demanded, we can point to St Peter and most of the apostles. Moreover, there are still thousands of liturgically knowledgeable nuns who are spiritually mature and could be ordained at short notice,

---

[371] Why must we have unanimity on the historical precedent of ordaining women as deacons, when a simple majority was enough to define two dogmas of much greater consequence in 1870?

although not all would want to be female adjuncts to a patriarchal clerical elite. (Pope Francis has written of the danger of clericalizing women if they were to become priests.) There could be women priests, part-time priests, worker priests, temporary priests, non-stipendiary priests or authorised lay men and women. Each of these solutions, however, would impinge on the exaggerated veneration of the sacrament of Orders which underpins Catholic ecclesiology. They would affect the privileges and prerogatives of those already in the profession. The leaders of the profession, who have a monopoly of decision making in the area, are unlikely to make the necessary decisions. The group dynamic is such that only the bravest propose solutions and the rest stay silent. Expressing support would preclude advancement to any level that could influence management policy.

Every solution would involve a change in some previous papal position, and this would tarnish the carefully promoted aura of generalised infallibility. This factor will distort the priorities until the bishops, who cope with the shortage every day, and who form the supreme authority with the pope, are permitted to make the necessary decisions.

When first the laity were forbidden to celebrate the Eucharist, the ban must have assumed the availability of enough ordained priests, or else it would have directly contradicted Christ's mandate. It cannot be justified now, when the effect is to prevent the celebration with a frequency that is appropriate for the building up of the community or for the spiritual development of the faithful. We noted earlier that one of many implications of the meal at Emmaus is that Jesus did not mean the Lord's Supper to be an occasional event or linked to a special feast day. He took the first available opportunity to repeat the celebration. He used bread and wine, the ordinary food and drink that would have been on the table, not turkey and pumpkin pie. His example suggests that he meant his disciples to celebrate his memory and join their self-offering with his, whenever they came together in his name. The long-established precedent is for a weekly celebration on the Lord's day. It must have been the professionals that introduced the ban to meet the need for order or perhaps even to enhance their own importance, or both. The leaders of the profession can therefore remove the ban and should do so now because, under current conditions, their by-laws conflict with the foundational mandates—directly in the case of "Do This" and indirectly in the case of "Make Disciples".

SMF 3: Earlier discussion of married clergy

The curia opposed the ordination of married men when it was discussed previously by the Synod, in 1971. A change at that time might have prevented the acknowledged shortage of priests from reaching crisis proportions now. The shortage of priests had been admitted and the change had been requested or supported in presynodal submissions, by the Episcopal Conferences in missionary areas and by some in countries where the Church was not yet desperately short of priests. It seemed to command widespread support. Yet, surprisingly, it was voted down when the Synod met. Such an outcome was possible because the proportion of curial cardinals and bishops is normally enough to block unwanted decisions. The Synodal structure was designed from the outset to give the curia control.

While Synodal decisions are purely advisory, the aura of generalised infallibility suffers if the subsequent Papal Exhortation is seen to be at variance with the recommendations. In 1971, the curia voices were opposing the ordination of married men, which was likened during the debate to "the thin end of the wedge" that might lead God-knows-where. This reluctance to deal with a real and immediate problem for fear of possible unforeseen problems in the future revealed a deplorable lack of trust in the guidance of the Holy Spirit. The unwillingness to change could be interpreted, however, at a more worldly level as bureaucratic inertia or as an example of the leaders of the profession prioritising the traditional privileges of the group over the Church's founding mandates.

The missionary bishops had principle on their side. They had a manifest shortage of priests and a failure to adequately provide the sacraments. They could quote from the recent Council:

"missionary activity ... is the greatest and holiest task of the Church" (LG §23).

The right of Pope Paul VI to govern as he pleased was not being questioned, but the missionary bishops wanted the Synod to assert unequivocally that "by reason of pastoral needs and the good of the universal church" a pope could "allow the priestly ordination of married men". The curia officials proposed instead the self-contradictory resolution: "Without denying always the right of the Supreme Pontiff, the priestly ordination of married men is not permitted, even in particular cases".

As the discussion progressed, it began to look as if the curial bloc vote might not be sufficient to win the day. Cardinal Seper, Prefect of the Holy Office, publicly proposed that the religious superiors (who had supported the change in respect of diocesan clergy) and the bishops of the Eastern Churches (who were already well accustomed to a married clergy) should be excluded from voting on the issue. Paul VI scotched this attempt at gerrymandering.

Then it was announced that the voting would not be secret. Ballots had to be signed! This worried missionary bishops who rely heavily on financial support from Rome, lest it might foreshadow future repercussions depending on how they were seen to have voted.

In the end the curial vote decided the issue. The self-contradictory resolution was passed by 107 votes to 87.[372] The latter part; "the priestly ordination of married men is not permitted, even in particular cases" was effective. It meant that the sacramental shortfall in mission areas could be allowed to continue for another fifty years without disturbing any senior ecclesiastical conscience ... or sleep.

---

[372] Peter Hebblethwaite, *Paul, the First Modern Pope*, London, 1993, HarperCollins, P585.

The fatuity of a self-contradictory resolution became apparent in November 2009 when the papacy wanted to facilitate the conversion of entire Anglican parishes with their pastors. Without so much as an apology to tradition, Benedict XVI approved the ordination of married men, 'based on … the needs of the Ordinariate',[373] There are now three Ordinariates, located in the USA, the UK and Australia. Together they number less than 12,000 and include some 200 clergy. (2016). How the 'needs of the Ordinariate' could be stretched to justify a ratio of one minister for every 60 former Anglicans has not been explained. Nor did Pope Benedict explain why the same derogation, from Canon 277 §1, could not be applied to meet the similar, but much more pressing, needs of the faithful in mission dioceses.

SMF 4: The Enlightenment.

In the eighteenth and nineteenth centuries Rome was faced with a number of challenges from the ideas of the Enlightenment, not least among them the preposterous ideas in the American Declaration of Independence, that:

> … all men are created equal and that they are endowed by their Creator with certain unalienable Rights, that … Governments are instituted among Men, deriving their just powers from the consent of the governed.—Paragraph 2, Declaration of Independence.

Had the management learned anything? Did the papacy embark on any attempt to modify derived teaching to take account of a new situation or make the gospel relevant to a world of growing scholarship, scientific discoveries and new ideas about human dignity, sociology, physiology, liberty and accountability of governments? Far from it. There would be no recognition or adaptation to modernity. Rather than apply the teaching of Jesus to the new situation the papacy issued condemnations. These doubtless won the approval of the peer group in Rome but had little chance of halting worldwide trends, let alone of reversing them. The attitude was firmly grounded in scholasticism, a system based on first principles. And first principles do not change. The Church was a perfect society. The papacy could never err, and therefore Church teaching could never need reinterpretation. The faithful could be reassured that the answers would always be right, even when the context or understanding of the question, had changed.

Unknowingly, the management was thus condemning the Church to a century or more of growing irrelevance. Pius IX issued the Syllabus of Errors (1864), which summarised no less than 80 condemnations that had been promulgated in earlier papal documents, mainly his own. Shorn of their original context they appeared to condemn even more than they did in the original texts. A few years later, the first Vatican Council raised the defensive bulwarks higher again. It reinforced the papal claim to inerrancy by replacing it with Papal Infallibility. It also turned the long-standing

---

[373]Complementary Norms for the Apostolic Constitution *Anglicanorum coetibus, art. 6.*

Roman demand for Universal Jurisdiction into a dogma. For Catholics, from then on, assent to both would be necessary for salvation.

The papacy then needed to build and protect the aura of infallibility, so it could not risk debate nor admit the need for research or consultation. This distracted it further from applying Christianity to modern knowledge, society, and ideas.

Building on the good in the existing culture and showing how the Gospel can complement and enhance it, has been the mark of the great evangelists like Paul, Patrick, Ricci, de Nobili, Shanahan, Fulton Sheen and indeed Billy Graham. The papacy had effectively debarred itself from evangelising modernity. Regrettably, it would not allow Catholic scholars to fill the gap. As we noted in Chapter 9, it embarked on a policy of coercion and persecution of Catholic intellectuals, accusing them of 'Modernism', a catch-all title for a variety of ill-defined abstract 'isms' considered to be heretical or unorthodox at the time.

Fr Gabriel Daly, OSA, an Irish theologian and historian is an expert on this period in Church history. He did his doctoral studies in Oxford on the development of what is known as the Modernist crisis of the late nineteenth and early twentieth century.

> My research showed me that the Modernists were a small group of Catholic scholars trying to face the challenges thrown up by the Enlightenment, an intellectual movement beginning in the late 17th century and providing the modern world with philosophies that were hostile to religion.[374]

Pope Pius X, in his intemperate encyclical letter, *Pascendi*, (1907) condemned the Modernists in extravagant and emotional terms, going so far as to say: " [W]e should define it as the synthesis of all the heresies".

Fr Gabriel Daly has described how they were treated:

> They were a group of honest and learned scholars who were treated outrageously by a pope who was theologically deficient and convinced that he was protecting people from heretics who were a threat to the Catholic Church …

> Pius X, who was a much more pugnacious character than Leo [XIII], cast aside any gentleness and decided that Modernism was "the meeting-place of all the heresies". This was so obviously untrue and unjust that, in my article for the Tablet, I didn't mince my words when I wrote that describing Modernism as the meeting place of all the heresies was "one of the silliest and most unjust judgments ever made about a responsible group of scholars by their fellow Catholics". Strong words, I concede, but accurate.[375]

The papal condemnations proved insufficient and in 1910 Rome introduced the mandatory oath (can there be such a thing?) against Modernism. A secret network

---

[374] Fr. Gabriel Daly, OSA, in a talk to members of 'We are Church, Ireland' 15th January 2018.
[375] idem. The Tablet article was commissioned to mark Fr Daly's 90th birthday.

was set up to identify clergy who might be harbouring Modernist thoughts.[376] The persecution of clergy and theologians relied on spying and coercion to resist scholarly progress in the dialogue of Christianity with the world. This alienated the educated, who were an ever-growing proportion of the faithful.

It is not just fortuitous that the Church is growing in parts of the world where people are lucky to get ten years of schooling and shrinking where the median is nearer twenty.

SMF 5: Ecumenism

About the same time, the Reformed Churches were having a more constructive discussion. Focusing on the essentials, they were identifying disunity as the greatest obstacle to Christian evangelisation. They proposed ecumenism as a solution, as a way to restore unity. Any move towards unity by the Catholics, however, could be expected to reduce the powers of both curia and pope. Rome did not participate in the 1910 missionary conference. Pope Pius XI rudely rejected an invitation to the follow-up conference in 1927. He denounced the movement and forbade participation by Catholics absolutely. This was confirmed in his encyclical *Mortalium Animos* (1928) only to be overturned directly by Vatican II in *Unitatis Redintegratio* without so much as a mention. This made ecumenism a part of Church teaching … but fifty years too late. The change provoked no significant outcry from the faithful or no loss of authority, possibly because the *sensus fidelium* had recognised it long before as the truth and the way.

SMF 6: Discrimination against homosexuals.

The World Meeting of Families took place in Dublin in August 2018. The Archdiocese of Dublin was the local organiser on behalf of the Vatican Dicastery for the Laity, Family and Life. Initially, the preparations were following the guidance of Pope Francis. He had shown himself ready to face the reality of families as they are today and Archbishop Diarmuid Martin had said that Catholic bishops should not "allow ourselves to be become entangled in trying to produce definitions of the family" because different cultural values mean family "cannot be defined simply".[377]

The preparatory brochure as initially issued to the parishes reflected this sensitivity. However, it was changed, reprinted, and replaced because of objections to some of the pictures that seemed to accept that not all families are made up of a man, a woman, and some youngsters. As well as replacing these pictures with more conventional family shots, one important text paragraph was deleted, even though it contained an exhortation originating from Pope Francis. It read:

---

[376] Angelo Roncalli often wondered why he was left for 12 years on his assignment in Bulgaria. On becoming Pope in 1978, he called for his own file only to find that it was anonymously marked 'suspected of modernism'.

[377] Joe Little, RTÉ, 22 October 2017 reporting on Archbishop Martin's address at St Patrick's, Drumcondra.

> "While the Church upholds the ideal of marriage as a permanent commitment between a man and a woman, other unions exist which provide mutual support to the couple. Pope Francis encourages us never to exclude but to accompany these couples also, with love, care and support."

The paragraph that had called attention to the Pope's recommendation against exclusion was itself excluded!

The removal conveys the opposite message to our brothers and sisters to whom God has given a homosexual orientation. Is that how we should 'accompany them with love, care and support'? Is that where the curia is trying to lead the Church?

It is evident that the wishes of Pope Francis and Archbishop Diarmuid were overridden by the curia in this instance. The Dicastery for Laity, Family and Life which was in overall charge of the event has not commented at the time of writing. The incident confirmed that the real power of governance is the curia and demonstrates how easily discrimination and prejudice can take precedence over oaths of loyalty and over Christ's commandment to love and care for one another.

About the same time, it was reported that the former President of Ireland, Mary McAleese has been barred by the prefect of the same Dicastery, Cardinal Kevin Farrell, from speaking at a Vatican venue. Dr McAleese had been invited to join a panel discussion at a 'Voices of Faith' conference to mark International Women's Day which was originally due to take place in the Vatican. McAleese is a committed Catholic who has campaigned for more equitable treatment by the Catholic Church of people with homosexual orientation. Ssenfuka Joanita Warry was also barred. She is a campaigner for LGBT rights in Kenya; a very brave person in a country which has draconian laws regarding sexual orientation.[378]

It was predictable that both these speakers would have argued in favour of more humane and less discriminatory attitudes on the part of civil society and the Church. The bureaucracy does not like to be told how and why it should change. It might have been more astute, however, to listen to what these women had to say rather than to try to silence them in advance.

At a pragmatic level, and not for the first time, the management obsession with control has led it to achieve the opposite of what it wanted. It generated widespread disapproval by its offensive opposition to a Catholic leader who is held in extremely high regard by millions of people in Ireland and internationally. And the gesture was futile. The conference went ahead at a new venue, this one just outside the boundary of Vatican City, and Mary McAleese was invited to give the keynote address. Her comments, and those of Ms Warry thus reached an audience hundreds of times greater than could have attended the conference as originally planned. Their impact was multiplied many times over. Doubtless his colleagues within the curia approved the Cardinal's firm stance but the message for the rest of the world was that the

---

[378] Irish Times, February 2 2018

papacy anticipated that it would be unable to accept or rebut the opinions of the two women and tried to silence them instead. In Ireland it evoked memories of a banned meeting and the suppression of the Gaelic Society in Trinity College in 1914 because "a man called Pearse" had been invited to be a keynote speaker.

SMF 7: The cart before the horse?

In neglecting the recommended development of moral theology, the papacy got the post-conciliar priorities inverted. Management also got the timing wrong, missing the opportunity to tackle moral theology in parallel with the 17-year revision of the Code of Canon Law. Consequently, most of the Synods held since the Council have laboured under the constraints of a moral theology that had already been identified as inadequate by the highest authority of the Church yet could not be challenged in the discussions.

Nowhere has this been more evident than in the three synods on the family. The fact that the second and third were needed is evidence that the first dealt inadequately with the subject. The second and third proved very divisive; particularly on the question of Holy Communion for Catholics who have re-married after divorce. The official position is that the new marriage is invalid and therefore any sexual or genital activity whatsoever that is presumed to be occurring in the new marriage is judged to create a continuing state of mortal sin.

Issues around homosexuality and same-sex marriages were also very divisive. If sexual morality had been given the study and renewal suggested by the Council, these Synods would have had a better understanding of the issues and might have come up with more convincing not to say compassionate recommendations.

The acute anxiety in dealing with anything related to sex springs from the idea that every infringement of the sixth and ninth commandments, however trivial, is a mortal sin. As we saw in the previous chapter this follows an edict issued by the Inquisition at the beginning of the seventeenth century.[379] It became a belief that distinguished Catholics for four centuries. Nobody could question it at the time. To disagree with the Holy Roman Inquisition then was to risk torture and excommunication as a heretic and consequent loss of life, patrimony, and salvation.

Had the recommended renewal of Moral Theology been allowed to take place it is likely that a sense of proportion about sex would have prevailed. It would have informed the discussion and influenced the synodal bishops and the popes, enabling them to link Catholic teachings more closely to the example and values of Christ as found in the gospels and to make "appropriate use … not only of theological principles, but also of the findings of the secular sciences".[380] It might have promoted a more constructive discussion and greater consensus. It might have made sense of morality.

---

[379] Ute Ranke-Heinemann, *Eunuchs for the kingdom of Heaven*, New York, Penguin, paperback, p256
[380] *Gaudium et Spes*, §62

SMF 8: Managing the paedophilia crisis

Papal policy and regulations protected and enabled paedophile activity for the best part of a century. The bishops' obedience to Roman instructions ensured the spread and cover-up of child sexual abuse. As early as 1922 the problem had reached a scale that prompted papal action. Regrettably, the action taken was not designed to resolve the problem but, instead, to cloak it in secrecy. A document entitled *Crimen Solicitationis* was circulated to the bishops of the world in the reign of Pope Pius XI, commanding them to treat all cases of child sex abuse as 'secrets of the Holy Office', under pain of *automatic excommunication*, which could only be lifted by the pope personally. Furthermore, the secrecy extended to the very existence of the document itself. This was to be kept in a locked safe to which only the bishop and his chancellor had keys. This prevented church officials from reporting the cases to the civil authorities and effectively kept the problem from the knowledge of the faithful as it worsened for about sixty years until the secular media began to investigate it.

Successive popes maintained this law in effect. Kieran Tapsell, an Australian civil and canon lawyer, has written extensively on this issue,[381] putting the responsibility squarely on the papacy:[382]

> *Crimen Solicitationis* was reissued by Pope John XXIII in 1962. In 1974 Pope Paul VI, by his decree, *Secreta Continere*, renamed 'the secret of the Holy Office' as 'pontifical secrecy' and expanded it to include the allegation itself. Breach could still lead to excommunication, but it was not automatic …

> In 2001, Pope John Paul II modified the Code's procedures, and confirmed the requirement of secrecy over such allegations …

> The most that the Holy See would allow was reporting where the local civil law required it, in other words, just enough reporting to keep bishops out of jail. That is still the current position[383]…

> The cover up of child sexual abuse did not occur because of bad faith or incompetence on the part of bishops, albeit in some cases that existed, but because they were ordered to cover it up through canon law by six Popes since Pius XI in 1922.

The repeated confirmation of this policy in face of the unfolding crisis must have gone to the very highest levels in the papacy, probably to the popes themselves, three of whom have since been canonised.[384] Rome knew what was going on in the 1980s from regular reports through diplomatic channels. The reporting from the Vatican

---

[381] Kieran Tapsell, *Potiphar's Wife: The Vatican Secret and Child Sexual Abuse,* Adelaide, ATF Press, 2014, and many articles.

[382] Kieran Tapsell, The Second Cover-up, in *The Swag,* Quarterly Magazine of the National Council of Priests of Australia, Autumn 2014.

[383] On December 17th, 2019, Pope Francis removed clerical sex abuse cases from the ambit of Pontifical Secrecy. This reversed the self-serving decision but did not undo a century of damage.

[384] Is canonisation being used here as a pre-emptive defence mechanism?

Embassy in Washington is public knowledge. A summary report describing the problem in the USA and warning about its scale and implications, prepared by Fr Tom Doyle O.P. was handed to Pope John Paul II by the nuncio, Cardinal Pio Laghi, in 1985 but the Pope took no action until 2002. Fr Joaquin Navarro-Valls, the long-time Vatican spokesman tried to explain this neglect by saying that he didn't think that the pope or anyone else understood the gravity of the crisis.[385] If so, the people who boast a divine commission to *teach, sanctify* and *rule,* at the highest level, showed their inadequacy in relation to all three. They displayed:

- a remarkable *ignorance* of human realities,
- a readiness to tolerate the *scandalising* of innocent children, and
- an *inability to manage* their own ordained personnel appropriately together with legislation that facilitated serial immorality.

One can sympathise with the Chilean bishops who offered their resignations *en masse* over the issue. Was that a gesture of mute protest? They had indeed failed to deal decisively with paedophile clergy, but that was not all their own fault. The papacy had been protecting paedophiles to protect the institution. The Chilean bishops had been obeying orders under threat of excommunication. Yet they were now to be made the scapegoats, to further protect the papacy. Bound by the oaths of fidelity to the papacy that underlie, enable and justify so much that is wrong with the Church, they could not defend themselves by publicly implicating former popes, some now declared to be saints. What else could they do in the circumstances but tender their resignations simultaneously?

What is being prioritised over the children's well-being at this stage is not the good name of the Church. That has already been lost. It is the reputations of certain decision-makers that are being protected and together with them the claims of the papacy to authority and wisdom.

The policies and legislation are still in force despite recommendations for change from both the United Nations Organisation and the Australian Royal Commission into Institutional Responses to Child Sexual Abuse.[386] Apparently, as in Luther's time, the bureaucracy does not take kindly to being told what it ought to do.

SMF 9: Alleged abuse by priests of nuns

The papacy failed to respond to complaints that priests were sexually abusing nuns when the spread of aids made sexual intercourse with prostitutes too hazardous. This was reported to Rome in 1994 by Sr Maura O'Donohue MMM, based on a survey covering more than 20 countries. It first came to public attention when headlined by the *National Catholic Reporter* on the 16th March 2001. Nothing had been done about it at that stage and there has been no indication of an effective response from the papacy since then. As with child abuse for so many years, the response has been

---

[385] At a Vatican Press Briefing on Friday 24th April 2014.
[386] We noted earlier sex abuse cases were removed from Pontifical Secrecy in Dec. 2019.

to turn a deaf ear to the complaint and take no action. The priority in the bureaucracy has been to protect the reputation of the institution and maintain the fiction that clerical celibacy implies chastity. In response to questions from reporters, after an interval of 25 years, Pope Francis publicly acknowledged the existence of the problem on 5th February 2019.

SMF 10: Amazonia - a new approach?

Nowhere was the ambiguous position of bishops more apparent than in the recent Synod on Amazonia. The *Instrumentum Laboris,* the document that set the agenda, had summarised the pre-synodal research among the relevant bishops, and the widespread consultation that had taken place. It listed broad areas for discussion, presaging a free debate on topics that had been banned at previous synods. New pathways in ministry were to be sought to meet the sacramental needs of the indigenous cultures. Creative change was in the air.

At the Synod, however, the bishops discussed the regulations that are known to be obstructing the spread of the gospel and the celebration of the Eucharist among the indigenous cultures, but there was little creativity in their proposals.

The bishops were too respectful of existing regulations and not tenacious enough about the mandates. The mandates are surely central to God's eternal plan, while the regulations are peripheral and secondary. They exist to bring order to the achievement of the mandates, not to obstruct them. Most of the current regulations had their origins at the Council of Trent, which was addressing the problems of its own time in a predominantly European context. They were not designed for the evangelisation of indigenous cultures in far-away places.

After a month of consideration, the Synod could only find the courage to recommend the ordination of existing married permanent deacons. This was a totally inadequate response to the Amazonian problem. The proposal would have done nothing to increase the number of ministers in the area or to harness the influence of women in the indigenous cultures, which had been identified as a key factor in the pre-synodal research. It would, however, have had immense implications for the worldwide celibate ministry; something far beyond the remit of a local Synod.[387]

One can only guess what stopped them from recommending more significant changes in regulations which the research seemed to justify. Was this a repetition of the 1971 Synod where control by the curia decided the outcome? Missionary bishops are still financially dependent on maintaining good relations with the curia.

In the post-synodal Apostolic Exhortation, *Querida Amazonia,* Pope Francis officially presented the Report of the Synod to the Church in a way that would make it part of Church teaching. This was in marked contrast to some earlier Apostolic Exhortations which overrode or ignored the related synodal discussions and

---

[387] They also mentioned women deacons, but this was already the subject of a (second) expert commission studying historical precedents...

reports. While avoiding direct disagreement with the proposal, he pointed out that the Amazon needs more permanent deacons, not fewer.

As happened with *Ut Unum Sint,* however, all the promise so hopefully expressed in the main text gets overridden in a few short phrases. In *Querida Amazonia* we find them in Sections 87 to 103. First, the unique privileges accorded to the ordained priesthood under Canon Law are safeguarded. These are reaffirmed although, or perhaps because, they are at the root of the problem of ministry among the indigenous communities who are admitted to being "deprived of the Sunday Eucharist for long periods of time". Francis writes "We cannot remain unconcerned; a specific and courageous response is required of the Church". He calls for "Efforts ... to configure ministry in such a way that it is at the service of a more frequent celebration of the Eucharist, even in the remotest and most isolated communities". Love of neighbour would seem to require nothing less.

But the response that Pope Francis presents turns out to be neither specific nor courageous. He continues:

> 87. This is why it is important to determine what is most specific to a priest, what cannot be delegated. The answer lies in the sacrament of Holy Orders, which configures him to Christ the priest. The first conclusion, then, is that the exclusive character received in Holy Orders qualifies the priest alone to preside at the Eucharist. That is his particular, principal and non-delegable function. ... This function ... is "totally ordered to the holiness of Christ's members". ...

> 88. The priest is the sign of that head [Christ] and wellspring of grace above all when he celebrates the Eucharist, the source and summit of the entire Christian life. That is his great power, a power that can only be received in the sacrament of holy Orders. For this reason, only the priest can say: 'This is my body'. There are other words too, that he alone can speak: 'I absolve you from your sins'. Because sacramental forgiveness is at the service of a worthy celebration of the Eucharist. These two sacraments lie at the heart of the priest's exclusive identity" ...

> 89. [W]e can even say that "no Christian community is built up which does not grow from and hinge on the celebration of the most holy Eucharist"[388]. If we are truly convinced that this is the case, then every effort should be made to ensure that the Amazonian people do not lack this food of new life and the sacrament of forgiveness.

Here, the 'exclusive identity' of priests is being prioritised above Christ's basic mandate, "Do This", 'the source and summit of the entire Christian life'. To enquire what is specific to the priest that cannot be delegated, is to ask the wrong question. All the duties and privileges of the individual priests were originally vested in the community of Christians and later ceded to the individual priests. As we have seen,

---

[388] Second Vatican Council, *Presbyterorum Ordinis* §6.

in relation to the Mass, this happened over a period around the third and fourth centuries as the ordination of individuals as priests became the custom. Prior to that, the community itself celebrated the Lord's Supper on the Lord's Day. The person presiding was not credited with power to transform the bread and wine. Does anyone suggest that the Lord's Supper was illicit or invalid during the first few centuries in the life of the Church? Not at all.

Similarly, the right to forgive sins was given to Christ's disciples and all Christians were his disciples. They still are. It was Church discipline that stopped the laity, the deacons the sub-deacons, deaconesses and ordinary Christians from doing things that gradually became the prerogative of the ordained priests and bishops. Charity demands that these prerogatives be renounced.

Pope Francis writes: "these two sacraments lie at the heart of the priest's exclusive identity". If we were to substitute 'privileges' or 'prerogatives' in place of 'sacraments' we would get closer to understanding the weakness of the Amazonia Synod. It was a gathering of seminary-trained, ordained, celibate males all beholden to the Roman curia in one way or another, as homogeneous a group as one could imagine, considering the possibility of sharing their 'exclusive identity' with others who are deemed to be ontologically inferior. They could only bring themselves to recommend the ordination of existing trained married deacons. The involvement of women in ending the Eucharistic crisis was a bridge too far, however, although the need to give women some official authority had been clearly identified in the pre-synodal research as being especially important and the key to caring for souls in the indigenous cultures in isolated areas.

Querida Amazonia praises the "strong and generous women who, undoubtedly called and prompted by the Holy Spirit, baptised, catechised, prayed and acted as missionaries". It speaks of "how many [church] communities in the Amazon would have collapsed, had women not been there to sustain them, keep them together and care for them", that is to act as ministers. It thus identifies women as leading the Church in everything except what Jesus told us to do. If the Holy Spirit has called these women to be missionaries what is stopping Church management from confirming the call? The assembled management of the Church agreed that these women should be given recognition as the missionary treasures that they obviously are, but then failed to do anything about it. Does nobody in Rome see the contradiction? At a pragmatic level, does nobody see the danger that this treatment will alienate some of the most important people in the faith life of the same indigenous cultures? Does the exhortation find ways to make them more effective? No. The authorities are blocked by the pseudo-infallible teaching that says women cannot be ordained. So the exhortation downplays the missionary value and significance of admitting them to Holy Orders and enabling them to lead the Eucharist, that would "make the Church", within their communities. "But", we are told, "that approach would in fact narrow our vision; it would lead us to clericalize women … and subtly make their indispensable contribution less effective". This is about as narrow a vision as one could imagine and reflects an appalling assessment of the social side-effects of Holy Orders.

Not surprisingly, *Querida Amazonia* contains the customary insincere and condescending references to women and the important contribution they can make to the Church "in a way that is properly theirs". It calls for the emergence of forms of service and charisms that are "proper to women" and responsive to the "needs of the peoples of the Amazon". But this is what the Synod was summoned for, and what it failed egregiously to do. The exhortation compounds that failure by at once promoting the ideal and guarding against its realisation.

There is talk about the need "to promote an encounter with God's word and holiness through various kinds of lay service that call for a process of education—biblical, doctrinal, spiritual and practical—and a variety of programmes of ongoing formation". This is a distraction. There can be no substitute for doing what Jesus told us to do. *Querida Amazonia* itself recognises this in the excerpt shown above (§89) when it quotes Vatican II: "No Christian community is built up which does not grow from and hinge on the celebration of the most holy Eucharist". The papacy, however, being composed exclusively of ordained, ontologically superior beings, finds itself unable to share with lesser mortals the privilege and dignity of confecting the Eucharist and assuring people of the forgiveness of God, although it readily admits to the urgent need to make these sacraments more widely available.

The Exhortation recognises the need for women to have access to positions in the ecclesial structure with official commissions from the bishop, allowing them to participate in leadership and decision making "while continuing to do so in a way that reflects their womanhood". When translated this means: in a way that does not impinge on the male preserve and the overblown attitude to sacramental ordination that prioritises it above the Eucharist itself.

If, by some miracle in the future, a way can be found of providing male ordained priests for indigenous communities that have hitherto been led by women, the men had better be taught that being sacramentally 'configured to Christ' does not mean that they are consequently in command. If they do not accept this, the indispensable contribution of the women is likely to come to a quick and angry end. Hell hath no fury like a woman scorned.[389]

The Synod on Amazonia offered an exceptional opportunity to do something strategic for the mission of the Church. The management, as currently constituted, was unable to respond to the challenge. Secondary considerations were allowed to block the essentials of Christian evangelisation. Consequently, the most promising way to bring the sacraments to indigenous Catholic communities in Amazonia will remain closed off for another generation or more.

---

[389] Paraphrased from playwright William Congreve.

The above ten examples of management failings cannot be dismissed as exceptions. They are systemic. Each of them has its roots in the structure, traditions, and priorities of the curia, as strengthened by the decisions of 1870.

REINTERPRETING THE COUNCIL.

The confidence with which Catholicism could address the people of the world following the Second Vatican Council has been allowed to evaporate over the past forty years. The clear vision mapped by the Council has been muddied. Rome now blames secularism, consumerism, capitalism, individualism, and indifferentism just as it decried ecumenism, modernism, rationalism, relativism, and Americanism in the years after the previous Council. But is error not the normal state of mind of the people whom we are called upon to convert to Christ? Does Rome not understand that the Way can be followed in any society, be it secular, consumerist, capitalist or whatever, although it may sometimes call for heroic virtue? For a missionary church, handwringing and condemnations are no substitute for communication, persuasion, humility, creative engagement, scholarship, joy in the good news, commitment, and good example. The Church now has a highly centralised management system which is faltering in its mission and cannot recognise its own failings. It is not fit for purpose. Pope Francis has been reminding us that the Council saw the need for us, Catholics, to get our own house in order … first.

We have seen in the previous chapters, how the bureaucracy has ignored, stalled, and/or reversed many of the recommendations of the supreme authority in the Church[390]. They justify their actions, or inaction, by claiming that the Council has been 'misinterpreted'. They can do this safely, knowing that in revising canon law they carefully omitted any mechanism by which the faithful could appeal decisions or interpretations. They made communication in the Church a one-way street. How can any organisation flourish without free communication up and down the line?

Even the clergy have great difficulty in getting their opinions heard as has been demonstrated in Ireland by the inability of the Irish Bishops to work constructively with the Association of Catholic Priests. Bishops cannot dialogue as long as the curia cannot listen. Since the papacy created legal claims to worldwide jurisdiction and unlimited power to buttress exaggerated infallibility, it simply cannot let its officials be seen to listen, to the clergy, to the people or to academic research. Despite what they protest and notwithstanding the annual Holy Thursday gesture, the leaders have chosen the way of lording it over their subjects rather than washing their feet.

Confused priorities.

Apart from issues of doctrine, priorities in the church are visibly disordered. The papacy should reorder its priorities putting first things first:

---

[390] Particularly, when the bureaucracy saw the danger of a competing power centre emerging: See *Collegiality* on page 189, Enforced unanimity for Episcopal Conferences on page 191, and the ICEL affair on page 193

1. Christ prayed for unity among his followers. The papacy is the only office in the world with the status required to lead Christians to greater unity. It thus has a duty to prioritise ecumenism. The response of the other denominations to the initiative of John XXIII at the time of the Council was encouraging, proving that, in general, they too long for greater unity. Other considerations, no matter how costly, no matter how essential to the papal ministry they may seem, must be subordinated.

2. Jesus said: "This is my body" and "Do This". Rules that prevent a Christian community from celebrating the Eucharist together on Sundays, or maybe more often, must be considered perverse unless the contrary can be proven. The onus of proof is on those who make and enforce such rules. As of now, the rules appear to prioritise an exaggerated veneration of the ordained priesthood and its prerogatives over the very mandates it was ordained to serve.

3. Christians are united in accepting that the Eucharist is something we have been told to do. It is the unifying sacrament and a mystery of religion. Rules that make it conditional on agreement as to how the mystery is accomplished are silly. 'Mystery' means mystery. Moreover, regulations that require assent to all the doctrines, interpretations and practices currently proposed by Rome as a condition for communion prioritise subordination to men over obedience to Jesus. The priority given to the secondary details that gets in the way of the essentials is entirely disproportionate. The Council reminded us that there is a hierarchy of truths.

4. Love has been the distinguishing and identifying characteristic of Christians from the start. The real test of fidelity is the commitment of each person, and the organisation at every level, to the loving care of others—to the point of inconvenience and beyond. Love, of course, presupposes unselfishness and is never lacks elements of forgiveness, justice, and mercy. When Pope Francis prioritises these, he is accused of setting the Church on a new course. What does that tell us about the old one?

5. Preaching Jesus Christ demands an overwhelming commitment to the truth. If such a commitment were to be made it would lead to official admissions that Rome has erred at times and therefore can err. (See Chapters 9 & 12). Moreover, it would classify Vatican I and Vatican II as Councils of the Roman Catholic Church rather than as Ecumenical Councils, weakening the theory that the definitions of Vatican I can never be reformed. Prioritising truth here would be costly. The obstacles are pride and power. The tradition of bolstering teaching with coercion protects the aura of infallibility but cannot be reconciled with evangelisation in the name of Jesus.

6. The need to protect pseudo-infallible teaching has spawned the controlled Synods where participants have been carefully filtered, pre-synodal submissions kept secret from the faithful, selected relevant issues banned from the

discussion and the final report drafted by curial officials for the pope. Some modern synods have been orchestrated as if the Promise had never been made. Pope Paul VI was aware of the structural shortcomings of the Synod that he was instituting and expressed the hope that it would develop greater strength later. Pope Francis has begun to make the necessary changes, but the Synod is still controlled by the curia.

7. Careerism prioritises self before service. Careerism within the curia is so widespread that Pope Francis referred to it as a problem within days of taking office. The farmer only talks about fences when they are causing problems.

8. The pretence that the Roman Magisterium cannot err has created unnecessary anxiety among the more traditional members of the faithful who have been led for generations to believe that salvation depends on personal assent to, or lack of dissent from, an official list of detailed doctrinal propositions. The papacy will have to accept the view of St Augustine endorsed by Vatican II, that the charism of infallibility rests on the promise of Christ to his followers and extends only as far as does their agreement. It will also have to accept that, insofar as our salvation depends on ourselves, it depends not on what we profess but on what we do for love of God's other children and the ecology that sustains them.

9. Obedience is important for the sake of order, but management should never elevate it over conscience and justice.

10. The idea that the pope should be judged by no one may have seemed reasonable to canon lawyers and others who were accustomed to monarchical forms of civil government, when the king was deemed to be divinely appointed and could do no wrong. The consequent omission of checks and balances and of the separation of powers from canon law suggests that the curia has learned nothing about sociology or jurisprudence in the past four hundred years. By omitting provision for the separation of powers, canon law prioritises authority but facilitates corruption and injustice.

11. For centuries, the papacy has been unable to see that its way of exercising authority is the antithesis of the one described by Jesus to Peter and the other apostles.[391] Unwillingness to limit the power of the papacy had been a consistent factor in this. Pope John Paul II's call, in his encyclical *Ut Unum Sint,* (1994) to find a "way of exercising the primacy" [and promote unity] …" while in no way renouncing what is essential to its mission" speaks volumes. It shows the same attitude. The papacy is prioritising what it deems "essential to its mission" ahead of the *raison d'être* of the office, and ahead of "the will of Christ for his Church". (See Chapter 16). This kind of topsy-turvy thinking can be

---

[391] See reference to Fr Wilfred Harrington and Harrington's Law in Chapter 4.

shrugged off by cradle Catholics but will never bring our separated brethren to greater unity.

Decentralisation

Catholics believe in the Promise, but does the papacy? How come the papacy is so unwilling to authorise initiative or experimentation in pursuit of the mandates? Universal central jurisdiction and the need to maintain an aura of infallibility combine to exclude innovation.

In contrast, in a decentralised organisation or movement, local leaders who know the circumstance and the culture, make the decisions, sometime in consultation with those affected. They can make mistakes without committing the CEO and, consequently, make progress. If bishops and local churches were allowed to work on their own initiative and take responsibility for solving their own problems, trusting the guidance of the Holy Spirit, then their successes would be copied, and the failures forgotten.

Taizé has been successful in developing a practical ecumenism and in bringing tens of thousands of young people into contact with Jesus. Every diocese could learn from Taizé. It must be admitted however, that had Br. Roger been a Roman Catholic bishop or priest, he could not have done what he did.

Highly centralised management has vitiated the ability of subordinate officers to take responsibility for their actions and get on with their jobs. If your responsibility is to farm the field, you should not need specific permission to buy a spade and a rake, or to go and hire a ploughman.

My personal experience in Africa Concern (now Concern Worldwide) of young priests who worked with us as volunteers in famine relief and community development, was that they were wonderful people to work with. Removed from the stifling control mechanisms of Church structures, they were creative, resourceful, unselfish, honest, intelligent, self-reliant, and hard-working. One could depend one's life on them. Seminary training can certainly produce great people. By dint of over-regulation, however, the Church system appears to make poor use of extraordinary talent and dedication. Given a looser rein, they could work wonders.

The lesson is obvious. Micro-managing a spiritual organisation of 1.33 Billion people from the centre has been a failure. It overworks the pope and leaves him hopelessly dependent on the bureaucrats. There are more than 5,000 well educated bishops who know the faith. A proportion of them also know the faithful in their own dioceses. Individually, they should be let run their dioceses. Collectively they should run the Church with the pope as their leader. A scaled down curia should be at their service.

Recapitulation and conclusions

The Church suffers from bad strategic management because the members of the papal team lack independence and variety in training and experience. The papacy is paralysed by a culture that treasures its infallibility and that accords unwarranted veneration to the sacrament of ordination which is shared by all its officials. For a century and a half, the papacy has governed as if virtually all current teaching and practices are infallible, and all current structures form part of some Divine plan that cannot be changed.[392] Significant changes are feared lest they undermine this position and lead to a diminution of power. The homogeneous management team seems incapable of making decisions that would impinge on the profession. Consequently, the prerogatives, privileges and dignity of the profession are habitually prioritised above the two foundational mandates.

This study does not attribute motives or judge anyone. It attempts to explain why an administration with so many intelligent, educated, prayerful, dedicated people can be so dysfunctional and corrupt and lose sight of its God-given objectives. It is in the nature of large bureaucracies to prioritise their own group needs. Therefore, a Church founded by Christ should not be governed by its bureaucracy. We have shown that the curia is an unchanging and homogeneous bureaucracy, with an unyielding structure and ethos and no legislature or board to control it. Its disdain for the separation of powers and resistance to financial auditing virtually guarantee arrogance, corruption, and injustice.

---

[392] Of course, the Divine plan can be reinterpreted. When the establishment wants to, it can find wriggle room. This can be done arbitrarily because canon law makes no provision for appeal or review of decisions or actions of the papacy. .

Chapter 16

Unity among Christians

"But in subsequent centuries more widespread disagreements appeared and quite large Communities became separated from the Catholic Church —developments for which, at times, men of both sides were to blame".

—Vatican II, Decree, *Unitatis Redintegratio,* §3

SHARED RESPONSIBILITY FOR DISUNITY

The statement above is circumspect, as befits a conciliar document. When translated, however, it is a remarkable admission that the papacy, which formed one of the 'sides', was at fault. Never had this been admitted officially. It took a Council of the Bishops of the Roman Catholic Church to face the truth and confess that the Church authorities had helped to turn Luther's attempt at reform into the division we have today.[393] The repentance was real. It led the Bishops to take four strategic reforming steps each of which opened possibilities for further reform:

1. They set up an inter-church dialogue with the Lutheran Church, even while the Council was still in progress, to seek resolution of doctrinal differences.

2. They reversed earlier papal teaching on the ecumenical movement making a virtue of what was previously a sin.

3. They decided unequivocally that the members of the churches and ecclesial communities arising from the Reformation are Christians and entitled to the name and that the Holy Spirit is at work among them.

4. They changed teaching on the issues of freedom of speech, freedom of religion, primacy of conscience, and the relationship of church and state.

Inter-church dialogue

The initiative of some Council bishops in setting up the Catholic/Lutheran dialogue formed a precedent which led the way for many joint commissions with other churches in the years after the Council, with some very encouraging results. The dialogue with the Lutherans persevered and after three decades led to agreement that 'the crux of the sixteenth century doctrinal dispute', the different positions on 'justification by faith', are not necessarily contradictory. This was a big step forward. It had been pointed out at the time by Cardinal Reginald Pole, the scholarly cousin of England's Henry VIII. He had argued that the differing views on Justification could be

---

[393] The way was paved for this repentance by Fr Yves Congar O.P. who was persecuted for his research and opinions by the CDF until his views were vindicated by the Council. His book, *True and False Reform in the Church,* published in 1950 had been read by Angelo Roncalli when he was Nuncio to Paris. His speech, as Pope at the opening of the Council, suggests that he had not forgotten it.

reconciled and therefore did not form grounds for schism.[394] He later got within one vote of being elected pope! If one more cardinal at the conclave, had voted for him , listening and reform could have taken the place of pride, anger, and schism.

In 1957, Hans Küng reached a similar conclusion to that of Cardinal Pole in his book, *Justification*, based on his doctoral thesis. In 1999 the Lutheran-Roman Catholic Joint Commission was 'able to articulate a common understanding',[395] based closely on Küng's work, and this was formally celebrated at a signing ceremony in Augsburg in November of that year. The theological issue did not justify a split then[396] and certainly does not justify it now.

To repair the division now, however, goes well beyond healing the original wounds. The papacy subsequently made itself infallible and centralised additional power in Rome. The churches have grown apart on many other secondary beliefs and practices. New grounds for division are used to rationalise the continuing scandal and ensure that the consciences of complacent church leaders are not disturbed.

Change of doctrine and attitude.

Pope John XXIII supported the College of Bishops when they overruled and reversed 60 years of papal teaching and policy on ecumenism. In consequence, the leaders of the Christian churches worldwide have been able to emulate the good-neighbourly attitudes of their congregations, follow the *sensus fidelium* and behave like Christians towards other Christians. Catholics have been able to respond to the invitation from the other churches to work together for unity and for the needy. The Christian churches have stopped vilifying one another.

The decree on ecumenism, *Unitatis Redintegratio* states openly that baptised members of other denominations are entitled to the name of Christians. This implies that they are members of the Mystical Body and that it is only at visible level that Christianity is divided. It humbly accepts that the divisions resulted from "developments for which, at times, men of both sides were to blame". It also decided that praying with other Christians, hitherto a sin, could be "allowable, indeed desirable".

Cecily Boulding O.P. condensed the introduction to the Decree:

> "Certainly, such divisions openly contradict the will of Christ … in recent times he has begun to bestow more generously upon divided Christians remorse over their divisions and longing for unity. Everywhere large numbers have felt the impulse of this grace … there increases from day today a

---

[394] Breifne V. Walker, C.S.Sp., *Cardinal Reginald Pole, Papal Primacy and Church Unity 1529-1536,* Unpublished M.A. Thesis presented to University College Dublin, 1972, pp 28-31

[395] Lutheran-Roman Catholic Joint Commission: Joint Declaration on the Doctrine of Justification, (JDDJ) http://www.vatican.va/roman_curia/pontifical_councils/chrstuni/documents/rc_pc_chrstuni_doc_31101999_cath-luth-joint-declaration_en.html .

[396] The seminal work on this issue in modern times was done by Hans Küng in his doctoral thesis. He has since then attracted the ire of Rome for his views on infallibility and was stripped of his licence to teach as a Roman Catholic theologian in 1979. Reflecting the small-minded and mean-spirited nature of curial thinking, Küng was omitted from the invitation list for the Augsburg celebration.

movement fostered by the grace of the Holy Spirit for the restoration of unity among all Christians … the Council gladly notes all this … it wished to set before all Catholics guidelines, helps and methods by which they too can respond to this divine call".[397]

A prominent and highly respected Lutheran theologian, Dr Oscar Cullmann, who was an observer at the Council, commented: "This is more than the opening of a door; new ground has been broken, No Catholic document has ever spoken of non-Catholic Christians in this way".[398]

The Decree recommends that the laity have a part to play in

" … keeping the separated brethren … informed about the Church, making the first approaches towards them. But their primary duty is to make an honest and careful appraisal of whatever needs to be renewed and achieved in the Catholic household itself, in order that its life may bear witness more loyally and luminously to the teachings and ordinances which have been handed down from Christ through the apostles" (§4) (Emphasis added).

The kingdom is building

The kingdom is one of love and when Christ repeated that it was very near, he was recognising that there were many loving, caring, individuals in the community. Over the centuries, the People of God have played a big part in making disciples (people who love) of all the nations. The *sensus fidelium* among Christians has helped to make the world a more humane place, albeit mostly indirectly. Society has become more loving, more respectful of human dignity. We don't stone adulterers or crucify thieves anymore. Torture of prisoners and suspects is rejected as barbaric. We don't stoop to mutilation or deportation to punish criminals. The death penalty is being phased out internationally. We don't burn heretics at the stake. Society has stopped the slave trade and disapproves of modern slavery. We don't allow child labour in the coal mines. Annexing of weaker nations is now disapproved of although in USA as recently as the presidency of Theodore Roosevelt, it was fair game. Nations now try to settle their disputes at the United Nations, and in at least one case, this has been successful to the point of averting war.

Most nations now use taxation to redistribute wealth from rich to poor and try to provide medical services for the needy, a work in which the churches led the way. The writer is personally aware that the generosity of ordinary people now enables Concern to employ 3,500 indigenous people in bringing disaster relief and development aid to 24 of the world's poorest countries at a cost of $200M per annum. The spread of democracy has prompted governments to give generous expression to the concern their citizens have for their less fortunate brothers and sisters.

---

[397] M. Cecily Boulding, OP, *Ecumenism Forty Years on – Are we Still in the Desert?* in Dermot A. Lane and Brendan Leahy (eds), *Vatican II, Facing the 21ˢᵗ Century,* Dublin, Veritas Publications, 2006, p187.

[398] Walter M. Abbott, S.J., in *Ecumenism,* in Walter M. Abbott, S.J. (ed) The Documents of Vatican II, London – Dublin, Geoffrey Chapman, 1966 p 338

Amazingly, 192 nations have signed up to Agenda 2030 a UN brokered agreement in which they have agreed to work together within a framework of 17 Sustainable Development Goals, designed to help ease hunger, poverty, disease and deprivation among mankind but primarily in the less developed countries. This is an extraordinary development, unprecedented in human history. Concern is love in action. The kingdom of God is nearer than we think.

Not every nation has been converted to the Christian faith, but, with notable exceptions, they are gradually coming around to the gospel values that have marked genuine Christianity since its foundations; the pursuit of justice, peace and care for the other. It is probably fair to say that the changes in attitude have been inspired more by the mindset and lives of the People of God than by the initiative of official leaders, spiritual or civil. Leaders often follow.

The main thrust of Christian evangelization should be to teach people and nations to let love guide their actions and to take care of the least ones and of the ecology on which everybody depends for life and well-being. There has been great progress in this over the centuries. It is the many faithful Christians living the Gospel message who have gradually made society more humane and civilised.

AMBIVALENT ATTITUDES TO ECUMENISM

The modern ecumenical movement is widely agreed to date from the Edinburgh Missionary Conference in 1910[399] when the division among Christians was identified as the greatest obstacle to the missionary work of the Christian churches.[400]

The Roman Catholic Church did not participate in that meeting and stayed aloof from ecumenism for 54 years although its own provenance, founder, scale, influence, and ubiquity make it the natural centre around which other churches might coalesce.

An invitation to participate in the subsequent *Faith and Order Conference* in 1927 was harshly rejected by Pope Pius XI.[401] In his uncompromising Encyclical *Mortalium Animos,* (1928) he taught that ecumenism was a "most grave error" and "that the Apostolic See cannot on any terms take part in their assemblies, nor is it anyway lawful for Catholics either to support or to work for such enterprises".

This position was grounded in the idea that the papacy was the exclusive channel for the authentic inspiration of the Holy Spirit and that the Roman Magisterium could never err. Thus, the papacy could only envisage Christian Unity in terms of reunion— a return of all 'misguided Christians' to the Roman fold. In contrast, the ecumenical idea implies a possible route to unity in Christ other than that of total submission to Roman doctrines, practices, and jurisdiction.

---

[399] In fact, the World Student Christian Federation and other youth organizations had already worked with the ecumenical idea.—Pastor Robra of WCC in interview with Antonio Spadaro S.J., Civiltá Cattolica May 31, 2018

[400] At this stage it may be affecting the survival of the churches as well as the expansion.

[401] M. Cecily Boulding, OP, Ecumenism Forty Years on – Are we Still in the Desert? in Dermot A Lane and Brendan Leahy (eds), *Vatican II, Facing the 21st Century*, Dublin, Veritas, 2006, p190.

At a pragmatic level, the curia could see that if Rome were to be part of any such unification, it would be at the cost of some significant watering down of papal claims and curial hegemony. The curia had another reason to resist the ecumenical movement. To encourage it would be in breach of the bureaucratic principle that any potential competition that cannot be controlled, must be weakened, or eliminated.

In contrast, when summoning the Second Vatican Council, Pope John XXIII was able to say: "We, instead, like to reaffirm all our confidence in our Saviour, who has not left the world[402] which he redeemed". Pope John did not share the group priorities of the curia but favoured reform, reconciliation, magnanimity, and some self-sacrifice. He understood that 'the seed must die'. The genuine warmth of his invitation enabled other churches and denominations to send observers and he arranged that they could play a constructive role. He wanted the Council to bring forward ecumenism. His view found widespread support among the faithful and among the diocesan bishops and heads of major religious congregations all of whom were given freedom to speak their minds[403] at the Council. The curia resisted as strongly as it could without being too obviously in opposition to its leader.

Pope John's successor, Paul VI was deeply committed to the ecumenical movement, as was apparent from his decision to continue the Council and to his opening address to the second session.[404] Furthermore, in his address to members of the Secretariat for Promoting Christian Unity in 1967 he recognised that the papal household could not be exempted from the 'careful appraisal of what needs to be renewed' saying: *"The Pope, as we well know, is undoubtedly the gravest obstacle in the path of ecumenism".*

Ut Unum Sint

Pope John Paul II seems to have been committed personally to ecumenism, although much of his thought was filtered through the curia which continued to oppose it. Thus, his encyclical, *Ut Unum Sint,* (1994) wholeheartedly endorses the search for unity, quoting extensively from the Council documents and from St Augustine, but reinforces rather than removes the traditional obstacles. One can get a feel for his personal commitment from a few excerpts:

> 1. "If they wish truly and effectively to oppose the world's tendency to reduce to powerlessness the Mystery of Redemption, they must *profess together the same truth about the Cross. The Cross!"*
>
> " … the commitment to ecumenism must be based upon the conversion of hearts and upon prayer".
>
> 2. 'What is needed is a calm, clear-sighted and truthful vision of things".

---

[402] In the apostolic constitution *"Humanae Saluti",* dated December 25, 1961.

[403] This demonstrated a divergence between the beliefs as witnessed by the bishops and by the Papal Magisterium. In theory, this can never happen since each benefits from the inspiration of the same Holy Spirit. It assumes, of course, that no churchman ever ignored the promptings of the Spirit.

[404] Walter M. Abbott, S.J., in *Ecumenism,* in Walter M. Abbott, S.J. (ed) The Documents of Vatican II, London – Dublin, Geoffrey Chapman, 1966 p 337

3. "There can be no ecumenism worthy of the name without a change of heart", (quoting *Unitatis Redintegratio* §7)

4. "By God's grace, however, neither what belongs to the structure of the Church of Christ nor that communion which still exists with the other Churches and Ecclesial Communities has been destroyed".

5. "To the extent that these elements are found in other Christian Communities, the one Church of Christ is effectively present in them. For this reason, the Second Vatican Council speaks of a certain, though imperfect communion. The Dogmatic Constitution *Lumen Gentium* stresses that the Catholic Church "recognizes that in many ways she is linked 'with these Communities by a true union in the Holy Spirit'". (quoting from LG,(§15)

6. "Likewise, we can say that in some real way they are joined with us in the Holy Spirit, for to them also he gives his gifts and graces and is thereby operative among them with his sanctifying power. Some indeed he has strengthened to the extent of the shedding of their blood". (quoting from *LG*, §15)

7. "In all of Christ's disciples the Spirit arouses the desire to be peacefully united, *in the manner determined by Christ, as one flock under one shepherd"* (emphasis mine).[405]

The last three excerpts are taken from the Second Vatican Council, *Lumen Gentium* (§15). However, the phrase highlighted in the final excerpt provides a convenient escape route. It would allow the pope, or the CDF as currently constituted, to veto any specific move towards unity by ruling authoritatively that it is not 'in the manner determined by Christ'. (Elsewhere, as we have seen, the manner specified by Christ has been ignored for centuries.)

While stressing the importance of unity in the mind of Jesus, Pope John Paul II goes on to set the bar uncompromisingly high. He insists on doctrinal, sacramental, and hierarchical communion, and quotes *Lumen Gentium* in support.[406] Thus, in one sentence the encyclical lays down conditions for ecumenism that are scarcely distinguishable from reunion and are known to be unacceptable to the other traditions. The concept of ecumenism as a pathway to unity is effectively dismissed. Church policy is thus out of step with Church teaching.

Furthermore, having confirmed Pope Paul VI's statement that the papacy is the 'gravest obstacle', John Paul II expresses the hope that a way might be found "of exercising the primacy which, while in no way renouncing what is essential to its mission, is nonetheless open to a new situation". He appeals for help in reconciling these two goals but fails to face the contradiction between the two objectives.

---

[405] Reading the last three quotes from the Vatican II one cannot but question why the disciples who share the blessings of the Holy Spirit, are not allowed to share in Christ's sacrament of unity.

[406] The phrase in *Lumen Gentium* §14 that he relies on confirms this interpretation: "the bonds of professed faith, of the sacraments, of ecclesiastical governance and of communion". He merges the last two items into "hierarchical communion".

This is the pivotal point in the encyclical. Regrettably, it can be read in two ways. Does it reflect a virtuous adherence to principle at all costs? Or could it be a determination never to compromise on the powers and privileges of the papacy? On a more careful examination, however, it becomes clear that he wants to remove the papacy as an obstacle to what he believes is 'Christ's will for the Church' but considers that some unidentified characteristics of the office as currently defined merit a higher priority. What on earth (or in heaven) can they be? He does not disclose the characteristics to which he attaches such idolatrous importance. To do so would reveal the inconsistency, not to say contradiction, of the entire encyclical. What if the things that he deems essential to the papal mission are the very things that are perpetuating disunity?

John Paul left us to figure out what precisely he had in mind as 'essential', although his focus on doctrinal, sacramental, and hierarchical communion leave us in little doubt. The dogmas of papal infallibility and universal papal jurisdiction would surely have figured prominently in his list. They would be part of 'hierarchical communion'. They are important in Rome. Within the curia, they are considered essential (just as was the independent existence of the Papal States at one time). Within the curia the credibility of the Church seems to hang on them. Outside, it survives despite them. They are not, however, essential to mission. The Church took shape and grew without them for nineteen centuries.

It is vital that whatever John Paul II considered 'essential' should be identified and evaluated against the unity that Christ prayed for. If in doing so, the faithful find a conflict between that unity and some of the things deemed 'essential to the papal mission', then there can be little doubt as to which objective ought to be prioritised.

Reviewing the mission?

The fruits of the dogma of Papal Infallibility have been reviewed in chapters 8 and 9 above and shown to be almost entirely negative. In chapter 17 we show how this 'irreformable' teaching can be reformed or revoked, given the will and the grace of humility. Stripped of it, the church could be more honest and more ready for greater unity. Moreover, the *sensus fidelium* might be able to find better expression.

Universal Jurisdiction with *plenitudo potestatis* is just what Lord Acton was referring to when he warned of absolute power corrupting absolutely. The Church now has a management crisis and a credibility crisis like never before. If, as we have seen, Theodore McCarrick, with un-investigated allegations of sexual abuse against him could rise, in spite of the guidance of the Holy Spirit, to become an influential cardinal with a right to participate in papal elections, it suggests that the corruption goes very close to the top.

Since 1870 the papacy has downgraded diocesan bishops and gathered to itself virtually all the power, control and decision making in an organisation that is grounded in the personal and freely chosen commitment of its individual members to love God and their fellow men and women. This makes it very vulnerable in the democratic era. The papacy has taken on the impossible task of micro-managing directly the spiritual lives and the consciences of 1.3 billion individuals of different cultures and levels of development. The successor of Peter has taken over the decision-making for all the successors of the apostles. If, as we are told, the Holy Spirit guides the selection of our 5,000 bishops, each of whom is a successor of the apostles, it is crass to deny them the authority to match their responsibilities.

Confused objectives

Ostensibly, *Ut Unum Sint,* is a panegyric on ecumenism. Regrettably, however, John Paul (or some official editing the text) slipped back into the old mind-frame of reunionism in one crucial sentence defining unity in terms of 'doctrinal, sacramental and hierarchical communion'.[407] This becomes the operative phrase, overriding all the inspiring rhetoric in the encyclical. It substitutes a demand for a unity characterised by the profession of one set of doctrinal propositions and seven sacraments,[408] and by acceptance of one form of governance. One looks in vain for any hint of a readiness on the part of the papacy to modify its position on any of them. These are not the elements of unity, but the focal points of division. We will consider them individually, bearing in mind that the demand for perfection can be the enemy of progress.

One faith

All the divisions in Christianity relate to secondary issues. Christians have long been in agreement on the fundamental doctrines: the Unity and Trinity of God, the Incarnation, Death and Resurrection of Jesus, the Second Person of the Trinity, and his great commandment to love God and neighbour, on which depend all the lesser commandments. We accept that he prayed that his followers would be united, and he promised to be with us forever. He gave us the Holy Spirit to fulfil this promise.

We are also in agreement on his two great mandates to his followers: "Make disciples of all the nations, baptising them … ", and "Do This in commemoration of me". For the first, Jesus defined disciples as people who would love one another. For the second, he did not try to explain *how* bread and wine could become his body and blood nor did he ask us to solve that mystery. He just told us to *do* it as he demonstrated at the Last Supper and at Emmaus.

These are the extraordinary and overwhelming blessings that unite us in a spiritual way, and they inspire a challenge, a Way of life that can be lived in any age, culture, or situation. It is easy to lose sight of the basics in the complexity of implementing them in different times and circumstances. At times, we can't see the forest for the trees. Being human, we need a visible organisation, called the church, to guide us, to preserve and pass on the teaching and to unite our efforts. Philosophers, scholars, inspired saints, and fellow members of our missionary churches teach us and guide us. We trust their judgement and authority on many issues that we have not studied

---

[407] Here the encyclical quotes the description in *Unitatis Redintegratio* (§14) of the unity said to exist in the Roman Catholic Church and uses it to set the standard for Ecumenical Unity. This is not ecumenism. In effect, it is a reiteration of the invitation to repent and return to the one true fold.

[408] CCC 1117: "…there are seven that are, in the strict sense of the term, sacraments instituted by the Lord".

or explored personally. If there is a hierarchy of truths, then we can be sure there are some that matter more and some less. We can be united with our siblings in love and in purpose without being unanimous about all the details. Regrettably, failure to understand this has led to divisions in the visible church *"for which, at times, men of both sides were to blame"*.

Providentially, the theological disagreement about Justification that turned the call for reform into a schism, has now been resolved. Many of the specific commissions for inter-church dialogue set up during the Ecumenical Spring have led to gratifying levels of doctrinal reconciliation. In the ensuing Winter, however, the CDF has been slow to let the pope 'confirm' the work of the theologians.

Cardinal Avery Dulles has described how some promising doctrinal dialogues came to a stop when they reached the more difficult issues. The examples he gave for the "sticking points" were women's ordination and the infallibility status of the pope. Obviously, these were "sticking points" for both sides of the discussion. But should they have been? Have the Catholic authorities lost all sense of proportion? These are not essential issues. How can relative trivialities such as these be allowed to obstruct progress towards the unity that Christ prayed for?[409] Could the churches not agree to differ on them? They are only indirectly linked to salvation, if at all. If wriggle room cannot be found, these differences could be dismissed on the grounds of triviality, of their low position in the hierarchy of truths or their very tenuous relationship with the great commandment.

Dr Coggan proposed that the priestly ordination of women should be considered a 'legitimate diversity'. Christ's instruction "Do This" was addressed to all his followers, so the onus of proof is on those who would deny the legitimacy.

Papal infallibility should revert to the status of a permissible belief for people who think it is true. The Orthodox Churches have kept the faith without a forced recognition of papal infallibility and while enjoying the legitimate diversity of ordaining married men. Papal Infallibility has only been used once and then only to reassure Catholics of something that they already believed and hoped was true. Infallibility could therefore be abandoned with scarcely any downside other than the loss of face. In the next Chapter, we offer a number of formulas that would allow the reform of this hitherto irreformable dogma. Only one will be needed, whenever the Church authorities get their priorities sorted out.

Seven sacraments

The Catechism of the Catholic church describes the sacraments as a treasure and the Church itself as a sacrament. It states that "the Church, by the power of the Spirit who guides her 'into all truths' has gradually recognized this treasure received from Christ". "Thus, the Church has discerned over the centuries that among liturgical

---

[409] Division "openly contradicts the will of Christ, provides a stumbling block to the world, and inflicts damage on the most holy cause of proclaiming the Good News to every creature". —Second Vatican Council, Decree on Ecumenism *Unitatis Redintegratio*, §1, quoted in *Ut Unum Sint*.

events there are seven that are, *in the strict sense of the term,* sacraments instituted by the Lord". The number seven was settled upon at the Council of Trent. Regrettably, some decisions of Trent are treated as irreformable, as if the guidance of the Spirit, or the process of gradual recognition, had come to a full stop at that point. This has put limits on Catholic thinking. The process of discernment and development of thought in relation to the sacraments has been brought to an official halt. Most of the other Christian churches make a shorter list of sacraments 'in the strict sense of the term', while not denying that the others are sacramental in a less strict sense. By demanding unity to the point of agreement on how they are to be ranked and classified, *Ut Unum Sint* maximises the divisive effect of the different traditions.

Nowhere is this more divisive than in relation to the sacrament of ordination, which pervades the structure and ecclesiology of the Catholic Church and on which Protestant attitudes are said to be 'inadequate', as we will learn later from Cardinal Kurt Koch who is an authority on the subject (page 253). He makes it clear that it is not just their classification that the Protestants must change but also their attitude to ordination, if ecumenism is to make progress. One must wonder why the People of God cannot be allowed to believe and live by what they think is true without being excluded from communion with one another. It is not simply the Roman domination/subordination syndrome that is at work here. One must remember that the Catholic attitude to ordination, as described by Cardinal Koch, has been developed over centuries by a[410] management team of which every single member has had the distinction of being ordained.

Is the sacrament of ordination itself necessary even for Eucharistic celebration? The expression 'priestly people', if permitted any meaning, would allow congregations to celebrate together as they did for centuries in accordance with Jesus' command and example.[411] We have seen how a member of the group, possibly one of the elders, the host or hostess would preside at the celebration. This was when presiding simply meant leading the proceedings. He or she did not have any 'power' to consecrate. The power that was needed came from Jesus, present in the people gathered in his name. This understanding changed with the introduction of the individual priest. 'Presiding' gradually became 'celebrating', 'consecrating', and/or 'confecting'. Catholic priests came to be understood, after the Roman and Jewish pattern of the time, as intermediaries between the people and their God, offering sacrifice on their behalf. This would have appalled Saints Peter and Paul, who both taught that we are a priestly people. As members of the Mystical Body of Christ, we do not need mediators. Christ,

---

[410] It is worth recalling here that the unity talks in the 1930s between the Anglicans and Presbyterians and between the Anglicans and Methodists foundered in each case on issues relating to the ordained ministry.

[411] Bermejo, op. cit., in a footnote on p 249 notes that Küng was condemned by the CDF for holding that in cases of necessity an unordained person can preside over the Eucharist but that Küng's opinion is shared by several other theologians. He cites works by Y. Congar, H. Legrand, and E. Schillebeeckx and adds Rahner, Grelot, Lehman and 'to some extent' Kasper to the list. Bermejo also cites an article by the Anglican Bishop Colin Buchanan.

who was God and man, is our one and only mediator. "No one comes to the Father except by me".[412] When we come together in his name, Christ is present in the community of the faithful. It is Christ who renews his total offering of self to the Father so that we can join our offering of self with his. We do not need anyone to take the place of Christ. The expression *in persona Christi* and its limitation to the ordained celebrant is directed more towards the honour of the profession than to the worship of God.

Two thousand years ago Jesus told us to "Do This". Fifteen hundred years ago, Church authorities decided that effectiveness of the sacraments follows from "the very fact of the activity's being done"[413] *(ex opere operato)*. Eight hundred years ago, St Thomas pointed out that the sacraments were wrought by the power of God. In 1983, with a shortage of priests already obvious and officially admitted, Pope John Paul II promulgated a revised Canon Law:

> Canon 900 §1 The only minister who, in the person of Christ can bring into being the sacrament of the Eucharist is a validly ordained priest.

> Canon 1378 §1 1 "a person who, not being an ordained priest, attempts to celebrate Mass" incurs a *latae sententiae*[414] interdict.

Thus, in the circumstances in which we find ourselves today, Canon Law at first sight seems to conflict with Christ's instruction to "Do This". It reads like a constructive negation of the mandate. In this situation, where it is impossible to keep both the divine mandate and the regulations, a proper sense of proportion must prioritise the first and break the latter. The catch here is that while Jesus leaves us our freedom, Canon Law relies on coercion, with the sanction of automatic interdict. Why not meet the needs of today by changing back to the practice of apostolic times? Why not remove the ban and the interdict, thus permitting communities that do not have the regular service of an ordained priest to offer Mass without a minister, chanting or singing the words of consecration in unison as a community? The priestly people must have the competence to do this. It was from the priestliness of the People of God that the individual priesthood was derived.

The lay groups who currently celebrate the Eucharist without an ordained celebrant are not breaking canon law but interpreting it exactly. When they meet, nobody purports to act *in persona Christi,* so Canon 900 §1 is not applicable. Moreover, there is no person celebrating. The group believes that Jesus is present among them and they are following his instructions. He is the one who confects the Eucharist, who transforms the bread and wine, so Canon 1378 §1.1 does not apply either. An official confirmation of this by the Council for the Interpretation of Texts is all that is needed to bring a quick and permanent end to the Eucharistic famine.

The possibility of some minor changes going in this direction associated with the development of an Amazonian Rite seems to be implicit in the final report of the

---

[412] John 14:6
[413] Catechism of the Catholic Church §1128.
[414] A penalty *latae sententiae,* is incurred automatically upon the commission of an offence.

Synod on Amazonia which Pope Francis has recommended to the Church in general in his post-synodal exhortation:

> "At the same time, I would like to officially present the Final Document, which sets forth the conclusions of the Synod, which profited from the participation of many people who know better than myself or the Roman Curia the problems and issues of the Amazon region, since they live there, they experience its suffering and they love it passionately. I have preferred not to cite the Final Document in this Exhortation, because I would encourage everyone to read it in full."

Pope Francis has thus endorsed the Final Document as agreed by the Synod. He does not want to rule like a monarch or a dictator. He seems to want the bishops and the faithful to respond to the Holy Spirit and discern the way forward together in freedom.

Hierarchical communion

The papacy is still confusing unity with uniformity and subordination. Christ's prayer for unity contains nothing to support the Roman preoccupation with governance, control, inerrancy, or uniformity in opinion. As we have seen in St John's Gospel it is for a unity of love, modelled on the unity of the Father and the Son. This is in the context of Jesus' last discourse with his disciples in which he exhorts them to remain in him so as to produce fruit in plenty.

The unity and fruitfulness of a team do not arise from the uniformity of its members. Its strength more often lies in their diversity. St Paul is eloquent on this. It derives from a group of people with various talents sharing love or commitment to a purpose. To be effective, of course, such a group needs structure, organisation, and leadership.

Belief in Papal Infallibility and Universal Jurisdiction only became essential for full communion with Rome in 1870. Why make obstacles to church unity out of them? Why burden consciences unnecessarily? The probability is that millions of Roman Catholics presenting themselves for Holy Communion know nothing about, disagree with, or doubt current teaching on these or other issues. Should they be refused communion? Should they be excommunicated? Denied Christian burial? If cradle Catholics need not bother too much about them, why should profession be made essential for churches seeking greater unity? On reflection, it becomes apparent to all but those in authority that the real issue is not one of beliefs, but one of authority, power, control, obedience, and/or subordination.

Is the obsession with governing just a continuing manifestation of the apostolic arguments about who should be the greatest or is it just the bureaucratic need for ever increasing power?

Not a binary issue.

Unity and disunity are falsely presented as alternatives—in binary terms. Here again, we are talking about a spectrum. We need to remember that gradations are things that change in stages, in steps that may sometimes be too small to be noticed, as a process rather than in one big event. The process is already well under way.

The thinking of the 2,500 bishops assembled at Vatican II brought all the churches up that gradient significantly. By courageously reversing Catholic teaching on ecumenism, they brought gospel values to bear on the relationships between the churches. They allowed the Christian denominations to love one another and local ministers and priests to cooperate as colleagues, even though some of their beliefs were different. They heralded an era of respect and co-operation between the papacy and the World Council of Churches and led to dialogue and joint studies that have uncovered agreement and reconciliation in many areas of doctrine and practice. The signing of the joint Lutheran/Roman Catholic agreement on Justification, referred to above, was a historic step, beyond what the Council bishops could have dared to hope for.

Under Pope Francis, the Catholic commitment to the ecumenical process has been reignited in face of the resistance in the curia.

If the denominations are to continue growing closer together, the discussion on the theoretical issues that divided them, initially and subsequently, must give way to a celebration of what unites. The progress made in dialogue should be confirmed in action. In my opinion, the faithful want this and are ready for it. The curial administrators must be persuaded to give the ecumenical movement the priority implicit in Christ's prayer. Some senior figures in the curia are resisting because each step threatens to weaken its authority and the carefully fostered aura of generalised infallibility.

Getting the priorities in order

An Italian Archbishop[415] at Vatican II, with a gift for prioritising, proposed a way to deal with doctrinal differences and increase unity:

> To arrive at a fair estimate of both the unity which now exists among Christians and the diversity which still remains it seems very important to me to pay close attention to the hierarchical order of revealed truths which express the mystery of Christ and those elements which make up the Church …
>
> Some truths are on the level of our final goal such as the mystery of the Blessed Trinity, the Incarnation and Redemption, God's love and mercy towards sinful humanity, eternal life in the perfect Kingdom of God . . . Other truths are on the level of means towards salvation such as that there are seven sacraments, truths concerning the hierarchical structure of the Church, the Apostolic Succession, and others. These truths concern the means which are given by Christ to the Church for her pilgrim journey here on earth; when this journey comes to an end, so also do these means.
>
> Now, doctrinal differences among Christians have less to do with these primary truths on the level of our final goal and deal mostly with truths on the level of means, which are certainly subordinate to those other primary truths.

---

[415] Andreas Pangrazio, Archbishop of Gorizia, Italy in *Council Speeches of Vatican II,* London, Sheed and Ward, 1964, pp125

But we can say that the unity of Christians consists in a common faith and belief in those truths which concern our final goal. If we explicitly make these distinctions in conformity with the hierarchy of truths and elements, I think the existing unity among all Christians will be seen more clearly, and it will become evident that all Christians are already a family united in the primary truths of the Christian religion.

In ecumenism, nowhere are the priorities more disordered than in relation to the Eucharist which both unites and divides the churches. Christians of all kinds currently do what Jesus commanded: "Do This" … "this is my body" … "take this all of you". If we believe that Jesus said words to this effect and shared the bread and (counter-culturally) the cup with all those present and if we believe that Jesus does not lie, then we should go ahead and do just what he says.[416] We can rely on him to work whatever transformation is required. We can agree that that transformation is a mystery and admit that we do not know how it is accomplished. If we demand agreement on the mechanics of the mystery, we will be chasing unity forever. Disputes about transubstantiation, consubstantiation or transfiguration are a distraction, as is the recipe for the bread and the initial content of the cup.

Jesus used the food and drink that were on the table. The bread was probably wheaten and unleavened.[417] If he had called for something special, it would have been noted. Christians in Mediterranean areas have used wine, others water and some a mixture. Priests recovering from alcoholism can get a dispensation from the curia allowing them to use *mustum*, an unfermented grape juice. This is not deemed to invalidate the sacrament.

The question must be asked: Do the trivial details matter? Are we giving them too high a priority? Should we not leave aside the trivia and simply *do* what Jesus told us to do, sharing the Eucharist with *all* his disciples just as he did, and as the apostles did? His instruction and example should be our priority. We know well that he is already present in the congregation, and in us and we in him (John 14:20), but the Eucharist is in some way a special encounter when he wants us to come together to worship in fellowship and when we have the opportunity of thanking him for his gift of himself and developing our relationship with him.

For the papacy to agree to sharing the Eucharist with other Christians who are not yet in full communion with Rome will be difficult. The ban on eucharistic sharing with our "separated brethren", had been around for a long time before Vatican II recognised them, as genuine Christians. To spell out the eucharistic consequence of that recognition at the time would have been a bridge too far. But the consequences are inescapable and must be admitted. Christ lives in other Christians, and they in Christ. They are part of his church. Regulations that debar them are misguided.

---

[416] Mary, in one of her few vocal contributions to the New Testament, said to the servants: "Do whatever he tells you" (John 2:5

[417] At the Passover celebration the bread would have been unleavened, In the inn at Emmaus, possibly leavened.

Rome's position has been ambiguous for centuries. The sacraments, we have been taught, are signs that achieve what they signify. Yet, for Rome there is one that doesn't; the most important sacrament, the one that brings us into closer union with Jesus and with one another, the unifying element among the People of God, the Eucharist. Instead of allowing Jesus in the Eucharist to create the unity it symbolises, however, we reserve that challenge to our own efforts and hold the Eucharist back to be used at some time to celebrate a future point on the path of unity.

The papacy sees unity in binary terms and in a way that is strangely unspiritual and un-sacramental. It seems we must meet some Roman definition of unity before we can share the sacrament of unity. That definition, as we have seen, is "doctrinal, sacramental and hierarchical communion". While nothing is impossible with God, these conditions in combination are beyond the possibility of human achievement. Individual members of the curia are aware of this, but the group dynamic distorts priorities and is best served by obstructing unity for as long as possible. It could be that eucharistic sharing, under the guidance of the Spirit, could gradually lead towards full ecclesiastical communion between denominations. The Pontifical Council for Christian Unity, as we shall see later, is putting the cart before the horse by making eucharistic communion dependent on ecclesiological communion.

Pope Francis sees things differently. In *Evangelii Gaudium* (§67) he describes the Eucharist as

> … not a prize for the perfect but a powerful medicine for the weak. These convictions have pastoral consequences that we are called to consider with prudence and boldness.

He is speaking here in terms of individual reception. But is he not hinting that the same principle should apply at group level?

Doctrinal unity – scope and granularity

The authoritarian frame of mind gets obsessed over compliance, with little concern for the gravity or triviality of the matter at issue. The Council saw fit to remind those involved in ecumenical contacts that there is a hierarchy of truths. Hopefully, this will lead to an acceptance that doctrines have an order of importance. Although we may never agree on their relative positions on the scale, we might be able to agree that some traditional tenets, while true, are not essential to life in Christ nor for eternal salvation.[418] Otherwise we could spend another five hundred years in dialogue on an endless list of ever more esoteric issues.

When we focus on the essentials of Christianity, however, like the Triune God, and belief in the incarnation, death and resurrection of Jesus, the practice of loving concern and forgiveness for others, and on Baptism and the celebration of the Eucharist after the example of Jesus, we realise the scale and overwhelming importance

---

[418] John Wesley preached that the basics were essential, and the rest were matters of opinion which people should be free to profess and thus live by what they think is true. He does not appear to have listed the doctrines that he would deem basic but has left them to be gleaned from his sermons.

of the unity that already exists. And that leaves room for a lot of legitimate diversity in opinion and practice.

While the various theological dialogues have made progress in reconciling attitudes and even doctrines, dialogue and reconciliation are still a necessary part of the process.

The Catholic side, however, has been better at participating in dialogue than at confirming and implementing the outcomes. As long as the authorities are preoccupied with their own position and maintain that everything in current Catholic teaching, policy, practice, and structure is the only appropriate response to centuries of divine guidance channelled exclusively through themselves, then they leave themselves with little room for adjustment and the papacy is forced to pursue a poorly camouflaged reunionism. Pope Francis seems to be willing to relativize some of the absolutes that have caused paralysis. Until he succeeds, ecumenism will depend on getting the Protestants to do all the adjusting.[419]

The goal

If the purpose of the unity Christ prayed for was "so that the world may believe that it was you who sent me", then the unity must be visible, palpable, and evident to the world, not just theoretical, doctrinal or aspirational. It must be a unity of love, visible in the lives of the disciples. The context of chapter 17 of St John's Gospel bears this out. Love is a gradation, not a binary. His many and disparate disciples have made tangible progress along that gradation, and the pace certainly quickened after Vatican II. The challenge is to maintain the momentum while bringing along those Catholics who still genuinely and loyally believe what they were taught: *i.e.* that fidelity means nothing can be changed.

Conditional Unity

For decades, the goal of ecumenism was understood as 'visible unity'. Since 2010, however, the Roman Catholic side has added two further, closely related, requirements; that unity demands a common understanding of the nature and structure of the church and a common attitude towards sacramental ordination.[420] Consequently, the churches no longer find themselves in agreement on the goal of ecumenism. This is comforting for those in the bureaucracy that fear any loss of power. It means that unity can be pushed further down the road, if ever it appears too imminent.

---

[419] I am indebted here to Peter De Mey (KU Leuven) and his academic paper, *The Commemoration of 2017 as Starting Point for a Joint Declaration on Church, Eucharist and Ministry?* —https://www.aca-demia.edu/login?post_login_redirect_url=https%3A%2F%2Fwww.acaemia.edu%2Ft%2Fbmum9-NmoZnASs3PiE%2Fresource%2Fwork%2F33790861%2F_The_Commemoration_of_2017_as_Starting_Point_for_a_Joint_Declaration_on_Church_Eucharist_and_Ministry_published_as_The_Commemoration_of_the_Reformation_as_the_Starting_Point_for_a_Joint_Declaration_on_Church_Eucharist_and_Ministry_in_Ecclesiology_24_2018_32-50_%3Femail_work_card%3 Dview-paper

[420] I must apologise to readers who find the rest of this section heavy going. The issues, debated in the early years of this century, are not easy to summarise. As obstacles on the path to unity they must be faced, although they have little to do with the kind of unity that Jesus was praying for.

In 2010, Cardinal Kurt Koch, the newly appointed President, gave the opening address at the biennial Plenary Assembly of the Pontifical Council for Promoting Christian Unity, in the presence of Pope Benedict XVI.[421]   It was an important occasion. The 13,500-word paper he delivered may be taken therefore as an official policy statement on ecumenism. It was entitled *Progress in the Ecumenical Journey: The State of Ecumenism Today.*

He spoke of "the contentious goal of ecumenism" and went on to say: "The various churches and ecclesial communities have not yet been able to reach a consensus on the goal of the ecumenical movement … " At that point in his paper, one would get the impression that the other churches and ecclesiastical communities are entirely to blame for this state of affairs. Later, however, he identifies the obstacle as the emerging divergence in ecclesiology[422] between Protestants and Catholics. A section of his paper is headed *"Ecclesiology as the Central Question in Ecumenism"* and it becomes clear that it is a Catholic demand for a common ecclesiology that has made the goal contentious. It is now the sticking point.

The ecclesiological divergence he describes is two-fold. In summary:

1. The first is on the nature of the church. He tells us that the Protestants see the visible church primarily in the local, 'concrete' assembly of worshippers. Taken together these form the Church of Christ, being related by a common faith and eucharist, the latter presupposing recognition of one another's ordination. For Catholics, in contrast, the Church is a global *'communio'* of worshippers which is manifested in microcosm in local worshipping communities that maintain a centrally defined orthodoxy and share the eucharist and a relatively consistent liturgy.[423]

2. The second divergence is in attitudes to the sacrament of ordination.

On the first divergence, one must ask: Does it matter if we say the flock is composed of sheep or the sheep together make the flock? The metaphor is not entirely satisfactory because it over-simplifies a complex situation. The 'sheep' we are talking about can make responsible decisions individually. And one of those decisions determines the level at which different kinds of decision should be made. While

---

[421] November 2010. —The speech may be downloaded in PDF from: http://www.vatican.va/roman_curia/pontifical_councils/chrstuni/information_service/documents/135_information_service_en.htm#top

[422] Oxford Dictionary: Ecclesiology: Theology as applied to the nature and structure of the Christian Church.

[423] The Reformed Catholic dialogue in the Netherlands has produced a text: *The Local and the Universal Dimensions of the Church*, which disagrees with the focus: "Developments in the various church traditions reveal that the issue of the priority of the local or universal church is not an ecclesiologically correct nor productive approach. Unity and diversity, the universal and the local, are rather to be understood as complementary, i.e. one cannot be properly interpreted without the other. They continually presuppose and refer to each other".—Quoted by Jeffrey Gros, in *Contextualizing Receptive Ecumenism:*—https://www.academia.edu/2175949/Contextualizing_Receptive_Ecumenism, accessed 8th October 2019

issues of ecclesiology would have been of professional importance to the Cardinal's audience on that occasion, they would scarcely merit to stand in the way of the unity Jesus prayed for. Jesus was certainly not praying for academic agreement on ecclesiology. The entire subject of his prayer is love and mutual indwelling (Jn 17:21-26). Nor will his followers be judged on their ecclesiology. Most of them would not know what the word means. Jesus was praying for a unity of unselfish love reflected in relationships and behavior towards others.

The family is our first church. As we grow to maturity, the local church is what is visible. It is the local congregation and its pastors, liturgy, buildings, and charitable activity that influence the lives of ordinary people. The universal *communio* is something much more distant and abstract, far less likely to move minds and hearts. The bishops and cardinals who manage the Catholic Church from the centre naturally have a top-down perspective. They relate to the Church as a single unit composed of national episcopates, diocesan bishops, secular and regular clergy and the faithful who worship in their local churches. Protestants have no similar central management. The different perspectives, however, should not be allowed to destroy unity. Quite the reverse. Toleration of the other's differences is a constituent part of any unity.

Cardinal Koch reports that there is limited agreement on the definition of the Church that Christ founded. The good news, the most encouraging news, is that there is general ecumenical agreement on the first two criteria: Preaching the Word[424] and the Celebration of the Eucharist. The disagreement relates to the third.

The third criterion is championed by the Catholic Church alone: "[T]he Catholic Church considers and recognises the apostolic ministry as a third criteria (sic) for the Church". The weakness here is that the phrase 'apostolic ministry' is much too woolly and carries too much potential baggage to be used in a definition of anything.[425]

Every Christian Church would see itself as continuing the ministry of the apostles. Thus, on a loose interpretation it would sound acceptable to our ecumenical partners. But the phrase could be interpreted as including one or other meaning of 'apostolic succession' which has been a contentious issue since the Reformation. Furthermore, the Protestants would have historically well-grounded fears lest Christ's appointment of Peter as head of the apostles would be authoritatively interpreted as endowing the papacy 'irreformably'[426] with Infallibility, Universal Jurisdiction, and unlimited powers. The two dogmas adopted at Vatican I were omitted from Cardinal Koch's

---

[424] The Cardinal makes a reservation here, that Protestants see the Word as something that stands alone while Catholics see it as being in 'mutual dependence and relation' with the Church. Is this true? This may be the understanding of senior clergy, but one would want to see some evidence before crediting it to the Catholic faithful in general.

[425] 'When I use a word,' Humpty Dumpty said in rather a scornful tone, 'it means just what I choose it to mean—neither more nor less'. 'The question is,' said Alice, 'whether you can make words mean different things——that's all'. 'The question is', said Humpty Dumpty, 'which is to be master—that's all'. —Lewis Carroll, *Through the Looking Glass*. Chapter 6. Profound and prophetic, from a brilliant son of the rectory.

[426] The question of reforming the irreformable is dealt with in the next chapter.

review of the current state of ecumenism, but they lurk behind the insistence on 'apostolic ministry' as a criterion for identifying the Church of Christ. Before this third criterion could hope to gain acceptance, it would have to be defined much more precisely, a process that would doubtless reveal a conflict with some things 'essential to the papal mission'. Readers will recall that these were not identified in *Ut Unum Sint*. They were left open, leaving the option to identify them later—yet the encyclical was uncompromising in their defence. John Paul II wanted to remove the papacy as an obstacle to unity "while *in no way renouncing what is essential to its mission*".

The second ecclesiological divergence stakes out much the same ground as would a broad interpretation of the third criterion. In Roman Catholic ecclesiology, the attitude to sacramental ordination is dominant and pervasive, and the importance of the laity has at times been undervalued, if not overlooked. (Newman had reason to protest that the church would look foolish without them.) Although it was not always so, administration of the sacraments is now reserved to the ordained.[427] All positions of authority in the hierarchical Church and in official decision-making are reserved to the ordained since the eleventh century, as is voting at synods even though synodal decisions are still only advisory. The Catholic attitude to ordination shapes Catholic ecclesiology making it unacceptable to Protestants.

Having described the ecumenical movement as the great work of the Holy Spirit, Cardinal Koch quotes Charles Péguy's lovely expression "patience is the little sister of hope" to make the lack of progress palatable. Yet he sets a new condition for unity by linking eucharistic communion and ecclesial communion, saying that you cannot have one without the other. Why not? He silently rules out toleration of diversity. He overlooks the teaching that a sacrament achieves what it signifies and that under the guidance of the Spirit, sharing the sacrament of unity would lead to greater unity of hearts and minds from which closer ecclesial understandings might well develop, in so far as it is important. The denial of intercommunion is the great symbol of division and it seems calculated to achieve what it symbolises—the maintenance of a safe ecclesial distance from the other denominations and the untrammelled authority of the papacy.

The Cardinal's audience on the occasion would have been made up largely of ordained men, members of the curia. None was likely to challenge his understanding of an ecclesiology permeated and dominated by veneration, one might almost say worship, of the sacrament of Orders. [428] At times it seems to be prioritised ahead of the Eucharist which it was undoubtedly intended to serve. To ask Protestants of many varieties to adopt what they would see as the overblown Roman Catholic attitude to

---

[427] Except baptism in case of necessity and for matrimony which is administered by the couple to one another. The catch here is that it is deemed to be *invalid* unless witnessed by a priest.

[428] In avoiding any reference to the institution of the sacrament of ordination, the Cardinal (inadvertently?) offers a formula which could facilitate the recognition of ordination in other churches. He speaks of "…a minister whose ordination and mission are founded in Christ and is therefore itself a sacrament". That formula skirts around the embarrassing fact that Christ never ordained a priest, but it opens a way to recognition of any Christian minister, male or female.

ordination, however, is to raise yet another barrier to the "great work of the Holy Spirit". The Cardinal seems unaware that the Church survived and shared the Eucharist for several centuries without ordained priests or an agreed ecclesiology. Here again, Church management finds itself paralysed by its pseudo-infallibilities. Consequently, its idea of ecumenism is, at heart, still reunionism under another name.

If unity is a process or a relationship, then to define a specific 'goal' is to treat a gradation as a binary. We might be better advised to pray in the words of our newly canonised saint, John Henry Newman, whom we venerate in common with other Christians, for guidance on our pilgrim way. He left us a poem which is also both prayer and hymn, *Lead Kindly Light*:

> Keep thou my feet,
> I do not ask to see,
> The distant scene,
> One step enough for me.

The Second Vatican Council taught unambiguously that the baptised members of the other denominations are entitled to the name of Christian. Accordingly, all are already united in the Mystical Body of Christ. It is only the visible church that is disunited. The importance of this is not adequately appreciated. The churches and ecclesiastical organisations that give the Mystical Body its visibility are indeed divided on many secondary matters. It is a mistake, however, to emphasise the differences. We should be cooperating to fulfil the two mandates in the manner Jesus described. But this cannot happen while one party is setting conditions about what the others must think or profess on inessential issues or what attitudes they must adopt. Jesus may well have had the domination/subordination pattern in mind when he told his disciples not to follow the Gentile leaders of this world by 'lording it over' those in their charge.[429]

Among the 1.33 billion Catholics and 1 billion other Christians, who agree on the fundamentals of the faith, the Catholic demand for detailed uniformity in professed beliefs and attitudes going far beyond the essentials is more ordered to the exaltation of the papacy than to the glory of God.

There is more to ecumenism than doctrinal convergence.

Christianity is a way of living and should not be reduced to a system of beliefs. There is a limit to what dialogue among theologians can achieve or what it needs to achieve. Doctrinal alignment, even if officially sanctioned must be genuinely received by the faithful if it is to have any meaning. Doctrine is an adjunct of faith, not *vice versa*. You do not change people's beliefs by edict. What counts in Christianity is what people really believe in their innermost hearts and how it shapes their lives, and their treatment of one another. What counts is the Way. Whatever doctrinal convergence is necessary will come about gradually through the working of the Holy Spirit as we

---

[429] You know that among the pagans their so-called rulers lord it over them, and their great men make their authority felt. This is not to happen among you. —Mark 10: 42-43.

respond to the call for a greater unity in our hearts and in our relationships. Mercifully, the judgement of our lives will not be an examination in doctrinal propositions; we have been told clearly, it will hinge on how we have related to our neighbours, most particularly the needy ones.

All this is not to espouse the error of indifferentism. Instead, it is an attempt to identify and oppose the hierarchical failing which we will call 'differentism'– making disunity more apparent than real and exaggerating the significance of differing opinions on inessentials to resist movement towards unity and to protect the *status quo*. It is high time the official church prioritised the essentials of Christ's message that have always survived among the faithful and their pastors and that should allow us to recognise and treat people with different opinions and hierarchical traditions as brothers and sisters in Christ. Families don't agree on everything, but they can love one another, work together, and dine at the same table.

After he had retired as Archbishop of San Francisco, John R. Quinn, took the opportunity to respond to *Ut Unum Sint*. His book, *The Reform of the Papacy*[430] is subtitled *The Costly Call to Christian Unity*. In it he spells out that there is more to Christian unity than doctrinal convergence; it would also require a reform of the Roman curia and its policies and procedures and a reversal of the ever-growing centralism. As a retired archbishop, he knew more about the system than most. He refers to the structures and practices of the papacy in the first millennium as a justification for doing things differently although he too is careful not to recommend first millennium answers to third millennium problems.

If a solution is possible it will be found in a new understanding and a new prioritising of the two conflicting elements: 'unity' and the 'essentials of the papal mission'. Several elements that have been looked upon as binary will have to be recognised as gradations instead. Several positions traditionally held to be essential will have to be humbly abandoned. It will be necessary to expand the category of legitimate diversity which was approved in the context of inter-church relations by John Paul II in *Slavorum Appostoli* (1985).[431] Furthermore, the 'hierarchy of truths' must be allowed to have the meaning obviously intended by the Council.

Love in action

In the early days of the ecumenical movement, there was a slogan: "Doctrine divides while service unites". That is seldom heard today but is true in one sense. It is not basic Christian doctrine that has divided us, but pride in our own derivations and opinions on secondary issues together with attachment to our own comfortable rituals

---

[430] John R. Quinn, *The Reform of the Papacy*, New York, The Crossroad Publishing Co., 1999

[431] 'Legitimate diversity' can be stretched a surprisingly long way when the issue is not the subject of public attention–when it is not seen as a hot button challenge to authority. For instance, in 2001 the Vatican accepted that the Anaphora (Offering) of Addai and Mari is a genuine celebration of the Eucharist even though it does not contain the exact wording of the institution prayer "This is my body", "This is my blood". This led to a declaration of intercommunion with the Assyrian Church of the East. (See Peter Phillips in *Receptive Ecumenism and the Call to Catholic Learning*, p 24)

and traditions. When the denominations work closely together for the poor, the suffering and the marginalised, doctrinal differences become less important. A proper sense of priorities emerges.

I have been greatly influenced by the involvement of Africa Concern in the JCA airlift during the Biafran War in Nigeria, 1967 to 1970. JCA stood for Joint Church Aid (and humorously, but aptly, Jesus Christ Airlines). It grew out of a joint effort by the overseas development arms of the major Christian churches who put aside theological differences to alleviate the war-induced famine in Biafra by flying supplies from the tropical island of Saõ Tomé to a jungle airstrip under cover of darkness. It was the biggest civilian airlift in history, providing over 35,000 tons of relief supplies in 3,500 flights over a two-year period. Africa Concern (now known as Concern Worldwide) was part of JCA and at the same time ran a supplementary airlift of 350 flights from Libreville, Gabon, delivering a further 3,500 tons. Both airlifts brought out emaciated children on return flights, virtually all of whom recovered with TLC in makeshift camps in Saõ Tomé, Ivory Coast and Gabon. This was ecumenical 'love in action'. None of the participants had to disavow any cherished beliefs. Admittedly, two related traditions failed to survive. Disparagement and distrust of one another on denominational grounds disappeared rapidly.

From its very beginnings in response to the Biafran famine, Concern has been ecumenical. Like their supporters worldwide, Concern volunteers have been of every religion and none, but they have exemplified gospel values. In the first thirty years, each of 1700 volunteers gave two years or more to bring their skills and knowledge where they were most needed. They endured privation, discomfort, and risk to life and limb in the care of the most needy, in 50 of the world's poorest countries. And I have never seen a more united or happier bunch of people.

Stepping back from the details and reading between the lines, it becomes evident that the papacies of John Paul II and Benedict XVI were strongly influenced by curial values and did not share the determination of Pope John XXIII, Pope Paul VI, and the Bishops of Vatican II to reach out warmly to other Christians and find ways to greater unity, even at a cost. The curia, as long it combines legislative and executive functions and can keep the College of Bishops in deep freeze, will prioritise its own power and ambitions as it has always done. It will take all the reforming energy and zeal of Pope Francis, and maybe one or two additional reforming popes after him, to change that.

Are precedents always necessary?

The widespread recourse to pseudo-infallibility has forced the authorities to canonise continuity making Catholic churchmen very conscious of precedents. But are detailed precedents always necessary? Is there a commandment to that effect? Should the mandate not be taken as authorising whatever seems conducive to its achievement? Should the greatest commandment not be allowed sometimes to compensate for the lack of specific instructions or apt scriptural example in certain areas? We Christians should be guided by the overall mandates to teach the world to love, to forgive, to celebrate the Eucharist. We have a job to do—given to us in one sentence. We should feel free to innovate—to try any promising approach that has not been specifically forbidden. We should be seeking strategies and structures to make the best of the conditions of our own time and exploit the opportunities on offer. The fact that something was not done in the past, or that the surviving record is ambiguous, does not imply divine disapproval. The Council said we should read the signs of the times. The servants who traded the talents in their master's absence took risks and earned his commendation. Only the fearful one who carefully buried the talent was reprimanded.

Giving a high priority to precedents tends to maintain the *status quo* and suit those currently in power. It offers tempting formulas for opting out of collective responsibilities. As has been demonstrated since Vatican II, however, any attempt at updating seems destined to end in conflict with the self-serving Roman bureaucracy. The papacy needs to learn that structures and personnel should be adapted to mission, not *vice versa*.

Humble learning

Archbishop Quinn suggested that the Church could learn from the experience of other large international organisations like the Red Cross or the UN. A colloquium held at Ushaw College, near Durham in 2006 entitled 'Receptive Ecumenism' looked at a new approach to Ecumenism; focusing on what the denominations could learn from one another. This led to the publication of a useful book of thirty-two essays[432] exploring what it might mean for Catholicism.

Vatican II and John Paul II have taught us that the Holy Spirit assists the other denominations also. Catholicism could benefit from some of the 'gifts and graces' the others have received but reception would call for both humility and courage. The readiness of the bishops at Vatican II to admit to limitations in the church's knowledge and faults in its actions would have to be revived and some of the teachings and structures that masquerade as irreformable would need to change.

The Church could also learn something from the foundation and management of the Visa International Settlements Association which oversees the VISA CARD system. In his book, Dee Hock[433] describes an alternative to the 'Domination-Subordination' paradigm of traditional management. The grounding principles were agreed between the parties in a way that left them free to compete and work together at the same time. Hock has coined the word 'chaordic' to describe the consequent mix of chaos and order. For VISA, it has proved successful and enduring on a large scale, while interfacing with various cultures and regulatory systems worldwide.

From my experience I can say that one policy that enabled Concern Worldwide to be so effective and to grow into a large international relief and development

---

[432] Paul D. Murray (Ed), *Receptive Ecumenism and the Call to Catholic Learning*, with foreword by Cardinal Walter Kasper, Oxford University Press, 2008,

[433] Dee Hock, *Birth of the Chaordic Age,* Published by Berrett-Koehler Publishers, ISBN 10: 1576750744 ISBN 13: 9781576750742

organisation, caring for the poorest and those in the greatest difficulty in 50 different countries, is its tradition of responding to the situation encountered and of backing the judgements of the people on the spot. The Country Directors know the Concern ethos and principles and they adapt them as best they can. They are given authority to match their responsibilities. While most of the development aid is delivered in the form of programs that have been carefully planned and tested, scope is always maintained for innovation and improvisation and also for the prompt response which can be so important in disaster situations. The need for food, water and shelter is always immediate and the situation is always different. It is from accumulated field experience of dealing with humanitarian relief and development that the Concern principles and ethos have evolved. Because of the Promise, Church management would not be acting irresponsibly if it too were to put the principle of subsidiarity into practice and allow a high degree of freedom in implementation to the energy, creativity and judgement of the local churches and their elected bishops. Christ's promise to be 'with us' relates not just to what the faithful believe but to everything they are and do. Response to the gifts of the Spirit sometimes demands innovation and risk-taking and always demands trust.

The character of unity

In any group activity, unity abides essentially in the minds and hearts of the participants. It is an expression of love for one another and for the shared objectives for which everyone is prepared to make some sacrifice. It is a thing of the spirit and, for the Church, a thing of the Spirit. The Council understood this; *"There can be no ecumenism worthy of the name without a change of heart.* For it is from renewal of the inner life of our minds, from self-denial and an unstinted love that desires of unity take their rise and develop in a mature way"*. If the bureaucracy is unable to understand this, then *Censeo Curia Romana Delenda Est.*[434]

Ecumenism is grounded in the prayer of Christ already quoted above: *"Father, may they be one in us, as you are in me and I am in you so that the world may believe it was you who sent me"* (Jn 17:21). The continuation of Christ's prayer in St John's gospel gives us an insight into the kind of unity: *"that they may be one as we are one"* and *"so that the love with which you loved me may be in them.* Earlier (Jn 13:35) Jesus had given them as a new commandment: *"Love one another … by this love you have for one another; everyone will know you are my disciples".* Love is the identifying characteristic of his followers. God is love and the unity Christ is seeking is a unity in himself, a unity of love. He did not pray for a unity of governance, of catechism, of liturgy, of branding, pecking order, dress, titles, language, ecclesiology, or forms of ministry. It was unity of love encompassing the mind-boggling variety of his children in every time place or circumstance and moderating the self-love which is itself an essential for the survival of the species.

---

[434] Here I am echoing Cato, who used to end his speeches *"Censeo Carthago Delenda Est"* (In my opinion Carthage must be destroyed) but I give the curia the place of Carthage.

Love was conspicuously lacking in the Roman response to Luther's criticisms. The Bull of Leo X,[435] *Exsurge Domine* was written in obvious anger at the effrontery of this Augustinian monk in challenging the very source of truth itself, the papacy that could 'never err'.[436] Even today, one could scarcely accuse the Roman curia of being driven by love. Like every large and powerful bureaucracy, it is pathologically unsympathetic to unselfish action. It always finds virtue in protecting and enhancing its own hegemony. In Chapter 6, we have quoted the letter from Rome of Yves Congar to his mother on this subject.

The consequence of the unity of love that Christ prayed for—"*so that the world will realise it was you who sent me*"—demands that the love be visible in what we say, in how we relate, and in what we actually do, individually and collectively. Structural unity is just one element in the mix.

Since Vatican II, Christians have made enormous progress towards a unity of love. Parish clergy from different denominations are now openly friendly. They now see one another as colleagues, even as sharers in mission. The popes have promoted a unity of love by praying together with leaders of other denominations and religions, exchanging visits, and openly promoting good relationships. Papal journeys abroad now routinely include some ecumenical event or contact. The initiative of Pope John XXIII is still bearing fruit.

The participating churches in any form of Christian unity must, of course, be Christian. Vatican II has dealt with the need for a definition by confirming that churches and assemblies in the Reformed tradition are properly classified as Christian as of now.[437] If further definition of a Christian church is called for, the way of love will be to seek inclusion rather than exclusion. The principle of not burdening consciences unnecessarily should be applied. Associated churches will be encouraged to keep their distinguishing and treasured traditions as far as practical.[438] St Paul would have looked only for belief in the resurrection of the Lord which of course implied belief in the incarnation and the crucifixion. Baptism and the celebration of the Eucharist would appear to be essential, but these the churches already have in common. Full agreement on the mechanics of the mysteries would be self-contradictory. They are, after all, mysteries—beyond human understanding.

---

[435] Leo X was a Medici pope, second son of Lorenzo the Magnificent. He grew up in affluence, groomed to secure the banking family's influence on the papacy. He had been made an abbot at 7 years of age, a canon at 8, a cardinal at 13 and pope at 37. (—Brian Moynahan, *The Faith,* London, Aurum Press, 2002, pp 343/4) He grew up in an environment of abuse of ecclesiastical authority, influenced by Machiavelli. It was a pity that someone with his background spoke for the Church at such a critical time.

[436] The Bull, of course, includes a politically correct wish that Martin will be saved … by repenting, accepting, and submitting to the papacy in all respects.

[437] "Nevertheless, all those justified by faith through baptism are incorporated into Christ. They therefore have a right to be honoured by the title of Christian". —*Unitatis Redintegratio, §*13.

[438] This principle has already been conceded in the arrangements for the Anglican Ordinariate.

Since patterns of liturgical celebration have changed over time, then change can be tolerated contemporaneously as between cultures and participating churches. If worshipping together is good, is there not a case for encouraging people to participate by catering to their cultural and linguistic preferences? The ritual should be adapted to the culture. Jesus could say:" The sabbath was made for man, not man for the sabbath". In the same spirit, we might decide that the celebration can be adapted for the people, not the people for the celebration. Uniformity in worship may have its origins in the worship of uniformity.

Did Jesus speak about governance? Not much, except in his exhortation that those in charge of his followers should not behave like the civil rulers of his time (See Chapter 3). He spoke about a shepherd who knows his sheep, and whose sheep know his voice and follow him to the good pastures. This would seem to call for an emphasis on local leadership rather than centralised micromanagement of a huge and diverse church. Universal jurisdiction, pseudo-infallibility and a selfish bureaucracy are all vastly different from the manner of leadership Jesus described and demanded. An episcopal structure with applied subsidiarity would probably find acceptance among the faithful provided arbitrary restrictions are kept to a minimum, and unnecessary uniformity in job description, lifestyle, gender, dress, and titles is avoided.

These are all secondary issues but tend to be blown out of proportion by those who would create division in men's minds. Christians of all varieties already share the Our Father and the Nicaean-Constantinopolitan Creed. The challenge is to live by them. This would be facilitated by allowing one another as much 'legitimate diversity' as possible.

There is a body of opinion that Benedict XVI made a mistake in 2007 by facilitating the extended use of the Tridentine Mass. It has been described as 'splitting' the Church.[439] There can only be validity in this, to the extent that one is seeking domination, uniformity, or a unity of ritual. Creation, however, speaks to us of a God who delights in diversity. For example, there are 60,065 different species of tree each with its own characteristics[440] and no two specimens are identical. God is glorified in diversity, in the wondrous blend of variety and order. So, what is against having a plurality of forms or rites? It is the Eucharist that unites the Christian churches, and this is the essence of the liturgy whatever rite is being followed or whatever language is being used. It can be celebrated in different ways. Originally, it was like-minded people sharing a meal. The setting or trimmings really matter little theologically, although they can matter greatly to the congregations that grow attached to them. Even in the Latin Rite, we were accustomed not long ago to High Mass and Low Mass, Votive Masses, Requiem Masses, Nuptial Masses, Ordination Masses, and Dominican

---

[439] By no less a commentator than the Church historian Massimo Faggioli, Professor of Theology and Religious Studies at Villanova University. He refers to 'splitting' in *La Croix International,* 24th February 2018.
[440] Journal of Sustainable Forestry, 4 April 2017.

Masses. Rome has allowed the Anglican Ordinariate to maintain much of its distinctive and traditional patterns of worship, without apparent ill effects.

The Church has tolerated many changes in the Lord's Supper over time (see Ch.10). Accordingly, variation as between cultures can be tolerated provided the essence is preserved. "Difference of customs in Holy Church does not destroy the unity of faith", says Pope Gregory the Great.[441] What is appropriate in one place may have negative connotations in another. "As a social animal, man is a ritual animal".[442] Local bishops and pastors are the best people to judge on the forms most meaningful and most edifying and socially attractive for their flocks at any given time. This might help to stem the erosion of congregations and devotion.

THE ESSENTIALS OF THE PAPAL MISSION

The East-West schism resulted from the centuries-long ambition of the Apostolic See to enhance the power of the papacy. It was triggered by a unilateral and unnecessary attempt to add to the creed. The definitions of the Marian dogmas were similar exercises in papal power that capitalised on popular devotion. They did not cause schisms but served to reinforce the existing ones.

The protection of the truth of Revelation is often claimed as an essential mission of the papacy. That mission, however, is not peculiar to the pope. The Truth of Revelation is Christ. Thus, its protection is the concern of the whole church, fundamentally of the *sensus fidelium,* under the guidance of the Holy Spirit. Christ's Promise, "Behold, I am with you ... even to the end of the age", was addressed to all his disciples and to all who would be his disciples, not exclusively to the clergy. His inspiration is always there. But let us repeat, he never takes away the freedom of decision on which our capacity to love depends.

The way forward

There is now a real possibility, albeit a slim one, that Christianity could move towards a unity of love. This is the pearl of great value. This is the treasure hidden in the field which stirs the finder to sell everything he owns and buy the field (Mt. 13:44). Jesus used the pearl and the treasure parables to illustrate the kingdom of God. For a pope, would unity not be that pearl, that treasure? "That they may be one ... so that the world may believe it was you who sent me". The successor of Peter must surely be aware that when Peter and his fellow fishermen found Jesus, they *left everything* to follow him.[443] Similarly with the tax collector, Levi.

St Peter had neither silver nor gold but his successors since then have considered it appropriate to amass substantial possessions. Beyond property, artwork, investments and cash, the papacy has garnered immense international dignity and prestige. It has acquired a degree of legislative, executive, and judicial power over Roman Catholics that Peter never aspired to including the exclusive legal right:

---

[441] Quoted in Dáibhí Ó Cróinín, *Early Medieval Ireland*, Harwell, Longman/Pearson, 1995, p 151

[442] Mary Douglas, 1966

[443] (Cf. Luke 5:11)

- to revise Canon Law which sets the operating framework and boundaries for everything in the visible organisation,
- to govern the Roman Catholic Church with *plenitudo potestatis*.
- to govern the Vatican City State,
- to appoint all the bishops in the world,
- to summon them to meet and, more significantly, to prevent them from meeting,
- to nominate cardinals who get to elect future popes, usually from among themselves,
- to teach infallibly, *ex cathedra,*
- to give dispensations from canon law, moral law, and natural law,[444]
- to forgive the 'sin' of breaching Pontifical Secrecy, and
- to create indulgences that apply the merits of Christ to souls in purgatory.

These are all secondary privileges acquired over a long period in the days when people thought that a unifying leader had to have dictatorial powers and a medieval court, and when the ambition of the Roman See was to turn a primacy of honour and the forum of final appeal into a total earthly sovereignty. The creation and maintenance of these 'possessions' contributed in no small way to the divisions in the church, yet some people still think them 'essential' to the papacy. The price of unity will therefore include a lot of painful voluntary divestment. Christ's statement: "[N]one of you can be my disciple unless he gives up all his possessions" (Luke 14:33) can be applied to the office as well as the officeholder.

For the papacy to divest itself of some of these inessentials would be much more than a grand gesture. It would open the door to achieving what has eluded the Church for a millennium, full communion with the Orthodox Churches and maybe more. This is not as extravagant a hope as one might think.

In a circumspect way, Fr. Paul McPartlan, professor of Systematic Theology and Ecumenism at the Catholic University of America, makes a somewhat similar suggestion involving papal divestment. Fr McPartlan is something of an insider, He has served two terms on the International Theological Commission. As a long-serving member of the Joint International Commission for Theological Dialogue between the Catholic Church and the Orthodox Church, he knows the issues, the needs, and the mindset of both sides. In his book *A Service of Love*[445] he proposes

> for consideration by both Catholics and Orthodox, three particular roles for a universal primate which might possibly form the basis for a consensus

---

[444] —Dominic M. Prummer O.P., *Handbook of Moral Theology,* Cork, Mercier Press. 1956, Fifth (first English) edition, *p*434. (Original edition was in German, 1921)

[445] Paul McPartlan, *A Service of Love: Papal Primacy, the Eucharist and Church Unity,* 2013, The Catholic University of America Press, Washington. D.C., *p*13.

between us, namely: moderating disputes, presiding at ecumenical councils, and serving Eucharistic communion.

Earlier in the same book, Fr McPartlan quotes from the Ravenna Document issued in 2007 by the same Joint International Commission:

"the fact of primacy at the universal level is accepted by both West and East"— a remarkable point of agreement already between Catholics and Orthodox—but that, nevertheless, "there are differences of understanding with regard to the manner in which it is to be exercised, and also with regard to its scriptural and theological foundations".

The manner of leadership

So, having come to agreement on the crucial point, a primacy at universal level, they find themselves blocked by differences about the way it should be exercised. Since it might be considered impertinent for a lay man to suggest that the Joint International Commission for Theological Dialogue should look to the gospels for guidance, we will revert to Fr Wilfred Harrington, whom we met in chapter 4, and who writes:

I have noted for some time now a strange and disturbing feature. What Jesus has to say about the conduct of his disciples is regularly unambiguous and very pointed. What disturbs me is the discovery of what seems to be an inflexible rule. Simply stated, it is this: the clearer the words of Jesus in regard to Christian conduct, the more certainly have Christians done exactly the opposite! Once I had noted the pattern, I could see that the rule had been followed with quite impressive fidelity. I have subsequently taken to referring to this phenomenon as 'Harrington's Law'.

The most glaring inconsistency identified by Fr Harrington is that between Jesus' teaching on the exercise of authority in his church and the actual church practice. [446] He references extracts from the four gospels. For the convenience of the reader, we show them here as they appear in the Jerusalem[447] translation:

Mt 20:25-29 (echoed in Mk 10:42-45) But Jesus called them to him and said, "You know that among the pagans the rulers lord it over them, and their great men make their authority felt. This is not to happen among you. No; anyone who wants to be great among you must be your servant, and anyone who wants to be first among you must be your slave, just as the Son of Man came not to be served but to serve, and to give his life as a ransom for many."

Mt 23: 8-12 "You, however, must not allow yourselves to be called Rabbi, since you have only one Master, and you are all brothers. You must call no one on earth your father, since you have only one Father, and he is in

---

[446] Wilfred J. Harrington OP, *Scribalism in the Church,* in Angela Hanley and David Smith (Eds.) Quench not the Spirit, Dublin, The Columba Press, 2005. P45

[447] Acknowledgement: Taken from The Jerusalem Bible, published and copyright 1966,1967 and 1968 by Darton, Longman & Todd Ltd and Doubleday and Co. Inc, and used by permission of the publishers.

heaven. Nor must you allow yourselves to be called teachers, for you have only one Teacher, the Christ. The greatest among you must be your servant. ·Anyone who exalts himself will be humbled, and anyone who humbles himself will be exalted.

Mk 9:33 They came to Capernaum, and when he was in the house, he asked them, "What were you arguing about on the road?" They said nothing because they had been arguing which of them was the greatest. So, he sat down, called the Twelve to him and said, "If anyone wants to be first, he must make himself last of all and servant of all."

Lk 22:23-27 A dispute arose also between them about which should be reckoned the greatest, but he said to them, "Among pagans it is the kings who lord it over them, and those who have authority over them are given the title Benefactor. This must not happen with you. No; the greatest among you must behave as if he were the youngest, the leader as if he were the one who serves.

Jn13:12-15 When he had washed their feet and put on his clothes again he went back to the table. "Do you understand," he said, "what I have done to you? You call me Master and Lord, and rightly; so I am. If I, then, the Lord and Master, have washed your feet, you should wash each other's feet. I have given you an example so that you may copy what I have done to you.

These quotations cannot be dismissed as convenient proof texts. They are drawn from all four gospels and fit in perfectly with the general tenor of Jesus' teaching and the totality of his message. They should be treated as imperative, not optional.

Jesus did not leave us a definition of what 'lording it over' one's subjects means, but the history of the papacy could be an object lesson in what he was talking about. When applied to the manner of exercising the papacy, the words of Jesus read like an indictment.

The pagan College of Pontiffs in Rome was certainly the 'greatest' in all matters relating to religion and liturgy when it was Christianised by edict. The Christianised college remained as the unquestioned religious authority throughout the Empire for a century until the Western Empire was lost. Its efforts to dominate the Eastern Empire came to an end with the mutual excommunications of 1054. Undeterred, the bureaucracy continued its quest to be the greatest throughout the second millennium. From the eleventh century on, Rome was developing its claims to temporal power, speciously turning the gospel reference to the two swords into a doctrine that gave it a divine right to approve and depose monarchs and to allocate territories to them. By the nineteenth century, papal ability to influence governments waned as monarchies declined. As the century progressed, the spread of ideas of liberty and democracy and the loss of the Papal States brought a downturn in its temporal power. The papacy responded by enhancing its spiritual authority—introducing the 'irrevocable' doctrines of Papal Infallibility and Universal Jurisdiction.

There is no reconciling the manner of exercising authority that Jesus enjoined (and exemplified) with the dictatorial manipulation of Vatican I by Pius IX that led to the defining of the two dogmas in face of the witness of a significant proportion of the

266

attending bishops. The dogmas did not represent the mind of the Church, but rather the ambition of pope and curia. The result of the pope's initiative was to endow his own office with theoretical infallibility and universal jurisdiction and change the structure of the Church from a hierarchical one into a totalitarian one, dominated by a bureaucracy that has made its position almost impregnable. In Chapters 8 and 9, we have discussed the fruits of these 'irreformable' teachings and the way they have been used and abused since then. It is difficult to see how the Church could now adopt the style of governance prescribed by Jesus without jettisoning the two dogmas and installing a working legislature to govern the bureaucracy.

For a century after Vatican I, the papacy was *in effect* saying to Catholics and, through them, to the rest of the world:

- We are in charge of everything related to religion and must be obeyed without question. We are infallible and even when we decline to invoke infallibility, you must treat us as the custodian of all truth. Our conclusions continue to be right even when the underlying thought processes have been shown to be faulty. Pastors and theologians must never disagree openly with what we say because of the divinely endowed dignity of our office—and because we will persecute them mercilessly if they so dare.

- While reserving to ourselves, under the guidance of the Holy Spirit, the exclusive right of appointing bishops, we also reserve the right to interfere and override these bishops in any matter pertaining to their allocated responsibilities under God's eternal plan and to demote or fire them at our discretion without due process.

- In countries having a Catholic majority, the State has a duty to recognise and tolerate the Catholic religion only, but where Catholics are in a minority, the State must actively support and guarantee the principle of freedom of religion for all.

The assembled bishops at Vatican II rejected this kind of posturing. They had the courage to admit that the Spirit moved in the other churches and to recognise that the teaching of Pius XI that ecumenism was a "grave error" was in itself a grave error. When the Council taught instead that ecumenism is a "movement, fostered by the grace of the Holy Spirit" that could ultimately lead to Christian unity, the revised teaching found an immediate resonance in the *sensus fidelium,* among Christians of almost every denomination. It evoked promising ecumenical encounters worldwide and dialogue during the remaining fifteen years of the pontificate of Paul VI. After he died, however, the resistance of the curia re-asserted itself. Another open reversal at that stage would have been ludicrous, so Catholics began to hear from the leadership that the Council had been 'misinterpreted'. Some thought it was being betrayed. Ecumenical activity was slowed to a crawl. This met the deep-seated needs of the bureaucracy.

Christianity is made up of local churches which have developed a variety of governance structures, traditions, practices, and customs. All these are secondary issues.

Among Christian churches, unity *and* identity depend on the lived discipleship of love, of shared purpose in spreading the Good News and of commemorating Christ's life and sacrifice in the Eucharist. Nothing else.

It is time the Catholic Church found the courage to take the next step in prioritising what is important and putting its own house in order, starting at the top. A unilateral initiative would probably evoke another constructive response from many brothers and sisters in Christ who have no great desire to be separated from us and who started to work for ecumenical unity long before Catholics were allowed to do so. Chapter 17 suggests some of the housekeeping that needs to be done and Chapter 18 summarises and lists some action areas.

Chapter 17

Putting the house in order

Christ died for us while we were yet sinners.

—St Paul (Romans 5:8)

Jesus always took the initiative. He gave himself, without negotiating a *quid pro quo*. He died for us while we were yet sinners. He forgave sins without being asked.

The unique duty of the papacy is to be a symbol and a force for unity. When John XXIII took an initiative aimed at promoting unity, the other denominations were quick to respond. The papacy should follow the example of his courageous and strategic leadership and take unilateral initiatives to expand the unity that currently exists among Christian and to focus greater attention on it.

Prior to Vatican II, popes thought their unifying role applied exclusively to the Roman Catholic Church, it being deemed the only true Church. By recognizing that the other denominations share the presence of the Holy Spirit and have the right to be called Christian, the Council conceded that the Promise applies to them also and thus extended the pope's unifying remit to encompass all the Christian churches.

The bishops at Vatican II understood this. In the Decree on Ecumenism they accepted that the discord between the churches openly contradicts the will of Christ and provides a stumbling block to the world. They were not constrained by pseudo-infallibility or by the abiding groupthink of the curia. They changed papal teaching radically on ecumenism itself, and espoused the idea of continuous reform:

> "Christ summons the Church, as she goes her pilgrim way, to that continual reformation of which she always has need, insofar as she is an institution of men here on earth"—*Unitatis Redintegratio*, §6

> "There can be no ecumenism worthy of the name without a change of heart. For it is from newness of attitudes, from self-denial and unstinted love, that yearnings for unity take their rise and grow towards maturity".(§7)

They recognised the need for further changes and initiatives on the Catholic side to facilitate greater unity:

> "Catholics must assuredly be concerned for their separated brethren …
> But their primary duty is to make an honest and careful appraisal of whatever needs to be renewed and achieved in the Catholic household itself …
> For although the Catholic Church has been endowed with all divinely revealed truth and with all the means of grace, her members fail to live by them with all the fervour they should."—*Unitatis Redintegratio*, §4

This call for all Catholics to prepare for greater unity by removing the obstructions on our side, by taking the initiative and putting our own house in order, applies with even greater force to the central managers of the Church. For the curia as a group and as individuals, this will involve significant self-sacrifice. The call to unity, as Archbishop Quinn has shown so clearly, is a costly one.

Having interviewed Pope Francis, Fr Anthony Spadaro, S.J., reported[448] that his primary objective is not the reform of institutions but of people in their hearts; in how they think and behave. In the papacy, however, there is no shortage of good and dedicated people, as Congar, who suffered so much at their hands, has attested. The problem is that excellent people are overwhelmed by the group dynamic and the system they have inherited. They are bound by vows of obedience and oaths of fidelity to the current teaching and the traditions and rituals of the curial institution. The precondition for significant reform in the behaviour of the officials, therefore, is an enabling reform in the ethos and culture of the curia. This is unlikely to be achieved without a radical change in the structure.

Dismantling the obstructions.

With the issue of Justification out of the way, the most intractable of the remaining obstructions to unity are the two dogmas of Vatican I. These twin sources of power were acquired in 1870. The history we have outlined shows that they are unnecessary and have done more harm than good. They are worldly goods cunningly dressed up as essentials to mission. They are inimical to mission. The papacy should divest itself of them unilaterally. At very least, Rome should confirm that people who do not think they are true can still be part of the communion and worship God as Catholics. Belief in them is not essential to salvation. Removing them from the obligatory list is just one part of that costly call to unity and truth. The curia, being a bureaucracy, will never relinquish power voluntarily, but a pope, while he still has the legal power can and should take that decision, so "that the world may know that it was you who sent me". That would be witness to the world indeed. The choice here lies between retaining the powers conveyed by the two dogmas and removing the greatest current obstacle to the unity that Jesus prayed for.

In practice, the dogma of papal infallibility would not be much to part with. It is already of questionable value. Since it was defined, only one pope out of twelve has seen fit to use it.

To renounce it would merely be to officially recognise an open secret. It has virtually no positive value in the lives of Catholics and immense negative implications for the other churches and for Christian unity. Abandoning it would remove the typically Protestant fear of being forced to profess inessentials in which they do not genuinely believe.

As to universal jurisdiction, renouncing this claim would undoubtedly reduce the workload on the pope and the power of the papacy. This would be more than compensated for by unleashing the capabilities and creativity of 4,000+ diocesan bishops. A more active role in the management of the church would revert to them while

---

[448] *National Catholic Reporter,* 9th September 2020

among them the pope would continue to be *primus inter pares*. There will always be disagreements and tensions but, relying on the Promise, to let them exercise their authority would be well justified.

If the management principle of giving someone a job to do and then letting them do it was seen to be applied in the Roman Catholic Church, then one justified fear among Protestant bishops would be allayed.

Downgrading the two dogmas would not require another Council. All that is needed is a formal papal acknowledgement that Vatican I was not an ecumenical council but rather a general council of the Roman Catholic Church. This would be nothing more than an admission of the manifest truth.

The Church survived until the second half of the nineteenth century without these dogmas and devotion to Our Lady survived without the two Marian ones. Their loss will not invalidate the Promise. The pope will would not be the divider, but rather the leader, of a church united under the guidance of the Spirit rather than under the control of a self-perpetuating curia.

Vatican II changed the institutional Church radically but, at that time, to question Vatican I would have been a step too far. It would have been interpreted as disloyalty to the pope. Yet, its specific endorsement of the dogmas was out of harmony with the Council's own general spirit and direction, which can be interpreted as opening a door to all the above.

REFORMING THE IRREFORMABLE?

Can the dogma of infallibility be, so to speak, undefined? Is it open to development or refinement as the mind of the Church develops? Are we not stuck with it because some past ecumenical council arguing in a circle; definitively deciding that a definitive decision of an ecumenical council is infallible, irreversible and irreformable? Are we stuck with having to pretend that every definitive decision of an ecumenical council is irreformable, even though Councils have contradicted one another in the past and even when the faithful no longer believe it, when the *sensus fidelium* has rejected it? It seems evident now, that senior hierarchs, even some members of the curia, have sufficient doubts about papal infallibility that they carefully avoid preaching it. Has the ambition of the papacy created a legal situation where the main obstacle to union or communion can never be removed? These questions have not had the theological discussion they deserve.

The letter here appears to be overwhelming the spirit. If, at some point in the future, a consensus emerges that this roadblock to unity should be removed, then some acceptable legal formula for unwinding the dogma will have to be found, if only to satisfy people with a legal mindset. On examination, it appears that the Holy Spirit has provided us with a dozen ways to reform the 'irreformable', in anticipation of the day when Church authorities agree that it should be done. These are outlined below. No doubt, the professional theologians could find more. If just one formula were to be found acceptable, however, it would be enough to allow the revision:

1. The dogmas were never signed. The intention had been that the bishops would follow the long-established tradition of previous councils, indicating their agreement or disagreement by writing '*placet*' or '*non placet*' with their signatures on a definitive document. The council adjourned for the hot Roman summer intending to continue their deliberations in the autumn, but the outbreak of the Franco-Prussian war and the capture of Rome by the army of the Kingdom of Italy made this impossible. Although the bulk of the published agenda had not been dealt with, the papacy had no incentive to reconvene it in the next 90 years. Pope Pius IX and the curia had got what they wanted. Papal infallibility had been approved, albeit with conditions. The chapters relating to the pope which had once been part of the schema on the church, *De Ecclesia,* had been hived off and dealt with as a separate document entitled *Pastor Aeternus,* (Eternal Father). By the providence of God, the legal status of this document is that of an agreed draft that has never been signed. This led to the extraordinary situation at Vatican II where the bishops, not wishing to contradict Vatican I, yet anxious to reclaim their historic role in the management of the Church ended up by defining not one but two 'supreme' authorities; the pope alone and the bishops acting in union with the pope. The bishops at Vatican II, however, had followed Pope John's example by determining that none of their decisions was to be deemed infallible, so the way is also clear for the Vatican II affirmation to be revisited. This would require a change of heart. In the meantime, the bureaucracy does not tolerate competing power centres, so the second "supreme authority"—the one that included the rest of the college of bishops with the pope—has since been legislated into impotence. The draft was never signed, it can be changed.

2. The council had adjourned with the onset of the Roman summer. But it was never reconvened, initially due to the Franco-Prussian war and the capture of Rome by the Piedmont Army. The bishops had addressed the issues relating to the Pope in 4 chapters out of a planned 15 chapters in *De Ecclesia.* They intended turning their minds next to the closely related question of the status of the bishops themselves. In her excellent study of the relationship between Vatican I and Vatican II, Dr Kristin Colberg quotes a letter written by Bishop William Clifford of Clifton confirming that there was a "distinct promise" that it would be the next item on the agenda. Consideration of these issues might have occasioned some amendments to the previously approved chapters. This the bishops would have been perfectly entitled to do. They were aware that discussion of the 'head' had taken place outside of the context of the 'body'.

> "[F]or many in the minority, it was only the belief that such discussions were merely delayed that had allowed them to consent to what they saw as an incomplete and flawed presentation of ecclesiastical authority".[449]

---

[449] Kristin M. Colberg, *Vatican I and Vatican II: Councils in the Living Tradition, 2016,* Collegeville, Minnesota, Liturgical Press, p 74. The whole of her Chapter 4 is relevant to this issue.

According to Bishop Clifford's letter, some bishops and at least one cardinal had decided to vote for *Pastor Aeternus,* only because of this 'distinct promise' that the relationship between the pope and the bishops would be the next item on the agenda..[450]

Moreover, they would surely have wanted to revisit the exact wording of the dogmatic definition itself because there had been no opportunity for them to debate it. It had only been given its final formulation in the closing days by the influential Cardinal Cullen, Archbishop of Dublin, in an effort to find agreement. The attempt to dismiss the need for reception by the faithful by the inclusion of "*and not by the consent of the Church*" is said by some to have come from Archbishop Senestréy and/or Archbishop Manning[451]. It was never debated and would surely have been revisited if the Council had been reconvened.

3. Infallibility could be annulled, just like a failed marriage. Find a legal flaw in the original process and, suddenly, it never was. This is akin to the couple who thought they were married all those years, only to discover a technicality that rendered the contract invalid. If a legal technicality can annul a marriage that the couple and the community had accepted as real, then why not annul a dogma? If the indissoluble can be legally annulled, so can the irreformable.

4. The role of an ecumenical Council regarding doctrine is to elucidate the belief of the whole church 'down to the last member of the laity'.[452] Thus, the duty of the attending bishops is to give witness to the beliefs of their flocks. There may be many variations in belief and many shades of difference. The Council tries to establish if there is a common or shared element and, if so, to formulate it. Because the infallibility is grounded in the People of God as a whole, ecumenical councils have aimed to gather as many bishops and educated notables as possible and, from the very first Council of Nicaea, they have looked for unanimity or virtual unanimity in identifying the beliefs of the church. Pius IV would not let the Council of Trent rule on issues where opinions were significantly divided[453]. A few *non placets* can be tolerated; they demonstrate a level of freedom among those voting. Many *non placets,* however, indicate that the faithful have a diversity of beliefs on the matter at issue so it cannot be categorised as infallible. At Vatican I there was nothing remotely like moral unanimity or consensus on the issue. About 20 per cent of the bishops opposed the definition strongly and they had the better of the arguments, both historical and theological. When it became

---

[450] Ibid. p 72.

[451] O'Malley, *Vatican I,* p. 229. Fr O'Malley is no mean authority on the subject. He credits the inclusion of this phrase directly to Pius IX.

[452] Lumen Gentium §12 quoting St Augustine *"De praed. Sanct.,"14, 27:PL 44, 980.* Augustine's is a remarkably limited definition. Its corollary must be that a teaching may well be true but cannot be considered infallible if a significant proportion of the faithful do not believe it.

[453] cf S. Pallavicini, *Vera Concilii Tridentini Historia,* III (Antuerpiae 1670), 336, quoted by Bermejo *op. cit.*

evident, however, that there would never be a consensus that would satisfy his ambitions, the Pope abandoned tradition by ruling that the proposal (relating to his own infallibility!) could be decided by a simple majority vote. On this basis, it was bound to get through. Despite centuries of claims and self-promotion by Rome, it had been evident that papal infallibility did not represent the mind of the Catholic faithful. It represented rather the ambition of the Pope, the curia and the Ultramontane faction in Europe.

But the opposing bishops had been put in an impossible position. The change of procedure had decided the issue. Once it had been ruled that a simple majority would suffice, it became inevitable that papal infallibility would be legislated without a consensus as a dogma within a matter of days. Most of the bishops of the day believed that a Council decision was infallible. They would be arguing and voting against something that was certain to become an article of faith within days. Some threw in the towel. Others absented themselves and went home.

Had the voting been weighted to reflect the number of Catholics in each bishop's diocese, the majority decision might have gone the other way. However, it would still not have reflected a belief of the whole Church. Even if one accepts that a solemn definition of an ecumenical council is infallible, (and that is a big if) the deep divisions that characterised the lengthy debate on this occasion must undermine the validity of any definition. If it is accepted that doctrines cannot be decided by majority vote, the Dogma of Papal Infallibility loses all its binding force.

5. The proceedings at Vatican I were held in secret. Despite Christ's disapproval of oaths, each participant was required to take a permanent oath of secrecy. This was interpreted by some as preventing a bishop from consulting his advisor or theologian about a draft document. However, several pro-infallible spokesmen, notably Cardinal Edward Manning, were absolved of this oath by the Pope so that they could promote the infallibility cause more effectively outside the Council at the time and subsequently.[454] The oath inhibited the minority forever from publishing their personal accounts of the Council. Providentially, Bishop William Ullathorne of Birmingham kept a detailed diary. This enabled Dom Cuthbert Butler, OSB, to publish the story of the Council for the general reader some 60 years later.[455] While defending the definition, Butler does appear to give a balanced and historically fair account of the history and of the arguments advanced on both sides. Thus, it was only after an interval of two generations that the general public could become aware of the extent and cogency of the opposition to the definition and the abandonment of the long-established conciliar tradition of moral unanimity that got the definitions adopted. In view of

---

[454] Cf. Cardinal Manning, *The True Story of the Vatican Council,* London, Westminster, Henry S. King & Co., 1877,

[455] He also had access to the papers of Félix Dupanloup, Bishop of Orléans who never wrote his memoirs of the Council, despite being a prolific author.

Christ's condemnation, the enforced secrecy could reasonably be deemed to invalidate the entire proceedings and/or the subsequent 'reception', such as it was.

6. Infallibility is grounded in all the faithful, ordained and lay. Therefore, any definition of a doctrine must originate in the belief of the faithful and be 'received' by the faithful. The Orthodox Churches and the Christian churches that are not controlled by Rome have never 'received' the theory of infallibility. In fact, they have firmly and consistently denied it, before and since. Coercion was used to make some of the bishops who had opposed the definition at Vatican 1 toe the line and proclaim the teaching in their dioceses subsequently. The reception, to the extent it was achieved among Roman Catholics, was vitiated by keeping the extent of the diversity of belief among the bishops from them. There is evidence now that Catholics, other than the doctrinaire conservatives, have abandoned whatever reception of papal infallibility they once had. The laity ignore it, the clergy do not preach it. The bishops of the Second Vatican Council followed the lead of Pope John XXIII, in declaring from the outset that they did not wish to make any infallible pronouncement. Of twelve popes who have reigned since the definition in 1870, only one has invoked the power; in 1950 Pius XII used it for the Assumption of the Blessed Virgin Mary, having (it was claimed[456]) consulted the bishops and thus confirmed that this had long been a pious belief among Roman Catholics. The conclusion must be that the authorities in Rome either (a) do not really believe the doctrine of papal infallibility at this stage, or (b) consider it imprudent to test publicly whether the faithful hold it or not. The available evidence on the current readiness of Roman Catholics to dismiss Roman teaching on contraception, celibacy, women priests, same-sex marriages, co-habitation and pre-wedding sex would not suggest a consciousness of, let alone any belief in, Papal Infallibility. It is therefore questionable whether the dogma has been received by Roman Catholics. It has very clearly been rejected by the rest of the Christianity. Ergo it can be abandoned or reformed on the grounds of non-reception by the faithful.

7. The definition relies on itself for validity, creating a circular argument. It attempts to outmanoeuvre the need for reception by including the phrase: *Therefore, such definitions of the Roman Pontiff are of themselves, and not by the consent of the Church, irreformable.* But if reception is a valid requirement (and John 2:20 gives this a biblical basis), the definition itself, including the italicised phrasing above, would itself require reception to become binding.

8. Vatican I was a strictly Roman Catholic affair. If it had been representative of the universal church, papal infallibility would have had no chance of approval. The Council was not ecumenical. It could not be. Relations between Catholics and their neighbours at grassroots level were tolerant to friendly at that time in

---

[456] But the curia has demonstrated a readiness to lie on the issue of episcopal consultation. See Chapter 9 page 136

most places but at institutional level, the churches were hostile and tribal. Each side dutifully condemned the others as being apostates; implying that they were rather worse than pagans. They lacked the mutual respect and trust necessary to gather an ecumenical meeting together, let alone sustain constructive dialogue. Consequently, Vatican I ranks as a General Council of the Roman Catholic Church and not of the Universal Church. This distinction was lost on most of the participants at the time. It was deemed to be ecumenical on the assumption that the Roman Catholic Church is equivalent to the Universal Church of Christ. That mistake was easier to make then than now. The Second Vatican Council refrained from saying that the Church of Christ *'is'* the Catholic Church but deliberately used the phrase *'subsists in'*.[457] It put paid to the implied legal fiction by recognising that all the Christian churches have baptism in common and by acknowledging that the Holy Spirit is at work in the other Christian churches and ecclesial communities, albeit to a lesser degree. This was something that any thoughtful Catholic who lived among Protestant or Anglican neighbours could have told them. If Vatican I was not genuinely ecumenical, then its decisions lose all claims to infallibility, and are open to reform.

Vatican II did not go on to draw the consequent conclusion that any future Council will need to invite the bishops, or equivalent ranks, of all the Christian Churches to participate fully if it wishes to claim the title of 'ecumenical'. The use of the expression 'ecclesial community' in some Roman documents does not change the fact that they are Christian churches in the ordinary meaning of the words. It means that they too will have to be participants in any future council that would purport to be ecumenical.

9. Vatican I was very unevenly representative of the Catholic Church itself. It was a heavily biased sample. The disproportionally high presence of Italian bishops, who might in the circumstances of the time have favoured any boost for the traditionally Italian papacy, was the inevitable result of the multiplicity of tiny dioceses in Italy. (Italy has 225 dioceses, compared to the USA with 195). It is reported that there were 62 bishops in attendance from the recently overrun Papal States whose care *averaged* 11,290 souls,[458] the equivalent of a small parish. Ethnically and politically, they could be depended upon to support the pope. Many bishops coming from overseas spoke for several dioceses numbering millions, or even for nations. It is beyond the scope of this book to enquire whether the imbalance in the attendance was fortuitous or contrived.

A deliberate bias was evident, however, in the make-up of the *deputationes*—the commissions that had control of what was to be discussed and of the amendments to be brought forward after each debate. The *deputatio* for the schema on the powers of the pope was composed solidly of bishops known to be in favour

---

[457] Lumen Gentium §8.

[458] Gertrude Himmelfarb, *The Vatican Council*, http://www.anthonyflood.com /actonhimmelfarb.htm

of infallibility, with one exception – the Hungarian Primate who got included by mistake. He was known to have published something favouring infallibility but had meanwhile changed his mind![459]

10. "By their fruits ye shall know them". We have dealt with the fruits of infallibility in Chapters 8 and 9 and found them overwhelmingly negative. If the Church were to make a similar discernment, papal infallibility could be simply accepted as a mistake and abandoned on solid biblical grounds.

11. St John Henry Newman and others questioned whether the Council had the necessary freedom. If this objection were to be accepted, the Church could simply walk away from the claim to Papal Infallibility.

12. This final approach is for the legalistic minds. The wording of the definition of infallibility is faulty. It reads:

> When the Roman Pontiff speaks ex cathedra, that is, when, in the exercise of his office as shepherd and teacher of all Christians, in virtue of his supreme apostolic authority, he defines a doctrine concerning faith or morals to be held by the whole Church, he possesses, by the divine assistance promised to him in blessed Peter, that infallibility which the divine Redeemer willed his Church to enjoy in defining doctrine concerning faith or morals. *Therefore, such definitions of the Roman pontiff are of themselves, and not by the consent of the church, irreformable.*

Papal infallibility was thus defined as being the same as that given to the church in general. If the infallibility with which Christ endowed his church is limited to doctrines finding universal agreement "from the bishops down to the last member of the laity", then the same infallibility when exercised by the pope must meet the same requirement, i.e. it needs reception[460] Otherwise, it is a not the infallibility with which Christ endowed his church.

Furthermore, papal infallibility was defined in terms of the infallibility of the church which itself has never been "infallibly" defined or delimited.[461] It was known at the time that this definition was due to come up on the agenda later on.[462] This leaves open another possibility. The church's infallibility could now be defined in appropriately modest, truthful, and humble terms, thus modifying the former indirectly without having to admit to an earlier error. Hans Küng's important work, *Infallibility?* would be helpful here, particularly Chapter 4, Section 6, which suggests some more appropriate and felicitous terminology.

---

[459] Archbishop Simor of Esztergom. Primate of Hungary. Cf. Dom Cuthbert Butler, *The Vatican Council,* p 175-6.

[460] Adding a clause at Vatican I to deny this was whistling in the wind. It changed nothing.

[461] "Vatican I stated that the pope enjoys that infallibility with which Christ endowed the church—without ever saying just what the infallibility of the whole church was. Those ideas stand in need of further exploration."—James Heft, University of Drayton: https://ejournals.bc.edu/ojs/index.php/ctsa/article/download/2986/2600 by J Heft - 2013 accessed 13 June 2017

[462] Colberg Opus cit., P 77 gives a reference to a letter to this effect from Bishop Clifford.

Consequences of rescinding infallibility

When papal infallibility is discarded, the pseudo-infallibility attributed to papal documents will be buried with it. Faith will still be a gift from God but some of the obligatory beliefs that now obstruct both faith and unity will be reduced to matters of opinion, dependent on the quality of preaching, scholarship, and the mind of the faithful, the *sensus fidelium,* to which the Promise ultimately relates.

Among the casualties will be Pope Leo XIII's dismissal of Anglican Orders as "absolutely null and utterly void". The idea that Jesus would renege on his part in a sacrament because of a technical flaw is no longer acceptable. This judgement, in *Apostolicae Curae,* was based on a narrow legalistic argument that allowed nothing for the justice and love of God who can grant the grace of a sacrament even when the wording of the prayer is faulty, or when the intention of the minister does not comply exactly with canon law. We considered *Apostolicae Curae* on page 104 above.

Moreover, the papacy has by now controverted the 'absolutely null and utterly void' teaching contention of Leo XIII by giving a special status to former Anglican and Evangelical ministers. It qualifies them uniquely, to become Latin rite priests without fulfilling the normal requirements of canon law and without committing to celibacy. So 'absolutely null and void' it is not.

Another casualty among pseudo-infallibilities will be the exclusion of women from ordination. As we have seen in Chapter 12, this exclusion was never a teaching of the Church although it has been the practice, starting in the fourth or fifth century when representative priests were introduced. It was classified as a barrier to unity by Pope Paul VI in correspondence with Dr Coggan, Archbishop of Canterbury but could be re-classified, as Dr Coggan had suggested, as a legitimate diversity, helping to ease the Eucharistic famine.

If Church authorities cannot bring themselves to ordain the women leaders, they would be better to revise canon law and allow the Christian community to celebrate Mass as Jesus commanded.[463] The Christian community does not need ordination. It was given an instruction at the Last Supper and that was enough for three centuries or more. That is what being a priestly people meant. It could mean the same to-morrow with the removal of a few prohibitions from canon law. The ordained priest and bishop would still have a leadership and preaching role and could still celebrate Mass individually for the community whenever their declining numbers allowed.

Hierarchical structure

Papal documents obsessively reiterate the teaching that the hierarchical structure is a part of God's eternal plan for his Church. Yet, while honouring this by appointing bishops, the papacy has gutted the very concept of hierarchy. Nobody proposes that the Church should dispense with bishops, but in 1870 the Bishop of Rome, and the

---

[463] Economists like to watch trends. The terminal trend in the celibate male ordained priesthood was clearly evident about forty years ago and I made this suggestion in the October 1981 edition of *Doctrine & Life,* p 526.

curia, became in many ways the Bishop of Everywhere. Since then, the papacy has progressively taken away the authority that once corresponded with the bishops' responsibilities. The link between authority and responsibilities is of the essence of hierarchy. The Roman Empire, on which Church structure was modelled, entrusted diocesan and provincial officials with the discretion and authority needed to match their responsibilities. The papacy's pursuit of control, however, has disempowered the rest of the Church. Universal jurisdiction has produced a plethora of rules that inhibit flexibility and limit both creativity and cultural adaptation. It has favoured obedience and uniformity at the expense of initiative, capability, and diversity in a culturally diverse world. Christ's commandment to 'make disciples of all' implies his authority to try whatever seems conducive to achieving that objective.

The papacy must return to the bishops their traditional administrative, sanctifying and teaching responsibilities and give back to the faithful and their clergy the right to choose their bishops.[464] Building community and commitment today demands that leaders in voluntary organisations be chosen by the members. This is one of the signs of the times to which church leaders should be adapting. Appointments by external authority should normally be avoided and only used as a fall-back. The idea that selection by a curial committee allows the Holy Spirit to make the most suitable choice is now fully discredited. Manifestly, the secretive, central selection from a list of three candidates submitted in secret by the relevant nuncio has not worked for the good of the Church. The scriptural precedent of choosing an apostolic successor from a short list by lot, as in the case of Mathias, has been ignored. It would give the Holy Spirit a role in the process. At the very least, it would help to frustrate simony and cronyism.

Having bishops selected locally by people who know the and have worked with them would be no panacea. In general, they would probably be no worse than those selected by the present system. They would provide a better mix of talents and ideas. If the selected bishops were given back traditional authority it would help avoid institutional scale disasters in future. Mistakes would tend to be localised and would normally be identified and corrected at local synod level. Sacramental famine could be ended without delay.

As for maintaining doctrinal purity, if a locally selected bishop were to express novel or unorthodox views, this would not reflect on the authority of the Church. His ideas would be subject to challenge and could be discussed in synods and ultimately accepted or rejected by the *sensus fidelium*. This slow process would deprive some Catholics of the pride and comfort of official certainty of being right. It would

---

[464] The papacy did not take away the selection of their bishops from the faithful. Feudal monarchs and princes had already done that, to a large extent. If feudal overlords wanted their own men in these influential positions, their subjects were in no position to resist. At that time only the papacy could provide a counterforce. This is still true with dictatorial and authoritarian regimes. The situation has changed now to the extent that democratic governments are in power. Some may wish to influence the selection but generally they stop shot of claiming selection as a right.

be preferable to centralised decision making that relies on the coercive support of the CDF. The papacy should be an example of trust in the Holy Spirit to protect the truths of Revelation in the mind of the faithful … where, even now, infallibility is theoretically grounded.

Key role for the bishops

Canon law affects every detail of Church life.[465] So the road to greater Christian unity will demand many revisions. Putting the house in order will involve taking initiatives that the curia is incapable of contemplating. For the bureaucracy, the cost of unity is too high. Concerted action by the bishops is the only human solution to a curia that does not change. For two pontificates, compliance was a criterion in selecting bishops. But they do not have to remain docile. Pope Francis seems to want the bishops to make themselves felt.

In 2010 Hans Küng suggested to the world's bishops that they should not keep silent but set about reform and begin to act collegially.[466] The bishops should use their collective authority, reaffirmed by Vatican II, to call for changes. Ironically, Pope John Paul II helped to prove the value of solidarity in dealing with authoritarian regimes. An open demand for reconsideration supported by a significant number of Episcopal Conferences could not be ignored by a pope. The dispersed bishops are entitled under Canon Law to put forward proposals for acceptance by a pope.[467]

Some areas where changes in Canon Law could be considered:

- Allow the bishops freedom to end the Sacramental Famine in their dioceses.
- Allow freedom of assembly to the College of Bishops.
- Tone down the veneration and unique privileges attaching to ordination which are being used as obstructions to Christian unity.
- Call for Church governance by a collegial body, including the pope that would control its own procedures and agenda. It would be superior to a trimmed down curia and would be in some way representative of the Church as a whole.

For the pope to agree would require active and visible trust in the guidance of the Holy Spirit. It would begin to give life to the College of Bishops with its head, the

---

[465] It contains 1752 Canons. The index alone in my copy (in English) runs to 112 pages!

[466] https://www.associationofcatholicpriests.ie/2012/05/hans-kungs-letter-to-bishops-is-worth-re-reading-chris-mcdonnell/ —accessed 05/09/2020

[467] Canon 337, §1 The College of Bishops exercises its power over the universal Church in solemn form in an Ecumenical Council.

§2 It exercises this same power by the united action of the bishops dispersed throughout the world when this action is as such proclaimed or freely accepted by the Roman Pontiff so that it becomes a truly collegial act.

§3 It belongs to the Roman Pontiff to select and promote, according to the needs of the Church, ways in which the College of Bishops can exercise its office in respect of the universal Church in a collegial manner.

pope, as the supreme authority. In time, Collegial governance would address the issues that cannot be addressed now.

ECUMENISM IN PRACTICE

Pride, we are told, is the greatest of the seven deadly sins. Apart altogether from its being immoral, it involves collateral damage of many kinds. It blinds people to the truth, creating slow learners. In the sixteenth century, the papacy was so puffed up about its own importance that it could not admit that there was an element of sense in many of Martin Luther's suggested reforms. No provocative, presumptuous, brash Augustinian professor from far off Wittenberg was going to teach Pope Leo X and the Roman authorities about the faith.[468] More than four centuries later, the bishops at Vatican II were able to accept several ideas that the sixteenth-century papacy could not entertain.

We have noted above how the Edinburgh Missionary Conference in 1910 identified disunity as the greatest single obstacle to mission. The link is scriptural, foreseen in Christ's prayer "may they be so completely one that the world will realise that it was you who sent me". (John 17:23, Jerusalem Bible). The Conference accepted the imperative. The papacy could not but agree with the reasoning but was unable to take the logical action of participating. So, the drive for unity was spurned by the largest Church accounting for more than half of Christianity. For Rome, it would have meant responding to a suggestion from the Protestants! At that time, emboldened by the dogmas of Vatican I, the papacy was focused on establishing its spiritual sovereignty, condemning anything and anybody that might modify the unchanging eternal truth of which it considered itself the sole custodian. Sometimes it behaved as if it were the source.

Undoubtedly, the rejection of ecumenism for 54 years reflected the bureaucratic fear of competing power centres. The assembled bishops at Vatican II took the matter out of the hands of the curia by directly reversing the teaching and policy of Pope Pius XI, as set out in his encyclical, *Mortalium Animos.* The bishops knew what they were changing was not an infallible teaching, and few Catholics were scandalised by the change. Despite the official teaching that papal opinions were fallible, for three generations Catholics had been fed the fiction that every doctrine that issued from Rome should be treated as infallible. The papacy had fraudulently exaggerated the scope of infallibility to enhance its power, making it inevitable that there would be defections at the time, and again when the truth would emerge.

The Second Vatican Council committed the Church to ecumenism and began the process of putting the house in order. It changed the working relationship between

---

[468] Readers who feel that this presents the papacy of Leo X as driven more by emotion than theology, should read the relevant Bull, *Exsurge Domine,* (largely drafted by Johann Eck) and judge for themselves. Leo's grasp of theology may be gauged from the comment of the historian of the Council of Trent, Fra Paolo Sarpi: "He would have been a perfect pope, if to these accomplishments he had added even the slightest knowledge of religion".

the denominations at official level from a worldly one of rivalry, competition, and tribalism to one of respect and collaboration; we might almost say love. The papacy should continue to remove the obstacles that have been created on the Catholic side. We should not wait to trade concessions over some future bargaining table. Unity will not come in one cataclysmic event. It will grow in many steps, big and small, some trumpeted, others imperceptible. We should put right what is wrong, simply because it is wrong.

Furthermore, if Catholicism were seen to be honestly and actively engaged in reform, the fear among other Christians of arbitrary use of papal power would be reduced.

Doctrinal convergence

The need to resolve significant doctrinal differences cannot be ignored, but there must be no coercion in matters of religion.[469] We must be true to what we really believe, but must allow our neighbours the same duty and privilege. This calls for a careful mapping of what is deemed to be essential. We should all be guided by the principle agreed at the very first Council in Jerusalem, when St Paul met the other apostles and the community of the faithful; no burden should be imposed beyond what is indispensable.[470] We should adopt John Wesley's contention that the essentials of Christianity can be written on one sheet of paper and the rest are opinions.[471] We can be united on the essentials and for the rest we can respect the integrity of others and permit them the integrity of professing what they honestly think is true, or most probable.

A lot of constructive work has been done already by the various joint commissions, with some surprising common ground being revealed. The recognition that there is a hierarchy of truths allows some flexibility here, as would an open acceptance that pseudo-infallibilities are not infallible at all but are open to diversity of opinion. This will be difficult for the papacy which tends to see every difference as a challenge to its authority. Moreover, we should not expect everything to be settled at one time. The Holy Spirit works slowly, not overriding our freedom to make unhelpful choices and patiently giving us time for conversion of heart.

In the meantime, we can grow in a unity of love, peace, and purpose. It does not have to be a conquest, a legal or administrative take-over. The individual churches can retain most of the structures and liturgical practices to which their members are accustomed. They are not inimical to the service of the Mystical Body. This principle has already been conceded by the papacy in extending a welcome to recent Anglican converts and in allowing them to maintain most of their patrimony.

---

[469] See excerpt from *Dignitatis Humanae* under *Coercion* on page 212

[470] Cf. Unitatis Redintegratio §14-21. For a group of Jews, this was a momentous, brave, counter-cultural decision pertaining to their very identity. Gentiles could become disciples and Mosaic circumcision was not necessary for salvation in Christ.

[471] See footnote on page 252.

Rome managed to bypass many of the secondary doctrinal and disciplinary issues when setting up the Anglican ordinariate, by arranging for prospective converts to profess belief in the Catechism of the Catholic Church which runs to more than 700 pages. In effect, those who had not read it carefully were accepting bundled infallibility based on authority. There is a risk here of confusing profession with belief. This stratagem may be acceptable for reunion, but ecumenism must be prepared to recognise integrity and tolerate honest differences of opinion, belief, and practice.

Lessons can be learned from the separate attempts in the 1930s to structurally unite the Church of England with the Presbyterians and the Methodists. The negotiations with the Presbyterians broke down because the Anglicans were unable or unwilling to recognise the validity of Presbyterian Orders. Trust in a loving God to compensate for legal deficiencies would have helped at that point. Christ is not going to break faith with a group of his followers when they "Do This", because of some deficiency in the one who presides. Later discussions with the Methodists also broke down on an issue relating to ministry. The issue was 'itinerancy", the Methodist tradition whereby ministers move to a new congregation every seven years. Surely this was an area where 'legitimate diversity' could have been tolerated. To the outsider, the deal-breaker in each case was related to the professional ministry and of little consequence compared to the objective of greater unity that both sides were seeking. In human affairs, great issues can be disproportionally influenced by little ones.

The status of the papacy, as defined in 1870, is the main issue standing between Christians and the greater unity that Christ prayed for. It is of relatively recent origin and therefore cannot be essential to the life of the Church.

By abandoning the claim to infallibility, the door would be opened to cooperation with other Christians in the search for truth and in worship. The Holy Spirit inspires but will never coerce. There will always be differences among finite human beings in their understanding of the infinite. It would be better if these could be expressed and possibly resolved over time. This would mean abandoning some of our intellectual pride, tolerating and listening to others whom we judge to be mistaken and focusing on the essential good news that our Father in heaven loves us and wants us to love one another as much as we love ourselves. He wants us to be in him and him to be in us. He wants us to be happy, here and hereafter and he has given us the key: forgiveness and love for one another, siblings, beloved children of one Father. That is why it is called 'good news'.

More slow learning

The latest Conciliar pronouncement on the infallibility of the People of God is interesting in this context. It takes us part of the way. We will quote it again here for the convenience of the reader. It cannot be accused of novelty. It harks back to the New Testament and uses a quote from St Augustine:

> The body of the faithful as a whole, anointed as they are by the Holy One
> (cf. Jn 2; 20,27), cannot err in matters of belief. Thanks to a supernatural
> sense of the faith which characterizes the People as a whole, it manifests this

unerring quality when, "from the bishops down to the last member of the laity" it shows universal agreement in matters of faith and morals. (*Lumen Gentium* §12)

This means that in defining something as infallible, the pope must pay attention to what the faithful believe. It is not a question of telling the faithful what they must believe or what the pope would prefer them to believe. Nor is it a question of majority opinion. It is a question of a leader articulating a shared faith. This puts in place the sort of limitation that was raised (most effectively by Cardinal Guidi) in the discussion at Vatican I but which would not be accepted by the Pope or the extreme Ultramontane party of the time, who saw it as potentially undermining the supreme and unlimited authority with which they wished to endow the pope.

Because papal infallibility underpins its power and control, the bureaucracy is unable to accept the limits set down by St Augustine's teaching or apply the conditions legislated by Vatican I. Only an external force will make a bureaucracy relinquish power. An independent pope could do this by suppressing some curial congregations entirely and breaking up the remainder geographically. In 2015, Erny Gillen explored some proposals for this in an open letter to Pope Francis.[472]

Jesus did not pray for the perpetuation of the Roman bureaucracy, but he did pray that his followers would be one. The People of God is a thing of the spirit: it is the Mystical Body of Christ. It undoubtedly needs an organisation, a church, through which to become visible, to worship, teach and act. The tail, however, should not wag the dog. Every church needs the services of a bureaucracy, but no Christian church should be *governed* by one. They are not naturally altruistic, have no conscience and do not understand self-sacrificing love. In the Roman one, the largely homogeneous staffing, traditional secrecy, and reliance on oaths of loyalty make it even more unsuitable.

A Possible Solution

A pope as currently constituted, however, has the power to break up the curia and spread its necessary work among the bishops or some widely separated bodies. He could make the remnant of the curia subject to the newly created Governing Body representing the College of Bishops, each member of which would be advised and supported by his own episcopal conference and a national (or regional) synod comprising bishops, clergy and laity.[473] This new structure would reintegrate the Church. It would make the current Synod of Bishops redundant. (It could not be constituted through a revision of the statutes of the current Synod, because this is under the control of the bureaucracy which would never let it happen.) There is ample precedent in the history of the Church that would justify setting up national and regional synods. The main problem would be Roman fear of the reduction of central control.

---

[472] Cf. Erny Gillen, *How a pope might treat curial diseases,* Berlin, Eds Saint-Paul, (ePubli GmbH) 2015.

[473] In seeking to rebuild a synodal structure, the Catholic Church of today would have something to learn from the Orthodox and the Reformed Churches.

But dispersed control with checks and balances is less easily corrupted and, probably more sensitive to the guidance of the Holy Spirit. And we have the Promise.

In passing, it must be said that the current situation of the Church would scarcely have been allowed to develop if the governance of the Church had been transferred to the College of Bishops and the Pope in the aftermath of the Council that had recommended it. This was frustrated rather than implemented by the curia.[474] The bishops do not have the same commitment to pseudo-infallibility, so they would have been more flexible. They would doubtless have restored greater authority and discretion to the diocesan level and required the curia to redefine its own role as one of serving, rather than governing, the episcopate. They might well have legislated to make the College of Bishops representative in some way of the People of God by giving back to the faithful and their pastors the role of selecting their bishops. The signs of the times are democratic. If modern adults are to make a commitment to voluntary organisations, they expect to have a say, however diluted and indirect, in how they are managed and in the selection of leaders.[475] In the long term this would help to close the distance between the body of the Church and its independent and unaccountable government..

The proposed Collegial Governing Body would set policy with the pope openly and transparently.[476] The bureaucracy, whether centralised or dispersed, would no longer govern. Instead it would serve the government and the bishops, by administering the government's policies and adopting its priorities. This would implement the Collegiality already agreed by Vatican II but stymied by the 1983 Code. The representative bishops should probably serve for a fixed term of years, a proportion retiring annually. They would be elected by their peers in episcopal conferences, who would know the people they were voting for. The representatives should probably not be the Presidents of the Episcopal Conferences. Most of them already have more than enough extra-diocesan duties to cope with.

Any such body would have to be set up initially by edict, to create an immediate counterforce to the curia which would easily outmanoeuvre any gradual change of regime.[477] The pope would only need to set up the basic structure and appoint an initial caretaker Governing Body to work out its own Constitution, ground rules and

[474] Mary McAleese in *Quo Vadis* describes the uncertainties of *Lumen Gentium* and the explanatory note appended to it by a 'higher authority', presumably Pope Paul VI. This was followed by the failure of the 1983 revision of the Code of Canon Law to give any effective structure to collegiality.

[475] *Ibid.* Page 150 raises the issue of "long-standing resentment by the lay faithful (but also and more quietly the lower clergy) at the lack of accountability, transparency and opportunities for participation in church governance".

[476] An all-bishop Governing Body would receive advice and proposals openly from the regional synods which would include both clergy and laity and could give a voice to the *sensus fidelium*. The Governing Body would become less homogeneous over time. Doubtless, it would have working subcommittees that include lay men and women.

[477] "Power concedes nothing without a fight"—Frederick Douglas

way of working under his leadership. If the curia were to be given the job of writing the statutes, the Governing Body would end up emasculated.[478]

A Logical Response

Consider then the position:

1. Vatican II said the Church should be governed by the college of bishops with the pope

2. John Paul II said, "the curia *is* the pope". Here the word 'pope' is used figuratively to mean the papacy.

3. John Paul II and Paul VI both identified the papacy as the greatest obstacle to unity. This suggests that the curia may be the greatest obstacle to unity.

4. "[T]he fact of primacy at the universal level is accepted by both West and East—a remarkable point of agreement already between Catholics and Orthodox" and, we might add, with several other Christian churches. They think it is appropriate for Christianity to have a primate. What an opportunity this offers! The differences arise in how the primacy is to be exercised. It does not have to be totalitarian or controlled by a self-perpetuating curial oligarchy. The way is open. Would the group dynamic within the curia permit it to cede power? Probably not. Would charity, faith and trust win the day? If so, we could be celebrating the end of the East-West Schism instead of sadly marking its millennium come 2054.

The solution follows logically: The pope renounces Infallibility and Universal Jurisdiction, the fruits of which have not been good, and accepts the more limited job description as proposed by Fr McPartlan: that of leading as primate, moderating disputes, presiding at ecumenical councils, preaching and serving Eucharistic communion. Of course, the pope would still be Bishop of Rome. He would also preside when representatives of the College of Bishops meet as the Governing Body of the Church, whatever form that takes. The curia would be downsized and divided; part to serve as curia for the diocese of Rome and part as the civil service for the new governing body. The curia would no longer govern the Church. Some of its dicasteries would be decentralised ans some abolished.

Of course, the pope's legal power of universal jurisdiction would only be rescinded after the key structural revisions have been put into effect and become established.

The dogmatic definitions of Vatican I, and the attitude of mind that they have created, have blocked the solution of many of the problems facing the Church today. The changes will cause short term discomfort for some but will enable others to be reconciled to the Church. It would solve the problem of eucharistic famine. It is

---

[478] As happened with the Synod of Bishops, the Episcopal Conferences, the International Commission for English in the Liturgy, and the College of Bishops as provided for in the 1983 revision of the Code of Canon Law.

unlikely to cause schism as the schismatics would find themselves denying the infallibility of a papal teaching that itself denied papal infallibility, which would mean tolerating it! The Pope would have to admit, openly and humbly, that the papacy has sometimes been wrong, unwise or sinful, and that the infallibility of the church resides fundamentally in the People of God, is limited to the deposit of faith, and does not provide a divine guarantee of validity in the short term. After the initial shock, this more humble position is likely to be received by the faithful because it fits well with the facts.

This would involve the papacy in emptying itself of some inessentials that are obstructing the Way. It would unilaterally remove the doctrinal grounds of the East/West Schism. If the two lungs could breathe together, each respecting the other's patrimony, the voice of the Church would be heard more clearly around the world. It would open the way to communion with many of the Reformed Churches.

Since the East/West break-up was finally triggered by the novelty of adding something to the creed, this would have to be remedied directly. The *Filioque* issue was really the last straw in the long-running row about the ambitious Roman claim to full doctrinal and jurisdictional authority.[479] It should be admitted that it makes no difference to salvation whether one thinks that the Holy Spirit proceeds from the Father alone or from the Father and the Son.

Biblically, the branches that do not yield good fruit are cut down and cast into the fire. On that principle alone, the Roman Catholic Church should abandon the twin dogmas of Vatican I which have done more harm than good. In relation to Universal Jurisdiction, the pope would only be giving back to the bishops the authority and power they exercised for most of the life of the Church.

Recapitulation

The conclusion, broadly speaking, must be that the administrative structures, regulations, and operating policies at the centre in the Roman Church are exactly what could have been expected to develop in any powerful secular bureaucracy. Their emergence necessitated little input from the Holy Spirit. The curia as a bureaucracy resists Christian unity (despite the best efforts of the Pontifical Council for Promoting Christian Unity, the Pontifical Council for Inter-Religious Dialogue, the two Popes of the Council, and Pope Francis). Some dicasteries are currently unfit for purpose, that is, if the purpose of the Church can be deduced from what scripture and tradition have taught us. Others pose obstacles to faith. The curia has tried and failed to reform itself.[480] The habitual abuse since 1870 of the "infallibility with which

---

[479] Pride is the big obstacle here. It is senseless and arrogant for finite beings to define the origins of the infinite. If we believe God exists outside of the time-space-energy-matter, cause-and-effect, number-and-distinction, male-and-female environment that he created for us, then it is foolish to apply our logic to the 'procession' of the Trinity. Moreover, it was certainly sinful to fight about it.

[480] Diarmuid Martin, Archbishop of Dublin, speaking about reconciling faith and reason at Trinity College Dublin 3rd July 2008. I was present.

the Divine Redeemer wished His Church to be endowed in defining doctrines of faith and morals" has put the bureaucracy beyond human redemption. It cannot reform itself now without admitting to the existence of pseudo-infallibilities and thus undermining its own hegemony. This would be against the nature of a bureaucracy.

Years of acting, and judging, as if everything is infallible and irreformable have concentrated power in the curia but have brought it to a state of constructive paralysis. Problems identified a century ago are still unresolved because every proposed solution involves change in some practice or tradition that has been presented as God's eternal plan for his Church or runs counter to some pseudo-infallibility.

It is clearly time for a lot of changes. The recommendations in Chapter 18 follow logically from the analysis in this book. They are not for the faint hearted. Luis M. Bermejo S.J. looks for much the same reforms, making four general proposals.[481]

If, as he has argued and as I have argued, there is a misfit between the way that Christ taught us by word and example and the traditional structure, operating style or ethos of management in Catholicism since the nineteenth century, then there can be no question as to which can and has to change. It is not enough to talk about a servant ministry. The ordained elite, from the papacy down must start divesting from status, power, dress, honour, and the comforts of the *status quo*. Changes are always painful. They upset the complacent and the comfortable. They will doubtless upset the people whose certainty of faith is grounded in the fiction that Rome has never been wrong.

Bermejo sounds a warning, that sudden and very radical proposals could be counter-productive if they were to lead to a loss of identity and further schism in Roman Catholicism. Division is, of course, the lurking danger in all reform. Pope Francis seems to understand this as he gradually undermines some of the certainties, and pseudo-infallibilities. Pride in the certainty of our own convictions or fear of uncertainty, can make us very intolerant of other people's views.

In this case, however, the danger could be minimised by accepting a number of inconvenient truths from the outset

- that the papacy can err and has erred[482]
- that there is a hierarchy of truths,
- that the doctrines that unite Christians are the important ones: Baptism, the Eucharist, the Creeds, the Our Father, and the call to love. The ones that divide us are secondary, tertiary, organisational or even less important,
- that different cultures can be served by different patterns of ministry,
- that Christian discipleship is a personal way of life marked by love of God and concern for one's neighbour that is characterised by unselfish action,

---

,[481]*Towards Christian Reunion,* Bermejo, Luis M., S.J., Anand, India 1984, Lanham, MD, University Press of America, 1987, pp 314-316.

[482].Admission of error after a delay of 500 or 1000 years is not enough. The possibility of current error must be admitted.

- that the unity we are seeking is one of shared purpose and love, leaving room for diversity in opinion, emphasis, liturgy, practice, structure, and governance.[483]

The homogeneous self-perpetuating bureaucracy will not allow these truths to be acknowledged because they would undermine its power and control.

If the Governing Body of Bishops, as proposed by Vatican II, were to be put in charge of a decentralised administration, these truths would gradually prevail. If the selection of their bishops was given back to the faithful, the scope for corruption and cronyism would be reduced and the homogeneous nature of the College would be gradually replaced with a more balanced mix of personalities, expertise, attitude, and experience. This process could be expedited by the representation, in some way, of vowed religious laity who are active in organised care for the least, in a deliberative or consultative role. If, as seems likely, the ban on women priests is abandoned, and go it must with the first steps towards structural unity, then the Governing Body itself will be enriched in due course by the addition of the feminine genius. The prophetic voices in the church would have a chance of being heard. The *sensus fidelium* would no longer be stifled.

We could indeed end up with an unrecognisable Roman Catholic Church because it would once again have become the Catholic Church. It would be a church of many kinds of people united by mutual love, the Eucharist and common purpose. It could possibly be a church that focuses on virtue rather than sin. Members, would be distinguished, not by their clothes, or headgear, or how they wear their hair or shave or grow their beards but because they teach the world to love unselfishly and are themselves seen to love and care for the least—sometimes to the point of inconvenience, significant cost or personal risk. We Christians are called to nothing less.

This time, instead of relying on ourselves, let us rely on the Holy Spirit who ensured that the Church flourished and grew under the most inhospitable conditions in the first three centuries without a dominating centralism and the structures of an empire. Those two elements were virtually unknown in Ireland[484] during the glorious six hundred years when 'the island of saints and scholars' sent a steady flow of missionaries to bring the message of Christ back to a Europe overrun by barbarians.

Is this too idealistic an objective? Not at all. It is the one Jesus Christ set us. Was he too idealistic?[485] A church that is concerned with the good of others at *every* level would foster the unity Christ prayed for and that so many Christians pray for. This would not be a unity of enforced beliefs, or of domination/subordination, but a unity of charity among those who share a common faith in the crucified and risen Christ, and a common calling to discipleship, and who commemorate him by offering their

---

[483] See footnote reference to John Wesley on page 252
[484] Dáibhí Ó Cróinín, *Early Medieval Ireland,* Edinburgh, Longman/Pearson, 1995, pp 147/8.
[485] Or Isaiah $2:4$: He will neither waver, nor be crushed until true justice is established on earth.

lives with him in worship. In so far as Christians respond to Christ's commandment to love one another they will humbly tolerate differences in understanding and they will be realising Christ's prayer in their lives, *de facto,* which is all that matters.

Chapter 18

Conclusions and proposals

But denunciatory rhetoric is so much easier and cheaper than good works
Yet is it far better to light the candle than to curse the darkness.

—William L. Watkinson[486]

ALWAYS IN NEED OF REFORM

The pope has an impossible job. The efforts of Pope Francis at reform would seem to confirm this. The Church has 1.33 Billion members and if united with the Orthodox and the churches of the Reformation, as it should be, it would have about 2.3Bn. Its management is centralised, increasingly so since 1870 as time goes on and communications improve. Nominally, the pope of the day combines the posts of President, Chief Executive Officer, Chief Justice, Head Teacher, and Head of Human Resources with responsibility for appointing a bishop nearly every day. He is also Head of State and Chief of the Vatican Diplomatic Corps. He is generally near or past retiring age when he takes on the job which Pope Benedict has described as an "enormous" office. In this overwhelming situation, the pope is managed by the Roman curia. Thus, the curia has become the effective government of the Church. Pope John Paul II confirmed this in the conversation with Cardinal Arns, when he said: "The curia *is* the pope".

The curia is a large bureaucracy with all the normal characteristics of a bureaucracy and a few unusual ones. The normal ones scarcely need repeating. Bureaucracies tend to be rule-bound, heartless, determined to protect their own interests and increase their power and control. The five unusual ones, which together make the Roman curia unique are:

1. It is not controlled by a government or board of directors.

2. It writes its own laws and acts as both interpreter and judge.

3. Its executives are bound by loyalty oaths and extreme secrecy.

4. For 800 years at least, its executives have been male and unmarried and for the past 400 years, very homogeneous, each having been shaped by the same seminary formation.

5. It controls its own recruitment and promotion, and this makes its ethos and culture virtually unchangeable.

---

[486] W. L. Watkinson *The Supreme Conquest and Other Sermons Preached in America,* New York. 1907, Fleming H. Revell Company, Sermon XIV, pp 217 and 218, https://quoteinvestigator.com/2017/03/19/candle/ accessed 23/12/2017

Pope John XXIII reckoned that the Church needed reform[487]. He knew the workings of the curia. He outmanoeuvred the officials with a surprise announcement that he would call the Second Vatican Council. Once he had done that, the bureaucracy had to maintain unity and be seen to support the initiative although, behind the scenes, senior officers worked against it as it had the potential to upset the *status quo*.

The assembled bishops, when they had the freedom to speak their minds, supported *Aggiornamento* and its corollary *Semper Reformanda*. They reversed some of the pseudo-infallible teachings and altered some long-established attitudes.

The implementation of the Council started with enthusiasm but was stalled by the bureaucracy. Significant reform would have involved the curia in ceding some of its power and control; a situation no bureaucracy will contemplate unless constrained by an external force. The bureaucracy used the post-Conciliar revision of Canon Law to deny power to the College of Bishops headed by the Pope, which is legally the supreme authority in the Church, and which could have pressed the reforms forward. This leaves the Pope isolated, in the classical position of a monarch who is totally dependent on his immediate circle of officials. And it leaves 1.33 Billion Catholics with absolutely no input into how the visible organisation of their Church is governed or by whom. This does not take account of the signs of the times.

The faithful of the Roman Catholic Church in the Third Millennium is witnessing the decay of the visible organisation and there is no practical or legal way it can do anything about it. Local management is clustering parishes, closing churches, and failing to provide the Eucharist due to human rules and 'irreformable' interpretations. The congregations get smaller as the parishioners get older. The priests now average 70 years of age or more.[488]

The papacy is failing to prioritise the two objectives that Christ set for his Church at its inception—the foundational mandates. It is also failing in the specific duty it has defined for itself, that of promoting Christian unity. It has made total subjection to itself and to a body of secondary teaching into a condition of communion. As we have discovered, some of this teaching requires deception to support it. This is not the way of the Good Shepherd.

The Roman Catholic Church can justifiably claim to be the original flock from whom the other sheep have strayed. Christ's prayer is that all sheep should be in one fold, but some of our earthly shepherds concentrate on strengthening the existing fences. They make a return to the fold unnecessarily difficult. There is evidence that many of the sheep on both sides of the fence do not approve of this situation. They see little merit in the division. They do not want it. But the shepherds cannot listen because to do so would strain their vows of loyalty and would involve breaking with

---

[487] He was persuaded that reform was possible, even necessary, by reading Yves Congar's, *True and False Reform* while he was nuncio to France.

[488] Fr Brendan Hoban, writing in *The Examiner* 23 April 2018.

existing structures, abandoning pseudo-infallibility, and questioning the dogmas of Vatican I. They see their flocks getting older and smaller but fear to take remedial actions that might affect the status of the profession. As in any secular profession, the leaders of Christ's shepherds make entry into the profession unnecessarily difficult and find ways to rationalise the group self-interest.

Disunity among Christians, meanwhile, diminishes the charity that would identify us as Christ's disciples. It devitalises the witness that we can offer to those who have not yet received Christ's message. This situation has been recognised for more than a hundred years by Anglicans and Protestants and for more than fifty by the supreme Catholic authority. Yet the Catholic leadership still balks at the costly call to unity.

We Roman Catholics and our clergy have been conditioned by 150 years of exaggerated infallibility into thinking that significant change in the Church is impossible. Yet we need to rethink our priorities and make changes if the current qualitative and quantitative decline in the Church is to be reversed. Some changes were achieved by the Council and others were foreshadowed but have been frustrated. The argument of this study points to 29 areas for immediate attention and these are listed below. Those relating to unity with other denominations of Christians should be considered for unilateral action by the Roman Catholic authorities because Jesus prayed especially for unity among his followers and because his example was consistently one of taking the initiative.

> But their [Catholics'] primary duty is to make an honest and careful appraisal of whatever needs to be renewed and achieved in the Catholic household itself, in order that its life may bear witness more loyally and luminously to the teachings and ordinances which have been handed down from Christ through the apostles.—Vatican Il, *Unitatis Redintegratio, §4.*

The table below summarises this study's 'honest and careful appraisal of what needs to be renewed'. It is a list of proposals for policy development rather than of glib solutions. The references in the right-hand column lead to supporting considerations in the text. However, since 'everything is connected to everything else' all the suggestions share all the reasoning.

	PROPOSALS	Some Links
1	*GIVE TOP PRIORITY TO THE GREAT COMMANDMENT AND THE TWO MANDATES.* They ought to be the first and overriding concerns among the managers of the Church that Christ founded. They always deserve top priority. *'Making disciples'* of all the nations does not necessarily mean making good docile Roman Catholics of them. Christ's defined his disciples as those who love others as themselves, *i.e.* without being selfish. The Christian Way influences and evangelises best by being lived. *'Do this in commemoration of me'* is unambiguous and should take priority over the privileges of professionals whose function was once to serve it. Simply by virtue of Christ's commandment, any group that normally lacks the services of a priest should be encouraged to celebrate the Eucharist together as a community. A proper sense of proportion would rank the mandate above traditional regulations and Canon Law, which should promote rather than prevent it. The celebration should be prioritised ahead of the choice of celebrant. In teaching that a priest is indispensable, the profession is acting out of group self-interest. Love demands that the needs of the congregation should take precedence.	Pages 239, 240 Pages 69, 229, 246, 247
2	*EXTRICATE THE CHURCH FROM VATICAN I DOGMAS.* The definitions of Papal Infallibility and Universal Jurisdiction were driven by human ambition and have done more harm than good. Most of the unresolved issues in the Church can be traced back to them. The good news is they are *not* irreformable. The Pope must admit, openly and humbly, that the papacy has sometimes been wrong, and that the Promise on which infallibility is based was made to the People of God. This admission will have to precede the review of moral theology in proposal *18* below. He should not renounce his Universal Jurisdiction or plenitude of power until the reforms have been instituted and begun to take root.	Pages 15, 23, 95, Pages 37, 270, 271, 287

3	*INSTITUTE GOVERNANCE BY THE COLLEGE OF BISHOPS WITH THE POPE,* probably on a representative basis. Agreed in principle by Vatican II as a supreme authority but outmanoeuvred at the time and put into deep-freeze later by the curia in revising Canon Law. This must be done by the pope before he relinquishes his absolute legal power because it will be resisted strongly by the bureaucracy.	Pages 9, 26, 52, 178, 285, 289
4	*ADOPT AN OVERWHELMING OPTION FOR THE TRUTH,* even when it is embarrassing, inconvenient, damaging, or likely to be used by the enemies of the Church. Abjure pseudo-infallibility absolutely. This option would have to exclude the disparagement of Christians who disagree on non-credal issues. It implies freedom of conscience at all levels and trust that the Holy Spirit will gradually guide the People of God to the truth through preaching, living the Way and dialogue without any need of coercion.	Pages 40, 66, 118, 119, 129, 130-131, 184.
5	*REDEFINE THE PAPAL ROLE.* Redefine what is essential to the mission to facilitate the unity Christ prayed for. The pope should renounce the disputed claims of the Apostolic See and redefine his own duties to be: *a.* Bishop of Rome, *b.* Symbol & force for progress in unity *c.* Final moderator in disputes, *d.* President at ecumenical or major councils and e. President of the Collegial Government.	Pages 264, 270
6	*IMPLEMENT SUBSIDIARITY THROUGH SYNODS* which include representatives of parish clergy, religious and faithful, male, and female. Make synods responsible for selecting local bishops and empower them to state a case to the governing College of Bishops on issues that exceed their remit.	Pages 26, 38, 260, 262
7	*ACCEPT THAT ALL WHO ARE BAPTISED AND WHO LOVE UNSELFISHLY MAKE UP THE MYSTICAL BODY.* This is Christ's own definition. The many institutional Christian churches, although disunited over secondary issues, together form the visible manifestation of the Mystical Body of Christ which is one and undivided.	Page 205

8	REAFFIRM THE PREFERENTIAL OPTION FOR THE POOR, and that poverty has many faces. Concern for his least ones should mark every Christian life and be visible at every level of Church organisation.	
9	END THE EUCHARISTIC FAMINE, which is indefensible, by making one or more of the following changes: a. Stop prioritising celibacy over the Eucharist. This contributes to the shortage of priests by deterring a large proportion of vocations. The marriage ban has led to the unnecessary loss of more than 100,000 priests, including many dedicated, educated, experienced, and humane pastors. b. Allow bishops to select and ordain suitable mature, people who can help to feed the lambs and sheep and immediately end sacramental famine. c. Abandon all discrimination against women. married or single. The ban on discussion of their ordination shows that the authorities are aware of the flimsy reasoning supporting their exclusion. The CDF made it pseudo-infallible, but the People of God to whom the Promise was given, have rejected it. d. As suggested in *1* above, stop restricting the celebration of the Eucharist to the ordained. This contradiction of the mandate can claim no precedent in the early Church. Allow any congregation without an ordained priest to say Mass as a community as Jesus commanded and as Peter and Paul taught. The doctrine of the priestly people can mean nothing less.	Pages 210, 65 Page 13, 144 Pages 142, 145 Pages 33, 22, 50, 69, 143, 246, 229, 278
10	THE EUCHARIST IS THE GREAT SACRAMENT OF UNITY. Sacraments effect what they symbolise. The use of the Eucharist as the defining symbol of disunity is a denial of its efficacy. All Christians accept that Christ's statement "This is My Body" is true although a mystery beyond human comprehension. Differences of opinion about how it is accomplished are therefore inescapable. Admit to the sacrament any baptised person who seeks it in good faith.	Page 251

11	*SCRAP THE OATH OF ALLEGIANCE TO THE PAPACY.* No man can serve two masters. Replace it with a solemn promise of loyalty to Jesus Christ or revert to the simple confession of faith which sufficed up to the twelfth century.	Page 44
12	*AFFIRM THAT THE CHRISTIAN UNITY WE SEEK IS THE UNITY OF LOVE,* respect, and the shared purpose of making disciples as defined by Christ.	Page 263,
13	*REALISE THAT THERE IS A HIERARCHY OF TRUTHS* and the unity of Christianity does not require a uniformity of belief, attitude, emphasis, or priority on every issue.	Page 288
14	*REASSERT THAT CHARITY IS THE OVERARCHING AND ETERNAL VIRTUE,* the foundation of all the law and the prophets. Take Christ at his word and accept that if something is not based on love, or the lack thereof, it is not part of Christ's moral teaching.	Page 203
15	*ACCEPT THAT THE GIFTS OF FAITH AND HOPE ARE LINKED* and enable Christ's disciples to trust in his Promise in a world of uncertainty. Accept: a. that whatever level of infallibility exists, it is a gift to the People of God that of its nature is limited in scope and presents difficulty in definition in human terms except for the basics. b. that the tenets of the faith find their best formulation in the moral unanimity of bishops or their equivalents, when they are acting in freedom and are witnessing to the beliefs of their flocks. c. that the infallibility of the People of God relates to the essentials of the faith and not to propositions that depend on human knowledge, judgement, and culture. d. that the infallibility of the People of God subsists even though individuals and groups have different opinions and beliefs on a wide variety of topics. e. that the search for truth is the great challenge for humanity, but that nobody will be condemned for being honestly wrong.	Page 37

16	*ACKNOWLEDGE THAT THE VIRTUALLY UNANIMOUS DECISIONS OF ECUMENICAL COUNCILS,* in which the bishops (or equivalents) of all Christian Churches have the opportunity to participate, is the highest teaching authority in the Church, but that such decisions are not infallible.	Pages 38, 83,
17	*ADMIT THE HISTORICAL FACT* that Councils of the Church held after the East/West Schism are not, and could not qualify as, valid ecumenical councils.	Page 79,
18	*INITIATE THE MAJOR REVIEW OF MORAL THEOLOGY* as called for by Vatican II. It would be more grounded in the gospel and less on canon law and human authority. No Christian should be excluded from this development of the *sensus fidelium* and no time limit should be set.	Pages 129, 199
19	*ACCEPT THAT ACHIEVING GREATER UNITY* is not a process of pressurising Christians to abandon genuinely held convictions or traditional practices. It is an effort to promote harmony and love among siblings and to focus on Christ's two mandates. In this exercise, all should start by reducing their own contribution to the current divisions.	Pages 238, 241 293
20	*ESPOUSE FREEDOM OF RELIGION FOR ALL.* Extend the rejection of coercion internally to include theologians, pastors and faithful. Recognise freedom of conscience in practice, internally and externally.	Pages, 99, 120, 138, 213, 222
21	*CONSIDER PROPOSALS FOR WRITTEN CONSTITUTIONS* for the Church, for Dioceses and for Parishes. Item 24 below would seem to require this. It could include the Bill of Rights for the faithful. The proposals could be taken up by the new Governing Body.	Pages 53, 197
22	*BREAK UP AND DECENTRALISE THE BUREAUCRACY* and make it subject to governance by the College of Bishops with the Pope. Extend legitimate diversity to adapt evangelisation to different cultures.	Pages 80, 235, 285, 284, 286

23	*GIVE BISHOPS BACK THE RIGHT AND THE AUTHORITY* to fulfil their diocesan responsibilities adequately. This would allow them to judge how many priests were needed in their diocese and ordain those they consider suitable without gender discrimination.	Pages 107, 187, 287
24	*INTRODUCE THE SEPARATION OF POWERS.* Legislative, Judicial, and Executive functions at national and international level should be separated to resist corruption.	Pages 53, 56
25	*SEVER LINK BETWEEN ORDERS & ADMINISTRATION.* This was reasonable when only clerics were educated. Good management requires inputs from people with a variety of skills, training, and experience. Recognise the administrative and management skills of women.	Pages 175, 255
26	*REBUILD CREDIBILITY OF CHURCH MANAGEMENT.* This will require a deliberate change of management style and structure. It will benefit from some of the other changes in this list, particularly the option for the truth. Let elected bishops run the Church, adhering to the style described by Jesus.	Pages 43, 53, 61, 91, 122, 188, 269, 265,
27	*REDUCE CAREERISM IN THE MINISTRY.* Revert to the practice that a bishop moves from his diocese only when this serves the identifiable needs of the Church. Match the discretionary authority of offices to their responsibilities, not to levels of rank or dignity.	Pages 36, 37
28	*LIKE CHRIST, BE MAGNANIMOUS WITH FORGIVENESS.* Remove restrictions on the third rite of reconciliation.	Pages 13 14, 72
29	*IMPLEMENT VATICAN II FULLY & HONESTLY.* Many of the needed elements have been listed above. The Council provides justification for these and other changes. Governance by the College of Bishops would probably achieve most of these objectives gradually.	Page 3 189

Many of these suggestions merely echo the decisions of Vatican II. All can be shown to be within the mainstream of Christ's message in the Gospels and in line with 2,000 years of Roman Catholic belief. Papal Infallibility and Universal Jurisdiction are relative novelties which were not defined until 1870 and have failed the test of time, the test of origins, the test of reception and the test of fruits, as we have shown. We have outlined a dozen formulas that would allow these apparently irreformable dogmas to be reformed. Only one will need to be found acceptable whenever the will to change is there.

If some of the above proposals imply imperfection in current practice, this does not negate Christ's promise to be with us. God has never taken away the freedom of decision on which our humanity and our ability to love depends.

Some traditional practices or misjudgements are currently obstructing the work of making disciples and celebrating the Eucharist. It is time to give the two mandates the priority they deserve.

If this would leave us with a somewhat unrecognisable Catholic Church, then so be it. It is better that it should be true to its founder than to its current profile. Fr Luis Bermejo S.J.[489] has written about this potential change of identity. The difference between the two indicates clearly that our leaders have been busy creating the wrong personality and trying to build the kingdom with an unsuitable system of governance. They too can be tempted to ignore the promptings of the Spirit. They too can get priorities inverted and get things out of proportion.

The church is always in need of reform.

---

[489] *Towards Christian Reunion,* Bermejo, Luis M., S.J., Anand, India 1984, Lanham, MD, University Press of America, 1987, p 315.

Glossary

A fortiori	There is stronger evidence for …
Agape	Christian love as distinct from erotic love.
Aggiornamento	Bringing up to date.
Apologia pro vita sua	Title of Newman's spiritual autobiography.
Arian Heresy	Denial of divinity of Christ. Condemned at Nicaea.
Catechumens	Converts being prepared for baptism in early church.
Computus	Knowledge of mathematics and astronomy required to calculate the date of Easter.
Confessio	St. Patrick's story written in Latin by himself.
Cui Bono?	Who stands or stood to gain?
De facto	In fact
De Fide	Of the faith. Essential to the faith.
De Jure	According to law. By right
Desiderata	Things that are needed or wanted
Equivocation	The use of ambiguity to conceal a false argument or to avoid committing oneself
Ecclesia	The church
En Passant	In passing. From the *en passant* rule in chess
En masse	In a group, all together
Ex opere operato	As a result of the action performed
Filioque	Latin; 'and the son'. Generally, refers to the controversy over addition of the word *Filioque* to the Creed
Homogeneous	Made up of parts of the same kind, or very similar.
In persona Christi	Symbolising Christ. Literally 'in the role of Christ'.
Lex orand, lex credendi	The law of prayer is the law of belief.
Magisterium	Teaching authority. Literally, guidance, direction.
Motu Proprio	An edict issued by a pope 'on his own volition'.
Non sequitur	The classic logical fallacy of a conclusion that does not follow from an earlier statement.
Par excellence	Better or more so that others of the same kind

Pater Familias	Latin, father of family. Roman male head of household.
Per se	By or in itself or themselves; intrinsically
Placet, Non placet	Way of voting at Councils. 'It pleases', 'it pleases not'.
Plenitudo Potestatis	Fullness of power
Pontifex Maximus	Greatest bridge-builder.
Primus inter pares	First among equals
Quid pro quo	Favour or advantage granted in return.
Quod Erat Demonstrandum	Latin, which was required to be shown. (Q.E.D.)
Primus inter pares	Latin, first among equals
Raison d'être	The purpose for someone's or something's existence
Recognitio	Confirmation or approval by the Apostolic See
Roma Locuta	Attenuated form of *Roma locuta est, causa finita,* (Rome has spoken, and the discussion is closed)
Sacramentum	Loyalty oath taken by a Roman soldier at enlistment.
Sceilig Mhichíl	Monastic rock located off the SW coast of Ireland
Sedea Gestatoria	Papal open sedan chair used in the past, carried by 8 men on public occasions.
Semper Reformanda	Latin; always in need of reform
Sensus Fidei	Alternate to *Sensus Fidelium*, sometimes, its content.
Sensus Fidelium	The supernatural grasp of faith of the People of God
Status quo ante	The previously existing state of affairs
Sub Secreto Pontifico	Under the highest level of secrecy in the church
Ultramontanism	The campaign to give unlimited authority to the pope
Ultra Vires	Beyond one's legal powers or authority